PLANTS & FUNGI

PLANTS & FUNGI

THE DEFINITIVE VISUAL GUIDE

DK LONDON

Senior Editor	Chauney Dunford
Senior Art Editor	Gadi Farfour
Senior Project Editor	Angela Wilkes
Editors	Anna Cheifetz, Alethea Doran, Tim Harris, Steve Setford, Rachel Warren Chadd
Senior US Editor	Megan Douglass
Project Art Editor	Katie Cavanagh
Picture Research	Laura Barwick, Kate Sayer
Jacket Design Development Manager	Sophia MTT
Senior Production Controller	Rachel Ng
Managing Editor	Gareth Jones
Managing Art Editor	Lee Griffiths
Art Director	Karen Self
Associate Publishing Director	Liz Wheeler
Publishing Director	Jonathan Metcalf

DK DELHI

Senior Art Editor	Chhaya Sajwan
Project Editor	Hina Jain
Project Art Editor	Shipra Jain
Assistant Art Editor	Mrunali Sanjay Likhar
Managing Editor	Soma B. Chowdhury
Senior Managing Art Editor	Arunesh Talapatra
Assistant Picture Researchers	Geetam Biswas, Shubhdeep Kaur
Picture Research Manager	Taiyaba Khatoon
DTP Designers	Ashok Kumar, Rakesh Kumar, Vijay Kandwal, Anita Yadav
DTP Coordinator	Jagtar Singh
Production Editor	Vishal Bhatia
Pre-production Manager	Balwant Singh
Production Manager	Pankaj Sharma
Jacket Designer	Juhi Sheth
Senior Jackets Coordinator	Priyanka Sharma Saddi
Creative Head	Malavika Talukder

First American Edition, 2024
Published in the United States by DK Publishing,
a division of Penguin Random House LLC
1745 Broadway, 20th Floor, New York, NY 10019

Copyright © 2024 Dorling Kindersley Limited
24 25 26 27 28 10 9 8 7 6 5 4 3 2 1
001–336907–Sep/2024

A catalog record for this book
is available from the Library of Congress.
ISBN: 978-0-5938-4407-6

Printed and bound in China

www.dk.com

Smithsonian

The Smithsonian is the world's largest museum and research complex, dedicated to public
education, national service, and scholarship in the arts, Smithsonian sciences, and history.

The name of the Smithsonian Institution and the sunburst logo are
registered trademarks of the Smithsonian Institution. For more information,
please visit www.si.edu.

Contents

DIRECTORY 364

Contributors

Lynne Boddy
Lynne Boddy is Professor of Mycology at Cardiff University. She has taught and researched into the ecology of fungi associated with trees and rotting wood for more than 45 years. She has written or edited ten books, and published over 300 scientific papers and popular articles. She has also talked about fungi on TV, radio, and in videos. Lynne has considerable acclaim for her work, and was awarded an MBE in 2019 for Services to Mycology and Science Outreach.

Chris Clennett
Now retired from the Royal Botanic Gardens Kew, Chris began a 40-year career in botanic gardens at Oxford, where he cultivated hardy, temperate, tropical, and desert plants. He studied for Master of Horticulture at Pershore College, before moving to Sussex and Kew Gardens in 1987. He has since studied for MSc and PhD in plant taxonomy, writing the Kew Monograph on *Erythronium*, and remains an active member of Royal Horticultural Society, Plant Heritage, and specialist society committees.

John Farndon
The author of hundreds of books on science and nature for both children and adults, John Farndon studied geography at Cambridge University. He has written extensively on earth sciences and the environment, focusing in particular on conservation and ecology. His books include *The Oceans Atlas*, *The Wildlife Atlas*, *How the Earth Works*, and *The Practical Encyclopedia of Rocks and Minerals*.

Tim Harris
After studying Norwegian glaciers at university, Tim Harris traveled the world in search of unusual wildlife and extraordinary landscapes. He has explored the dunes of the Namib Desert, climbed Popocatépetl in central Mexico, camped in the Sumatran rainforest, and searched the frozen Sea of Okhotsk in Russia. A keen amateur botanist, Tim is a former Deputy Editor of *Birdwatch* magazine in the UK, and has written books about nature for adults and children.

Sarah Jose
Sarah Jose is a science writer and editor who completed a PhD in Plant Science, before leaving the laboratory to share her deep love of plants with the world. Dr. Jose wrote DK's *Trees, Leaves, Flowers & Seeds*, and contributed to several other DK books about the wonderful world of botany, including *Flora: Inside the Secret World of Plants*, *Timelines of Nature*, and *Knowledge Encyclopedia: Plants and Fungi*.

 WARNING

Many plants and fungi found in the wild can contain substances that may be poisonous or cause allergic reactions. You should not pick wild plants or mushrooms to eat and must take care if handling them. The book aims to give general information on plants and mushrooms, and every effort has been made to ensure the accuracy of the information. However, in no circumstances can the publisher or the authors accept any liability for any loss, injury, or damage arising from the use of any information contained in this book.

The association between plants and fungi underpins all ecosystems, allowing animals such as the European hedgehog (*Erinaceus europaeus*), to flourish.

Introduction

Plants and fungi are amazing organisms. Both have evolved over millions of years to colonize every habitat on Earth—even the frozen wastes of Antarctica, where mosses, liverworts, and some flowering plants grow alongside fungi and lichens. Although they are quite different, plants and fungi share the same habitats and have developed mutually beneficial relationships. Animals, including humans, are entirely dependent on them, because they are the keystone of every ecosystem.

This book explores habitats all around the world, ranging from the vast cold forests of the Northern Hemisphere, through the rainforests of the tropics, to the Southern Hemisphere. Between these zones are temperate habitats filled with trees, shrubs, perennials, and annual plants, all of which have their own strategies for coping with the changing seasons. Many have evolved special features to help them grow in extreme conditions or live in water. Others are able to thrive in deserts or frozen mountain heights, while carnivorous plants have adapted to live in habitats that lack nitrogen. Some plants have even become parasites and steal their nutrients from others. Fungi have evolved alongside plants. Most of them obtain nutrients from decaying plants and animals, but here, too, there are parasites that invade other organisms to obtain the nutrients they need.

For thousands of years, people all over the world have found practical uses for the plants and fungi around them. From fruits and vegetables to fibers, timber, and natural medicines, plants provide a wide range of benefits that we still rely on today.

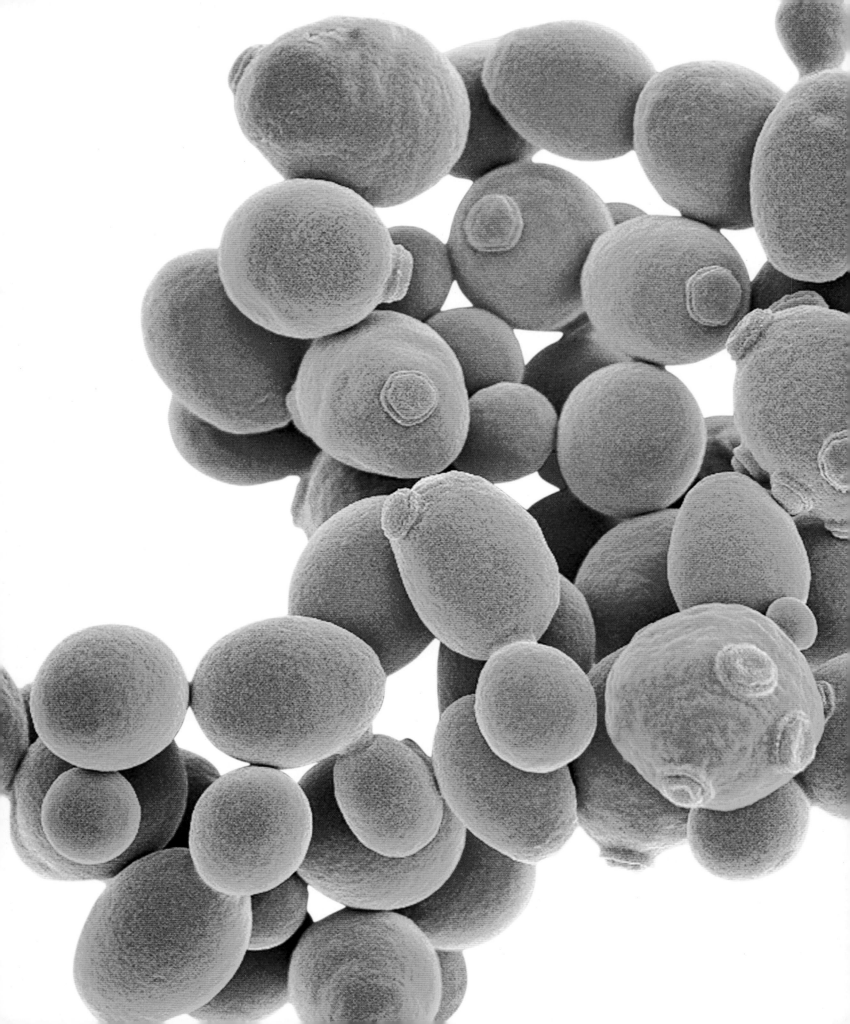

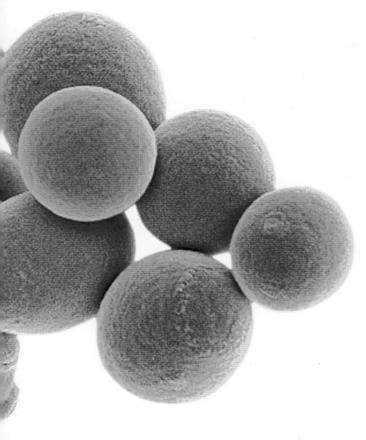

THE SCIENCE OF PLANTS AND FUNGI

Over millions of years, plants and fungi have evolved from microscopic algae into an astonishing variety of forms that have colonized nearly every corner of the Earth.

The plant kingdom

Plants evolved from microscopic algae and began to colonize land around half a billion years ago. Spreading across the planet, they transformed ecosystems, paving the way for a boom in animal evolution, too. The earliest plants were small and limited to wet habitats, but today more than 400,000 plant species are found in almost every biome on Earth, providing people with food, oxygen, shelter, clothing, medicine, fuel, and many other vital resources.

Leaves have a large surface area to absorb maximum light

What is a plant?

Most plants are autotrophic organisms—they make their own food using light, water, and nutrients in a process known as photosynthesis (see pp.34–35). All plant cells have rigid walls made of cellulose, which help retain their structure. Plants also have stem cells that divide and differentiate to grow new organs throughout their life cycle.

A timeline of plant types

The first plants were small and simple, but some evolved specialized vascular tissues to transport water and food, true leaves to increase photosynthesis, and flowers and seeds for efficient reproduction. All these features are seen in flowering plants.

Aquatic algae

Around one billion years ago, multicellular green algae emerged as simple strings of cells that could absorb light using a green photosynthetic pigment called chlorophyll. The earliest plants evolved from these algal ancestors.

Green algae Today, there are around 9,000 species of green algae, which are mostly found in fresh water.

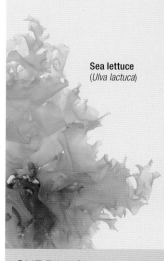

Sea lettuce
(*Ulva lactuca*)

Bryophytes

The first land plants appeared around 500 million years ago. They differed from algae in having more complex structures with specialized tissues, and reproduced using spores (see pp.18–19).

Hornworts There are 215 species of these small plants, which are named for their horn-shaped, spore-producing structures.

Liverworts There are around 7,500 surviving species of liverworts, which have flattened, leaflike tissues.

Mosses A diverse plant group with at least 15,000 species, mosses form clumps or mats of leaflike tissues.

Common liverwort
(*Marchantia polymorpha*)

Lycophytes and ferns

Plants with vascular bundles (veins) in their stems and leaves to carry water and nutrients around the plant body evolved around 450 million years ago. These rigid vessels enabled lycophytes and ferns to grow much larger than nonvascular bryophytes, but they still used spores for reproduction (see pp.20–21).

Lycophytes The 1,300 species of lycophytes that exist today are relatively small, feathery plants, but ancient species grew into towering trees that dominated the landscape.

Common club moss
(*Lycopodium clavatum*)

Ferns With distinctive leafy fronds that produce spores, the 10,500 surviving species of fern are derived from ancient forms that once dominated Earth's habitats.

Southern maidenhair fern
(*Adiantum capillus-veneris*)

Gymnosperms

The evolution of seeds allowed plants termed gymnosperms (meaning "naked seed") to germinate only when conditions were hospitable. These were the first plants to use pollen to reproduce (see pp.22–23).

Cycads Most of the approximatel[y] 300 surviving species of cycads ha[ve a] trunk of spongy wood with a crow[n of] large, divided leaves. Cones are us[ually] borne in the center of the crown.

Sago palm
(*Cycas revoluta*)

| ONE BILLION years ago | 500 MILLION years ago | 450 MILLION years ago | 360 MILLION years ago | 320 MILLION years ago |

Plant impersonators

Some organisms look like plants but actually belong to other kingdoms. Algae, including seaweed, are related to the unspecialized green algal ancestors of plants, but are separated from them by hundreds of millions of years of evolution. Fungi are often mistaken for plants, but they are actually more closely related to animals. Lichens often look like mosses, but are in fact a symbiosis (close beneficial relationship) between an alga or a cyanobacterium and a fungus.

Simple photosynthetic tissues

Golden kelp
(*Laminaria ochroleuca*)

Bracken fern
(*Pteridium aquilinum*)

Fossilized plants

The oldest preserved vascular plants

Fossils provide important information about plant evolution. This *Cooksonia barrandei* fossil is 432 million years old and shows a small plant with a simple structure. It has branched, leafless stems holding spore-producing organs, revealing how ancient plants developed and reproduced.

Spore-producing structure

Leafless stem

Fossil of *Cooksonia barrandei*

Siberian stone pine
(*Pinus sibirica*)

Angiosperms

The first flowering plants (angiosperms) quickly outcompeted other plants and dominated the landscape by the end of the dinosaur era, 65 million years ago. There are now around 369,000 species of angiosperms.

Ginkgo A large tree with unique, fan-shaped leaves, *Ginkgo biloba* is the only surviving species of the ancient *Ginkgoaceae* family.

Conifers Like cycads, the 615 species of conifers use male and female cones for reproduction. The females produce the seeds.

Gnetophytes This unique group of 96 species contains unusual and highly diverse shrubs, vines, and desert plants.

Magnoliids Around two percent of angiosperms are magnoliids. Some have very ancient flower features, such as scalelike stamens.

Monocots Including cereal crops and orchids, this group accounts for 25 percent of angiosperms. Their seeds hold one embryonic leaf.

Eudicots 75 percent of angiosperms are eudicots (sometimes called "dicots"). Their seeds hold two embryonic leaves.

Ginkgo
(*Ginkgo biloba*)

Douglas fir
(*Pseudotsuga menziesii*)

Melinjo
(*Gnetum gnemon*)

Dawson's magnolia
(*Magnolia dawsoniana*)

Crown imperial
(*Fritillaria imperialis*)

Korean mint
(*Agastache rugosa*)

250 MILLION years ago

Powering growth

Plants require water, sunlight, carbon dioxide, and nutrients in order to grow and reproduce, as well as the right location, and a suitable temperature. A lack of any one of these factors will affect the plant's health and its ability to reproduce and colonize an area.

Carbon dioxide from the air diffuses into the leaf through microscopic pores called stomata

Light, absorbed by cells in the leaves, provides energy for the plant to convert carbon dioxide and water into sugars for food (photosynthesis)

Stems draw up water, which is vital for photosynthesis. Water also acts as a solvent to transport nutrients at a cellular level, and helps the plant maintain its structure

Potato plant (*Solanum tuberosum*)

Plants require space and optimum temperatures to grow well.

Nutrients

Building blocks

There are 18 chemical substances called nutrients that plants have to obtain from their environment in order to grow. These include the elements hydrogen, carbon, and oxygen derived from water and atmospheric gases; the mineral elements nitrogen, phosphorus, and potassium (termed macronutrients); and smaller amounts of 12 minerals termed micronutrients (sulfur, calcium, iron, boron, cobalt, manganese, molybdenum, magnesium, copper, zinc, chlorine, and nickel). Plant roots take up both macro- and micronutrients from the soil.

Roots absorb nutrients that are essential for plant growth, including nitrogen, phosphorus, and potassium

Roots also anchor plants in the ground. The soil or other substrate supports the plant, and usually provides it with water, nutrients, and symbiotic microbes

What do plants need?

Plants live in a variety of habitats but they all share the same basic needs: water, air, sunlight, and essential nutrients. Given these, plants can create the cells and proteins that they need for growth, and can power activities such as photosynthesis. This is the process by which plants use sunlight energy to convert water and carbon dioxide into food (see p.35). By taking what they need for growth, plants play a crucial role in Earth's ecosystems, including the planet's carbon and nitrogen cycles.

Carbon and nitrogen cycles

Plants acquire carbon and nitrogen as part of ecosystem-wide nutrient cycles. They take these elements up and use them to grow; the elements then return to the soil when the plants are eaten or decompose. Human activities, such as burning fossil fuels, intensive farming, and deforestation, severely disrupt these natural cycles and the role that plants play in them.

Bamboo grasses
These very fast-growing plants absorb more carbon dioxide per second than most trees.

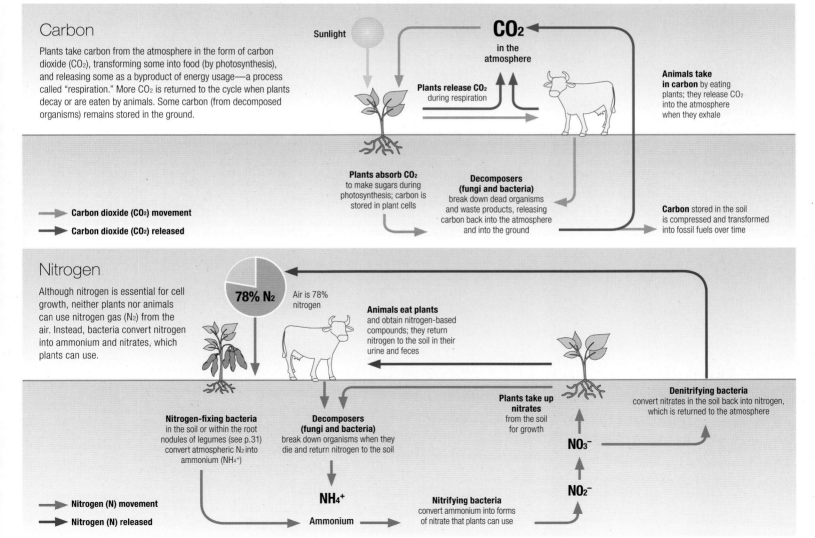

Carbon

Plants take carbon from the atmosphere in the form of carbon dioxide (CO_2), transforming some into food (by photosynthesis), and releasing some as a byproduct of energy usage—a process called "respiration." More CO_2 is returned to the cycle when plants decay or are eaten by animals. Some carbon (from decomposed organisms) remains stored in the ground.

→ **Carbon dioxide (CO_2) movement**
→ **Carbon dioxide (CO_2) released**

Sunlight

CO_2 in the atmosphere

Plants release CO_2 during respiration

Animals take in carbon by eating plants; they release CO_2 into the atmosphere when they exhale

Plants absorb CO_2 to make sugars during photosynthesis; carbon is stored in plant cells

Decomposers (fungi and bacteria) break down dead organisms and waste products, releasing carbon back into the atmosphere and into the ground

Carbon stored in the soil is compressed and transformed into fossil fuels over time

Nitrogen

Although nitrogen is essential for cell growth, neither plants nor animals can use nitrogen gas (N_2) from the air. Instead, bacteria convert nitrogen into ammonium and nitrates, which plants can use.

78% N_2 Air is 78% nitrogen

Animals eat plants and obtain nitrogen-based compounds; they return nitrogen to the soil in their urine and feces

Plants take up nitrates from the soil for growth

Denitrifying bacteria convert nitrates in the soil back into nitrogen, which is returned to the atmosphere

Nitrogen-fixing bacteria in the soil or within the root nodules of legumes (see p.31) convert atmospheric N_2 into ammonium (NH_4^+)

Decomposers (fungi and bacteria) break down organisms when they die and return nitrogen to the soil

NO_3^-

NO_2^-

→ **Nitrogen (N) movement**
→ **Nitrogen (N) released**

NH_4^+ Ammonium

Nitrifying bacteria convert ammonium into forms of nitrate that plants can use

Plant life

Plants live and die within a huge range of timescales. Some desert plants germinate, bloom, and die within two weeks of rare rainstorms, while a few ancient trees are known to be several thousand years old. All aspects of this life cycle, including germination, growth, reproduction, aging, and death, are processes that ultimately help a plant maximize how successfully it can reproduce and pass on its genetic material to the next generation. Plants can achieve this in two different ways—through sexual reproduction, which requires two parent plants, or by asexual reproduction, which is a form of cloning.

Asexual reproduction

Plants that reproduce asexually produce clones—offspring that are genetically identical to their parent. Because this method needs only one parent, it is often faster and more energy-efficient than sexual reproduction, enabling plants to colonize a favorable environment quickly. A downside of cloning is that cloned offspring are identically susceptible to new diseases or to changing climatic conditions.

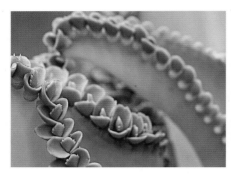

Producing plantlets
Some plants, such as this mother-of-thousands (*Kalanchoe daigremontiana*), produce small plantlets that develop their own leaves and roots while still attached to the parent, then detach and root independently. The plantlets that form along the creeping stems of strawberry plants are another example of this type of reproduction.

Spreading underground
Some plants have swollen storage organs or special stems beneath the soil that can form new plants. Corms and bulbs, such as the tulip above, produce new offshoots at their base; tubers (swollen stems or roots) and rhizomes (creeping underground stems) produce buds that sprout to form new plants.

Embryonic leaves
are known as cotyledons

Sunflower seedling

The lifespan of a plant

Plants can be divided into three groups based on their lifespans. Annuals grow, reproduce, and die within one year, while biennials grow during their first year then reproduce and die in their second. By contrast, perennials are long-lived plants that can grow and reproduce over several years; this group includes plants with tough, woody stems, such as shrubs, as well as trees.

Germination

The embryonic plant held within a seed is activated and sprouts to form a seedling during the process of germination. This first stage in the growth cycle can only occur when water, light, and temperature levels combine to create optimal growing conditions.

Growth phase

Plants strengthen and expand their root systems, stems, and leaves during this phase of growth. When plants reach maturity, they grow more slowly and redirect energy toward processes such as flowering, necessary for reproduction.

3 years or more

2 years

1 year

ANNUAL | BIENNIAL | PERENNIAL | SHRUBS | TREES

Sexual reproduction

For plants to reproduce sexually, separate male and female gametes (sex cells) must be introduced to each other (the action of pollination in flowering plants), then fuse together in the process called fertilization. Fertilization results in the formation of a cell known as the zygote, which contains genetic information from both parent plants. The zygote divides and develops into a plant embryo, and the surrounding cells form the seed that encases it. The seed holds the plant embryo in a dormant state until conditions are favorable for growth.

Female gamete ♀ + Male gamete ♂ = Zygote ♀♂

Genetic mix
Sexual reproduction combines the genetic material from two plants, which may give offspring beneficial new traits.

Reproductive plant types

Flowering plants have evolved different ways of distributing male and female reproductive organs between their flowers and timing their reproductive cycles to prevent self-fertilization. These methods avoid male pollen germinating on the female stigmas of the same plant, maximizing reproductive success while maintaining genetic diversity.

KEY

○ Plant

♀ Female flower parts

♂ Male flower parts

Flower A — Flower B   Flower A — Flower B   Flower A — Flower B

Monoecious plants
Male and female parts are present on the same plant, either on the same flower (hermaphrodites), or on different flowers on the same plant.

Dioecious plants
Individuals carry either all male or all female flowers. This means that more than one plant is needed for pollination and fertilization to take place.

Dichogamous plants
Male and female parts are present on the same plant but mature at different times. This means that more than one plant is needed for reproduction.

Ray flowers attract pollinators to help the plant reproduce

Disk flowers contain both male and female reproductive parts

Stems support leaves, supplying them with water and nutrients during the growth phase

Death

All plants eventually age and die in a process regulated by hormones and determined by DNA and environmental factors. Annuals, such as this sunflower, die at the end of the growing season to divert their energy into producing seed rather than trying to survive the winter.

Seeds contain the embryos that will form new plants

Sunflower seed head

Mature sunflower plant

Leaves use sunlight to provide the plant with energy for growth

Bryophytes

The most ancient type of plants alive today, bryophytes first appeared around 500 million years ago. They include thousands of species of mosses, liverworts, and hornworts, which are found all over the world. These plants' simple bodies and small size mean they are often overlooked, but they play vital roles in water storage and soil stabilization, and provide food and shelter for a huge range of animals. Scientific studies of bryophytes have revealed much about early life on our planet and how plants evolved.

Simple plants

Bryophytes do not have true leaves, roots, flowers, or seeds. They reproduce using spores, or vegetatively from fragments, and absorb nutrients and water from their environment through leaflike photosynthetic tissues or rootlike cells called rhizoids. Because their primitive tissues do not contain veins, water and nutrients can only passively diffuse through them. This is inefficient, and so most bryophytes are limited in size to only a few centimeters.

Liverworts

Most liverworts look like a flat, scaly, green sheet, or like moss. They reproduce via short-lived spore-producing structures on thin stalks (pictured), or asexually, by forming reproductive material in tiny cups which is then carried away by drops of water.

Hornworts

These plants have a distinctive, horn-shaped, spore-producing structure that splits when dry to release spores. Like all bryophytes, hornworts thrive in damp places, but they grow best in warm and tropical regions.

Mosses

The spirally arranged, leaflike tissues of mosses are only one cell thick but they can still function to absorb water and nutrients. Special rhizoid cells act like tiny anchors, attaching the plant to its substrate.

Mossy carpet
Due to their small size and modest needs, bryophytes such as this moss in the Sanzen-in temple moss garden, Kyoto, Japan, can live on hard surfaces that larger, more complex plants are unable to colonize.

Reproduction cycle of mosses

Bryophytes spend most of their lives as a ground-hugging, leafy body called the gametophyte. This has only one set of chromosomes, with either male or female sex cells. Male gametophytes produce sperm, which have to swim through water to reach an egg in a female gametophyte. The sperm and egg fuse to produce a sporophyte—a spore-producing structure with a full set of chromosomes. The sporophyte produces spores containing half a set of chromosomes; each spore will germinate into a new gametophyte.

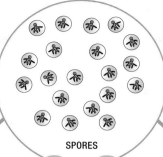

SPORES

♀ + ♂

Stalklike sporophytes grow from the leafy gametophytes

Spores are microscopic cells containing half a set of chromosomes; they typically disperse in wind or water.

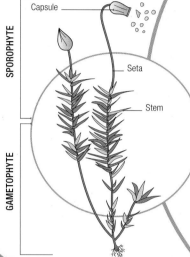

SPOROPHYTE

Capsule

Seta

Stem

GAMETOPHYTE

The sporophyte grows from, and remains attached to, a female gametophyte, which provides it with nutrition. The sporophyte does not live long and dies back as soon as it has produced and released the spores that will germinate into new plants.

After fertilization, a spore-producing capsule on a slender stalk (the sporophyte) grows from each fertilized egg.

Leafy male and female gametophytes grow from spores that land and germinate when conditions are suitable.

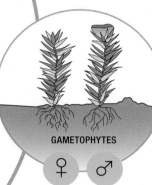

GAMETOPHYTES

♀ ♂

The gametophyte is a leafy body containing the sex organs that make sperm (male) and egg (female) cells. Bryophytes spend most of their lives as gametophytes; all other plants spend most of their lives as sporophytes, only forming tiny gametophytes when it is time to reproduce.

Sperm (the sex cells produced by male gametophytes) swim through water in damp environments to the female gametophyte, where they fertilize egg cells.

Common cord moss (*Funaria hygrometrica*) has spore capsules that spring open, flinging spores away from the plant.

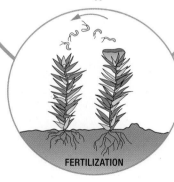

FERTILIZATION

Bryophytes are restricted to damp or wet environments because of the way they reproduce.

Extreme survivors

From deserts to the Arctic

While most mosses prefer cool, damp environments, some species can survive in extreme conditions. Mosses have been recorded photosynthesizing in temperatures as low as 5°F (-15°C) and as high as 104°F (40°C). When dried out, they have even survived periods at -457°F (-272°C) and 212°F (100°C).

Some desert mosses, like *Syntrichia caninervis* found in the Mojave Desert, US (above), can endure many years without water. They dry out completely and their cells go into hibernation mode. They grow and reproduce again only once it has rained.

+212°F (100°C)

More than 600 arctic mosses, especially *Racomitrium* species, survive in the freezing tundra and lava fields of Iceland (above). Although they grow very slowly (less than ½ in/1 cm per year), they provide essential food for animals and help maintain the surrounding temperatures.

-39.5°F (-39.7°C)

Fertile leaves
Fern fronds are divided into two types:
spore-producing sporophylls and sterile
tropophylls. The spore-producing structures
(sporangia) appear as brown or orange
clusters called sori on the undersides
of fertile leaves.

Mature leaf

**Sori form on the underside
of fertile leaves**

Fronds may be simple,
as here, or divided into
many leaflets called
pinnae, depending on
the species of fern

Fernlike fronds
formed a crown

Fronds grow in a
rosette from the base
and form a cup shape
that collects water

The first forests

Older than the dinosaurs

More than 300 million years ago, ancient relatives of
lycophytes and ferns appear to have colonized extensive
areas, establishing some of the world's first forests in
prehistoric wetlands. The first known tree, *Wattieza*, grew to
at least 26 ft (8 m) tall and resembled a modern tree fern,
shedding branches as it grew to maintain a crown at the top
of its trunk. *Lepidodendron*, a treelike lycophyte, grew to
around 164 ft (50 m) tall and had long, grasslike leaves
arranged spirally around a thick, green trunk.

Wattieza tree

Bird's nest fern
(*Asplenium
scolopendrium*)

Ferns

While ferns vary greatly in size, they all have leaves, stems, and roots with vascular tissues. Ferns have no flowers or seeds, but reproduce via spores.

Reproduction cycle

Like bryophytes (see pp.18–19), lycophytes and ferns require damp habitats in order to reproduce because their sperm cells need water to carry them to an egg cell. Unlike bryophytes, however, lycophytes and ferns spend most of their lives as sporophytes—the phase of growth after fertilization when the plant has a full set of chromosomes.

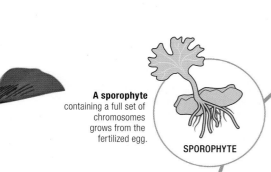

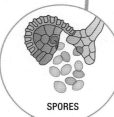

Lycophytes

Including the quillworts, club mosses, and spike mosses (not true mosses), modern lycophytes are low-growing plants that form carpets on tropical forest floors or grow as epiphytes on branches. They have tiny leaves and simple roots that grow from an underground stem.

MATURE FERN SPOROPHYTE

A sporophyte containing a full set of chromosomes grows from the fertilized egg.

SPOROPHYTE

As it matures, the sporophyte develops the leafy fronds characteristic of a fully grown fern.

Sporangia—tiny structures containing spores—develop on the underside of fertile fronds. Each spore contains half the chromosomes of the parent plant.

SPORANGIA

Egg cell

Female sex organ

Sperm

Male sex organ

FERTILIZATION

Female sex organ

Male sex organ

Mature spores are dispersed when a sporangium dries and opens to release them into the wind. Some sporangia act like a catapult to fling spores farther away from the parent plant.

SPORES

Sperm made in the male sex organs of the gametophyte move through a film of water, when conditions permit, to fertilize the egg cell in the female sex organs.

Rhizoids

GAMETOPHYTE

Spores that land in a suitable habitat grow into a tiny, heart-shaped plant called a gametophyte. This develops male and female sex organs and rootlike rhizoids.

New vascular tissues led these plants to dominate the planet more than 300 million years ago.

Lycophytes and ferns

Evolving more complex vascular tissues that could efficiently transport nutrients and water led new groups of plants—the lycophytes and ferns—to grow much larger than their primitive, nonvascular ancestors. Vascular tissue also made it possible for plants to develop more specialized features, such as the first true leaves and roots. Lycophyte leaves (microphylls) have remained small because they are supplied by a single, unbranched vein, but fern fronds (macrophylls) can be extremely large—those of the Australian giant fern (*Cyathea cooperi*) can reach 20 ft (6 m) in length. This great size, as well as the fact that each frond has many leaflets (a common feature in ferns) maximizes the amount of light that ferns can harvest in shady habitats.

Gymnosperms

The first plants to produce seeds, gymnosperms are a group of woody plants that include the conifers, cycads, ginkgo, and the gnetophytes. Unlike flowering plants, gymnosperms produce "naked" seeds that are not enclosed within fruits; instead, they develop on leaf scales, in cones, or on separate branches. The evolution of seeds meant that the plant embryos of the next generation could remain protected and dormant until conditions were optimal for growth. It also meant that plants did not need a damp environment in order to reproduce, which enabled them to diversify and colonize new habitats. Gymnosperms are now found on every continent except Antarctica and include many economically important plants. Conifer species are used for around half of all commercial timber, and to manufacture paper.

Conifer life cycle

The pines (*Pinus*), larches (*Larix*), spruces (*Picea*), firs (*Abies*), cedars (*Cedrus*), and cypresses (*Cupressus*) are all conifers and form cones of many shapes and sizes to carry their reproductive organs. Most conifers bear male cones (which produce pollen) and female cones (which contain egg-producing cells and form seeds) on the same plant. All are pollinated by wind; the female cones of some species even produce sticky droplets to draw in pollen.

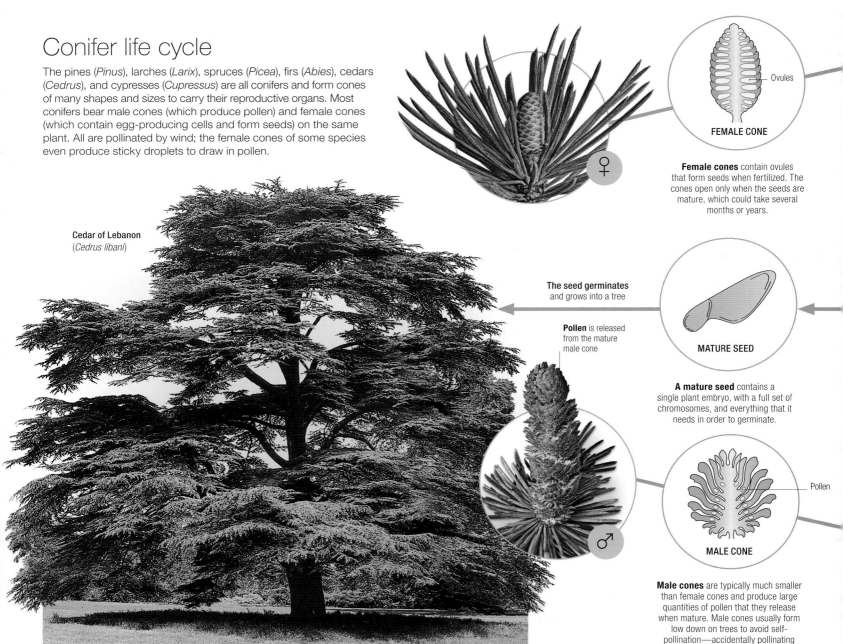

Ovules

FEMALE CONE

Female cones contain ovules that form seeds when fertilized. The cones open only when the seeds are mature, which could take several months or years.

Cedar of Lebanon
(*Cedrus libani*)

The seed germinates and grows into a tree

Pollen is released from the mature male cone

MATURE SEED

A mature seed contains a single plant embryo, with a full set of chromosomes, and everything that it needs in order to germinate.

Pollen

MALE CONE

Male cones are typically much smaller than female cones and produce large quantities of pollen that they release when mature. Male cones usually form low down on trees to avoid self-pollination—accidentally pollinating female cones on the same tree with their pollen.

Gymnosperms **are some of the longest-lived plants, with bristle-cone pines reaching at least 5,000 years of age.**

Female plants produce seeds in a fleshy coating

Ginkgo
The fan-shaped leaves of the ginkgo tree (*Ginkgo biloba*) set it apart from other gymnosperms, which usually have needle-shaped, scalelike, or feathery leaves.

FEMALE GAMETOPHYTE

The female gametophyte houses the egg; after fertilization, it nourishes the growing embryo and provides it with a protective seed coat.

Female life cycle

Inside a female cone, each ovule contains a female gametophyte—the reproductive organ that carries an egg cell. Once this egg has been fertilized by pollen, it will develop into a new plant embryo inside a seed.

DEVELOPING SEED

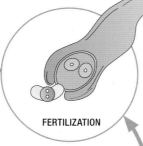

FERTILIZATION

Male life cycle

Pollen grains are the male gametophyte (the organ that carries male sex cells) and are formed inside male cones. When a grain of pollen lands on a female cone it develops a pollen tube which delivers genetic material into the ovule, fertilizing the egg cell inside.

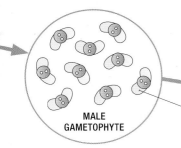

MALE GAMETOPHYTE

Some types of pollen have "wings" to aid their dispersal by wind

Types of gymnosperm

Gymnosperms once dominated the landscape, and still do in temperate coniferous forests. Many species are instantly recognizable by their cones, which can be up to 35 in (90 cm) long in certain tropical cycads. Although some gymnosperms may appear to produce berries, like the ginkgo and gnetophyte shown here, these are actually fleshy seed coatings.

Conifers
Most conifers have evergreen, needlelike leaves adapted to reduce water loss and repel predators. This helps them survive extreme conditions, such as alpine winters.

Cycads
The pinnate (divided) leaves of cycads superficially resemble those of tree ferns, but unlike ferns, cycads reproduce using seed cones rather than spores.

Gnetophytes
This small but diverse group includes tropical evergreen vines and shrubs, desert bushes (shown above), and a long-lived desert species with just two leaves.

Angiosperms

The most recent group of plants to evolve were the flowering plants, also known as angiosperms. Like gymnosperms (see pp.22–23), angiosperms have complex vascular tissues and produce seeds to protect the next generation of plants until conditions are right for germination. However, angiosperms additionally package their seeds in dry or fleshy fruits to protect

and disperse them better. They also produce flowers, which promote more efficient pollination and successful reproduction. The evolution of flowers and fruit led to a rapid explosion in the number of flowering plants in all habitats, ending the dominance of gymnosperms. Most of the plants on Earth are now angiosperms.

Lily flowers have three petals and three sepals, which look the same as each other

Each lily flower has six stamens, usually arranged in two groups of three

African lily (*Agapanthus praecox*)

Monocots

Around 25 percent of angiosperms are monocots—the embryonic plant contained within their seeds has only one embryonic leaf (called the cotyledon). Monocot flowers typically have parts in multiples of three, including stamens, petals, and sepals (petal-like structures that protect the emerging flower). Some of the most important food crops, including rice, wheat, and corn, are monocots.

Three petals and multiples of three

Endosperm
Cotyledon
Coleoptile
Epicotyl
Hypocotyl
Radicle

Seed
Monocots have a single cotyledon within their seeds. Most of the seed is filled with endosperm, a nourishing tissue that provides food for the germinating embryo.

Eudicots

The eudicots are named for the two cotyledons (embryonic leaves) within their seeds. Around 75 percent of angiosperms are eudicots, and most of them produce blooms with flower parts in multiples of four or five. The majority of fruit and vegetable crops are eudicots, as are most common garden plants.

Four or five petals and multiples of four or five

Flowers have five petals

Leaves have branching, netted veins

Dog rose (*Rosa canina*)

Epicotyl
First true leaves
Cotyledon
Hypocotyl
Radicle
Seed coat

Seed
Eudicots are defined by the two large cotyledons that occupy most of the seed; these contain the nutrients required for the germinating seedling.

Magnoliids

Around two percent of angiosperms are magnoliids, a relatively primitive group that includes magnolias, avocados, and black pepper plants. Their flowers can have many petals, or none at all, and their simple leaves usually have branched veins.

None, three, six, or more petals

Angiosperms represent around 80 percent of all plant species.

Pollen grains generally have only one opening

Petals are arranged in whorls, each often consisting of three elements

Stamens and multiple unfused carpels (female flower organs) are arranged in spirals

Southern magnolia
(*Magnolia grandiflora*)

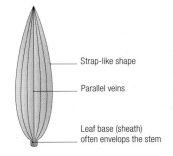

- Strap-like shape
- Parallel veins
- Leaf base (sheath) often envelops the stem

Leaf structure
Monocot leaves are usually long and narrow, with parallel veins running lengthwise or sometimes from the central midrib.

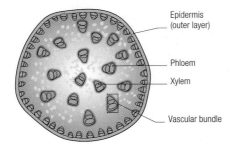

- Epidermis (outer layer)
- Phloem
- Xylem
- Vascular bundle

Stem structure
Monocot stems are usually unbranched, with bundles of vessels scattered throughout. Water-carrying xylem vessels (see p.33) point toward the stem center.

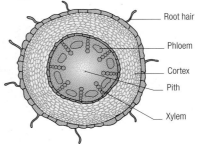

- Root hair
- Phloem
- Cortex
- Pith
- Xylem

Root structure
Monocot roots vary, but generally a circle of food-transporting phloem vessels divided by xylem arms surrounds a central pith; an outer cortex provides structure.

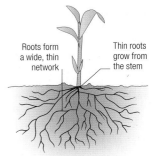

Roots form a wide, thin network

Thin roots grow from the stem

Root formation
Monocots typically form fibrous networks of roots, which branch out from the stem. Most of the root system remains in the upper layer of soil.

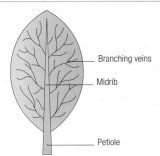

- Branching veins
- Midrib
- Petiole

Leaf structure
Eudicot leaves are often rounded, with networks of veins branching from a central midrib and a distinct leaf stalk (petiole).

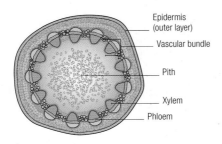

- Epidermis (outer layer)
- Vascular bundle
- Pith
- Xylem
- Phloem

Stem structure
Eudicot stems are typically branching, with bundles of vessels circling a central pith. Water-carrying xylem vessels are more central than phloem vessels (see p.33).

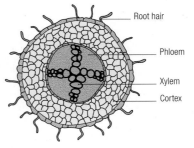

- Root hair
- Phloem
- Xylem
- Cortex

Root structure
In eudicot roots, phloem vessels develop around the two, three, or four arms of xylem vessels that radiate from the center of the root.

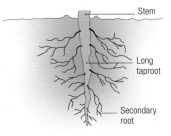

- Stem
- Long taproot
- Secondary root

Root formation
A single dominant taproot anchors eudicots in the ground, and smaller, secondary roots absorb most of the water that the plant needs.

Flowers

Evolving from modified leaves, flowers made the process of
reproduction more efficient, and enabled angiosperms to outcompete
nonflowering plants such as gymnosperms (see pp.22–23).
Gymnosperms use wind to transfer pollen, but flowers
give plants the alternative of attracting specific
pollinators, usually insects, to transfer their pollen
to other flowers of the same species. This greatly
increases the chances of successful pollination and
reproduction. Many flowers now have adaptations,
such as showy petals, nectar, and scent, to make
them more attractive to pollinators.

Stamens comprise slender
stalks (filaments) topped by
pollen-producing anthers

Reproductive role

Sexual reproduction in angiosperms involves the
transfer of pollen (the male sex cells or gametophyte)
from the male reproductive organs (stamens) of one flower to the female
organs (stigma) of another. The pollen germinates, growing a pollen tube that
carries genetic material through the stigma into the ovary beneath. The ovary
contains one or more ovules—tiny structures containing an egg cell (the female
gametophyte). Once the egg cell has been fertilized, a seed begins to form.

Leaflike sepals
protect flowers
as they develop

Pollination by insects

Flowers attract insects with sugary
nectar. This is located in the base
of the flower to ensure that
pollinators brush past the
reproductive parts and
transfer pollen.

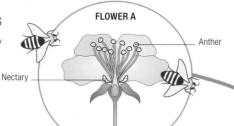

FLOWER A

Anther

Nectary

A pollinating insect brushes
past the anthers, collecting
pollen on its body while trying
to reach sweet food in the
nectaries of a flower (A).

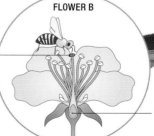

FLOWER B

Stigma

Ovary

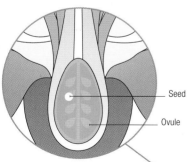

Seed

Ovule

The fertilized ovule
develops into a seed, which
contains a plant embryo and a
food reserve to sustain it
(endosperm tissue). A hard
seed coat protects the plant
embryo within.

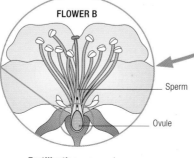

FLOWER B

Sperm

Ovule

Fertilization occurs when
sperm cells enter the ovary,
find an ovule, and fuse with
its egg cell.

Pollination occurs when
pollen grains are transferred by
the insect from one flower (A)
to the stigma of another (B).
Each pollen grain grows a
special tube along which sperm
cells travel into the ovary.

A pedicel is a
stem supporting
a single flower

Irish tutsan
(*Hypericum
pseudohenryi*)

Ancient flowers most likely resembled white magnolias.

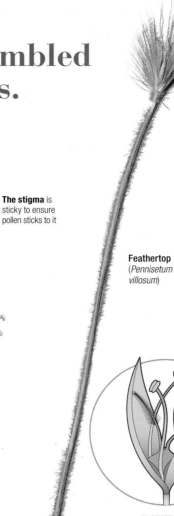

Each flower head holds millions of pollen grains

Featchertop (*Pennisetum villosum*)

Pollen

The stigma is sticky to ensure pollen sticks to it

Petals attract pollinators to visit the flower

Pollen is held on a flower's anthers

Pollen baskets carry pollen back to the hive

Bees transfer pollen from flower to flower when they visit them in search of food. Pollen sticks to hairs on the bee's body and brushes off on the next flower. Some female bees also carry pollen in tiny "baskets" on their hind legs.

Wind pollination

Pollen on anther

Feathered stigma

Inefficient wind-pollinated flowers produce vast quantities of pollen to increase their chances of success. These flowers have no need for showy petals, but often have feathery stigmas to maximize the area to which pollen can adhere.

FLOWER A

FLOWER B

Pollen, containing male sex cells, is produced by the anthers and carried by wind to a receptive female stigma.

Female stigmas receive the pollen, which produces a tube to access the ovule (within the ovary) and fertilize the egg cell.

Vertebrate pollinators

The birds and the bats

While insects are the most common pollinators, birds and bats can also pollinate flowers. Birds such as hummingbirds are attracted to brightly colored (especially red) flowers that also have large quantities of nectar. Bat-pollinated flowers are typically fairly large and pale in color, and may be heavily scented at night. Pollinating birds and bats often have long beaks or noses and tongues that can reach inside flowers; the flowers are usually tubular in shape to ensure that pollen is deposited onto the heads of the visiting animals.

Hummingbirds have long beaks so they can reach the nectar inside the flowers.

Fruits and seeds

Producing fruits containing seeds is the final stage in angiosperm reproduction. After a flower has been fertilized, its ovary undergoes a major transformation. Inside, the ovule containing the fertilized egg develops into a seed housing a tiny embryo—a future plant. The surrounding ovary develops into a fruit. This may swell, and become sweet and fleshy to attract animal seed dispersers, or may become dry or hard to aid dispersal by wind or water. Once dispersed, seeds germinate when conditions are favorable, and grow into new seedlings. These will become mature plants, produce flowers of their own, and restart the reproductive cycle all over again.

Cherry plum fruits are around ¾–2¼ in (2–3 cm) in diameter

How fruits develop

Fruits develop in four stages: fruit set, cell division, cell enlargement, and maturation. Fruit set is when the fertilized ovary becomes a developing fruit. In the second stage, cells in the ovary wall begin to rapidly divide, and then expand to further grow the fruit. Finally, the maturing fruit ripens.

Most fruit trees do not produce a crop of fruit until they are about four years old.

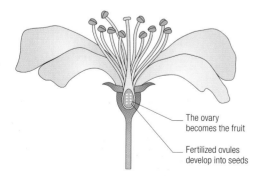

FRUIT SET

The ovary becomes the fruit

Fertilized ovules develop into seeds

After fertilization, the flower dies, the fertilized ovule develops into a seed, and the ovary wall becomes a fruit. Some plants have many ovules within an ovary, producing a fruit that contains many seeds. Each seed contains an embryo with one or two embryonic leaves, nutritious endosperm tissue, and a seed coat (see p.24).

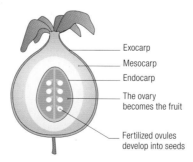

FRUIT GROWTH

Exocarp

Mesocarp

Endocarp

The ovary becomes the fruit

Fertilized ovules develop into seeds

In the second and third stages of growth, cells in the ovary wall rapidly divide then expand to form the pericarp (flesh) of the fruit. The pericarp consists of a thin outer skin (exocarp), a fleshy mesocarp, and the endocarp layer surrounding the seeds.

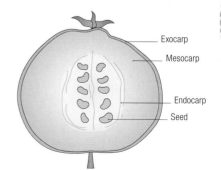

MATURATION

Exocarp

Mesocarp

Endocarp

Seed

The ripening fruit undergoes changes to maximize the dispersal of its seeds. This might involve becoming fleshy and sweet to attract animal dispersers, or drying out in order to aid wind dispersal.

Seed dispersal

Plants use various methods to ensure that seeds are carried away from them to avoid competition for space, light, and nutrients. They may make use of passing animals, or produce seeds with special features, such as parachutes or wings, to catch wind currents. Some plants have floating seeds that can be washed away by water.

Stone fruits
Also called "drupes," stone fruits such as the cherry plum (*Prunus cerasifera*) produce fleshy fruits with a hard stone or pit inside. The stone is a tough endocarp layer, which encloses a single large seed kernel.

Cherry plum
(*Prunus cerasifera*)

Hooked spines on the fruits of plants such as great burdock (*Arctium lappa*) catch on the fur of passing animals.

Water carries away the specially adapted seeds of plants from lake, pond, or marine habitats, such as the sacred lotus (*Nelumbo nucifera*).

Parachutes formed by a crown of tiny hairs catch the wind and carry dandelion (*Taraxacum officinale*) seeds away to colonize new areas.

Exploding seed pods, such as those produced by viola species, forcefully eject seeds, flinging them away from the parent plant.

Helicopter seeds, which have stiff wings to help them catch the wind, are formed by many trees, including maple (*Acer*) species.

Attractive fruits with sweet pulp, such as raspberries (*Rubus idaeus*), entice animals and birds to eat them. The seeds are passed in droppings.

Fleshy or dry

Adaptations for reproductive success

Fruits typically have either fleshy or dry pericarps (the part of the fruit around the seeds), depending on how they disperse their seeds. Fleshy fruits are nutritious to entice animals to eat them and carry their seeds to a new location, where they are deposited in fertilizer-rich droppings. Dry fruits, on the other hand, may split open to release their seeds. Some dry fruits, such as nuts, also rely on animal dispersal; many others have tough shells or chemical defenses to deter animals from eating them.

Fleshy fruits tempt animals to consume seeds along with the flesh. The hard seed coats protect the embryos within them during digestion, so they are still intact when the seeds are deposited.

Dry fruits, such as these poppy seed pods, sometimes need to dehisce (dry and break open) to release their seeds; others have different features, such as wings, to carry them off with the wind.

Anatomy of roots

Plants with vascular tissues have roots, which anchor them into the ground, and also absorb water and nutrients from the soil to help them grow. Some roots are more specialized and can also store energy or nitrogen. Most roots form symbiotic (mutually beneficial) relationships with mycorrhizal fungi, which gather nutrients and water from a much greater area of soil than roots can reach in return for sugars that the plant provides (see pp.52–53).

Tap roots

Gymnosperms (see pp.22–23) and eudicots (see pp.24–25) usually form a single dominant root, called a taproot, with smaller, branching roots along it. The main root anchors the plant and can access water and nutrients deep in the soil. Some plants, such as beets (*Beta vulgaris*), carrots (*Daucus carota*), and radishes (*Raphanus sativus*), store energy reserves of sugars in swollen taproots.

Feeder roots
take up most of
the plant's water

Beet
(*Beta vulgaris*)

The end of the tap root
is slender to penetrate
deep into the soil

Monk's hood cactus
(*Astrophytum ornatum*)

The main root
anchors the plant and can
store sugars used to fuel
growth and flowering

Fibrous roots

Monocots (see pp.24–25) and ferns (see pp.20–21) usually have fibrous root systems, with several main roots of equal diameter. These networks of thin, branching roots grow from the plant stem and are often concentrated near the surface of the soil, especially in areas where the water table is high.

Sprawling roots bind to soil
particles near the surface,
maintaining soil stability

Branching roots grow
from rapidly dividing
cells at the root tips

Spreading roots are mostly
found within the first 12–24 in
(30–60 cm) of soil, but deeper
branches provide extra anchorage

Root supports

Helping trees stand tall

In addition to underground roots, some plants—especially trees—have supporting roots that are visible above the soil surface. Prop and stilt roots grow down from the stem into the ground to provide a scaffold of support. Buttress roots are extensions of lateral roots, and are often produced by tall rainforest trees that have shallow roots.

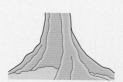

Buttress roots
provide strong, bracing
support. The largest
roots form on the side
of the prevailing wind.

Prop roots grow from
the stems of some plants
with narrow trunks, to
provide extra support
as they grow taller.

Stilt roots form at the base
of mangrove trees (*Rhizophora*
spp.), to anchor them into the
soft, shifting mud found in
their coastal swamp habitats.

How roots work

Plants send out fine lateral roots to explore the soil around them and search for resources. Water and dissolved nutrients in the soil enter root cells and hairs by osmosis, then move into conductive vessels called xylem in the root tissue (see p.33). These vessels transport the water and nutrients from the roots to the rest of the plant.

Stems transport water
and nutrients from the
roots to the leaves

Leaves make sugars
that are carried back
to the roots

Root nodules

Some plants, called legumes, form a symbiotic relationship with rhizobia bacteria, which can convert unusable nitrogen gas from the air into the nitrates that plants need for growth (see pp.14–15). Legume roots chemically attract the rhizobia, which in turn induce the roots to form small swellings called nodules to house them. In return for nitrogen compounds, the plant provides the bacteria with sugars and oxygen.

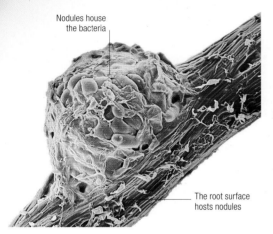

Nodules house
the bacteria

The root surface
hosts nodules

Root hair   Epidermal cells

Root hairs grow from the outer (epidermal) cell layer of a root. They increase the surface area of the root, greatly improving its ability to acquire water and nutrients and to anchor the plant. Root hairs grow behind the root tip and break off older roots as they grow.

Conductive vessels
move resources
through the plant

Branching roots
explore new areas

Water containing
dissolved nutrients enters
the roots by osmosis

Longer roots anchor
the plant and access
deeper resources

ROOT FUNCTION

Contractile roots

Many plants, particularly those with underground food storage organs such as bulbs and corms, have specially adapted roots that adjust the plant's position in the soil. These roots shrink and extend to pull the plant body deeper below ground. This can protect the plant from seasonal fluctuations in temperature and drought. Some species also use contractile roots to move new offspring plantlets away from the mother plant to reduce competition between them.

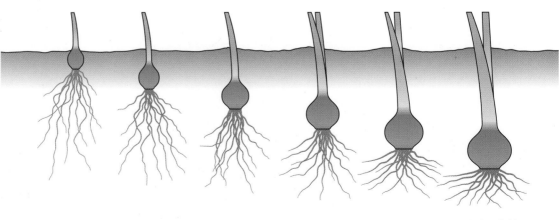

Bulb seedlings begin growing
near the surface of the soil.

Contractile roots widen then extend,
pulling the bulb deeper into the soil.

Mature bulbs sit deeply in the soil; this
supports the developing flower stem.

Anatomy of stems

Stems provide the main supporting structure of a plant, and connect the roots, leaves, flowers, and fruits. In vascular plants, stems house vessels that transport water and nutrients; some enlarged stems store nutrients for future growth, while green stems may feed the plant by photosynthesizing like leaves (see p.35). Stems also have special cells called meristems, which divide to produce new leaves and shoots.

Types of stem

Most stems grow upward to help the plant reach sunlight. For tall plants with particularly long stems, such as trees, this upward growth is often aided by the development of hard, woody tissue. Softer, flexible stems, often called "herbaceous" stems, may last for just one growing season before dying back, or may become woody with age.

Woody stems

In tough, woody stems, an outer layer of dead bark protects a live layer of phloem cells, which transport nutrients, and inner layers of xylem cells, which carry water. Cambium growth cells between the layers continually divide to produce new phloem and xylem cells as the plant grows.

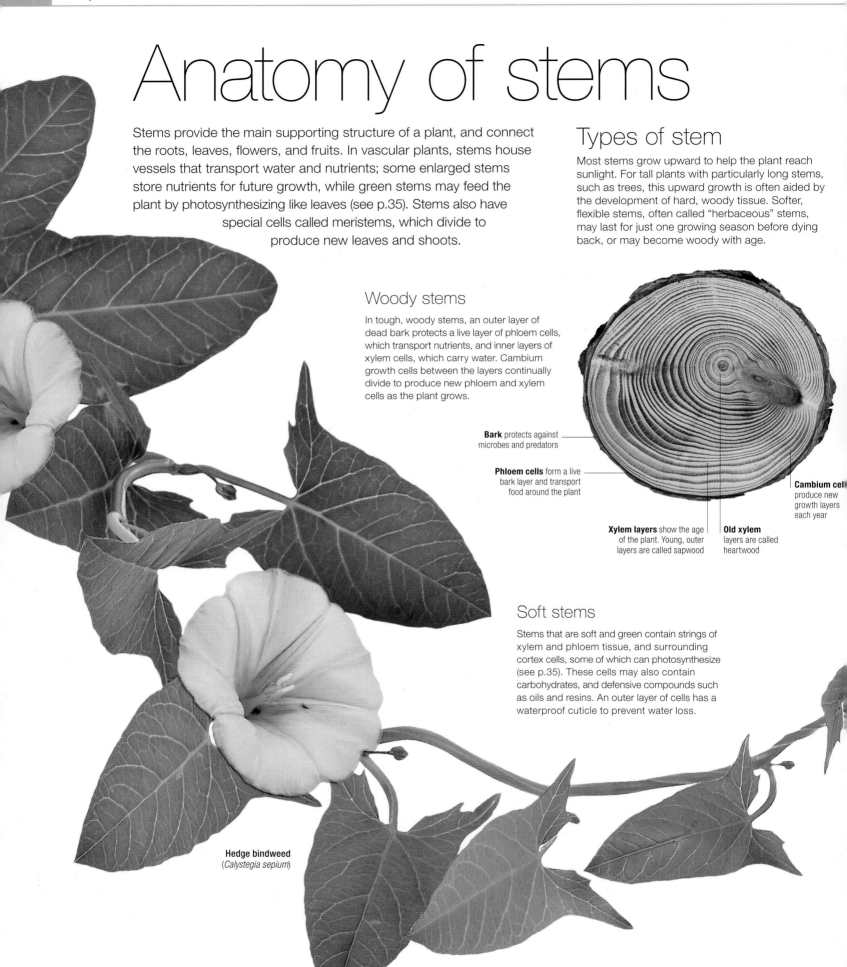

Bark protects against microbes and predators

Phloem cells form a live bark layer and transport food around the plant

Cambium cell produce new growth layers each year

Xylem layers show the age of the plant. Young, outer layers are called sapwood

Old xylem layers are called heartwood

Soft stems

Stems that are soft and green contain strings of xylem and phloem tissue, and surrounding cortex cells, some of which can photosynthesize (see p.35). These cells may also contain carbohydrates, and defensive compounds such as oils and resins. An outer layer of cells has a waterproof cuticle to prevent water loss.

Hedge bindweed
(*Calystegia sepium*)

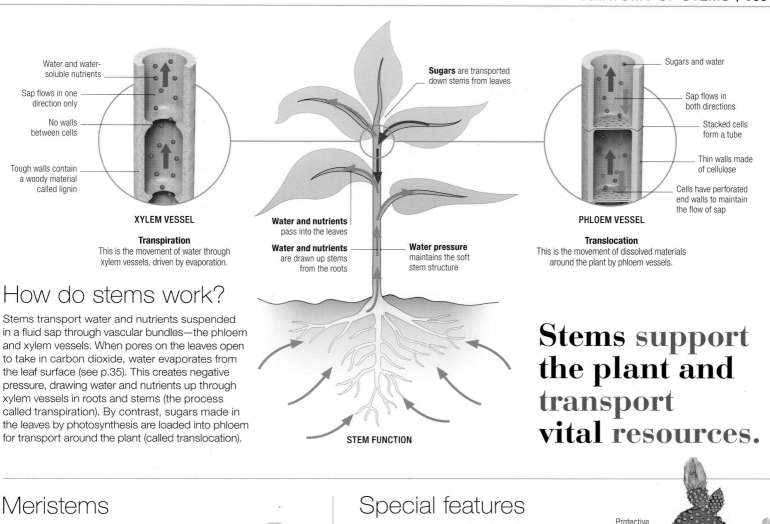

Water and water-soluble nutrients

Sap flows in one direction only

No walls between cells

Tough walls contain a woody material called lignin

XYLEM VESSEL

Transpiration
This is the movement of water through xylem vessels, driven by evaporation.

Sugars are transported down stems from leaves

Water and nutrients pass into the leaves

Water and nutrients are drawn up stems from the roots

Water pressure maintains the soft stem structure

STEM FUNCTION

Sugars and water

Sap flows in both directions

Stacked cells form a tube

Thin walls made of cellulose

Cells have perforated end walls to maintain the flow of sap

PHLOEM VESSEL

Translocation
This is the movement of dissolved materials around the plant by phloem vessels.

How do stems work?

Stems transport water and nutrients suspended in a fluid sap through vascular bundles—the phloem and xylem vessels. When pores on the leaves open to take in carbon dioxide, water evaporates from the leaf surface (see p.35). This creates negative pressure, drawing water and nutrients up through xylem vessels in roots and stems (the process called transpiration). By contrast, sugars made in the leaves by photosynthesis are loaded into phloem for transport around the plant (called translocation).

Stems support the plant and transport vital resources.

Meristems

Stems and roots have growing points called meristems, in which stem cells divide and specialize to produce new tissues. What type of cell they become depends on where they are in the plant.

Apical meristem

Intercalary meristem

Apical meristem

MERISTEM LOCATIONS

Flower

Leaf

Internode Node

Terminal bud

Special features

Some stems have special adaptations that benefit the plant. Cacti do not produce leaves, but photosynthesize in large succulent stems that also store water and nutrients. Other stems have protective thorns or chemical defenses, and some plants grow horizontal stems to spread rapidly across their habitat.

Above ground
Some climbing plants produce stems with long tendrils to help them scramble up neighboring structures. Other plants produce stems with defensive thorns—sharp outgrowths that deter animals from eating them.

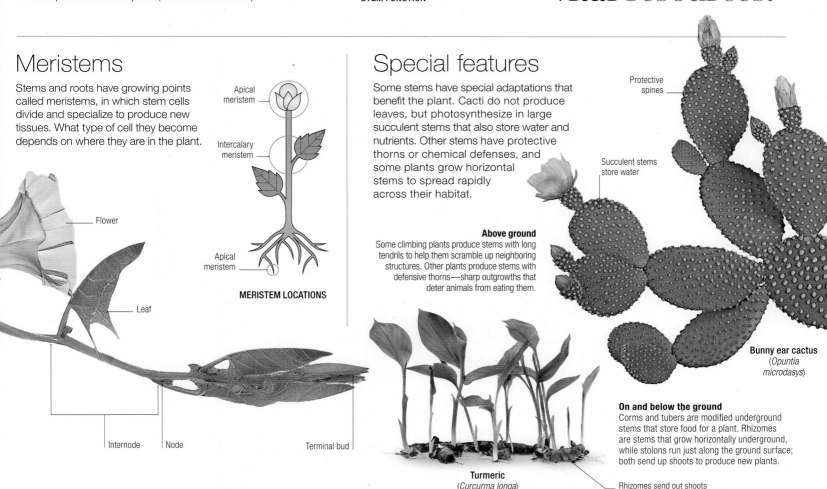

Protective spines

Succulent stems store water

Bunny ear cactus
(*Opuntia microdasys*)

On and below the ground
Corms and tubers are modified underground stems that store food for a plant. Rhizomes are stems that grow horizontally underground, while stolons run just along the ground surface; both send up shoots to produce new plants.

Rhizomes send out shoots

Turmeric
(*Curcurma longa*)

Leaf structure

Most leaves are flat to expose the largest possible area to sunlight. They have a thin transparent layer of epidermal cells that encloses densely packed photosynthetic cells supplied by veins. Stomata, microscopic pores on the surface of the leaf, let carbon dioxide in and oxygen out, and control water loss.

A waxy cuticle layer prevents water loss and protects against infection

Epidermal cells allow light to pass to photosynthetic cells beneath

Palisade mesophyll cells contain the chloroplasts that perform photosynthesis

Air spaces allow carbon dioxide to diffuse through eudicot leaves

Veins transport water, nutrients, and sugars, and provide support

LEAF STRUCTURE

Stomata open to take in carbon dioxide and close to avoid excessive water loss

Arum lily
(*Zantedeschia aethiopica*)

Leaf blade

Margin

Lateral vein

Base

Leaf stalk (petiole)

Midrib

Leaf types

Plants have evolved many types of leaf to adapt to their environments, balancing the surface area needed to absorb light with the risk of water loss, damage, or disease, and the availability of resources. Leaves of closely related plants often look similar, reflecting their shared evolutionary history; all grasses, for example, have long, narrow leaves.

Narrow leaves
Most monocots (see p.24), including grasses and palm species, have oblong or strap-like leaves that limit light damage and water loss in open, drier habitats.

Broad leaves
Eudicots (see p.24), such as deciduous trees, generally have broad "simple" leaves (undivided, not palmate or pinnate) to maximize light absorption in summer.

Palmate leaves
Compound leaves that are palmate have leaflets radiating from a single point. This spreads the leaf tissue and helps reduce wind damage and evaporation.

Pinnate leaves
Compound leaves that are pinnate have leaflets attached along a central stalk (rachis). This gives more photosynthetic surface area for the same resources.

Bipinnate leaves
The fronds of many ferns (see pp.21–22) have compound leaves in which leaflets are further divided into smaller "pinnae," creating a feathery effect.

Anatomy of leaves

Leaves harvest sunlight and use its energy to make a sugary food for the plant through the chemical process of photosynthesis. As the foundation of the food chain, everything that we eat originates in this process, and the oxygen we breathe is released as a byproduct. The sugars made in the leaves travel through stems and roots, and are broken down, releasing energy for plant growth and reproduction. Despite their shared function, leaves come in a great variety of shapes, sizes, and textures, ranging from tiny, scalelike forms to large, compound fronds many yards in length. These differences reflect how plants have evolved leaves to suit their specific environments.

Why are leaves green?

Leaves contain several pigments that harvest light, of which chlorophyll is the most abundant. Within leaf cells, chlorophyll is packed onto stacks of membranes in structures called chloroplasts. White sunlight is a spectrum of all colors, and chlorophyll absorbs the blue and red light wavelengths, leaving green light to be reflected from or pass through the plant. This makes leaves look green.

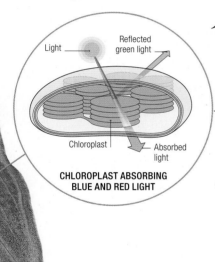

Light
Reflected green light
Chloroplast
Absorbed light

CHLOROPLAST ABSORBING BLUE AND RED LIGHT

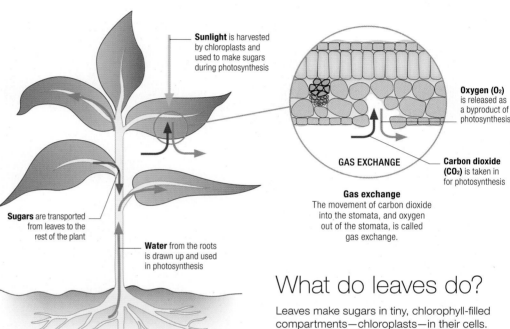

Sunlight is harvested by chloroplasts and used to make sugars during photosynthesis

Oxygen (O_2) is released as a byproduct of photosynthesis

GAS EXCHANGE

Carbon dioxide (CO_2) is taken in for photosynthesis

Gas exchange
The movement of carbon dioxide into the stomata, and oxygen out of the stomata, is called gas exchange.

Sugars are transported from leaves to the rest of the plant

Water from the roots is drawn up and used in photosynthesis

LEAF FUNCTION

What do leaves do?

Leaves make sugars in tiny, chlorophyll-filled compartments—chloroplasts—in their cells. Chloroplasts use energy from sunlight to convert carbon dioxide (absorbed from the atmosphere) and water (delivered via roots and stems) into sugars. During this process, leaves release oxygen. Water is also released from the leaves; as it evaporates, it draws water up through stems and roots by capillary action (see p.33).

Drip tips are common on plants native to wet habitats, such as this arum lily (*Zantedeschia aethiopica*). They let water run off leaves quickly without damaging them.

Variegation

Chimeric leaves

Leaves are produced from groups of dividing cells called meristems. In variegated plants, these include normal cells and those with a mutation that prevents them from producing chlorophyll. As the cells divide and the leaves grow, they will have patches of normal green cells and patches of yellow or white cells that lack chlorophyll. Variegated plants are rare in nature as they are less able to photosynthesize and therefore weaker than other plants.

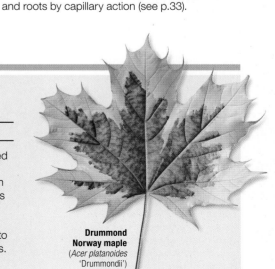

Drummond Norway maple
(*Acer platanoides* 'Drummondii')

The leaf life cycle

The lifespans of leaves vary widely—they can live anywhere from a few months to 20 years depending on the plant species. Environmental factors mainly determine these differences. Longer-lived evergreen leaves are found primarily in regions with extremely hot or cold conditions, while plants with short-lived leaves that are shed annually, such as deciduous trees, are found in temperate areas. Climate and habitat also appear to influence form—evergreen leaves are usually thicker and denser than deciduous leaves.

Evergreen or deciduous

Whether a tree has evergreen or deciduous leaves is largely down to climate. In tropical rainforests, it is wet and warm year-round, so plants invest a lot of energy to produce long-lived, large evergreen leaves that make the most of the continuous growing season. In temperate regions, plants produce more flimsy deciduous leaves to capture light as quickly as possible in the warm summers, but do not waste resources protecting them in winter when little photosynthesis can occur. In cold climates, plants produce slow-growing but tough, waxy, evergreen leaves that can withstand the extreme conditions.

Falling plane tree leaves (*Platanus spp.*)

Evergreen plants naturally grow in tropical, cold temperate, or Arctic regions and include conifers such as pine trees (*Pinus* spp.).

Deciduous plants, such as maple trees (*Acer* spp.), grow in temperate regions, and produce new leaves each spring.

Environment matters

Plants have evolved leaf shapes and sizes adapted to the climate in which they live. In the desert, many plants have tiny leaves to limit water loss, while in the rainforest this is not a concern, and most leaves have a large surface area. In addition to size, temperature seems to impact leaf shape. Leaves in cooler climates typically have lobed or serrated edges and those in warmer regions have smooth margins, although this is only a general pattern. Plants can also adapt their leaf shape to changing conditions. Some species form narrower leaves in response to climate change.

Succulent
Desert plants are often succulent, with thick, fleshy leaves adapted for water storage and a relatively small surface area to reduce water loss.

Needlelike
The waxy, needlelike leaves of many conifers minimize water loss and are resistant to wind, helping plants withstand extremely cold, dry conditions.

Hairy
Alpine plants often have hairy leaves. The hairs provide protection from excess light, insulate against extremes of temperature, and reduce the rate of water loss.

Large
Plants native to shady habitats, such as the understory of tropical rainforests, tend to have broad, large leaves to maximize light absorption.

Why do leaves change color?

Green chlorophyll is the dominant pigment in leaves, but plants stop producing it in the fall, revealing the less abundant yellow and orange carotenoid pigments. As these begin to break down, the plant produces red-purple anthocyanins (pigments with antioxidant properties) to protect leaves while their nutrients are reabsorbed and recycled. When the anthocyanins are lost, tannins and dead material make the leaves look brown.

Deciduous trees detect fall is coming by the shorter day lengths and cooler temperatures.

YELLOW / ORANGE
Fall color

Green pigment is reabsorbed by the plant, revealing carotenoid pigments

RED / PURPLE
Fall color

Red-purple anthocyanin pigments are produced by the leaf as carotenoids break down

LIFE CYCLE OF DECIDUOUS LEAVES

Most deciduous leaves burst from buds in spring, rapidly growing and maturing; they then age in the fall, turning from green to shades of yellow-orange and red-purple, before going brown, dying, and falling from the tree. The following year's leaf buds are formed from nutrients reabsorbed from dying leaves.

GREEN
Spring / summer color

Green pigments are dominant

Carotenoid pigments are masked

Tannins are hidden by pigments

BROWN
Winter color

Carotenoid pigments have been lost

Anthocyanins pigments break down

Brown tannins are revealed

Nutrients recycled from dying leaves are used to form leaf buds in the fall or winter, ready to open the following spring

BUDDING

LEAVES BEGIN TO DECAY

The plant produces enzymes that break down the layer of cells at the base of the leaf stalks, causing leaves to drop

Why do leaves drop?

After reabsorbing nutrients from the leaves about to drop, deciduous trees form a protective layer of cork cells at the base of each petiole (leaf stalk). The neighboring layer of "shedding" cells is broken down by enzymes produced by the plant, and the leaf falls. The cork cells seal the wound and are visible as a leaf scar.

Serrated
In cooler climates, plants often have leaves with serrated margins. This may increase the temperature around the leaf, speeding photosynthesis.

Smooth
In hot, tropical areas, plants tend to have leaves with smooth edges, smooth surfaces, and drip tips to enable excess water to run off efficiently.

The fungi kingdom

Fungi belong to their own kingdom and are not plants, animals, or bacteria. They were mistakenly classified as plants by the Swedish biologist Carl Linnaeus in the 1700s—probably because the fruit bodies of some fungi look a bit like plants—but they are more closely related to animals than plants. There are estimated to be over five million species of fungi across all habitats on Earth, but only around 155,000 have been named and cataloged so far.

A fungal timeline

The first fungi appeared as single-celled organisms living in water around one billion years ago. Some fungi, such as Chytridiomycota, still retain features of these early ancestors. Five major categories of fungi are well known, but there are several more; our understanding of how these groups evolved in relation to each other is still incomplete. We do know, however, that they evolved from a common ancestor rather than from each other.

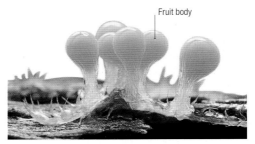
Fruit body

Myxomycete slime mold (*Trichia decipiens*)

What is not a fungus?

Water molds (oomycetes) form colonies and produce spores like fungi, but they are more closely related to types of algae. Some myxomycete slime molds also produce minute, spore-producing fruit bodies on delicate stems that superficially resemble fungal fruit bodies.

Chytridiomycota

Some of the simplest fungi, Chytridiomycota (commonly called chytrids) have a microscopic ball-shaped body (thallus), with filaments called rhizoids extending from the base. There are 1,050 named species, many of which live in water and wet soil, and feed on dead material. Some types of Chytridiomycota cause disease by growing in or on living animal or plant cells.

Chytrids These fungi reproduce by changing their body into a spore-producing structure called a sporangium (below). A plug in the top of the sporangium dissolves or detaches, releasing spores that can swim using a tail-like projection.

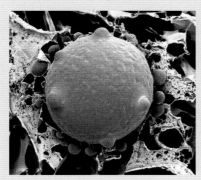

Chytrid fungus

650–800 MILLION years ago

Zoopagomycota

The first group of fungi to evolve spores that cannot swim, Zoopagomycota include about 550 named species. They form networks of hyphae called mycelia, and specialize in killing invertebrates. Masses of their hyphae can sometimes be seen emerging from their victims.

Entomophthora These fungi are an insect-killing form of Zoopagomycota. They produce spores on hyphae that have emerged from insect cadavers, which they shoot off to hit and infect further prey, such as the fly pictured below.

Entomophthora fungus (*Entomophthora muscae*)

650–700 MILLION years ago

Mucoromycota

There are two major groupings in this division, which contains about 1,300 named species. Mucoromycotina species feed largely on dead animal and plant material, while Glomeromcotina species are important plant partners, supplying their roots with water and mineral nutrients.

Mucoromycotina Species in this group of fungi are generally microscopic, but the dark structures that contain their asexual spores (the round structures shown below) are sometimes visible, such as on bread mold.

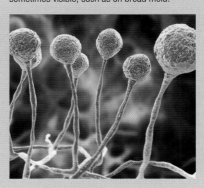

Bread mold (*Rhizopus stolonifer*)

650–700 MILLION years ago

Dikarya

Also known as "higher fungi," Dikarya are the most recently evolved fungi. Their name comes from the Greek *di*, meaning "two," as they form cells with two nuclei during sexual reproduction. Some Dikarya remain microscopic throughout their lives, but others form visible fruit bodies.

600–650 MILLION years a

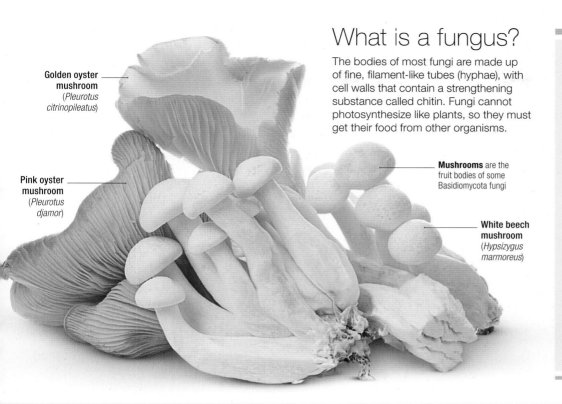

Golden oyster
mushroom
(*Pleurotus
citrinopileatus*)

Pink oyster
mushroom
(*Pleurotus
djamor*)

Mushrooms are the
fruit bodies of some
Basidiomycota fungi

**White beech
mushroom**
(*Hypsizygus
marmoreus*)

What is a fungus?

The bodies of most fungi are made up
of fine, filament-like tubes (hyphae), with
cell walls that contain a strengthening
substance called chitin. Fungi cannot
photosynthesize like plants, so they must
get their food from other organisms.

Fossil fungi

The oldest preserved fungi

Fossils suggest that fungi colonized land
more than 635 million years ago, but there
is evidence of fungus-like filaments in rocks
that lay beneath deep oceans millions of years
earlier. The earliest complete mushroom
fossils are from at least 99 million years ago.

A fossilized mushroom preserved in Burmese amber.

Basidiomycota

Commonly called basidiomycetes, 52,300 species in this
group have been named so far. After mating, most of them form large
fruit bodies, such as mushrooms, puffballs, or brackets—sometimes
very soon, but often weeks or months afterward. Sexual spores are
formed in the fruit bodies on small, club-shaped structures called
basidia, from which the group takes its name.

Trumpet chanterelle (*Cantharellus infundibuliformis*)

Ascomycota

This is the largest group in the fungal kingdom, with
97,300 species named so far. All ascomycetes make vast numbers
of asexual spores without mating. Some also mate and make spores
in a saclike structure called an ascus (from the Greek *askos*—
meaning "leather bag"). Asci are often housed in minute fruit
bodies, but some, such as truffles, are larger.

Scarlet elf cup (*Sarcoscypha austriaca*)

The fungal life cycle

Fungi reproduce by forming spores. These can be produced by sexual reproduction, which involves the fungus mating with a compatible partner, or produced asexually by an individual fungus without mating. Most fungi can reproduce using both sexual and asexual methods, though one method often predominates. Spores produced by some fungi have especially thick walls that help them survive until growing conditions allow them to germinate. Other spores, such as the sexual spores of many basidiomycete fungi, have thinner walls and rely on landing quickly in a suitable environment for germination. Spores are mostly dispersed by wind, but some are propelled from the parent fungus, or carried to new locations by passing animals.

Sexual reproduction

In some fungi, mating simply involves the hyphae from two individuals fusing. In others, different structures may fuse; or male or female sex cells may need to travel between reproductive organs. Sexual reproduction produces fungi with DNA from both parents, giving them new characteristics that can be an advantage in variable, challenging environments.

Basidiomycetes usually produce sexual spores in visible fruit bodies.

The hyphae of compatible basidiomycetes fuse during mating.

Young mushroom

A fruit body with a stem and cap develops. Once mature, it is ready to produce sexual spores.

IMMATURE FRUIT BODY

Mature mushroom

Sexual spores are carried on air currents

Microscopic sexual spores are released from the gills of the mature fruit body, and are dispersed by air currents. Most land within a few yards of the fruit body that produced them.

SPORE DISPERSAL

Growing hyphae

GERMINATING SPORES

Spores germinate, producing fine, threadlike filaments called hyphae. As they grow, these form a weblike network called the mycelium.

BASIDIOMYCETE REPRODUCTION CYCLE

Sexual reproduction in basidiomycete fungi involves hyphae from two individuals fusing together, which combines their DNA. This "mated" mycelium eventually produces fruit bodies and the next generation of spores.

Hyphae of fungus A

Hyphae of fungus B

Tight little knots of entwined, mated hyphae form when the temperature, moisture, and food supply are suitable. Each little knot (called a primordium) develops as a tiny, pinhead mushroom.

PRIMORDIUM

The mycelium finds a sexually compatible mate (this can take hours or months) and their hyphae fuse, sharing nuclei that contain DNA. Mated hyphae have two nuclei in each of their cells — one from each fungus parent.

MATING MYCELIUM

Fawn mushroom
(*Pluteus cervinus*)

Sexual spores are produced on cells in the gills of mushrooms

Most fungi reproduce using spores, but sometimes also bud or separate into fragments to produce offspring.

Asexual reproduction

Most fungi that reproduce asexually make spores—conidia—on the ends of special hyphae called conidiophores. Others form spores within hyphae, or in sacs (sporangia) on the tips of upright hyphae. Asexual reproduction requires less energy than sexual reproduction, so vast numbers of asexual spores can be made. Yeasts often reproduce asexually by budding—a small bud of tissue forms and detaches to form a new organism. Asexual spores and buds are clones of the parent fungus.

Individual conidia break away from the chain

The conidia detach easily from the conidiophore, and each has the potential to form a new fungus

Chains of asexual conidia

Onion skin

Aspergillus growth

Black mold (*Aspergillus niger*) colonizes onions by producing asexual spores (conidia).

Conidia are often produced in chains at the tip of individual conidiophores. Some species, such as the ascomycete *Aspergillus*, produce long chains of spores (shown here at around 700 times the actual size).

How fungi grow and feed

Mushrooms usually come to mind when thinking of fungi, but these are just fruit bodies that appear when a fungus reproduces. The main body of most fungi is the mycelium—a network of hyphae hidden underground or within its food source. Fruit bodies develop from the mycelium, and may be produced many times during the lifetime of long-lived species. Some fungi, known as yeasts, consist of a single cell that replicates by budding (see p.41), or cell division. Certain fungi can switch between a mycelial and a yeast-body form, depending on their environment.

Yeasts

Single-celled bodies

Saccharomyces ("sugar fungus") yeasts use enzymes to break down carbohydrates into sugars, which they absorb. They ferment these sugars to obtain energy, producing carbon dioxide and alcohol as byproducts.

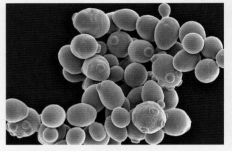

Yeast cells with scars where buds have detached.

What is the mycelium?

Forming the main body of most fungi, the mycelium is a network of fine filaments called hyphae. These threads are usually a few micrometers wide, so can only be seen with a microscope. Hyphae can penetrate solid materials using physical force or digestive enzymes, and can also grow through narrow gaps and across empty spaces. Although hyphae are thin, their weblike network has a large surface area, helping them find and absorb food. This far-reaching network also helps certain fungi find and partner with plant roots in mutually beneficial relationships (see pp.52–53).

The mycelium is crucial to the existence of most fungi.

Hyphae grow in whatever material they are feeding on, forming long-lived networks. Spore-producing fruit bodies, such as mushrooms, sometimes develop above ground from these mycelial networks.

Button mushroom
(*Agaricus bisporus*)

Mushroom fruit body

Hyphae diverge as the colony expands

Hyphae at the margins maintain a regular distance

Spore

Mycelial growth
Hyphae emerge from the tip of a germinating spore and then begin to branch outward, forming a mycelium.

Hyphae interconnect to form a network

Side branches grow to fill the gaps between diverging hyphae

What do fungi feed on?

Every chemical made by plants, animals, and microorganisms can be broken down by a species of fungus and used for food. However, across the fungal kingdom, food sources and preferences vary widely. Most fungi are saprotrophic, meaning they feed on dead material; other fungi parasitize living organisms, causing disease; while others form beneficial partnerships.

Plant partners
Some fungi partner with organisms that can make food for them. In mycorrhizal partnerships (see pp.52–53), the roots of plants provide fungi with sugars, and the fungi supply the plants with water and nutrients in return.

Fruit bodies of the mycorrhizal fungus *Boletus edulis*

Decomposer fungi
Feeding on dead plants, animals, or other fungi, saprotrophic fungi absorb nutrients from dead or decaying material that they break down.

Killers and parasites
Some fungi kill other organisms and then feed on them. Others, like this leaf rust, are parasites, keeping their food alive while they feed on it.

Visible cords

Hyphae are usually microscopic, but in a few fungi species, parallel hyphae join together to form visible cords. Sometimes these are quite tough and have a thick outer rind. Cords may be seen above ground on rotting wood, or stretching through leaf litter.

How fungi digest their food

Plants make their own food by photosynthesis, but fungi and animals cannot do this. They need food that has already been made by other organisms. Animals eat this food and digest it in their guts, using enzymes to break down large food molecules into smaller ones that their bodies can use for energy and growth. Fungi use a similar process, but break down the food outside their bodies using enzymes secreted by hyphae.

Hyphae secrete digestive enzymes to break down large food molecules (for example, starch) into nutrients such as glucose that can be absorbed by their hyphae.

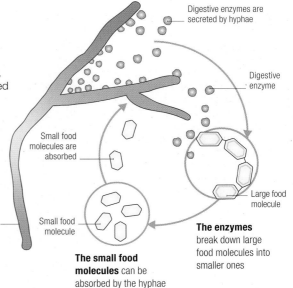

Digestive enzymes are secreted by hyphae

Digestive enzyme

Small food molecules are absorbed

Large food molecule

Fungal hyphae

Small food molecule

The enzymes break down large food molecules into smaller ones

The small food molecules can be absorbed by the hyphae

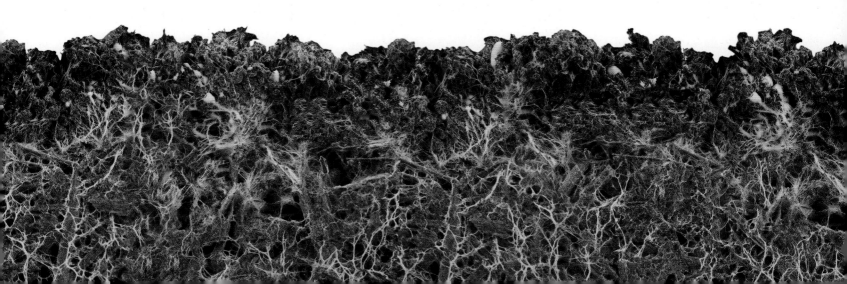

Ascomycetes

The largest and most diverse group in the fungal kingdom, ascomycetes include fungi with microscopic fruiting structures and some with large fruit bodies, such as morels, truffles, and cup fungi. Regardless of size, all ascomycete fruit bodies produce sexual spores in tiny sacs called asci. Ascomycetes can also produce vast numbers of asexual spores (conidia) that are clones of the parent fungus (see p.41)—this is often the most common method of reproduction. Some ascomycetes, such as *Penicillium* and *Aspergillus*, are visible to the naked eye only when they form a mass of colored, asexual spores.

The lid opens to release mature spores

Detail of an individual ascus
Morels have club-shaped asci that shoot out spores.

Each ascus typically contains eight spores

DETAIL OF ASCUS

Mature spores

Multiple asci sit on the inner surface of the cup, creating a fertile layer

Small cups
This illustration shows one of the many small cups that form the head of a morel fruit body.

Cup

INNER SURFACE OF CUP

Morel (*Morchella* spp.)
Their fruit bodies are covered in deep cups lined by asci. The open honeycomb design helps spores catch air currents and disperse widely.

Common morel
(*Morchella esculenta*)

Special spore sacs

Ascomycetes are sometimes called sac fungi because their sexual spores are made in microscopic sacs called asci. These are usually cylindrical or club-shaped, but may be spherical in some fungi. An ascus usually contains eight sexual spores (called ascospores), but some contain four or sixteen. Most asci form inside fruit bodies, but some fungi form asci on the leaves or fruits of their plant host.

Asci in fruit bodies
The fertile layer that contains the asci may be exposed (as in fungi with cup- or saucer-shaped fruit bodies), held in tiny, flask-shaped structures, or fully enclosed within a fruit body.

Ascus

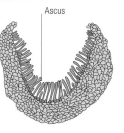

Cups and saucers

Ascus

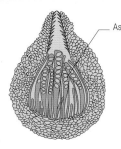

Flask-shaped structure

Ascus

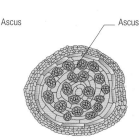

Closed structure

Types of fruit body

Ascomycete fruit bodies vary greatly in form, depending on the arrangement of the fertile layer that holds their asci. Some ascomycetes produce tiny, spherical fruit bodies on the stems and leaves of host plants, which break open to release their spores. Others have large, fleshy cups and saucers with asci on their upper surface. Fruit bodies with flasks hold their asci in minute, bottle-shaped structures.

Closed bodies

Truffles are examples of ascomycetes with enclosed asci. These tuber-like structures develop underground, and have closed, spherical asci packed into a dense, warty, fruit body. Truffles have a strong scent to attract mammals. These dig up and eat the fungus, then spread its spores to new locations in their droppings.

Summer truffle (*Tuber aestivum*)
Found throughout Europe, the summer truffle has fruit bodies 1–4 in (2–10 cm) across.

Parasites

Fungi living on other organisms

Many ascomycetes cause plant diseases, such as scabs and powdery mildews. The fungus *Erysiphe alphitoides* commonly causes powdery mildew on oak trees in Europe. It colonizes young leaves and shoots, covering the surfaces with a felty, white mycelium. The mycelium uses tiny pegs to penetrate and feed from leaf cells.

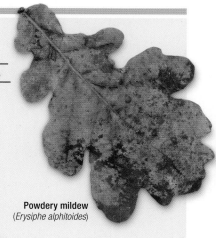

Powdery mildew
(*Erysiphe alphitoides*)

Scarlet caterpillar fungus
(*Cordyceps militaris*)

Tiny flasks protrude from the fruit body surface

Asexual spores

Flasks

The fertile layer of some ascomycetes is covered in minuscule, bottle-shaped structures (flasks) with many asci inside. Spores are discharged from one ascus at a time, through a pore at the top of the flask.

The tiny flasks look like black dots

Nail fungus
(*Poronia punctata*)
Feeding on horse and donkey dung, the nail fungus produces tiny fruit bodies that look like the head of a carpenter's nail.

Candlesnuff fungus (*Xylaria hypoxylon*)
Asexual spores form first on white fruit bodies. The fruit bodies later darken as sexual spores develop in tiny flasks on their surface.

Dead man's fingers (*Xylaria polymorpha*)

Club fungi
Cordyceps and *Xylaria* species are examples of fungi that hold their asci in tiny flasks embedded in the firm tissue of their club-shaped fruit bodies.

Cups and saucers

Fungi with cup- or saucer-shaped fruit bodies have an exposed fertile layer that contains asci. Spores are forcibly ejected from many asci at the same time, causing an updraft that lifts them into air currents above the fruit body surface.

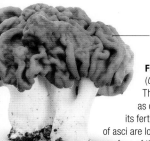

Fertile layer

False morel
(*Gyromitra esculenta*)
This fungus is classed as cup-shaped because its fertile, spore-bearing layer of asci are located on the outer surface of the fruit body.

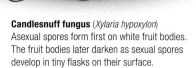

Fertile layer

Beech jelly disk (*Neobulgaria pura*)
Found on fallen broadleaved trees in Europe and eastern North America, this fungus has tiny cups less than ½ in (1 cm) tall.

Orange peel fungus (*Aleuria aurantia*)
Common on gravelly soil in Europe and North America, this fungus has cups that can reach 4 in (10 cm) across, with a bright orange, fertile layer inside.

Fertile layer

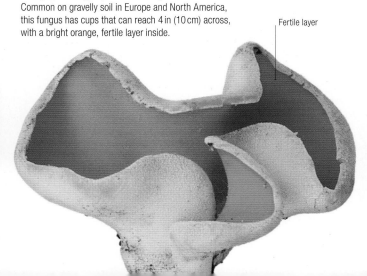

Basidiomycetes

This division of the fungal kingdom includes mushrooms, smuts, rusts, and some yeasts. The structure of their fruit bodies varies enormously, and includes jelly- and crust-like forms, coral-shaped fungi, brackets, puffballs, and mushrooms with gills or pores (see pp.48–49). These structures evolved to spread spores efficiently in different environments. At the microscopic level, however, they all have a special form of spore-releasing cells—little club-shaped structures called basidia, which may protrude from gills, tubes, or spines, or sit in pores, or on the smooth underside of fruit bodies, depending on the species.

Spore structures

Basidia form a fertile layer on the fruit body. They are reproductive cells that each usually produce four sexual spores (basidiospores). These spores contain genes from two fungus parents. Once the spores are released, they will germinate in suitable conditions to produce a new fungus.

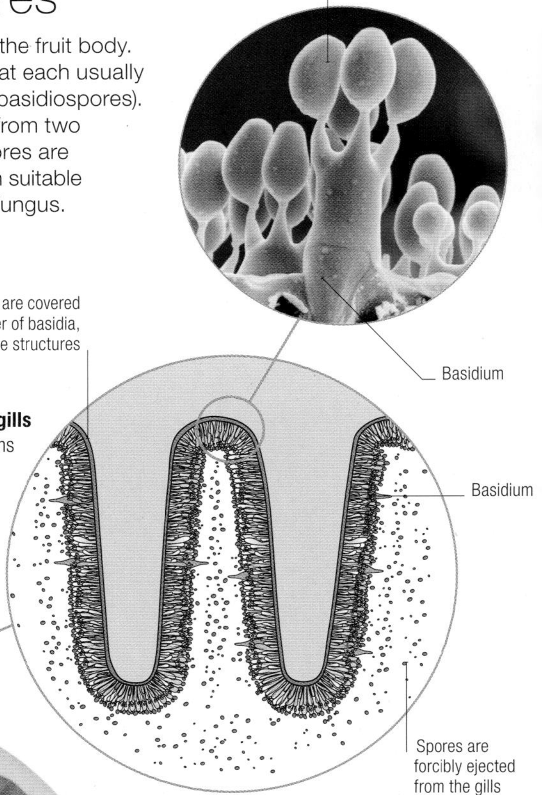

A basidiospore attached to a basidium

Basidium

Gills are covered with a fertile layer of basidia, as well as sterile structures

Basidium

Basidia on the gills
On mature oyster mushrooms (*Pleurotus* spp.), basidia are located on the gills on the underside of the cap.

Spores are forcibly ejected from the gills by the basidia

CLOSE-UP OF GILLS

The top of the cap protects the exposed gills beneath

Golden oyster mushroom
(*Pleurotus citrinopileatus*)
This fungus grows on decaying hardwood trees and produces mushroom-shaped fruit bodies.

Fruit bodies

Basidiomycete fruit bodies differ in the form and location of the fertile layer where sexual spores are made. This layer may consist of gills, tubes, veins, spines, or teeth; coral- or rosette-shaped structures; flattened tongues; or smooth, warty, wrinkled, or spiny crusts. Each form has evolved to disperse spores as efficiently as possible.

Wind dispersal

The spores of most basidiomycetes are dispersed by wind, but the chance of each spore landing in the perfect site for growth is small. To compensate for this, fungi make billions of spores to hugely increase the chances of reproducing. Spores are usually ejected away from the basidia and then carried off by air currents.

Spores are produced on the surface

Grows on rotting wood

Strict-branch coral fungus (*Ramaria stricta*)
The fruit body of this basidiomycete grows to around 4 in (10 cm) tall. Each branching arm is covered with basidia.

Blushing bracket (*Daedaleopsis confragosa*)
Spores are released through pores on the undersurface of the fruit body, which turns pink or red if bruised.

Puffing and exploding

In puffballs and earthstars, spores are formed in spherical sacs, in tubes, or on other exposed surfaces, rather than on gills. When a twig, raindrop, or animal disturbs the fruit body, it puffs out spores.

Common puffball (*Lycoperdon perlatum*)
Spores are made in a pear-shaped sac, 1–2 in (3–6 cm) across, and are puffed out from a small hole at the top of the fruit body.

Cannonball fungus (*Sphaerobolus stellatus*)
Each tiny fruit body of this earthstar fungus contains a minute spore package that can be shot up to 18 ft (5.5 m) away.

Raindrop propulsion

Bird's nest fungi use a unique "splash cup" method to disperse spores. When drops of rain land in the fruit bodies, spore packages are ejected at a speed of 16 ft (5 m) per second. Each package has a tiny, coiled cord to help it latch onto a landing site.

Spore packages

A membrane protects the spore packages while they form

Fluted bird's nest (*Cyathus striatus*)
The packages of basidiospores, held in tiny cups around ¼ in (6 mm) wide, resemble eggs in a bird's nest.

Animal attraction

Using insects or other invertebrates, such as slugs, to transport spores is a more reliable way to ensure they reach a suitable site for germination. Some fungi have special adaptations to attract these spore couriers.

Fruit bodies may reach 8 in (20 cm) in diameter

Basket stinkhorn (*Clathrus ruber*)
The cage-like fruit body produces a dark, smelly substance on the inside to attract the flies that will disperse its spores.

Spores are held in a smelly slime that sticks to the bodies of insects

The white, spongy stem is hollow inside

Common stinkhorn (*Phallus impudicus*)
This fungus attracts insects by producing spores in a putrid, slimy mass that smells like rotting meat.

Mushroom fruit bodies

Many basidiomycetes produce fruit bodies in the form of mushrooms. Fruit bodies are equivalent to the fruits of flowering plants, and the spores they produce play a similar role to seeds. While mushrooms vary greatly in size, color, and shape, they all form sexual spores in special cells called basidia (see pp.46–47) on the undersides of their caps. These cells may be held in gills; in the walls of tubes; or on the spiny, toothed, veined, or smooth undersurface of the mushroom cap. Fruit bodies can only form once the mycelium has mated (see p.40), and when conditions are optimal for growth—this may be many weeks, or even months, after mating. Once they begin to form, mushroom fruit bodies develop quickly, and often last only a few days when mature.

> ## Mushrooms are visible signs of the fungus, most of which lies hidden below ground.

Gills are the spore-producing layer on the mushrooms of some species of basidiomycetes.

Sexual spores project from cells (basidia) in the gills

Fruit body development

In many types of basidiomycetes, fruit bodies form after hyphae that have mated come together in knots, called pinheads or primordia (see p.40). These develop into immature fruit bodies that eventually grow into larger, mushroom-shaped forms, raising their spore-producing surfaces above ground. All mushrooms with gills develop in a similar way, but the tissues that protect their gills while the spores develop vary. In some mushrooms, the gills are protected by a weblike tissue; in some, the tissue is slimy; in others, it forms a type of veil (see box, opposite). In *Amanita* mushrooms, such as the fly agaric (*Amanita muscaria*) below, the fruit body emerges shrouded in a protective outer veil (the "universal veil"), and the gills are covered by a second, partial veil.

Scales are remnants of the universal veil

Remnants of the partial veil that protected the gills

Stipe elongates

Swollen base (volva) retains remnants of the universal veil

Fly agaric
(*Amanita muscaria*)

Emerging fruit body protected by the universal veil

Cap begins to show

Stage one
The young mushroom looks like a white egg and is completely enclosed in a veil.

Stage two
The stipe (stalk) elongates, rupturing the universal veil. This starts to reveal the cap.

Stage three
As the cap expands, the universal veil breaks further, revealing the red cap beneath.

Stage four
As the cap enlarges, the partial veil that encloses the gills ruptures, forming a skirt or "annulus."

Stage five
The stipe lengthens further, and the cap expands, creating a classic mushroom shape.

Stage six
The gills are exposed when the mushroom is fully grown. They hang vertically, so ejected spores drop from between them and catch the wind.

Remnants of the
universal veil

Protective fringe
Panther cap (*Amanita pantherina*) often
has a distinctive, shaggy ring of
scales on the stipe beneath its
cap—the remnants of the
partial veil that protected
the gills in early growth.

Panther cap
(*Amanita pantherina*)

Webs, veils, and slime

Protecting the spore-producing structures

On mushrooms, the spore-producing surface
underneath the cap is often protected by a special
layer of tissue. In *Agaricus* species, it can take the
form of a membrane-like partial veil that covers only the
gills. *Cortinarius* mushrooms form a thread- or weblike
structure, while *Gomphidius* species have a slimy
coating. *Amanita* mushrooms (opposite) have two levels
of protection—a membrane that fully encloses the young
fruit body (universal veil), and a partial veil that covers the
gills. As the fruit bodies enlarge, remnants of the veils,
webs, or slime are often left on the surface of the stalk,
and can be used to help identify mushroom species.

A cobweb-like veil covers the underside of the cap in a
Cortinarius "webcap" mushroom.

The partial veil of an *Agaricus* mushroom has been
pulled back to reveal the spore-producing surface beneath.

Lichens

Although lichens look like plants, they are actually a combination of organisms that live together—fungi, green algae, and sometimes cyanobacteria. The algae and cyanobacteria are known as "photobionts" because they contain photosynthetic pigments; they make carbohydrates that they feed to the fungi. In return, the fungi protect the photobionts and supply them with mineral nutrients obtained from rain, or from the substrate they are attached to. Lichens generally grow very slowly—less than a millimeter each year—but they can reach a large size because they live for so long. Some lichens have a lifespan of hundreds or even thousands of years.

Symbiotic structure

The body (thallus) of a lichen is made up of photobiont cells embedded in a mesh of fungal filaments (hyphae). This close contact makes it easy for water, nutrients, and carbohydrates to diffuse between the organisms. Some fungi also have hyphae with tiny pegs or tubes that tap into the photobiont cells to reach the carbohydrates inside. When algae and cyanobacteria are both present as photobionts, the cyanobacteria are held in special structures on the lichen surface.

Lichens are the product of a mutualistic partnership.

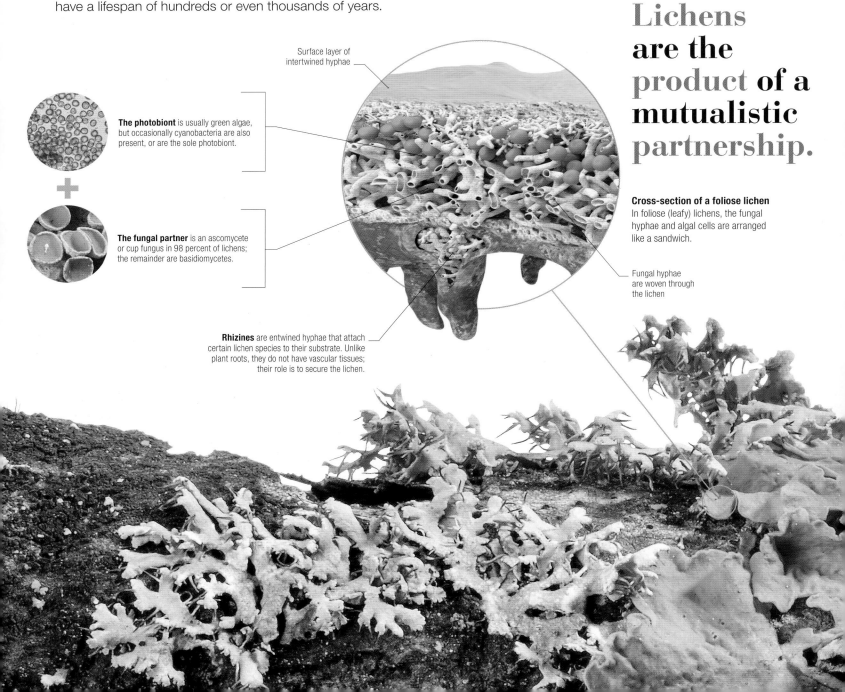

Surface layer of intertwined hyphae

The photobiont is usually green algae, but occasionally cyanobacteria are also present, or are the sole photobiont.

The fungal partner is an ascomycete or cup fungus in 98 percent of lichens; the remainder are basidiomycetes.

Cross-section of a foliose lichen
In foliose (leafy) lichens, the fungal hyphae and algal cells are arranged like a sandwich.

Fungal hyphae are woven through the lichen

Rhizines are entwined hyphae that attach certain lichen species to their substrate. Unlike plant roots, they do not have vascular tissues; their role is to secure the lichen.

Types of lichen

Lichens vary greatly in shape and form. The latter is determined by the fungus that makes up the main part of its body. Leprose lichens—the simplest form—have a powdery appearance, and consist of fungal hyphae that envelop small clusters of algal cells or even single cells. Other lichens are larger and more complex, sometimes forming conspicuous crusts (called crustose lichens), leaflike forms (foliose lichens), or collections of tubules (fruticose lichens).

Crustose lichens
Bonding onto soil, bark, or rock, these lichens consist of algal cells covered by a layer of fungal tissue, or a mixture of tissue and particles from the substrate.

Foliose lichens
These leaflike lichens have distinctly different upper and lower surfaces. They are commonly found in humid conditions on trees or on fallen wood.

Fruticose lichens
These lichens are made up of small tubules that form branched, shrubby, upright tufts, or dangle from the branches of trees.

Reproduction

Lichens can reproduce by forming clones, when tiny parts containing both the photobiont and the fungus break off the main body. The fungus and photobiont may also reproduce separately, each making asexual spores that must meet to form a new lichen. Fungi can also reproduce sexually, producing fruit bodies that release spores. These have to join photobiont cells to form a new lichen.

Fruit bodies of the powdered trumpet cup, *Cladonia fimbriata*.

Tough survivors

Desert lichens

Lichens can often survive in harsh environments, where neither the fungus nor the photobiont would be able to live on their own. These include areas with extreme temperatures and little rainfall, such as deserts, places low in nutrients, and those that fluctuate between extreme wet and dry. Some lichens, such as *Ramalina maciformis*, can absorb the water they need for photosynthesis from the air if humidity is over 80 percent. Others can tolerate pollutants, such as sulfur dioxide or heavy metals, which would kill many other organisms.

Drought-tolerant *Teloschistes capensis* can survive in the hot deserts of southern Africa.

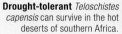

Fruit bodies of the fungal partner

Shared habitats
Different lichen species commonly grow on the same substrate, such as this branch.

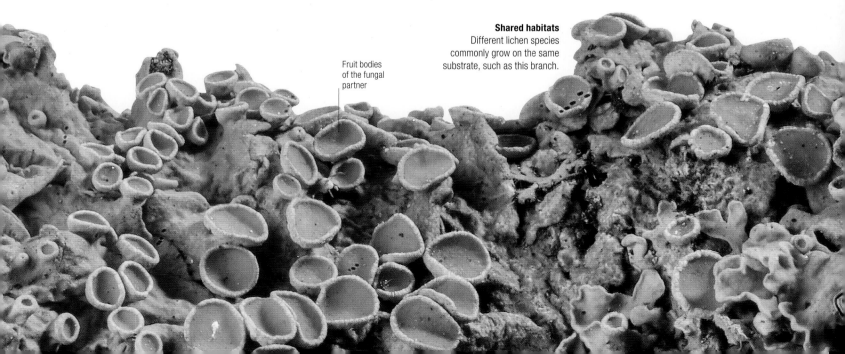

Plant and fungal relationships

In natural environments, the roots of 90 percent of plants work together with fungi in mutually beneficially partnerships. These associations are called mycorrhiza, from the Greek *mykes*, meaning fungus, and *rhiza*, meaning root—literally "fungus root." In mycorrhizal partnerships, fungi colonize the roots of host plants, then extend through the soil, forming large networks of mycelia that extend the plants' root systems. Networks that link neighboring plants in a forest are sometimes referred to as a "wood-wide web" (see pp.70–71). Mycorrhizal partnerships take slightly different forms, depending on the type of plant and fungus. Most flowering plants and ferns, for example, partner with fungi that penetrate their root cells (arbuscular mycorrhizas). Many trees in temperate and boreal woodlands, however, partner with fungi that envelop their root cells but do not penetrate them (ectomycorrhizas). Two further types of mycorrhizas are formed by acid-loving plants, such as camellias, and by orchids.

How the partnership works

Mycorrhizal partnerships are mutually beneficial. Since fungi cannot make their own food, they rely on plants to supply them with sugars produced during photosynthesis. In return, fungi provide plants with water and nutrients that their hyphal filaments have absorbed from the soil, or from breaking down dead organic matter (see p.43). Some mycorrhizal fungi can also protect plants from threats, such as toxic substances in the soil, extremes of temperature, or diseases that attack plant roots. In order to thrive, young plant seedlings need to establish mycorrhizas quickly. They can do this easily if there is already a well-established network of mycorrhizal mycelium, or spores from mycorrhizal fungi, in the surrounding soil.

The larch bolete (*Suillus grevillei*) usually partners with larch trees (*Larix*). While some fungi form mycorrhizas with a wide range of plants, others, like this example, only form a partnership with one species of plant.

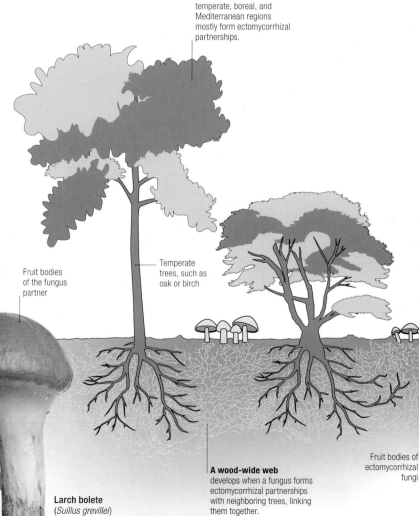

Trees and shrubs from temperate, boreal, and Mediterranean regions mostly form ectomycorrhizal partnerships.

Fruit bodies of the fungus partner

Temperate trees, such as oak or birch

A wood-wide web develops when a fungus forms ectomycorrhizal partnerships with neighboring trees, linking them together.

Fruit bodies of ectomycorrhizal fungi

Larch bolete (*Suillus grevillei*)

The first mycorrhiza

The first organisms on Earth evolved in aquatic environments, where they were surrounded by the water and nutrients they needed to survive. When plants evolved on land, they found it difficult to access these resources because they did not have roots. Mutually beneficial mycorrhizal partnerships developed between these early plants and fungi, which used their threadlike hyphae to extract water and mineral nutrients from soil and rock to feed the plants in return for sugars.

Archaeopteris hibernica
fossilized in sandstone

This fossil of **Archaeopteris hibernica** from the early Devonian period shows the type of plants that began to thrive and colonize new areas with the help of mycorrhizal partnerships. These plants formed the first forests.

Mycorrhizal partnerships begin when the first plants to evolve roots partner with the earliest forms of fungi in a mutually beneficial relationship. These mycorrhizas are similar to modern arbuscular mycorrhizas.

The first forests begin to flourish with the help of mycorrhizal fungal partners. The forest trees were only a few yards tall and included species such as *Archaeopteris hibernica*.

The evolution of pines, followed by broadleaved trees, leads to the evolution of ectomycorrhizal partnerships between plant roots and fungi.

450 MILLION years ago

398 MILLION years ago

145 MILLION years ago

The mycorrhizal network that links the roots of different plants is often called the wood-wide web.

The roots of most plants, including many perennials and shrubs, partner with fungi that form arbuscular mycorrhizas.

Common bluebell
(*Hyacinthoides non-scripta*)

Cross-section of root tips

Fungal hyphae penetrate young plant roots and also extend widely into the soil. Within the root, the hyphae are in close contact with plant cells. They supply the plant cells with water and mineral nutrients in return for sugars.

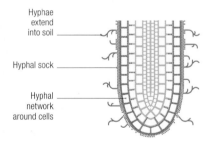

Hyphae extend into soil

Hyphal sock

Hyphal network around cells

Ectomycorrhiza
Fungal hyphae grow into and over the root, sometimes forming a complete sheath or sock.

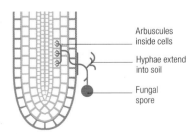

Arbuscules inside cells

Hyphae extend into soil

Fungal spore

Arbuscular mycorrhiza
Fungal hyphae grow into root cells and form branching, tree-shaped structures called arbuscules.

Ectomycorrhizal partnerships can help trees cope with drought and nutrient-poor soils, because fungal hyphae supply them with water and nutrients.

Mycorrhizal fungal mycelium extends the area of soil that a plant can reach to obtain the water and nutrients it needs for growth.

Supporting Earth's ecosystems

Plants and fungi power Earth's terrestrial ecosystems and recycle their resources. They regulate the atmosphere, and make the planet habitable for the diverse animals and organisms that depend on them directly or indirectly for food and habitat; without them we would not be here. Plants and fungi have also become crucial components in human ecosystems. In addition to food, we have come to rely on them for fibers, fuel, medicine—even building and packaging materials. All ecosystems must remain balanced in order to work efficiently.

The first forests, with plants similar to these modern tree ferns, began to alter Earth's atmosphere

Regulating Earth's atmosphere

Plants take carbon dioxide from the air for photosynthesis, releasing oxygen as a byproduct. Before Earth was colonized by land plants, the carbon dioxide content of air was ten times greater than it is today. This began to change around 500 million years ago, when the first mycorrhizal relationships began to form between plants and fungi (see pp.52–53). These special partnerships helped plant life to flourish, which led to reduced carbon dioxide and increased oxygen levels—atmospheric changes that enabled the planet to sustain animal life as we know it.

Recycling material

For a natural ecosystem to remain balanced, the amount of dead plant material broken down must equal the amount of new material produced. Decomposition fuels this process—as dead material decays, it releases mineral nutrients that can be used by plants. Fungi play a crucial role in this system—they are the only organisms that can quickly break down the complex lignocellulose that forms the bulk of woody plant tissues. These tissues are a reservoir of carbon and nutrients, which fungi help to release and recycle.

Sulfur tuft (*Hypholoma fasciculare*) can break down all components of wood

Dead wood provides a nutrient-rich habitat for fungi

Every year, land plants make over 55 billion tons of new plant material to fuel the Earth's food webs.

Fungal fruit bodies provide food and habitats for many invertebrates

Supplying food

Plants and fungi form the basis of many interconnected food chains or webs. Both are eaten in what are called "grazing" food webs. But fungi also play a role in two other types of web. In detrital webs, they recycle nutrients into forms that other organisms can use. In mycorrhizal partnerships, they feed nutrients and water to plants.

Birds and other animals eat the insects that feed on fungi

Tree trunks host fungi, and also provide a habitat for insects and birds

Creating habitats

Plants and fungal fruit bodies provide habitats and breeding grounds for many invertebrates in all biomes. Fungi are particularly important in creating habitats because they can rot wood and hollow out trees, providing cavities to shelter animals such as birds, mammals, insects, and other invertebrates. Fungi also nourish and support the soil, creating a hospitable environment for microorganisms and invertebrates.

Fungal hyphae and fine roots bind soil particles together

Sustaining soil

Fungi play an important role in soil formation. They make humus by decomposing dead organic matter, and promote good soil structure by binding tiny soil particles together with a substance called glomalin, to make crumbs. Some fungi even grow into rock and fragment it. Both fungal hyphae and fine plant roots help to stop soil from being blown or washed away.

Networks of hyphae absorb and redistribute soil nutrients

Balanced systems

Established ecosystems, such as this temperate deciduous woodland, contain plants, animals, fungi, and other microbes linked by complex interdependencies. These include mutually beneficial partnerships and one-sided feeding relationships. Disrupting these networks, for example by removing fallen wood, damages the stability of the system and can reduce biodiversity.

TREES AND SHRUBS

Tough and woody, trees and shrubs include some of the oldest and largest plants on the planet. Many of them have close, beneficial relationships with fungi.

Previously covered with ice during periods of glaciation, lakes, streams, and bogs are common features of boreal forests.

Boreal forests
Trees of the cold north

△ **Mature cone of lodgepole pine** (*Pinus contorta*) open to shed seeds

The trees and shrubs of the northern boreal forests grow all around the Arctic region. These plants are tough enough to withstand extreme cold and deep snow in winter, but also hot summers with periodic forest fires. Conifers dominate the forests. Their narrow, evergreen leaves (often termed needles), which are coated with wax, repel winter snow and retain water within the trees in summer.

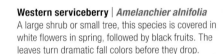

Berries begin red, but ripen to black

North America

Boreal forests extend throughout Canada, Alaska, and the northernmost parts of the continental US. Often acidic, wet, and boggy, the soils here make for slow-growing, resilient plants.

Western serviceberry | *Amelanchier alnifolia*
A large shrub or small tree, this species is covered in white flowers in spring, followed by black fruits. The leaves turn dramatic fall colors before they drop.

Female cones stand upright on the branches

Short shoots bear small male cones between the needles

Black spruce | *Picea mariana*
This slow-growing conifer is widespread across North America, often living on swampy ground. Its mature height varies depending on where it grows.

The cones are the smallest of any of the spruces, just 1½-in (4-cm) long

Tamarack larch | *Larix laricina*
Like all larches, this is a deciduous conifer that loses its needles in winter. This tree can survive extreme cold, then burst into life with new needles and cones in spring.

Balsam fir | *Abies balsamea*
This conifer reaches more than 66 ft (20 m) high. Intolerant of fire, it is in decline. Its upright, blue cones disintegrate as they shed their seeds.

Edible white berries contain two seeds with a tough covering

Bog Labrador tea | *Rhododendron groenlandicum*
This small rhododendron favors wet acidic soils at or beyond the tree line. Clusters of white flowers attract pollinating insects, such as bees.

Young trees have a characteristic conical shape

Common snowberry | *Symphoricarpos albus*
This shrub has underground suckers and spreads to form large patches. Its white berries are eaten by birds and bears.

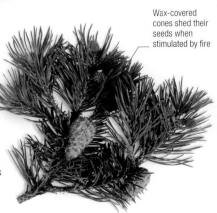

Wax-covered cones shed their seeds when stimulated by fire

Lodgepole pine | *Pinus contorta* var. *latifolia*
So named for its use as a central pole in Indigenous American dwellings, this pine can grow up to 160 ft (50 m) tall.

Sitka spruce | *Picea sitchensis*
Now widely planted in European commercial forests, this valuable timber tree originates in the cold forests of Alaska. It grows slowly, reaching up to 330 ft (100 m) tall.

Europe and Asia

The boreal forests of Europe and Asia look very similar to those of North America, since the trees and shrubs there are often related. Similar environments lead to almost identical plants, all adapted to cold winters and hot summers.

The small leaves change color in the fall, before they drop

Resting buds can survive extreme cold throughout winter

Dwarf birch | *Betula nana*
This is one of the smallest birches, reaching a mere 3 ft (1 m) high. The deciduous leaves only start growing once the harsh winter is over.

Little-leaf linden |
Tilia cordata
This deciduous tree is often found in ancient forests. Several rounded seed pods share a papery bract, which acts like a wing to disperse them.

Manchurian fir |
Abies holophylla
Similar in appearance to balsam fir, this Asian species has brown, upright cones and dense, flattened needles on its twigs.

> ## "Forests are the lungs of our land."
> Franklin **Roosevelt**
> 32nd President of the United States

The triangular-ovate (heart-shaped) leaves are mostly hairless

Small flowers attract pollinating bees, wasps, and moths

Carbon sink

Climate change

The boreal forests represent billions of individual trees and smaller shrubs. Each plant draws carbon out of the atmosphere and incorporates it within its dense tissues. Despite their slow rate of growth in these harsh climates, the trees and shrubs of the forests capture and hold a colossal amount of carbon. Increasingly hot summers due to climate change are triggering fires that destroy the forests. The fires release vast amounts of CO_2 into the atmosphere, accelerating the rate of climate change.

Pines, spruces, and birches dominate the boreal forests of Finland.

Clusters of white flowers attract bees in spring

Siberian crab apple |
Malus baccata
This wild apple species produces white flowers in spring, followed by clusters of small red or yellow apples that are sour.

Young berries are green

As they ripen, each berry turns deep red

Lingonberry | *Vaccinium vitis-idaea*
Across northern Europe and Asia, the lingonberry grows in dense mats under trees and on open hillsides. Small, bell-shaped flowers are followed by deep red berries.

Long, hanging female cones shed hundreds of seeds

Norway spruce | *Picea abies*
This species is native across large parts of the far north. Now used as a Christmas tree, it is widely cultivated in forests farther south.

Dahurian larch | *Larix gmelinii*
A deciduous conifer, this larch has distinctive, bright pink young female cones. The cones fade to brown when mature, and shed their seeds in their second year.

Siberian spruce | *Picea obovata*
This species grows in Siberia, where it is able to survive bitterly cold winter temperatures. Slow growing, it can reach 115 ft (35 m) tall. It is used for timber and to make paper.

Catkins appear with the new leaves in spring

Silver birch | *Betula pendula*
This birch grows across much of Europe and Asia, but is replaced in the Far East by other species of birch. Mottled white bark gives the tree its common name.

Siberian fir | *Abies sibirica*
This fir can tolerate extreme cold, down to -58°F (-50°C). Despite this, it seldom lives more than 200 years, because fungi attack its soft wood.

The flattened needles look silver from underneath

Large clusters of orange-red berries attract birds to feed

The leaves are divided into up to 15 leaflets

Cones take three years to mature and shed seed

Scots pine | *Pinus sylvestris*
This widespread species survives extreme cold and very poor soils. Slow-growing, mature trees can reach around 65 ft (20 m) tall.

Siberian alder | *Alnus hirsuta*
Like most alders, this species grows best in damp soils. The reddish catkins of spring are followed by oval, woody, cone-like fruits. The tree is native to northern Asia.

European mountain ash | *Sorbus aucuparia*
A tree of poor soils and open forests, it bears flat heads of cream-colored flowers in spring. It rarely reaches 39 ft (12 m) tall.

Paper bark birch can form dense woodlands where it is free from competition.

Paper bark birch
A northern pioneer

Paper bark birch (*Betula papyrifera*) gets its name from its stringy, papery bark. Like most birches, it is a pioneer species—it colonizes new habitats before other, often longer-lived, trees gain a foothold. The papery wing that surrounds each seed carries it on the wind, sometimes for long distances. In northern North America, paper bark birch will grow wherever forests are felled or destroyed by fire.

Male catkins shed pollen in spring

Paper bark birches grow fast and live for a relatively short time—typically 80 years, sometimes longer. They can form dense stands, but over time birch woodland naturally dies away, being replaced by slower-growing trees.

> **"A birchbark canoe is the only craft suitable for navigation in Canada."**
> Samuel **de Champlain** French explorer, c. 1600

Mastering the water

Indigenous resources

Paper bark birch was a vital resource for the Indigenous peoples of Canada. They used its waterproof bark to make wigwam covers, pots, buckets, and, most importantly, birchbark canoes which enabled them to move efficiently through flooded woodland. These light, maneuverable craft are an example of a superior Indigenous technology that was adopted by European colonizers. Many Europeans were animal trappers and used these canoes to expand the fur trade.

Birchbark canoes were used by many Indigenous peoples in North America.

Kelo trees
Abundant life after death

In healthy, old-growth forests, more than 20 percent of the trees stand dead. These form a specialized habitat for many fungi and invertebrates that are rarely found elsewhere, yet such trees are generally not retained in managed forests. In northern Europe, Scot's pine (*Pinus sylvestris*) trees can live for 300–500 years but may then remain standing dead for a further 200 years or more. Named kelo trees in the Finnish language, these dead pines provide a different habitat from fallen trees, and from other standing dead trees.

Kelo trees lose their bark after about 40 years and become extremely desiccated. Their heartwood is rich in terpenes and resins, which inhibit many fungi, but the sapwood is rapidly colonized by blue stain fungi, which do not rot the wood. The sapwood eventually decays, and rain, wind, and ice erode it. The trees may also be charred by forest fires, making an already harsh environment even harsher for fungi. Olive duster fungus (*Coniophora olivacea*) is one of a few basidiomycetes that can cope with the stressful environment of standing kelo trees. When long-dead trees fall to the ground, the improved microclimate encourages a range of specialized fungi. These include *Antrodia crassa* and *Phlebia cornea*, but they are very different from fungi in felled pine trees.

Standing dead trees provide a unique habitat for invertebrates, vertebrates, and specialized fungi.

Eurasian three-toed woodpecker (*Picoides tridactylus*) is a keystone species in natural coniferous forests.

The bark has been lost from this standing kelo pine in Urho Kekkonen National Park, Finland.

Once a kelo tree has fallen, a different range of fungi and invertebrates colonize its heartwood.

Red-banded polypore (*Fomitopsis pinicola*) on standing and fallen non-kelo pine (*Pinus*), spruce (*Picea*), and beech (*Fagus*).

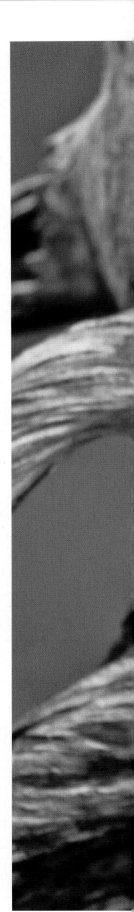

A red squirrel (*Sciurus vulgaris*) looks out from a hole in a dead Scot's pine tree (*Pinus sylvestris*).

Western North America
Pacific coast giants

△ **Mature cone** of a giant redwood (*Sequoiadendron giganteum*)

The trees and shrubs of this region have evolved to survive an often hostile climate. Very cold winters, with deep snow, are followed by short springs and long, hot, and dry summers. Forest fires are frequent. The plant species here have evolved ways of overcoming these problems, with some obtaining additional moisture from the sea fogs that roll in from the Pacific Ocean. However, an increasingly extreme climate is stretching their survival strategies to the limit.

Conifers and shrubs

The waxy, needlelike foliage of conifers minimizes water loss during the Pacific Northwest's hot, dry summers. Many shrubs have also evolved special features to help them survive periods of heat, cold, rain, and drought.

Flowers are borne in dense heads

Flowering currant | *Ribes sanguineum*
This deciduous shrub can be found in forests along the Pacific coast. In spring, it is covered in hanging heads of deep pink flowers, attracting bees and hummingbirds.

Male plants grow long, gray-green catkins (female catkins are shorter and silver-gray)

Silk tassel bush |
Garrya elliptica
This large evergreen shrub grows in the Pacific Coast Ranges and can reach 15 ft (6 m) high. Flowers are held in long, hanging catkins.

Small green cones are held upright

Western red cedar | *Thuja plicata*
Flat twigs of small, almost scalelike evergreen leaves make this species distinct. Although it grows relatively slowly, mature trees can reach 164 ft (50 m) tall.

Male flowers appear before the leaves in spring

Black cottonwood |
Populus trichocarpa
This tree reaches more than 100 ft (30 m) tall. It has very soft wood because it grows so quickly, and has a very extensive root system.

Stems have a weeping habit

This species has very long hanging cones

Brewer's spruce | *Picea breweriana*
A very narrow growth habit and weeping branches make this conifer unique. Although it can reach 164 ft (50 m), it is often only 20 ft (6 m) wide.

Needles are twisted

Beach pine | *Pinus contorta*
Related to the lodgepole pine, this conifer is often twisted and gnarled by its exposed coastal habitat. In these situations, it may only grow to 10 ft (3 m) tall.

Dense forests provide a vital winter habitat for wildlife.

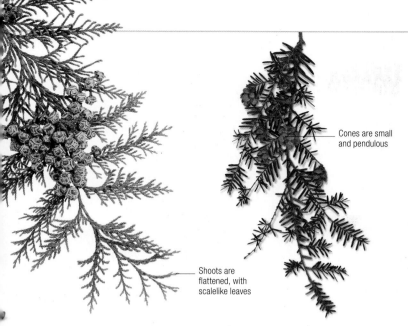

Cones are small and pendulous

Shoots are flattened, with scalelike leaves

Lawson cypress | *Chamaecyparis lawsoniana*
This conifer is native to Oregon and northern California but has been planted in gardens and parks throughout the Northern Hemisphere.

Western hemlock | *Tsuga heterophylla*
This tree can reach 230 ft (70 m) in height, forming vast, coniferous forests with other species. The cones grow on trees more than about 25 years old.

A sanctuary for the mice

Indigenous legends

Indigenous peoples of the Pacific Northwest tell a tale of a great fire that swept through the western forests. Animals scurried to escape the flames, but the mice could not run fast enough and asked the trees to help them. All the trees of the forest turned the mice away until the Douglas fir allowed them to hide in its cones. When seen up-close, a female Douglas fir cone has bracts projecting from between the scales, which resemble the tail and back legs of a mouse.

The female cones of Douglas fir have prominent bracts between the cone scales.

Young shoots appear reddish

Tiny rounded male cones nestle amongst the foliage

Coast redwood | *Sequoia sempervirens*
Found only in California and Oregon, these are some of the tallest trees on Earth. They can reach a great age because their thick, spongy bark insulates them from fire.

Douglas fir | *Pseudotsuga menziesii*
Growing alongside other conifers, this species is widespread along the western side of the continent. The female cones have protruding bracts above the scales.

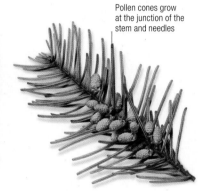

Pollen cones grow at the junction of the stem and needles

Feltleaf ceanothus | *Ceanothus arboreus*
Almost all species of *Ceanothus* are found in California, this one is native to islands off the Californian coast. Showy, pale blue flowers are borne in conical panicles.

Giant fir | *Abies grandis*
This conifer is often found growing with Douglas fir. It has upright green cones and its long needles grow in flattened rows on the shoots.

Red alder | *Alnus rubra*
This is one of the largest alders, reaching 100 ft (30 m) tall. Fast growing, it favors damp habitats, particularly riversides at the south of its range.

Large leaves are shed in the fall

Female catkins are green when young, later turning brown

The canopy of old redwood forests towers high over the landscape.

Giant redwood
Long-lived and tough

The giant redwood (*Sequoiadendron giganteum*) is native to only a relatively small part of California, in the Sierra Nevada mountains. This tree lives to a great age (more than 3,000 years) and reaches an enormous size. In the 19th century, the lumber industry felled many colossal, ancient redwoods, but public outcry led to the creation of protected groves, national parks and, ultimately, the Giant Sequoia National Monument.

Mature cones are relatively small

Giant redwoods have a particular significance for Indigenous peoples, whose ancestors tended the forests long before the arrival of European colonizers. Many of the remaining ancient trees have been named and celebrated, such as the General Sherman tree—which, at 275 ft (83 m) tall and 36 ft (11 m) in diameter at the base, is the largest known tree in the world. Redwoods are threatened by climate change.

> **"Despite our wealth, we cannot create a redwood forest ..."**
> Lyndon **B. Johnson**
> 36th President of the United States

Withstanding fire
Adaptations to adversity

Giant redwoods have evolved spongy, fire-retardant bark that is often more than 1 ft (30 cm) thick. This protects the inner trunk, where nutrients and water are transported, from damage during forest fires. Generally, these trees can continue growing with little interruption after a fire. However, as climate change makes both droughts and fires more intense and frequent, even giant redwoods are beginning to suffer.

Thick bark often saves redwoods, but since 2015, fires have been much fiercer, and are now killing more trees.

Wood-wide web
Fungal networks

Mycorrhizal fungi grow in association with plant roots (see pp.52–53). They use fine filaments (hyphae) to forage in soil for water and mineral nutrients, but get most of their sugars from the plants they partner with. In exchange, the fungi supply the plants with mineral nutrients and water. Individual trees partner with many different mycorrhizal fungi, and a single fungus can sometimes form mycorrhizas with the roots of more than one tree. The fungus forms a network of hyphae, called a mycelium, that links several trees, sometimes even trees of different species. This mycelial network—through which nutrients, sugars, and water can move—has been dubbed "the wood-wide web." However, the extent to which food made or obtained by one tree can pass into and be used by another tree is not yet clear.

The mycelium of some fungi that live on decaying wood and leaf litter can also grow into soil in search of other food supplies. Their hyphae often aggregate to form linear structures called cords, which can look similar to plant roots. Cords form when the fungus encounters new resources, connecting its existing food sources with the new one. Water, sugars, and mineral nutrients can move through these extensive, long-lived mycelial networks to parts of the system where they are needed.

A single gram of soil can contain 656 ft (200 m) of fungal hyphae.

Mycorrhizal fungi create a dense network of fine, foraging, hyphal filaments in soil.

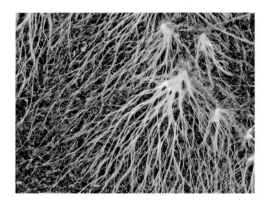

The mycelium of a *Piloderma* fungus extends from the roots of its partner tree.

A ring of fruit bodies indicates the underground presence of mycorrhizal mycelium partnering with the tree in the center.

Ectomycorrhiza root tips (see p.53) on spruce trees, with masses of hyphae extending beyond the root.

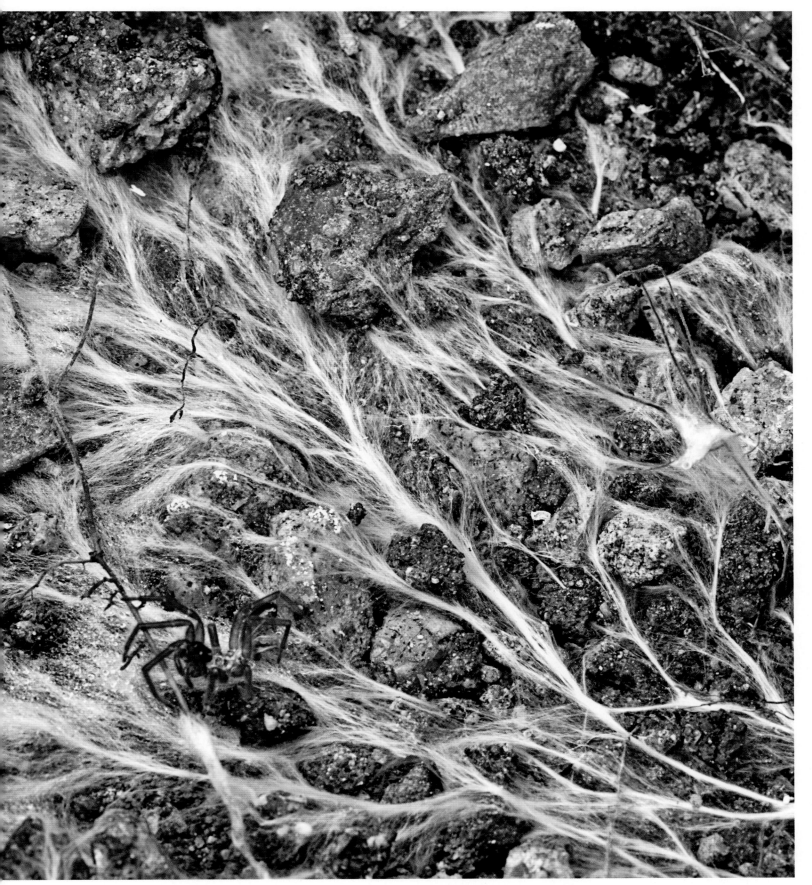

A spider crosses individual hyphal filaments that have aggregated together to form larger cords.

The forest of the Upper Peninsula, Michigan, which is home to a 2,500-year-old honey fungus.

Armillaria ostoyae fruit bodies growing from a tree trunk in the Bavarian Forest National Park, Germany.

Rhizomorphs of a honey fungus (*Armillaria* spp.) that have grown beneath the bark of a tree.

Honey fungus
A humongous fungus

Worldwide, there are many species of honey fungi (*Armillaria*), most of which decompose dead wood and cause disease in tree roots. Fungi usually form fine networks of microscopic filaments (hyphae) underground (see pp.42–43), but in honey fungi, they often aggregate to form black, rootlike "bootlaces" called rhizomorphs, measuring $1/32$–$1/16$ in (1–2 mm) in diameter. These structures are covered in a protective layer of melanin and water-repellent proteins. Rhizomorphs grow from their tip and can form networks connecting trees that the fungus has killed, or decaying wood. They also grow under the bark of trees and can be seen when bark is removed from a standing dead or fallen tree trunk.

Some honey fungi form huge rhizomorph networks beneath the surface layer of leaf litter in woodlands. The current record breaker is an individual *Armillaria ostoyae* in Malheur National Forest, Oregon, which covers $3^{1}/_{2}$ sq miles (9.5 km²), weighs at least 394 tons (400 metric tons), and is more than 2,000 years old.

Bulbous honey fungus
(*Armillaria gallica*)

Honey fungi are among the largest and longest-lived organisms on Earth.

The fruit bodies of a honey fungus (*Armillaria* spp.) growing from a dead birch (*Betula*) tree.

Eastern North America
Shades of Asia

△ **Sweet gum** (*Liquidambar styraciflua*) has spiky seed capsules and leaves with five points.

The trees and shrubs of eastern North America are very different from those of the western side of the continent. In fact, they are more similar in many ways to the trees of eastern Asia. The climate in the east is wetter and generally less cold than in the west, which favors deciduous species. Many shed their leaves in a spectacular fall display of yellow, orange, and red.

Deciduous dominance

Forests in the east are dominated by broadleaved trees, such as oaks and hickories. This makes eastern forests much more colorful than those in the west, where conifers proliferate.

White fringe tree | *Chionanthus virginicus*
This small tree bears drooping flower clusters at its branch ends in late spring. Each flower has four long, thin petals, creating a fringed effect.

Shagbark hickory |
Carya ovata
A large species growing to 98 ft (30 m) tall, this tree bears an edible fruit, like all hickories. Some shagbarks can live for up to 300 years.

Young leaves grow rapidly in spring

A cluster of tiny flowers is surrounded by four large, pink bracts

Flowering dogwood | *Cornus florida*
A small tree, reaching 33 ft (10 m), this deciduous species has clusters of tiny flowers (inflorescences), like all dogwoods.

Threadlike petals drop after a week or so

Strong fragrance attracts pollinators in winter

Witch hazel |
Hamamelis virginiana
The source of the astringent liquid of the same name, this deciduous shrub bears tiny flowers, each with several threadlike, yellow petals.

Fall brings a riot of color to the abundant forests of eastern North America.

Kentucky coffee | *Gymnocladus dioicus*
Although this tree can reach 50 ft (15 m) tall, it usually lives for no more than 100 years. Male and female flowers are found on separate trees.

The large leaves are divided into as many as 30 leaflets

Staghorn sumac | *Rhus typhina*
This deciduous shrub or tree can form large patches of stems, as it spreads by underground suckers. The leaves turn bright orange and red before they drop in the fall.

Black locust | *Robinia pseudoacacia*
This fast-growing tree can spread by underground suckers, forming colonies where it grows. Where it is not native, it can become an invasive pest if not controlled carefully.

In spring, large sprays of white flowers appear

Large pink to white flowers are borne in summer

Southern catalpa | *Catalpa bignonioides*
This deciduous species can reach 39 ft (12 m) in both height and width. Its flowers are followed by long, thin pods of seeds, resembling beans.

The tulip-shaped flowers are green and orange

Tulip tree | *Liriodendron tulipifera*
A large tree, up to 164 ft (50 m) tall, this species is related to magnolias. The spring flowers develop into cone-like seed pods in the fall.

Typical oak acorns are up to half enclosed in a woody cup

Scarlet oak | *Quercus coccinea*
This species sustains many animals in its canopy and with its fallen acorns. It produces male and female flowers in spring. The lobed leaves turn bright orange and red in the fall.

American sweetgum | *Liquidambar styraciflua*
The maplelike leaves on this tree change through many shades before they are shed in the fall. Unusual knobbly bark on the trunks explains its other common name of alligator bark.

Similar—but separate

Species diversity

The flora of eastern North America and eastern Asia are remarkably similar. Despite their separation, many species are closely related, since a continuous forest once extended from eastern Asia across North America. Similar woody plants grew across the region, but as the Rocky Mountains uplifted, the climate and flora of western North America changed, leaving two widely separated regions today.

Foamflowers (*Tiarella* spp.) are native to both regions.

As the fall temperatures drop, green chlorophyll breaks down and leaves turn fiery red and orange.

Sugar maple

Living national treasure

Sugar maple (*Acer saccharum*) is native to eastern North America. Its forests form a valuable habitat, because the species supports a wide range of wildlife. For thousands of years, Indigenous peoples have tapped the tree for its sweet sap, a practice adopted by European colonizers. Sap runs before the trees come into leaf in spring, so harvesting takes place in late winter. Indigenous peoples celebrated the first full moon of spring as the "sugar moon." The sugar maple's sap season is very short and trees need to be at least 10 in (25 cm) in diameter to tap.

The long process of boiling down raw sap into maple syrup remained unchanged for thousands of years, until evaporators and other technologies made the process more efficient in the second half of the 19th century. Today, the Canadian province of Québec produces 90 percent of the world's maple syrup, and the product is virtually synonymous with Canada. Sugar groves capture more carbon than the refining process emits, so maple syrup is "climate positive."

Leaf is palmate in shape

Sap for commercial use is extracted from sugar maple trees grown in sugar groves.

Metal taps, or spiles, are pushed into holes drilled into the sugar maple trunks.

Buckets hanging from hooks on each spile collect the flowing sap.

Over several weeks, a single tree can produce up to 8 gallons (38 liters) of sap.

A country reborn

The Canadian flag

Before 1965, Canada had no official flag. For much of the 20th century, the Canadian red ensign was used as an informal flag. This bore either red or green maple leaves, along with other symbols. After designs combining the maple leaf with British and French symbols were rejected, a flag with two red bars and a central 11-pointed, red maple leaf was chosen. The new flag was first raised in January 1965.

In 1964, the Canadian parliament voted for a new flag to unify the country.

Quaking aspen woodlands may consist of thousands of trunks, but a single, shared, root system.

Pando

One tree, vast and ancient

Quaking aspen (*Populus tremuloides*) is a widespread tree in cooler parts of North America. It grows quickly and spreads by means of underground suckers, allowing it to colonize large areas quite rapidly. Eventually, a colony of clones can produce an entire woodland, in which the trees all share one root system. Each tree may live for 60 to 100 years and reach a height of 60 ft (18 m). However, when an individual tree dies, the colony carries on living, regularly producing new trunks.

Pando is a single colony of male clones in Fishlake National Forest, Utah. It covers an area of 108 acres (43.6 hectares) and is thousands of years old. Like similar aspen groves, Pando is suffering dieback. Increased grazing pressure, climate change, and insect infestations are all cited as possible causes.

Fall colors on aspen leaves

Pando is the oldest, largest, and heaviest organism on Earth.

The Pando aspen grove forms drifts of yellow and orange as the leaves drop in the fall.

Galleries are formed by elm bark beetles beneath the bark of dead and dying elm trees. Female beetles burrow under the bark to lay eggs, and their hatched larvae tunnel as they feed.

Dutch elm disease
Changing landscapes

An English elm (*Ulmus procera*) coming into leaf in spring. Mature elm trees are now a rare sight in the UK.

Elm bark beetles (*Hylurgopinus* and *Scolytus* spp.) carry spores of the fungus *Ophiostoma novo-ulmi* on their bodies.

Emergence holes are created by young adult elm bark beetles that lived beneath the bark as larvae.

Signs of Dutch elm disease include yellowing of leaves, which eventually wilt and fall.

The landscape of temperate and northern Europe was once adorned with majestic elm trees (*Ulmus* species) until they were destroyed by Dutch elm disease. The disease, called "Dutch" because early research on it was carried out in the Netherlands, hit as two pandemics. The first began in 1910 and was caused by the fungus *Ophiostoma ulmi*. It killed more than 10 percent of elms in Europe, spread to North America and eastern Asia, but abated in the 1940s. During this decade, a far more destructive epidemic began in eastern Europe and the southern Great Lakes region of North America. Caused by the closely related fungus *Ophiostoma novo-ulmi*, it killed millions of elm trees across the northern hemisphere, then later in western Asia.

The fungi make toxins and block the trees' xylem—the vessels that conduct water and nutrients—causing the trees to wilt and die. They are carried between trees by elm bark beetles, which feed in the forks of twigs and introduce fungal spores into the small wounds they make. Female beetles excavate tunnels under the bark to lay eggs; the larvae burrow more tunnels. They emerge as adults and move on to other trees.

Standing dead elm tree

Fungal diseases of trees can dramatically change the landscape.

Southern North America
Spanning borders

△ **Big cone pine** (*Pinus coulteri*) bears its long, stiff needles in groups of three.

The **southern US and Mexico** make up a region of wildly contrasting habitats, from the vast swamps of Florida to the bone-dry deserts of the US southwest and northern Mexico, and southward into subtropical forests. Not surprisingly, an enormous variety of trees and shrubs flourish in this region, with particular diversity seen among species of oak and pine. Many other smaller trees and shrubs grow in the shelter of the subtropical pine-oak woodlands, which also offer a haven to a multitude of animal species.

Rising to the challenge

Each species has evolved to overcome the challenge of its particular habitat, whether it be withstanding coastal winds, growing in swampy soil, finding water in arid conditions, or competing for pollinators.

Mexican orange blossom | *Choisya ternata*
This large shrub reaches 8 ft (2.4 m) in both height and width. Evergreen leaves, divided into three lobes, are joined by sprays of fragrant, star-shaped, white flowers during spring.

California allspice | *Calycanthus occidentalis*
This shrub or small tree bears deciduous oval leaves. Its maroon flowers are short-lived, lasting 1–2 days. Numerous tepals form whorls around the central cluster of stamens.

Coulter pine | *Pinus coulteri*
The exceptionally large cones of this conifer grow to more than 12 in (30 cm) long and weigh up to 11 lb (5 kg). Each scale, or segment, of the cone is tipped with a talon-like hook.

Twigs carry minute, scalelike leaves

Monterey cypress |
Cupressus macrocarpa
A conifer native to California, this tree reaches 82 ft (25 m) in height. It thrives near the sea and shows great tolerance of salty ocean winds. Large, globular cones appear on older specimens.

Narrow leaves, which reduce water loss, grow from the tips of shoots

Joshua tree |
Yucca brevifolia
This desert-dwelling evergreen can live for up to 300 years. Its creamy-white flowers appear in spring and are pollinated only by yucca moths, *Tegeticula* spp.

Tree lupin | *Lupinus arboreus* Many lupins are herbaceous, dying down each year. The tree lupin is an exception, living for up to seven years and standing up to 5 ft (1.5 m) tall.

Bald cypress | *Taxodium distichum* This deciduous conifer can stand 120 ft (37 m) tall. It develops roots above the water that enable it to breathe in swamps.

Leaves are composed of five to seven leaflets

Pure white flowers are borne in spring

Hanging, bell-shaped flowers will later develop into winged green fruits

California buckeye | *Aesculus californica*
Related to horse chestnut, *A. hippocastanum*, this species grows as a shrub or small tree up to 39 ft (12 m) high. Dense heads of white, sweet-smelling flowers form in spring.

Southern magnolia | *Magnolia grandiflora*
Evergreen and glossy-leaved, this magnolia grows in the southeastern US, where it can be 125 ft (38 m) tall. Large, goblet-shaped flowers attract beetles as pollinators.

Madrona | *Arbutus menziesii*
This species is characterized by its bright orange bark and clusters of small, white flowers. The flowers are followed by orange to red, strawberry-like fruits.

Carolina silverbell | *Halesia carolina*
Pendent white flowers resembling snowdrops emerge at the same time as the fresh green leaves. Native to the southeastern US, this small tree grows to around 40 ft (12 m) high.

Large yellow flowers appear in summer

Tree anemone | *Carpenteria californica*
In its native California, this bushy evergreen shrub produces large, white flowers with bright yellow stamens in early summer. Its long leaves are paired and lance-shaped.

California flannelbush | *Fremontodendron californicum*
An evergreen shrub of California, Arizona, and Mexico, the flannelbush is covered with irritant hairs that deter browsing animals.

Marvelous Madrean

Biodiverse woodlands

The Madrean pine-oak woodlands of Mexico—and small areas of southern Texas, New Mexico, and Arizona—hold the greatest concentration of pine and oak species in the world. These woodlands are home to more than 5,000 species of plant (most of which are found nowhere else), more than 500 bird species, and in excess of 300 mammal species. They are also the winter roost of millions of migrating monarch butterflies. Like many forest habitats, the Madrean is threatened by logging and the expansion of farming.

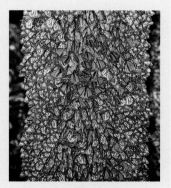

Monarch butterflies (*Danaus plexippus*) cluster in vast numbers on trees in the Madrean during winter.

Bristlecone pines
Ancient sentinels

High in the mountains of the western US, ancient and gnarled bristlecone pines (*Pinus aristata*, *P. balfouriana*, and *P. longaeva*) can be found. The Great Basin bristlecone pine (*Pinus longaeva*), is one of the longest-living tree species, regularly reaching 2,000 years old. Great Basin bristlecones grow extremely slowly in the hostile mountain climate. They live in poor, stony soils, with little rainfall, they are blasted by icy winds in winter, and have a short summer growing season. Two specimens, one in California known as Methuselah and another in Nevada called Prometheus, are known to be almost 5,000 years old. Even the needles of these pines last for a long time, often staying alive on the branches for 40 years.

The wood of bristlecone pine trees is dense and resinous, which makes it highly resistant to insects, helping the trees to reach a great age. The wood rarely rots, even after a tree dies. Instead, it is sculpted like stone in the wind, creating the characteristic writhing, twisted shapes of these trees. Although bristlecone pines are not resistant to wildfires, they are mostly found in high mountain habitats, where few other plants grow, so forest fires are not a major threat. The risk is much greater, however, for bristlecones that grow at lower altitudes.

Young, purple
P. aristata cones

Tree-trunk timeline

Dendrochronology

Using tree-trunk growth rings to study the past is called dendrochronology. Each ring is one year's growth, so the total number of rings gives the tree's age. Because the thickness of a ring reveals if the weather that year was good or bad for growth, the overall ring pattern shows climate variations during the tree's life. Old wooden objects can be dated by comparing growth rings in the wood to those of ancient trees. Bristlecones are useful for this, as they record thousands of growing seasons.

Core samples extracted from ancient trees show the pattern of growth rings.

Ancient bristlecone pine trees are battered by the weather, but they still survive for thousands of years.

Temperate Europe
A feast of color

△ **Hawthorn** (*Crataegus monogyna*) produces red berries called haws in the fall.

The forests of northwest Europe enjoy a relatively mild climate, with strong seasonal variations. Winters can be cold with snow, but not to the extent of those in the far north. Springs are longer and run into warm summers, in which day length and temperature regulate the speed and rate of growth. In the fall, shorter days and colder nights trigger the development of fall color and leaf drop.

Varied woodlands

Species from many plant families enjoy these temperate conditions, leading to varied and—at times—colorful forests. Ancient woodlands, undisturbed for centuries, still exist in many places, increasing their value as ecosystems.

European beech | *Fagus sylvatica*
Often called the queen of the forest, beech trees have dense foliage that prevents many other plants from growing below them. Their distinctive dry fruits are termed beech "mast."

Young leaves are lime-green, becoming darker as they mature

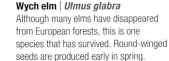

Wych elm | *Ulmus glabra*
Although many elms have disappeared from European forests, this is one species that has survived. Round-winged seeds are produced early in spring.

Long, green needles grow in pairs

Austrian pine | *Pinus nigra*
A more southerly counterpart of Scots pine (*P. sylvestris*), this species has darker trunks and deep green needles. Its cones mature over three years before shedding their seeds.

Bright yellow, sweetly scented flowers attract many bees and butterflies

Gorse | *Ulex europaeus*
Gorse flowers appear among its spines in the fall, blooming through winter to late spring. The plant is an invasive pest when introduced elsewhere in the world.

Large leaves are divided into five slightly toothed lobes

European horse chestnut | *Aesculus hippocastanum*
The conical flower panicles of this deciduous tree produce spiny cases containing shiny "conkers." It was spread across Europe by the Romans.

Common holly | *Ilex aquifolium*
This evergreen tree can reach 49 ft (15 m) in height. Its tiny, four-petaled white flowers appear in spring, followed by red berries on the female trees.

Yellow flowers are borne in long heads termed racemes

Golden chain tree |
Laburnum anagyroides
Also called laburnum, this tree grows to 26 ft (8 m). Flowers appear in early summer, followed by highly toxic, green-black pods.

Characteristic double seeds, each with a wing, hang in small clusters

> **"The most important factor that has changed the European landscape is the clearing of the woodland."**
>
> H. C. **Darby** Welsh historical geographer

Norway maple | *Acer platanoides*
A common and widespread tree, this is a fast-growing species of maple. Green flowers appear before the distinctive toothed, palm-shaped leaves grow.

Common hawthorn | *Crataegus monogyna*
This small tree is very common across Europe, especially in hedgerows. Clusters of white flowers appear in May, hence the alternative name of "May blossom."

Fungal tree-killers

Nonnative plant pathogens

Several nonnative diseases, such as Dutch elm disease (see pp.80–81), have spread across European woodlands in the last 50 years, wiping out trees that lack natural resistance to them. First recorded in Europe in the 1990s, Ash dieback (*Hymenoscyphus fraxineus*), is a fungal disease from Asia that is killing native ash trees (*Fraxinus excelsior*). It is gradually spreading westwards, devastating woodlands.

Ash dieback causes leaves and stems to wilt and die, gradually weakening and killing infected trees. It is expected to kill 80 percent of UK ash trees.

European spindle | *Euonymus europaeus*
A large shrub, or occasionally small tree, spindle bears small green flowers that develop into four-seeded pods. Spindle develops bright colors before losing its leaves in the fall.

Common ash | *Fraxinus excelsior*
This deciduous species can reach 98 ft (30 m) tall. Trees are either male or female, so only some produce the characteristic, narrow-winged seeds, called keys, in the fall.

English oak
Venerable woodland giants

The English, or pedunculate, oak (*Quercus robur*) is actually native to much of Europe and western Asia. It is because of the many ancient specimens found in England and its widespread use in old English naval ships that it gained its common name. Mature trees can be 130 ft (40 m) tall and have enormous trunks 33 ft (10 m) or more in circumference and often hollow. It is frequently the dominant tree species in woodlands, particularly in southern Britain.

Oaks support a greater range of organisms than other tree species, becoming centers for woodland biodiversity. The roots form mycorrhizal associations with fungi, gathering nutrients from the woodland soil. Other fungi attack dead wood in the trunk and old branches, producing dramatic brackets. The rough bark creates a perfect habitat for mosses and lichens, which often clothe the branches. From parasitic gall wasps, to moth and butterfly caterpillars, and wood boring beetles, more than 400 insect species are reliant on these trees. In turn, they provide food for numerous birds and foraging mammals. Oak acorns are also the main source of food for many animals in the fall. Squirrels, jays, wild boars, and domestic pigs all thrive on these fruits, sometimes burying them for later use. Where they forget their buried stash, new oaks spring up the following year.

Flowering catkins appear in spring

Often struck, oak is linked to lightning gods in Greek, Irish, and Norse myths.

In open fields, where there is no competition from other trees, oaks adopt a characteristic domed shape.

Hazel dormice (*Muscardinus avellanarius*) visit oaks in spring and summer to pick caterpillars from the leaves.

Oaks support more species of fungi than any other European tree, including hoof fungus (*Fomes fomentarius*).

Rough-textured bark allows mosses and lichens to establish on oak trunks and branches.

Many birds, including tawny owls (*Strix aluco*), favor oaks for shelter, lookout points, and nest sites.

Ancient oak trees, such as this English oak (*Quercus robur*), are often hollow inside, with their heartwood rotting away completely.

Heart rot
Standing tall but hollow

Some tree species can live for hundreds of years. By the time they are ancient—around 400 years old in oak trees (*Quercus* spp.), for example—most have hollow trunks. Fungi cause this hollowing, known as "heart rot," by decomposing the dead tissue (heartwood) in the center of the tree's trunk. This process can benefit the tree, by releasing nutrients to sustain new growth. It can also benefit the wider ecosystem, providing nutrients and habitats for plants, animals, and microbes.

The fungi causing heart rot vary among tree species. Only a few species of fungi, such as the beefsteak fungus (*Fistulina hepatica*) and chicken-of-the-woods (*Laetiporus sulphureus*) colonize oak trees, because its heartwood contains chemicals that inhibit fungal growth. Beech trees (*Fagus* spp.), on the other hand, support a wide range of heart-rot fungi.

Patterns created by heart rot in a beech tree

Hollows in ancient trees provide valuable habitats for wildlife.

A hollowing ancient sessile oak (*Quercus petraea*).

Wood-decay fungi
Complete rotters

△ **Silver leaf fungus** (*Chondrostereum purpureum*) grows on the dead wood of broadleaved trees and causes silver leaf disease.

Wood, the structural component of the trunks and stems of trees and woody shrubs, is made from lignocellulose, the most abundant renewable raw material on the planet. Lignocellulose is composed of the carbohydrates cellulose and hemicellulose, plus lignins. Lignins are the most complex biologically produced organic molecules, and relatively few organisms have evolved mechanisms to break them down. A few basidiomycete and ascomycete fungi can, however, break down some or all of the components of wood, and hence recycle it.

Polyporales

More than 1,800 species of polyporales have been identified. Most are annual, but some are perennial. They are basidiomycetes that produce their spores in cells on the walls of tubes on the underside of the cap.

Stinkhorn | *Phallus impudicus*
This wood-decay fungus forms networks of white, cord-like bundles of hyphae more than 1 mm thick below the woodland litter layer.

Caps measure 2–8 in (5–20 cm) wide. The stalk has a bag-like structure at its base.

Silky rosegill | *Volvariella bombycina*
Uncommon, but widespread in many countries, it is usually found on well-decayed wood of broadleaved trees from summer to late fall.

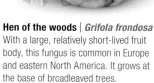

Hen of the woods | *Grifola frondosa*
With a large, relatively short-lived fruit body, this fungus is common in Europe and eastern North America. It grows at the base of broadleaved trees.

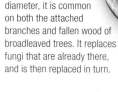

Turkey tail |
Trametes versicolor
Up to 4 in (10 cm) in diameter, it is common on both the attached branches and fallen wood of broadleaved trees. It replaces fungi that are already there, and is then replaced in turn.

Silver leaf fungus |
Chondrostereum purpureum
Its spores enter the branches of *Prunus* species via wounds. Toxins spread to the leaves, turning them a silvery color.

Spores are produced on the mazelike undersurface

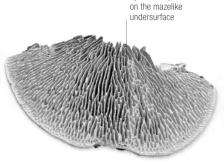

Oak mazegill | *Daedalea quercina*
Found on fallen oak (*Quercus*) and also sweet chestnut (*Castanea sativa*), it sheds spores in late summer and fall. Usually solitary, it can grow in overlapping groups.

Chicken of the woods |
Laetiporus sulphureus
This fungus grows on the dead central wood in the trunks of many tree species, especially oak (*Quercus*) and beech (*Fagus*).

Great variety of banding patterns and coloration

Dryad's saddle |
Polyporus squamosus
Up to 24 in (60 cm) across, it appears from spring to early fall on standing trees and fallen wood. It is common in Europe.

Ascomycetes

Few ascomycetes break down wood. Those that do often act slowly, without altering the lignin greatly. However, they are still important members of the decay community, and tolerate dry, wet, and variable conditions.

Cramp balls | *Daldinia concentrica*
When split open, concentric bands are visible inside this fungus. It grows on the dead branches of broadleaved trees, especially ash (*Fraxinus*); similar species grow on other trees.

Dead man's fingers | *Xylaria polymorpha*
This wood-decay fungus, which is widespread in Europe and North America, fruits on broadleaved tree stumps and buried wood, mostly in summer and fall.

Beech woodwart | *Hypoxylon fragiforme*
Patches of fruit bodies, up to ⅓ in (2–9 mm) across, form on attached dead and fallen beech (*Fagus*) wood. Brownish orange to start, they become almost black.

Green elfcup | *Chlorociboria aeruginascens*
The fungus turns the wood a blue-green color, making it highly prized for decorative items, such as antique Tunbridge Ware boxes.

Lemon disco | *Bisporella citrina*
With yellow, saucer-shaped fruit bodies just ⅛ in (3 mm) across, this common fungus forms on the dead wood of broadleaved trees all year round.

White or brown

The chemistry of decay

The two main types of wood decay are white rot and brown rot. Some wood decay fungi can use all of the chemical components of the wood, although they vary in the rate at which they do so, making it bleached and often fibrous. Other fungi just use the cellulose and hemicelluloses, and leave the lignin. This turns the wood brown, cracked, and crumbly.

Brown-rotted wood

Jelly fungi

These basidiomycetes are found in several different families, and vary greatly in color and shape. All have irregularly branched fruit bodies with a gelatin-like texture. They are mostly decomposers of dead material or live as parasites on other fungi or plants.

Basidiospores are produced on the underside

Jelly ear |
Auricularia auricularia-judae
Previously seen largely on the decaying wood of standing elder (*Sambucus nigra*), it is now found on a greater variety of tree species, probably due to climate change.

Often drying out, this fungus can produce spores again when rehydrated

Witches butter | *Exidia glandulosa* This fungus commonly grows on the recently dead wood, attached or fallen, of broadleaved trees, especially oak (*Quercus*).

Beard lichens (*Usnea* spp.) hanging from trees in a temperate cloud forest in Meili Snow Mountains National Park, Yunnan, China.

The branches of this hazel (*Corylus avellana*) are covered with epiphytes, and its exposed roots grow over a boulder.

A sessile oak (*Quercus petraea*) dominated by epiphytes, including common greenshield lichen (*Flavoparmelia caperata*).

Pannaria rubiginosa, a cool, temperate zone lichen, growing on common hazel (*Corylus avellana*).

Red beard lichen (*Usnea rubicunda*) is common in temperate coastal and other moist woodlands.

Temperate rainforests
Moss and lichen woodlands

Among the oldest ecosystems on Earth—more than 65 million years old—only about 3.8 million sq miles (10 million sq km) of temperate rainforests remain, a tiny fraction of the area of tropical forests. The last remaining examples are in mid-latitude coastal and mountainous locations with cool winters, warm summers, high rainfall, and frequent mist. The best examples are on the Atlantic coast of Europe, the Pacific Northwest coast of North America, and in New Zealand and southeast Australia. Some temperate rainforests are broadleaved, others sclerophyllous or coniferous, including coastal redwoods. They face multiple threats: harvesting or clearance for farming, drought, invasive species, and diseases such as ash dieback.

Though species diversity is far lower than in their tropical counterparts, temperate rainforests are also characterized by epiphytic ferns, mosses, liverworts, woody climbers, and lichens. Many of their plants and fungi are found nowhere else in the world, and are now under threat.

A threatened habitat with distinctive fungal communities.

Hazel gloves

Hypocreopsis rhododendri

Glue crust fungus (*Hymenochaete corrugata*) is common on hazel (*Corylus avellana*). It grows from one branch to another if they make contact, effectively gluing the two together with plates of dark tissue. In the Atlantic rainforests of the UK, Ireland, and France it is sometimes parasitized by the rare ascomycete fungus *Hypocreopsis rhododendri*, which fruits from late summer to early winter. It looks and feels like fawn-colored kid gloves.

Fruiting on old hazel trees, forming fingerlike structures, hazel gloves are temperate rainforest specialists.

Mediterranean
Drought-resisters

△ **Oriental plane** (*Platanus orientalis*) has spherical, spiky fruits, usually in pairs.

The trees and shrubs of the Mediterranean have evolved to survive long, hot summers almost devoid of rainfall, and wet winters. Since strong summer sunlight causes plants to lose water rapidly, many have adapted to combat this. Leaves are generally small, waxy, and shiny, reflecting bright sunlight and reducing water loss. Many have a dense covering of white hairs (trichomes), which increases the amount of light reflected. Most Mediterranean species flower after rain in fall through winter, or in spring.

Trees

Methods to combat water loss and extreme heat unify the native trees and shrubs of the Mediterranean. Small, leathery leaves and thick bark are characteristic of these plants.

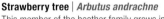

Waxy evergreen leaves have many culinary uses

Strawberry-like fruits give this tree its common name

Kidney-shaped leaves grow up to 4 in (10 cm) across

Rosy-pink flowers grow in clusters on older wood

Bay | *Laurus nobilis*
Bay laurel can grow into a large evergreen tree up to 59 ft (18 m) tall. Widely cultivated for its leaves, which are used for food seasoning, it can be pruned for hedges.

Strawberry tree | *Arbutus andrachne*
This member of the heather family grows into a small evergreen tree. Creamy-white, bell-shaped flowers attract bumblebees, and the bark is bright orange.

Cones mature from green to brown

Narrow acorns begin green and mature to dark purple-brown

Judas tree | *Cercis siliquastrum*
This member of the pea family is a small, slow-growing deciduous tree with distinctive, kidney-shaped leaves. In spring, bare branches are covered in small purple flowers.

Storax | *Styrax officinalis*
This species is a small deciduous tree or large shrub. The felted, oval leaves reduce water loss. White flowers with yellow anthers appear in May and June, followed by yellow fruit.

Phoenician juniper |
Juniperus phoenicea
This widespread species can tolerate sites exposed to hot, direct sunshine. Tiny leaves reduce water loss and the cones are berrylike.

Holm oak | *Quercus ilex*
This evergreen species of oak is characteristic of the region. Reaching 92 ft (28 m) tall, it bears leaves with a white, felted underside to reduce water loss.

"The first western gardens were those in the Mediterranean basin."

Penelope **Hobhouse**
Plants in Garden History, 1992

Columnar in shape, this dark green evergreen grows to 115 ft (35 m)

Narrow, green needles are borne in small dense clusters

Cedar of Lebanon | *Cedrus libani*
One of only four species of cedar, this large, majestic tree grows in the eastern Mediterranean. The upright cones disintegrate as they shed their seeds.

Pistachio | *Pistacia vera*
This is the largest and most valuable of several related species. Tiny green flowers lead to red-tinted fruits, in which each nut develops.

Cypress cones

Lombardy poplar |
Populus nigra 'Italica'
This narrow, upright form of black poplar is one of the most iconic Mediterranean trees. Yellow color precedes the loss of leaves in the fall.

Oriental planetree |
Platanus orientalis
Often growing beside streams, this deciduous species can reach 98 ft (30 m) tall and wide. Tiny flowers and seed heads are held in hanging, globular clusters.

Portuguese laurel |
Prunus lusitanica
This small evergreen tree, reaching 26 ft (8 m), grows in the western Mediterranean region. Heads of white flowers are followed by red to black fruit.

Italian cypress |
Cupressus sempervirens
Throughout the region, two forms of this iconic species are found: a wide, spreading tree, and the more common tall, narrow version.

Classic landscapes

Plants and art

The landscape of Italy is marked by the vertical accents of Italian cypress and Lombardy poplar. Although both were wild trees in antiquity, they have been cultivated throughout the Mediterranean for centuries, and particularly in Italy. The Italian cypress originated in the eastern Mediterranean, but as an ancient symbol of mourning it is often planted in cemeteries elsewhere. These trees, complementing the region's landscapes and architecture, have been the inspiration for many artists.

The characteristic, upright forms of cypress trees punctuate the Italian landscape.

Mediterranean shrubs

Plants of many unrelated families have developed similar strategies to survive here, often including aromatic oils that increase heat resistance. As a result, they are much valued for their medicinal or herbal uses.

Oleander | *Nerium oleander*

This species can grow as a shrub or a tree. All parts of oleander are highly poisonous. Despite this, its large, attractive flowers have led to it being widely planted.

Flowers are most usually pink, but may be red or white

The lance-shaped, dark green leaves are thick and leathery and grow in pairs or groups of three

Colorful bracts attract bees and butterflies to the flowers

French lavender | *Lavandula stoechas*

As in many lavenders, dense hairs on the leaves and stems reduce water loss. The small flowers grow in dense, upright heads. Many pollinators visit the purplish flowers.

The reddish fruit husk surrounds chambers containing many seeds

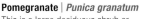

Pomegranate | *Punica granatum*

This is a large deciduous shrub or occasionally a small tree. It bears large orange flowers that are followed by its characteristic fruits.

Large, papery flowers last only a single day

Gum rockrose | *Cistus ladanifer*

Cistus species are found throughout the region. The evergreen foliage of gum cistus is covered in glandular hairs that make it sticky. The hairs reduce water loss and deter grazing animals.

Yellow composite flowers are held on tall stems

Lavender cotton |
Santolina chamaecyparissus

This low-growing evergreen has silvery leaves and stems. Hundreds of tiny florets merge together in a dense, flat flower head.

Silverbush | *Convolvulus cneorum*

Native to coastal areas from Spain to Albania, this evergreen shrub is covered in short, silver hairs that help it conserve water. The flowers can almost completely cover the plant.

Yellow flowers have crinkled petals, each with a maroon blotch at the base

Woolly rock rose | *Halimium lasianthum*

This small shrub grows just 3 ft (1 m) tall. It is found in Spain, Portugal, and France, growing in dry, rocky areas. Its felty leaves help reduce water loss.

Butcher's broom |
Ruscus aculeatus
This spiky shrub reaches 3 ft (1 m) tall and spreads into large clumps. It has tiny leaves, but the stems are modified into flattened, leaflike structures called cladodes.

Red berries contain seeds, which are dispersed by birds

Irish heath | ***Erica erigena***
This species is native to the Iberian peninsula and also Ireland, hence its common name. It flowers in winter, when there are few other blooms for pollinators.

Sprays of flowers are followed by very thin pods

The seed pods contain up to 12 segments

Waxy leaves retain water year-round

Spanish broom |
Spartium junceum
This shrub reaches 10 ft (3 m) tall. Its tiny leaves are shed as soon as temperatures rise in late spring— an adaptation to reduce water loss.

Flowers appear in summer, when most plants are dormant

Stinking bean trefoil | ***Anagyris foetida***
This species grows throughout the Mediterranean. After flowering and setting seeds, stinking bean trefoil loses its leaves in summer to conserve water.

Scorpion senna | ***Hippocrepis emerus***
A medium-size shrub, scorpion senna can reach 6½ ft (2 m) in height. The deciduous leaves are divided into many small leaflets. The yellow flowers resemble those of peas.

Large, yellow flowers are borne in long racemes

Myrtle |
Myrtus communis
Myrtle's thick evergreen leaves lose little water, and it can regrow from the base if damaged by fire or cutting.

Spanish gorse | ***Genista hispanica*** This deciduous shrub has spiny stems to deter grazing animals. Tiny leaves grow between the spines in spring, but are lost as temperatures rise.

"There are riches enough for all of us, no matter our abilities or circumstances."

Robert D. **Kaplan** American author

Japanese maple | *Acer palmatum* Growing to 32 ft (10 m) tall, this deciduous tree has deeply lobed leaves that develop vivid fall colors.

Temperate East Asia
Sheltered evolution

△ **The leaves of the empress tree** (*Paulownia tomentosa*) can measure 12 in (30 cm) long.

East Asia escaped the periodic glaciation that so devastated the flora elsewhere, allowing its plants to evolve for millions of years without any drastic climate changes. The result was zones with stable climates, known as refugia, where a vast array of different species emerged. Today, these are among the most species-diverse areas of the world. They are also the source of many of the plants currently grown in the gardens of Europe and North America.

Sprays of pink blossoms appear in spring

Trees

East Asia's temperate forests and woodlands boast a rich variety of trees. Some species are similar to their eastern North American relatives (see box p.75) but many more are distinct and some are unique to the region.

Fragrant white flowers are held in large heads (panicles)

Tiny flowers lack petals

Japanese cherry | *Prunus serrulata*
The cherry blossom cultivars of China and Japan have been developed from this tree. It is a small species with serrated leaves and large, pink flowers.

White fruits develop from many individual flowers

White mulberry | *Morus alba*
As the food plant of silk worms, this tree has been central to the silk trade for centuries. Its tiny flowers grow in dense clusters.

Katsura |
Cercidiphyllum japonicum
Known for their fall color, katsura grow to 100 ft (30 m) tall. Male flowers appear before the leaves emerge—female ones as the foliage expands.

Glossy privet |
Ligustrum lucidum
This small evergreen tree gets its Latin name from the shiny surface of its leaves. Flowers are followed by black berries in the fall.

Siebold's magnolia |
Magnolia sieboldii
Large, fragrant, cup-shaped, white flowers adorn this small deciduous tree during the summer months.

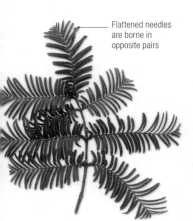

Flattened needles are borne in opposite pairs

Empress tree |
Paulownia tomentosa
A large tree, this deciduous species can reach 82 ft (25 m) in height and width. Flower buds develop in the fall, but remain dormant until spring.

Large, funnel-shaped flowers

Flower buds, which are visible on the bare branches all winter, open in spring

Winged seeds follow the tiny yellow flowers

Dawn redwood | *Metasequoia glyptostroboides*
Long thought extinct, this species was rediscovered during the 1940s, and subsequently introduced to Europe. The dawn redwood is a deciduous conifer and loses its needles every fall.

Tree of heaven | *Ailanthus altissima*
This fast-growing species spreads by sending out underground suckers, creating thickets from a single tree. The tree of heaven is an invasive weed in some countries.

Shrubs

The attractive shrubs of East Asia's temperate forests were widely collected during the 19th and early 20th centuries. As a result, many are now familiar as garden plants.

Matrimony vine | *Lycium barbarum*
The deciduous shrub grows as a sprawling mass, often over other plants. Long, wiry stems bear small flowers and berries at the same time.

Young leaves are bright red but mature dark green

Pieris | *Pieris formosa*
A large evergreen shrub, pieris will form dense thickets. The white, bell-shaped flowers are held in branched, pendant chains.

Paperplant | *Fatsia japonica*
A relative of ivy, the paperplant grows multiple tall stems. Globular heads of white flowers are followed by round, black berries.

Weeping forsythia |
Forsythia suspensa
One of several forsythia species in temperate East Asia, this shrub can be 10 ft (3 m) tall and wide. It flowers before the leaves develop.

Leaves unfurl after the flowers have faded

Large, four-petaled flowers are produced in spring

St. John's wort | *Hypericum forrestii*
One of several Asian species going by the common name of St. John's wort, this usually deciduous shrub produces a dense mass of stems. Large, yellow flowers appear at the shoot tips in midsummer.

Large panicles of small flowers attract pollinators

Butterfly bush |
Buddleia davidii
Native to temperate East Asia, the butterfly bush is a common garden shrub that is now naturalized in many countries. Tall shoots grow each year to bear long panicles of flowers at their tips in midsummer.

Camellia |
Camellia reticulata
Wild camellia bears single flowers, with a central mass of yellow stamens. However, since antiquity, varieties with multiple petals have been bred in China and Japan.

Chinese witch-hazel | *Hamamelis mollis*
This deciduous shrub produces clusters of highly fragrant flowers on bare branches during winter. The felted leaves, when they emerge, resemble those of hazel (*Corylus avellana*).

Japanese dogwood | *Cornus kousa*
The large bracts surrounding the small flowers of Japanese dogwood draw pollinators to the blooms. Each flower head develops into a single multi-seeded, edible, red fruit.

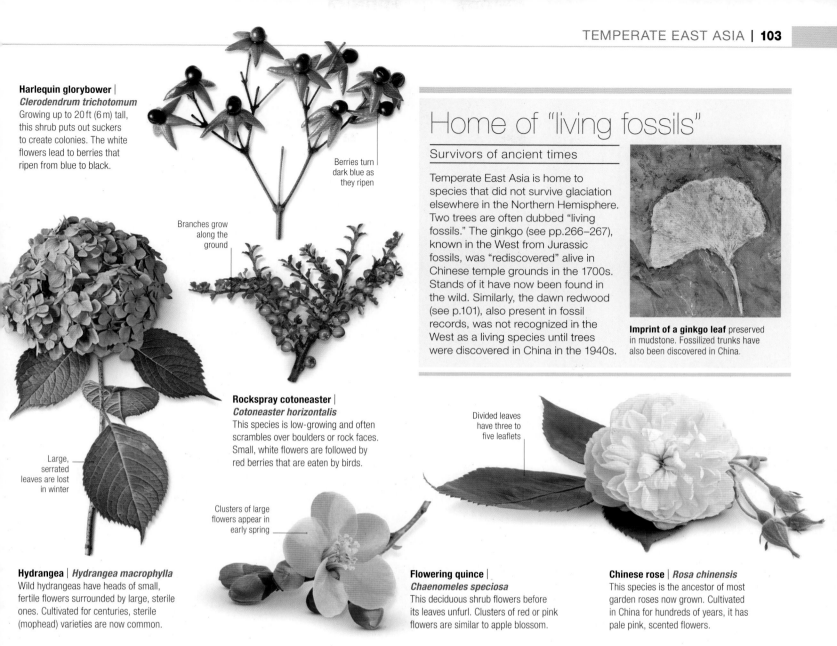

Harlequin glorybower |
Clerodendrum trichotomum
Growing up to 20 ft (6 m) tall,
this shrub puts out suckers
to create colonies. The white
flowers lead to berries that
ripen from blue to black.

Berries turn
dark blue as
they ripen

Branches grow
along the
ground

Home of "living fossils"
Survivors of ancient times

Temperate East Asia is home to
species that did not survive glaciation
elsewhere in the Northern Hemisphere.
Two trees are often dubbed "living
fossils." The ginkgo (see pp.266–267),
known in the West from Jurassic
fossils, was "rediscovered" alive in
Chinese temple grounds in the 1700s.
Stands of it have now been found in
the wild. Similarly, the dawn redwood
(see p.101), also present in fossil
records, was not recognized in the
West as a living species until trees
were discovered in China in the 1940s.

Imprint of a ginkgo leaf preserved
in mudstone. Fossilized trunks have
also been discovered in China.

Large,
serrated
leaves are lost
in winter

Rockspray cotoneaster |
Cotoneaster horizontalis
This species is low-growing and often
scrambles over boulders or rock faces.
Small, white flowers are followed by
red berries that are eaten by birds.

Divided leaves
have three to
five leaflets

Clusters of large
flowers appear in
early spring

Hydrangea | *Hydrangea macrophylla*
Wild hydrangeas have heads of small,
fertile flowers surrounded by large, sterile
ones. Cultivated for centuries, sterile
(mophead) varieties are now common.

Flowering quince |
Chaenomeles speciosa
This deciduous shrub flowers before
its leaves unfurl. Clusters of red or pink
flowers are similar to apple blossom.

Chinese rose | *Rosa chinensis*
This species is the ancestor of most
garden roses now grown. Cultivated
in China for hundreds of years, it has
pale pink, scented flowers.

Unlike their wild cousins, cultivated mophead hydrangeas do not set seed and can only reproduce by artificial propagation.

Japanese domestic scene, c.1790, painted by Katsukawa Shunchō, depicting a servant carrying a bonsai tree into a home.

The art of bonsai

Re-creating the beauty of nature

The cultivation of dwarf trees in containers originated in China, where it was called *pun-sai*. Potted plants portrayed on a 2,000-year-old Han dynasty tomb are probably the first evidence of this, and by 700 CE it had become an established pastime among society's elite. Pun-sai probably reached Japan when Buddhism spread there, although this is not recorded. It had certainly appeared in Japanese culture by the late 12th century, when the Saigyo Monogatari Emaki picture scroll, which shows the life of poet-priest Saigyo, depicts a bonsai plant. This suggests that it was considered a sign of status.

By the time of the Edo period (1603–1868), the practice of potting, pruning, and nurturing small trees had become a popular pastime in Japan, and scholars of the Chinese arts named it *bonsai* in around 1800. During the 19th century, many different styles developed, and exhibitions were held where growers could show off their skills. The art form has since developed a global following.

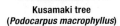

Kusamaki tree
(*Podocarpus macrophyllus*)

Buddhism and bonsai

Spirituality

Zen Buddhist philosophy values deep connections with nature. When Chinese monks fled to Japan after the collapse of the Song dynasty in the 13th century, they took this idea with them. One of the main spiritual influences of Zen Buddhism on bonsai is the notion of *wabi* and *sabi*. Wabi is reflected in the beautiful nature of a bonsai tree—its simplicity. Sabi indicates respect for the natural flaws and defects of bonsai—valued signs of a tree's age.

For Buddhists, the routine care of bonsai is a time for personal meditation and reflection.

Asian fungi
Fungal hot spot

△ **Dried cordyceps** (*Cordyceps* spp.) have long been used in traditional Chinese medicine.

Asia encompasses diverse habitats—grasslands, alpine regions, mixed coniferous and broadleaf forests, and subtropical and tropical rainforests, many of which contain undiscovered fungi. The Greater Mekong subregion alone has two global biodiversity hot spots, in which high numbers of new species of mammals, plants, and insects are being found. One in five species of fungi collected here is new to science; many have spectacular coloring and features, and some are bioluminescent species.

Crown-tipped coral |
Artomyces pyxidatus
This coral fungus is found on moss-covered, decaying wood in pine forests in northeastern India, as well as in Europe and North America.

Vast diversity

The variety of fungal species in Asia reflects the wide range of food sources, plant communities, soil types, and climate. In wet seasons, fungi fruit prolifically, and fruit bodies can often be found for many weeks.

The vaselike cap has wrinkled ridges

Luminous porecap |
Favolaschia manipularis
Found on rotting wood in tropical Asia, this fungus is sometimes faintly bioluminescent and has a cap $1/5–2^1/5$ in (0.5–6 cm) across.

Cordyceps | *Cordyceps militaris*
Feeding on many different insect species, this entomopathogenic (insect-killing) fungus is often found in damp forests during the rainy season.

Woolly chanterelle | *Turbinellus floccosus* This fungus partners with the roots of conifers (see pp.52–53). It grows among older trees where there is decomposed wood on the forest floor.

Bristly tropical cup |
Cookeina tricholoma
This fungus decays twigs and other woody material in lowland tropical areas. Spores are formed inside its goblet-shaped fruit bodies.

Termite mushroom |
Termitomyces microcarpus
In broadleaf forests, this fungus partners with termites in their underground nests. It breaks down plant material delivered by the insects.

Beefsteak fungus | *Fistulina* spp.
This species slowly rots the heartwood that forms the inner core of tree trunks—even in trees where this wood is rich in chemicals that inhibit the activity of most fungi.

Gongsay | *Hymenopellis raphanipes*
As the toxic fruit body starts to emerge from a white, egg-shaped sac, the protruding orange-yellow cap looks like the yolk of a chicken's egg.

Mauve parachute |
Marasmius haematocephalus
Also called the purple pinwheel, this fungus decomposes fallen leaf litter and wood in southern Asia and other tropical regions.

False turkey-tail | *Stereum ostrea*
This fungus looks similar to a common turkey-tail (*Trametes versicolor*). It rots the wood of broadleaved trees in Asia and many other regions.

Bamboo mushroom | *Phallus indusiatus* Widely distributed in southern Asia, this fungus decays wood and commonly produces fruit bodies on the ground in bamboo forests after rain.

Some fungi are heavily harvested for food and traditional medicines in Asia.

Shiitake | *Lentinula edodes*
Native to Southeast Asia and Japan, this fungus grows on the dead wood of many species of broadleaved trees. It has been cultivated for food for centuries.

Glowing fungi

Fungal bioluminescence

A relatively few fungi have caps, stalks, or mycelium (the underground network of fungal filaments) that glow in the dark. These bioluminescent fungi are all mushroom-forming basidiomycetes (see pp.48–49) that cause white rot wood decay. Bioluminescence occurs as part of the processes used by some fungi during wood decomposition. The greenish glow emitted by these fungi often attracts insects that may help spread their spores.

Roridomyces phyllostachydis is a wood decomposer that has been discovered recently in northeast India.

Himalayas
Life at high altitude

△ **The cones of deodar** (*Cedrus deodara*) disintegrate completely when the seeds are shed.

To survive in the Himalayas, Earth's highest mountain range, plants have had to adapt to hostile conditions that place considerable demands on them. The air is thin at high altitude, reducing both oxygen and carbon dioxide density, and the sunlight is intense. Temperatures can also be extremely low. Trees and shrubs in the Himalayas tend to have small, waxy or leathery, evergreen leaves to minimize water loss, or they are deciduous and remain dormant throughout the dry winter.

Large, lance-shaped leaves are lost with the first frosts

Himalayan honeysuckle | *Leycesteria formosa*
Fast-growing Himalayan honeysuckle develops new shoots from its base each year. The shrub's white, tubular flowers are protected by large, colored bracts.

Trees and shrubs

Tough conifers, such as cedar, fir, and pine, and deciduous trees, like magnolia and birch, make up the forests of the Himalayas, with many smaller shrub species growing beneath the forest canopy.

Blooms are arranged in rings around the flower spike

Orange and yellow interiors attract pollinators

Deodar | *Cedrus deodara*
Slow-growing at first, the majestic deodar can tower 164 ft (50 m) above the ground. Young branches droop, but this characteristic is lost with age.

Himalayan fir | *Abies spectabilis*
Of a similar height to the deodar (left), this conifer bears short, flattened needles. It produces upright cones that turn from blue to brown as they age.

Campbell's magnolia | *Magnolia campbellii*
This deciduous species can grow up to 80 ft (24 m) tall. Large pink flowers appear before the leaves emerge in early spring.

Himalayan mint shrub | *Colquhounia coccinea*
In summer, spikes of bright red flowers decorate this semi-evergreen or deciduous shrub. The soft, downy leaves have a whitish underside.

Leadwort | *Ceratostigma griffithii*
After the fall flowering of this small shrub, which rarely exceeds 3 ft (1 m) in height, its leaves turn orange and drop.

Wilson's barberry | *Berberis wilsoniae*
A small, spiny, deciduous shrub, Wilson's barberry has narrow, oval leaves. Its yellow flower clusters develop into pink berries.

Winters in the Himalayas are dry, while the summer is monsoon season.

Himalayan birch | *Betula utilis*
Reaching up to 40 ft (12 m) in height, this variable species can have white or brown bark. Like all birches, it is deciduous.

Young leaves appear just as the catkins begin to fall

Black berries form after flowering

Sweet box | *Sarcococca hookeriana*
This small, evergreen shrub uses suckers to spread and form large clumps. Its minute winter flowers are highly scented.

Sacred paper

Making paper from shrubs

For Buddhists living in the harsh high Himalayan climate, finding a source of paper for religious texts was a challenge. Lowland peoples utilized a number of fast-growing plants and even wool, but Himalayan plants offered few options. The most suitable was *Daphne bholua*, a shrub with stringy stems that can be made into long-lasting, insect-resistant paper. (The related *Edgeworthia chrysantha* provided paper in Japan and China.)

Nepalese paper plant (*Daphne bholua*) has scented flowers.

High valleys in the Himalayas, especially in the western part of the range, are dominated by deodar forests. These trees, which grow at an elevation of between 6,200–9,800 ft (1,900–3,000 m), support a variety of ground flora and fauna.

Sal tree (*Shorea robusta*) groves provide food and shelter for wild elephants and other animals.

Sal tree

Versatile and sacred

An Asian species, the sal tree (*Shorea robusta*) grows from the Himalayas southward, and throughout the Indian subcontinent. Fossil evidence suggests that it has been present in the region for almost 50 million years; today, it is a dominant forest species. The sal has a long tap root that makes it highly windproof. Since it is also resistant to wildfire and can regrow when coppiced—meaning periodically cut to the base—it is enormously beneficial to the environment, creating stable habitats for many other species.

Sal tree resin, or dammar

The sal tree has sacred importance for Hindus – being associated with Vishnu in India – Buddhists, and Jains. It is often depicted in religious architecture and, as a valuable hardwood, its timber is often used in temple construction.

Sal tree resin is used to mount microscope specimens.

Sal value

Myriad uses

Sal trees provide several valuable materials. The resinous wood is resistant to termites, which makes it particularly good for door and window frames. The resin is used to create varnish, paints, and batik (wax-treated cloth). Sal seeds are ground into a flour or made into porridge, while the oil the seeds contain can be extracted and used as a substitute for cocoa butter. When dried, the large, rounded leaves are used to make disposable plates and bowls (*patravali*).

Sal leaves are stitched together for use as plates in India and Nepal. They can then be fed to goats or cattle afterward.

Tropical Asia

Threatened paradise

△ **Soapberry** (*Sapindus trifoliatus*) has leaves composed of three leaflets.

The tropical forests of south and southeast Asia are rich in their diversity of plant and animal species. However, tropical forest is such a closely interwoven biome that the loss of a few keystone species can lead to the collapse of the entire system. Many of the woody plants that grow in the region's tropical forests are sources of useful and valuable materials. While Indigenous peoples traditionally harvested sustainably, the insatiable demands of modern international trade and the quest for land for cash-crop plantations have led to devastating deforestation.

Tiny, globular figs are eaten by animals; the seeds are then deposited on treetops

White fig | *Ficus virens*
The seed of this strangler fig sprouts in the canopy of another tree. It sends roots down to the ground, encircling and outgrowing its host, which it eventually smothers and kills.

Arabian jasmine |
Jasminum sambac
Found throughout the region and cultivated widely, this shrub can be up to 10 ft (3 m) tall. Clusters of highly scented flowers appear year-round at the branch tips.

Teak | *Tectona grandis* Demand for the wood of this seasonally deciduous tree was once a cause of deforestation. Teak is now grown sustainably.

Flowers change shade from white, then pink, to red to attract varied pollinators

Rangoon creeper | *Combretum indicum*
This vine can scale heights up to 39 ft (12 m), using modified leaf petioles as grappling hooks. The tubular, fragrant flowers are adapted to long-tongued pollinators.

Water pine |
Glyptostrobus pensilis

The water pine is a deciduous conifer of Laos and Vietnam. Once common, it now only survives in swampy forests, which are also now being drained for agriculture.

Hanging flowers can cover the entire tree when it is in blossom

Young seed cones are green, maturing to yellow-brown

"Reversing deforestation is complicated; planting a tree is simple."

Martin **O'Malley,**
Former governor of Maryland (2007–2015)

Seeds are rich in compounds called saponins, which are used by Indigenous people for soap

Flowers are arranged in branching clusters called panicles

Soapberry |
Sapindus trifoliatus

Native from Pakistan to Myanmar, this tree grows to 82 ft (25 m) tall. Its common name refers to the fact that its seeds contain chemicals that can be used to make soap.

Australian pine |
Casuarina equisetifolia

Resembling a conifer, this evergreen tree has drooping branches; tiny, scale-shaped leaves; and cone-like fruits. It often grows near the sea or beside rivers and streams.

Golden shower tree |
Cassia fistula

Originating in South Asia, this deciduous tree is often planted as an ornamental. Growing to 50 ft (15 m), it has large, pinnate leaves. It has been used in herbal remedies for millennia.

Lanceleaf marble tree |
Elaeocarpus lanceifolius

This tree of South and Southeast Asia has many uses, providing timber, seeds that are used as jewelery beads, and edible fruit.

Camphor tree | *Cinnamomum camphora*

An evergreen, this tree is widely cultivated for timber and camphor—a waxy solid distilled from the bark that has long been used for its scent and in folk medicine.

Forest crisis

Biodiversity hot spot under threat

Southeast Asia possesses around 15 percent of the world's tropical forests. However, the deforestation rate in the region is also the highest globally, posing a grave threat to many unique forest species. Indonesia, which is home to some of the most biodiverse of all tropical forests, is now among the top ten countries for carbon dioxide emissions. This is mainly due to the clearance and burning of forests, and the soil degradation that results.

Indonesian forests are at risk of clearance to create palm oil and timber plantations, or grazing land for animals.

The Indian banyan (*Ficus benghalensis*) is able to develop an immense canopy by growing hundreds or even thousands of extra trunks.

As banyan trees mature, adventitious roots—those that sprout from its stems—grow down to support the spreading branches.

Mature fruits turn bright orange, attracting birds and monkeys, which spread the seeds to the branches of new host trees.

The Moreton Bay fig (Ficus macrophylla), or Australian banyan, has large buttress roots growing from the base of its trunk.

Banyan
Growing down and out

The Indian banyan tree (*Ficus benghalensis*) has the largest canopy in the world, but starts life as a small epiphyte on the branch of another tree. An animal carries seeds from a juicy fig it has eaten to the host tree, where they germinate. For 15–20 years, the banyan grows unobtrusively in the canopy of its host. As it develops, aerial roots grow down toward the ground. Once these reach the soil, the banyan grows much faster and it starts to look more treelike, as the roots merge to form a trunk. In time, it outgrows the host tree and smothers it, eventually killing it. The banyan is a type of strangler fig, and they all grow in this way.

Free of competition from its host, the banyan continues to spread. To support its increasing weight, more aerial roots grow down from the branches. Gradually, these "prop" roots become trunks themselves, enabling the canopy to spread wider and wider. This is what defines a tree as a banyan. Several fig (*Ficus*) species are banyans, but the Indian banyan is the biggest by far.

The trunk of a banyan tree is hollow, where the host tree used to be.

Hinduism

Sacred symbol of longevity

To Hindus, the banyan is the tree of life, and symbolizes both life and death. The tree's apparent ability to grow forever is linked to Lord Brahma, Lord Vishnu, and Lord Shiva. Its spreading branches are associated with the gods' shelter provided to devotees. The unusual manner in which the banyan grows—its roots above ground, and the way in which it strangles its host—are described in the *Bhagavad Gita* as reflecting the relationship between the material and the spiritual world.

This is a popular depiction of Krishna as a savior god, called Vatapatrasayi, Lord of the Banyan Leaf.

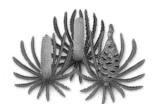

Australia

Isolated evolution

△ **The upright flower heads** of banksia become cone-like when in seed.

Australia is a vast landmass that encompasses a range of climatic conditions. Separated from other continents for millions of years after the breakup of the ancient supercontinent called Gondwana, its isolated plants have often evolved in unique ways. Australia's trees and shrubs include the wattles and several members of the *Protea* family—perhaps more often associated with southern Africa. Many of these plants are evergreen, with small leaves that reduce water loss.

Trees and shrubs

Most trees and shrubs rely on fungi in the soil, mycorrhizas, to enable them to access nutrients in the soil. Some Australian trees and shrubs lack this fungal association, which means that they can only grow where the vital trace elements are readily available to them in the soil.

Branch tips bear fragrant, ball-shaped, fluffy yellow flowers

Finely divided, fernlike leaves are blue-green to silvery gray

Silver wattle | *Acacia dealbata*
Also known as mimosa, this medium-size tree can grow up to 82 ft (25 m) tall. An evergreen species, it has finely divided leaves and globular heads of petalless flowers.

Gondwanan inheritance

The *Proteaceae* family

Many native Australian plants also grow on other land masses that were once linked as Gondwana (Africa, India, New Zealand, and South America). The centers of diversity of the *Proteaceae* family, for example, are Australia (where *Banksia*, *Grevillea*, and *Telopea* grow) and southern Africa (home to *Leucadendron* and *Protea*). Related plants grow in New Zealand and South America. Finding related plants on isolated land masses is known in botany as vicariance.

Gondwana was an ancient supercontinent that began to break up 180 million years ago into the landmasses that exist today, helping to spread plant and animal species.

Oyster Bay pine | *Callitris rhomboidea*
This conifer has minute leaves on wiry stems. Male and female cones are carried on the same tree. Tiny male cones grow at the shoot tips, while larger female cones form clusters on the fruiting branches, where they may remain for several years.

Crimson bottlebrush | *Callistemon citrinus*
Like eucalyptus, this shrub is a member of the *Myrtaceae* family, and has an arching habit. Cylindrical flower heads appear in summer, with shoots continuing to grow beyond them. The leaves give off a lemony aroma when crushed.

Kerosene bush | *Ozothamnus ledifolius*
The common name of this slow-growing shrub, up to 5 ft (1.5 m) tall, derives from its highly flammable leaves. Clusters of small white flowers grow from red buds at the shoot tips.

Rigid leaves have a sharp tip

Coast banksia |
Banksia integrifolia
Able to reach a height of
33 ft (10 m), coast banksia
has evergreen leaves and
produces flower spikes
directly from older branches.
The flowers are pollinated by
honey possums.

Sydney golden wattle |
Acacia longifolia
This species has no leaves, except when it is a
seedling. Instead, its leaf stems are modified into
flat structures called phyllodes, which perform the
same photosynthesizing role as leaves.

White, four-petaled
flowers appear in
spring and summer

Oval, evergreen leaves
have a glossy upper
surface

Leatherwood | *Eucryphia lucida*
This evergreen tree can grow up to 98 ft (30 m),
occasionally more. The strongly fragrant flowers
attract bees, making it popular with beekeepers.

> "Trees are, after all, our largest
> and oldest living things. They are
> Australia's natural, national treasures."
>
> Richard **Allen** *Australia's Remarkable Trees,* 2009

Spreading correa |
Correa decumbens
This is a small shrub that grows up to
3 ft (1 m) high. Tubular flowers appear
among the evergreen glossy leaves
during summer.

Colorful, five-petaled
flowers lure pollinators

Manuka | *Leptospermum scoparium*
An evergreen shrub, manuka grows
multiple erect shoots up to 10 ft (3 m) tall.
It is one of the first species to reestablish
itself on recently burned land.

New South Wales waratah |
Telopea speciosissima
Numerous vertical stems emerge from the
tuberous root of this evergreen shrub. Flower heads,
surrounded by colorful bracts, form at the shoot tips.

Silky oak | *Grevillea robusta*
The large, evergreen silky oak, which may
grow 100 ft (40 m) tall, is a member of the
Protea family. It bears compact, brushlike
heads of orange flowers in spring.

Eucalyptus
Icon of the Outback

The genus *Eucalyptus* is confined to Australia and a few islands to the north of it. From the enormous mountain ash (*Eucalyptus regnans*), reaching 300 ft (90 m) tall, to the shrubby *E. vernicosa* of Tasmania, eucalyptus trees have adapted to a range of habitats across this huge continent, becoming the dominant trees in many areas. The leaves and stems are rich in natural oils that deter predators, but burn easily. Most species have dormant buds under the bark of their trunk, or at its base, which are known as "lignotubers." Both types sprout new shoots very quickly after wildfires, enabling the trees to regrow.

Eucalyptus is adapted to survive hostile conditions, with spreading roots that obtain every molecule of moisture they can and tough, evergreen foliage that loses little water. The flower buds are protected by a cap, or operculum, which drops off as they open. The flowers have no petals, but brushlike masses of stamens that attract bees and coat them in pollen. Large amounts of seed ensure that some seedlings survive, making these trees invasive pests in countries where they are introduced.

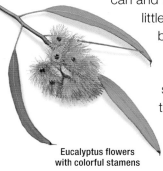

Eucalyptus flowers with colorful stamens

Toxic oil

Removing competition

Eucalyptus leaves are highly toxic to most insects and mammals. The koala (*Phascolarctos cinereus*) is one exception. It has specialized bacteria in its gut that neutralize the toxin and digest the leaves, although few other animals can do the same. However, it is not only animals that eucalyptus trees can repel. Their roots emit chemicals that stop other plant seeds from growing near them, an example of allelopathy. This means trees face no competition for water or nutrients.

Few other plants grow near eucalyptus trees, which are known as "gum trees," because of the gooey sap they exude.

Koalas (*Phascolarctos cinereus*) are dependent on eucalyptus, the mainstay of their diet.

New Zealand
Mammal-free evolution

△ **Kauri** (*Agathis australis*) cones take 18 months to develop and contain winged seeds.

New Zealand broke away from Gondwana 85–100 million years ago. Some of its native plants were already present, but others arrived via sea currents and birds. Insects and birds—including the huge, now-extinct moas—played a key role in shaping New Zealand's ecosystems. Plants evolved free from the influence of grazing mammals until European colonizers introduced sheep, goats, deer, and cattle.

Trees and shrubs

Most trees and shrubs are evergreen and intolerant of extreme cold. Some are highly variable in appearance, or have very different juvenile and adult forms, which can make identification difficult.

Common broom |
Carmichaelia australis
This shrub soon loses its small leaves. Photosynthesis then occurs in the flattened green shoots. Tiny pea flowers appear at the stem joints.

Tree fuchsia |
Fuchsia excorticata
Small flowers grow from the old stems of this tall deciduous shrub. They open green, but turn red as they age. The bark is papery and flaking.

New Zealand holly | *Olearia macrodonta*
One of several *Olearia* species in New Zealand, this shrub can grow 20 ft (6 m) tall. Although it's leaves resemble those of holly, *Ilex aquifolium*, they are not closely related.

Kauri | *Agathis australis*
Soaring up to 165 ft (50 m) above the forest floor and dominating the forest canopy, the kauri is one of the world's tallest trees. An ancient conifer, it has small, narrow leaves and bears globular cones.

Brushlike flower heads consist of many small flowers

Pōhutukawa | *Metrosideros excelsa*
Related to eucalyptus, this species produces vibrant midsummer blooms between November and January that do not have petals. Instead, a mass of bright red stamens provide the attraction for pollinators.

Vital pollinator

Native mammals

Because New Zealand became isolated before mammals rose to dominance on land, its only native mammals were bats. New Zealand's long-tailed bats are insect-eaters, but its short-tailed bats also feed on nectar, pollen, and fruit. The lesser short-tailed bat is the sole pollinator of the threatened wood rose (*Dactylanthus taylorii*), a parasitic plant that entices bats with a sweet musky scent.

New Zealand lesser short-tailed bat

Willow-leaf hebe |
Veronica salicifolia
One of the largest hebe species, the fast-growing willow-leaf has long, lance-shaped leaves and large, often drooping, heads of small flowers.

Cabbage tree | *Cordyline australis*
The cabbage tree begins as a single stem, forming side branches only after its first flowering. Long, narrow leaves are accompanied by sprays of white flowers.

Wire-netting bush |
Corokia cotoneaster
The common name of this small shrub, typically no more than 10 ft (3 m) tall and wide, derives from its distinctive zigzag gray stems.

Glossy evergreen leaves have undulating margins

Kohuhu |
Pittosporum tenuifolium
The highly variable kohuhu can grow as a shrub or small tree. Dark maroon-red flowers develop among the leaves and lure night-flying insect pollinators.

Ribbonwood |
Hoheria sexstylosa
A small tree, this evergreen species has large, serrated leaves. Insect pollinators are drawn to the fragrant white flowers that appear in late summer and fall.

Growth has a dome-shaped habit

Pōhutukawa (*Metrosideros excelsa*) is also known as the New Zealand Christmas tree.

Parana pine | *Araucaria angustifolia* Intensive logging has made this conifer critically endangered. Several bird species and many invertebrates depend on it for food and shelter.

Tropical South America
Tapestry of plants

△ **Parana pine** (*Araucaria angustifolia*) seeds are widely eaten by Indigenous people of southern Brazil.

Encompassing habitats as varied as Amazonia's lowland rainforest, the dry forest of northeast Brazil, the grassland and shrubland of the Andes Mountains, and even areas of desert and semi-desert, this region has the most diverse plant life on Earth. The Amazon rainforest—the world's largest—is one of the wettest and hottest terrestrial habitats, with emergent trees towering over a dense canopy.

Trees of the forest

The trees of the region exhibit an extraordinary variety of sizes, fruits, and relationships with animals. For millennia, people have used their wood, fruit, leaves, and roots for building, food, and medicine.

Flowers are a key source of nectar for many birds and insects

Lignum vitae | *Guaiacum officinale*
For centuries, people have used this tree's very hard wood to make furniture and dwellings. Its resin is a remedy for rheumatism and respiratory disorders.

Wild sweetsop | *Annona mucosa*
This evergreen has a dense crown and can grow to 65 ft (20 m) tall. *A. mucosa* has edible fruit (green, ripening to yellow), and its leaves are used to make medicine.

Guanacaste |
Enterolobium cyclocarpum
Now dispersed only by people and farm animals; native species that ate and spread the seeds are now extinct.

Acai palm | *Euterpe oleracea*
The globular black fruits of the acai, a native of eastern Amazonia, provide food for birds such as channel-billed toucans. Candies and drinks are made from the fruit pulp, and the palm hearts are eaten as a vegetable.

Floss silk tree | *Ceiba speciosa*
The trunk of this semi-deciduous tree is studded with large, conical thorns. Its seed pod fibers are used as a stuffing for upholstery.

Large flowers have five pink petals, yellow at the base

Walking palm | *Socratea exorrhiza*
The saplings can "escape" light-blocking vegetation by growing new roots on the opposite side, gradually shifting ("walking") to a brighter spot.

Ant tree | *Triplaris americana*
When in bloom, this tree produces thousands of pink flowers. The female flowers are larger and more numerous than their male equivalents.

Brazil nut | *Bertholletia excelsa*
Towering over its neighbors, this tree can be more than 165 ft (50 m) tall. Up to 24 nuts are held in spherical pods; mature trees bear more than 300 pods.

Understory shrubs

Shrubs play a vital role in tropical South American ecosystems, stabilizing the soil and maintaining the water balance. Not only do these plants offer shelter, their pollen, fruits, buds, and leaves support a huge variety of bird, mammal, and invertebrate life. Humans have long exploited them, too.

Jabuticaba | *Plinia cauliflora*
The flowers and purplish-black, grapelike fruits of this large shrub grow directly from the trunk and branches. The sweet pulp of jabuticaba fruit is used to make jam and wine.

Cat's-claw creeper | *Dolichandra unguis-cati*
This liana scales tree trunks by means of claw-shaped tendrils and aerial roots, climbing up to 65 ft (20 m) into the crown of trees. It produces bright yellow, trumpet-shaped flowers.

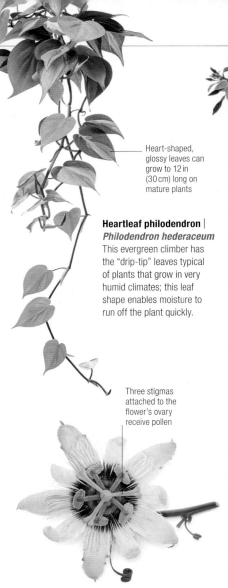

Heart-shaped, glossy leaves can grow to 12 in (30 cm) long on mature plants

Heartleaf philodendron |
Philodendron hederaceum
This evergreen climber has the "drip-tip" leaves typical of plants that grow in very humid climates; this leaf shape enables moisture to run off the plant quickly.

Three stigmas attached to the flower's ovary receive pollen

Passion fruit | *Passiflora edulis*
Spectacular flowers followed by edible, oval fruits are produced by this evergreen vine. It is pollinated by bees, butterflies, moths, hummingbirds, and bats.

Lesser bougainvillea | *Bougainvillea glabra* Hummingbirds feed on nectar from the tubular, creamy-white flowers of this shrub, which blooms all year. The small flowers are held within large, pinkish, petal-like bracts.

Cinchona | *Cinchona officinalis*
The bark of the "fever tree" contains quinine as a defense against insects. Before the advent of synthetic drugs, quinine was used to treat malaria.

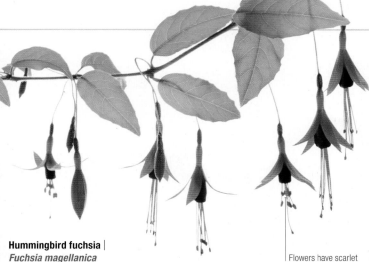

Hummingbird fuchsia |
Fuchsia magellanica
Drooping, tubular flowers are pollinated by hummingbirds that probe the blooms for nectar. This fuchsia is native to subtropical regions of southern Chile and Argentina.

Flowers have scarlet sepals and purple petals, with protruding stamens and stigma

Jaborandi | *Pilocarpus jaborandi*
An established folk remedy, jaborandi leaves contain chemicals, such as pilocarpine, now used in commercial pharmaceuticals.

Achiote | *Bixa orellana*
The fruit pods of this tall shrub are covered in soft spines. Mature pods dry, harden, and then split open, exposing the seeds within.

Spiked pepper | *Piper adancum*
Indigenous Amazonian people use this shrub's aromatic, lance-shaped leaves as an antiseptic and its fruits as a condiment.

Hot lips | *Palicourea elata*
The bright red bracts ("lips") at the base of the scentless flowers of *P. elata* attract butterfly and hummingbird pollinators.

The fight for light

Photosynthesis in a forest environment

Forest plants have evolved different ways to obtain sunlight needed for photosynthesis. Trees grow tall, competing to reach the canopy where light is abundant. Lianas and vines do not have massive trunks, so they climb large trees to access sunlight, while epiphytes grow on branches high above the gloomy forest floor. Plants that live in shade have thin leaves with a large surface area to capture more light.

Plants competing for light in a dense Costa Rican forest

Swiss cheese plant | *Monstera deliciosa* Seedlings sprout in soil but climb tree trunks in search of light. The plants become epiphytes once they leave the ground.

Yellow-chevroned parakeets (*Brotogeris chiriri*) in South America use the fluffy seed fibers from kapok fruits as nesting material.

A rainforest giant, this kapok dwarfs the surrounding trees. Kapoks are among the largest of all flowering trees.

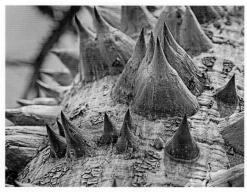

The flowers of the kapok tree produce a scent that is appealing to bats—but unpleasant to the human nose.

Strong, conical spines protect the trunk and larger branches from attack by browsing animals.

Kapok tree
Giant of the rainforests

The kapok (*Ceiba pentandra*) is an enormous tree of Central and South American rainforests, and also of west Africa. Typically growing to 230 ft (70 m), it towers over other rainforest species. Reaching such a height helps its seeds, with their fluffy fibers, disperse more widely. The kapok is deciduous, and sheds its leaves in the dry season. Like most rainforest trees, it grows on relatively poor soils, so it needs a wide, shallow root system in order to obtain enough nutrients. Being so tall and having shallow roots would make the tree unstable, so it has developed a system of buttress roots around the base of its trunk for additional support. Bats are the principal pollinators of kapok trees, attracted by the scent of their pink or white flowers, which open after dusk. The flowers appear when there are no leaves, giving the bats a clear flight path to the nectar-laden blooms.

Dried kapok fruit

The kapok tree was sacred to the Maya people of Central America, and ceremonial masks are made from its wood in west Africa. Commercial kapok plantations are concentrated in Southeast Asia, where the tree was introduced. The fluffy, cotton-like seed fibers have been used for centuries as stuffing material for pillows, mattresses, and soft toys, but they are difficult to spin into yarn. The fibers are also highly flammable, so they are no longer used for upholstery in modern furniture.

Buttress roots, which anchor the tree in the ground, can grow 65 ft (20 m) out from the base of the trunk.

Kapok trees can produce up to 4,000 fruits in a season, with each one containing 200 seeds.

South American fungi
Unimaginable variety

△ **Mealy bonnet** (*Mycena cinerella*) has distinctive tiers of gills beneath its cap; it feeds by decomposing leaf litter on the forest floor.

South America is one of the most biodiverse regions on Earth, with ecosystems that include equatorial, temperate, and Mediterranean forests, grassland, and desert habitats. More than 14,000 plant species have been found so far in the Amazon rainforest but it has been estimated there are more than 40,000, most of which are associated with at least one species of fungus. Many of these fungi are found only in South America, and while some are recognizably relatives of species found elsewhere in the world, others have exotic shapes, patterning, and coloring that make them unique.

Conical, grayish cap is up to 1 in (3 cm) across

Nitrous bonnet |
Mycena leptocephala
Found in parts of South America—and widespread in Europe and North America—it decomposes dead organic matter on the forest floor.

Rotters, partners, and parasites

As in forests worldwide, South American fungi include species that decay or recycle dead plant matter. Others form beneficial partnerships with the roots of plants (see pp.52–53), or live as parasites on plant or animal hosts.

Entoloma necopinatum
Listed as a vulnerable species, this fungus is only found in southern beech (*Nothofagus*) forests in coastal areas and foothills in Chile. It decomposes leaves on the forest floor.

Stephanopus azureus
A rare inhabitant of the forest floor in Chile, it is a mycorrhizal partner with the roots of *Nothofagus*. It is one of only five species of this genus, all found in South America.

Stalked orange peel fungus |
Sowerbyella rhenana
An ascomycete mycorrhizal partner with *Nothofagus* roots in Chile—it is also found in North America, Europe, Japan, and Australia.

Southern bracket fungus |
Ganoderma australe
Found worldwide, this fungus decays dead wood in the trunks of living broadleaved trees and causes white rot.

Fistulina antarctica Endemic to southern Chile and Argentina, this fungus decays dead wood in the trunks of old standing trees in native forest. *Fistulina* species cause brown rot.

Aleurina argentina
An ascomycete found on forest floors in Patagonia and Southeast Australia, it forms cups ³/₄ in (2 cm) wide. It is a mycorrhizal partner with the roots of *Nothofagus* species.

Hallingea purpurea
A basidiomycete mycorrhizal with *Nothofagus* species in Patagonia. It forms truffle fruit bodies below the surface, and is spread by ground-dwelling birds that seek it out.

Cyttaria berteroi
The fruit bodies of this parasite are seen only on the cankers it causes on the branches of southern beech (*Nothofagus*) trees. It grows in South America and Australia.

Hypholoma frowardii
Unlike *Hypholoma fasciculare*, which is found worldwide, this species only grows in Andean-Patagonian forests on the stumps of dead southern beech (*Nothofagus*) trees.

Cortinarius magellanicus Endemic to South America, and confined to the Patagonia region, this webcap is a mycorrhizal partner with the roots of *Nothofagus* trees.

Descolea antarctica
Native to Chile, it grows on forest floors as a mycorrhizal partner with roots of *Nothofagus* trees. The genus is named after Raúl Descole, an Argentinian botanist.

Boletus bresinskyanus
One of six species so far found to be native to Chile, in Patagonian forests, it is an ectomycorrhizal partner with the roots of southern beech (*Nothofagus*) trees.

Preventing extinction

Sustainable collecting

Butyriboletus loyo forms large, edible mushrooms up to 12 in (30 cm) across and weighing up to 11 lb (5 kg), which are a valuable commodity for many Indigenous people in southern Chile. However, over-picking, the loss of native forest, and wildfires have led to its decline and it is now listed as endangered. Only collecting mature fruit bodies that have already deposited some spores—a form of sustainable harvesting—may be one way to ensure that the fungus survives.

The natural population of *Butyriboletus loyo* has reduced by half over the last 50 years—the rate of decline is increasing.

Widely used as an herbal remedy, boldo (*Peumus boldus*) reaches 65 ft (20 m) high.

Temperate South America
An ancient ancestry

△ **Juvenile flowers** on a Prince Albert yew (*Saxegothaea conspicua*)

Many of the trees and shrubs of South America trace their ancestry to the ancient continent of Gondwana, which long predates the joining of South and North America. Many of South America's trees and shrubs have red flowers, which attract birds as pollinators. Adaptations such as this have meant that the flora of temperate South America has remained unique, whereas its fauna evolved as North American species moved south.

Brush bush |
Eucryphia glutinosa
This is the only deciduous member of a genus found in South America and Australia. Its divided leaves turn red, yellow and orange in the fall.

Trees

Often closely related to those of Australasia— also once part of Gondwana—the trees are unrelated to those of the Northern Hemisphere. Convergent evolution means that despite this, some look like their northern equivalents.

White flowers characteristically have numerous stamens

Chilean myrtle |
Luma apiculata
This smooth-barked tree can reach 49 ft (15 m) tall. Its trunk is orange-brown and its pointed oval leaves are evergreen.

Small leaves have minutely toothed margins

Small leaves are borne on flattened shoots

Chilean cedar | *Austrocedrus chilensis*
This slow-growing conifer eventually reaches 78 ft (24 m) tall. It is related to similar conifers in Australasia and, like them, has small upward-pointing cones.

Southern beech |
Nothofagus antarctica
A large, deciduous tree, this species can reach 49 ft (15 m) high. The leaves turn yellow or orange in the fall before they drop.

Clusters of bright, orange-red flowers are pollinated by birds

Leaves are characteristically pointed at the tips

Large bell-shaped flowers hang profusely from branchlets

Prince Albert yew | *Saxegothaea conspicua*
This conifer belongs to an exclusively Southern Hemisphere family. It grows slowly to 82 ft (25 m) tall, with flaking bark and small, spiky cones.

Chilean lantern tree | *Crinodendron hookerianum*
This small evergreen tree reaches around 26 ft (8 m) tall, with glossy foliage and a gray trunk. Pendant red flowers attract nectar-seeking hummingbirds, which pollinate them.

Chilean fire bush | *Embothrium coccineum*
Native to Chile and Argentina, this evergreen grows to 59 ft (18 m) tall. It can grow multiple shoots to form thickets. Its soft wood is easily carved.

Shrubs

Many of these South American shrubs have unusual growth habits, and often brightly colored flowers. They have coevolved with their pollinators to maximize the chances of seed production.

Large, yellow flowers are held in loose heads termed corymbs

Argentine senna | *Senna corymbosa*
This member of a widely distributed genus grows to 3 ft (1 m) tall. It has a long flowering season and has medicinal use as a laxative.

Each shoot is tipped with a spine to deter grazing animals

Bright orange flowers ¼ in (2 cm) across grow in tight, globular heads

Stamens deposit pollen onto foraging hummingbirds

Orange ball tree | *Buddleia globosa*
Although Asian species of this genus are well known, this one is different. The flowers appear in separate heads, branching from a central stem.

Hummingbird fuchsia | *Fuchsia magellanica*
This is the wild ancestor of most garden fuchsias. Narrow, hanging flowers and a long flowering season ensure there is always nectar for its hummingbird pollinators.

Crucifixion thorn | *Colletia hystrix*
This large shrub has no leaves, so photosynthesis takes place in the green stems instead. Small, scented flowers appear in winter and attract bees.

Darwin's barberry | *Berberis darwinii*
This evergreen shrub reaches 10 ft (3 m) tall and wide. A network of thorny twigs and evergreen, spiny leaves discourages grazing animals but encourages nesting birds.

> "In a forest of a hundred thousand trees, no two leaves are alike."
>
> Paulo **Coelho** Brazilian writer

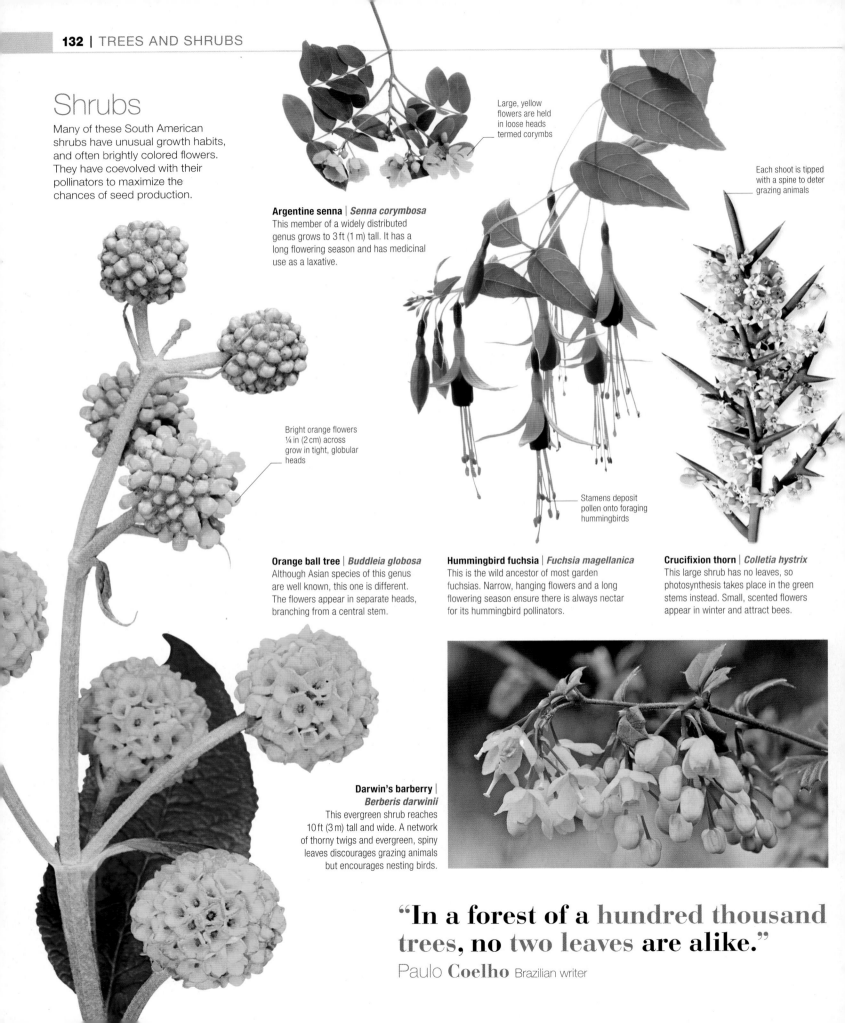

Sacred flower of the Incas |
Cantua buxifolia
This small-leaved evergreen shrub reaches 6 ft
(2 m) tall, grows in the high Andes, and is one
of the national flowers of Peru and Bolivia.

Clusters of
slipper-shaped
flowers appear
in summer

Red and yellow
tubular flowers
attract hummingbirds

Bird magnets
Evolution of flower shape and color

Many South American plants are pollinated
by birds, especially hummingbirds, which
are native to the Americas. These plants
often have tube-shaped flowers that
hummingbirds with long beaks can reach
into for nectar—but insects cannot enter.
Red or orange flowers attract birds, which
see red very well, and projecting stamens
deposit pollen onto the birds' plumage.

Hummingbirds are important plant pollinators

Large, white
to pink berries
grow on the
female plants

Bush slipperwort | *Calceolaria integrifolia*
This unusual small shrub reaches 3 ft (1 m)
tall. The stems have soft evergreen leaves
with bright yellow corymbs of flowers at
their tips.

Prickly heath | *Gaultheria mucronata*
This low-growing spiky shrub is widespread
above the tree line in Chile and Argentina.
Bell-shaped, white male and female flowers
grow on separate plants.

Red, tubular
flowers attract
hummingbirds
as pollinators

Yellow flowers have
a strong evening
scent, attracting
pollinating moths

Redclaws | *Escallonia rubra*
A dense evergreen shrub, this species
grows near the coast and is tolerant of salt
spray. The margins of redclaws leaves are
characteristically toothed.

Chilean holly | *Desfontainia spinosa*
The foliage of this shrub resembles that of
holly, (*Ilex aquifolium*), although it is unrelated.
The spiny evergreen leaves appear in opposite
pairs with flowers developing between them.

Palqui | *Cestrum parqui*
This toxic shrub can grow to 8 ft (2.5 m)
tall, with straggly branches. Strongly
fragrant flowers appear from spring
to fall, followed by black berries.

Red angel's trumpet |
Brugmansia sanguinea
The flowers of this shrub are so long that only the
sword-billed hummingbird (*Ensifera ensifera*), can
reach the nectar with its 5-in- (12-cm-) long beak.

Monkey puzzle tree
Jurassic bark

The monkey puzzle tree (*Araucaria araucana*) is native to the Andes mountains of South America. This ancient species of conifer is a member of the *Araucariaceae* family that grew in the Jurassic and Cretaceous periods, and is a relic from the age of the dinosaurs. The family was once widespread and very diverse—their fossils have been found in most parts of the world. Only three genera of these trees survive today—*Agathis*, *Araucaria*, and *Wollemia*—in South America and Australasia.

Monkey puzzle trees can grow to 164 ft (50 m) tall, and have a single trunk topped, in older trees, by a tuft of branches. The rigid, triangular, pointed leaves grow in spirals around the branches, which on young trees extend all the way down to the ground. In the mid-1800s, English barrister Charles Austin is said to have remarked, on first seeing the tree, that climbing the spiny branches would be a puzzle even for a monkey—hence the common name. In reality, no monkeys live near wild trees.

In its native range, Indigenous peoples harvest the tree for wood, resins, and its large seeds. The spherical female cones disintegrate as the seeds ripen, so obtaining them is not easy. The tree is protected in Chile, and international trade in its timber is banned, in order to help conserve the remaining populations.

Male cones growing at shoot tips

Wollemi pine
A surprise discovery

Both living and fossil relatives of the monkey puzzle have been extensively studied since the 19th century. In 1994, wildlife ranger David Noble discovered an entirely new member of this family in Australia's Wollemi National Park. After studies showed that the foliage was similar to fossilized *Agathis jurassica* leaves, the tree was identified as a completely new genus of "living fossil." The species was named after its place of discovery and the man who found it: *Wollemia nobilis*.

Wollemi pine is now widely planted. Proceeds from sales support wild trees.

On volcanic slopes in Chile, monkey puzzle trees tower over woodlands of southern beech (*Nothofagus* spp.).

Tropical Africa
Life in the rainforests

△ **Only about one-third of mature sapele** (*Entandrophragma cylindricum*) trees produce fruits each year.

The **vast rainforests** of the Congo basin are second only to Amazonia in size and variety, with a wealth of giant emergent trees, canopy species, lianas, and shade-tolerant shrubs. Elsewhere in tropical Africa, the Eastern Afromontane forests grow in mountainous regions from Saudi Arabia to southern Africa, and the Guinean forests stretch from Guinea to southern Cameroon. Even in drier areas, many rivers are bordered by gallery forest, which provides valuable corridors for wildlife.

African breadfruit |
Treculia africana
The huge fruits of this tree are eaten either cooked or raw, while the seeds are used to make porridge.

Individual fruits can grow to the size of a volleyball

Trees

African rainforest trees provide sustenance and shelter for animals, and wood, food, and medicines for people. They also absorb huge quantities of carbon, playing an important part in mitigating the rate of climate change.

Sapele | *Entandrophragma cylindricum*
Found in the rainforests of Congo, this slow-growing tree can live for 500 years. They provide habitat for rare primates, such as the Thollon's red colobus (*Piliocolobus tholloni*).

Alstonia | *Alstonia congensis*
In West and Central Africa, this tree is valued medicinally. People use extracts from the leaves to treat rheumatic pains and root extracts to treat malaria.

Iroko | *Milicia excelsa*
One of Africa's most valuable timber trees, this forest giant is revered by the Yoruba people. Sometimes called "African teak," it has been over-exploited commercially.

Bush mango | *Irvingia gabonensis*
People and animals, including elephants and gorillas, enjoy the juicy fruits and the protein-rich nuts of this lofty tree. The stone of each fruit contains a single nut.

Dibetou | *Lovoa trichilioides*
The dibetou is another colossus of the rainforest, reaching up to 148 ft (45 m) tall. Its small flowers bloom throughout the year, and its seeds are dispersed by the wind.

Mucous fig | *Ficus mucuso* This fast-growing tree produces vast quantities of fruits, which are an important food source for chimpanzees (*Pan troglodytes*).

Shrubs

Rainforest shrubs grow far below the forest canopy and are engaged in a constant battle to gain enough light. Many achieve this by clambering up larger trees. Others only thrive when a tree falls, creating a temporary gap in the canopy.

African forests contain more large trees and fewer small trees than the forests of Amazonia or Asia.

Velvet tamarind | *Dialium guineense*
Often found in gallery forest, this shrub or small tree has delicate white flowers and edible, grape-size fruits. It is slow-growing, and its dense, hard wood has a fine texture.

Christmas bush | *Alchornea cordifolia*
The leaves, fruits, and root bark of this straggling shrub are all used in traditional medicine. It has important antibacterial, antifungal, and antiparasitic properties.

Kamyuye | *Hoslundia opposita*
The kamyuye is a scrambling, woody plant with ribbed, colorful berries. The leaves are eaten as a vegetable and used as a medicinal herb for a range of ailments.

Royal poinciana | *Delonix regia* This tree is renowned for its bright red flowers, which are pollinated by butterflies and moths.

Cola nut | *Cola nitida* The beautiful flowers of the cola tree develop into caffeine-rich seeds, which were once used in the manufacture of cola drinks. The seeds are chewed as a mild stimulant.

Sunbird nectar thieves

Ecology

Many insects, birds, and mammals feed on the nectar of flowers. As they do so, they also pick up pollen, transferring it from one plant to another. In tropical Africa, long-tubed flowers are pollinated by long-billed sunbirds. The adaptation of the flower shape to the birds' bills increases the chance of the flowers receiving pollen from another flower of the same species. But shorter-billed sunbirds cheat—biting holes in the base of the flowers to "steal" nectar without transferring pollen.

A male double-collared sunbird pierces the base of a flower to feed on its nectar.

Fever berry | *Croton gratissimus*
This is a striking shrub with silvery, aromatic leaves. When its three-lobed fruit capsule matures, it explodes, scattering the seeds.

Glorybower | *Clerodendrum umbellatum*
This climbing shrub bears red or white flowers with red-tinged centers. In West Africa, the leaves, sap, and roots are used medicinally.

Emin's strophanthus | *Strophanthus eminii*
A shrub, small tree, or liana with extraordinary pink-and-white flowers, this deciduous plant grows in the upland forests of East Africa.

Camwood | *Baphia nitida*
The bark and heartwood of this small tree from Central and West Africa are a rich, deep color and are used to make red dye.

Egyptian star cluster |
Pentas lanceolata
The star-shaped, red or white flowers of this small shrub attract a wide range of pollinating insects, especially butterflies.

Stamens glittering with pollen protrude from the flowers

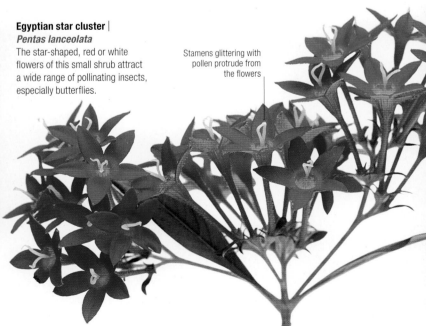

Yellow-dye root | *Cryptolepis sanguinolenta*
An extract from the roots of this climbing shrub, which grows in gallery forest, is traditionally used as a treatment for malaria.

Ira | *Bridelia ferruginea*
Many animals, including monkeys and forest antelopes, feed on the fruits of this straggly tree, dispersing its seeds in the process.

The whistling thorn tree (*Vachellia drepanolobium*) is a food source for many herbivores on the African savanna, including reticulated giraffes (*Giraffa reticulata*).

Acacia

Hosting an ant army

Many acacia trees (*Acacia* and *Vachellia* spp.) develop a characteristic flat-topped shape. This is often the result of grazing: herbivores eat the new shoots growing farther down as soon as they appear. Several species of acacia have evolved mutualistic relationships with ants that minimize this destruction. The trees form specialized structures that are beneficial to ants: hollow or swollen thorns provide ready-made homes for them, and nectaries on the leaf stems or fat globules on the leaf tips supply them with food.

Several ant species take up residence in acacia trees, but there is usually only one species in each tree. In return for food and lodging, the ants vigorously defend their territory, removing insect pests and attacking larger grazing animals—thereby protecting the trees. Adult giraffes can tolerate the bites, but calves are more sensitive, and so they are discouraged from eating the acacia's leaves. The ants may even nip off shoot tips themselves if they grow close to another tree, to prevent neighboring colonies from invading. The trees and ants can survive apart, but together they give each other a competitive advantage.

Pinnate acacia leaf

The **bullhorn acacia** (*Vachellia cornigera*) of Mexico and Central America has wide, hollow spines, ideal for ants.

Ants burrow into the enlarged spines of bullhorn acacia, and use them for shelter and as breeding chambers.

Swollen thorn bases on East Africa's whistling thorn tree (*Vachellia drepanolobium*) offer homes for ants.

Patas monkeys (*Erythrocebus patas*) will feed on the whistling thorn tree until persistent ant bites deter them.

Helping each other

Mutualistic plant relationships

Plant-insect relationships are not limited to acacias. Another species guarded by ants is the odd-looking ant plant (*Hydnophytum* spp.), in whose swollen stem base ants take up residence. Sometimes a plant needs help with reproduction, not protection. Female senita moths (*Upiga virescens*) in America's Sonora Desert pollinate and lay eggs on the flowers of senita cacti (*Lophocereus schottii*). While the caterpillars partly eat the fruits, seeds still develop on the parts that remain.

Ant plants absorb nutrients from dead insects delivered to them by ants.

African savanna
Open canopy

△ **The fruits of the sausage tree** (*Kigelia africana*) can reach 3 ft (1 m) long and weigh more than 20 lb (9 kg).

Savanna covers vast areas of sub-Saharan Africa. A mix of grassland and open-canopy woodland, it has distinct wet and dry seasons. Savanna woodland occurs in areas with higher rainfall, where trees such as mopane (*Colophospermum mopane*) are prominent. In drier areas, grassland dominates, and trees or shrubs, including many acacia (*Vachellia* spp.), are more scattered. The driest savanna is barren in the dry season, but bursts into life and color when the rains come.

Marula |
Sclerocarya birrea
In East Africa, the fruit and nuts of this deciduous tree are valued for food and oil, while the bark has many medicinal uses.

Leaves are used in traditional African medicine

Traditional value

People in Africa's savanna have utilized the fruits, leaves, roots, and wood of its plants for millennia. The rich habitat is home to some critically endangered species, such as black rhinos.

African fan palm | *Borassus aethiopum*
Growing to 82 ft (25 m) tall, this palm has multiple uses. Its fruit and young roots are edible, its wood and mature leaves provide timber and roof thatch, while its young leaves are used for medicine.

Pairs of spines line the stem ridges, where buds will form

Candelabra tree |
Euphorbia ingens
The milky latex produced by the succulent candelabra tree is toxic, but its wood is used for boat-building, and woodpeckers nest in its dead branches.

The branching stems give rise to this plant's common name

Porkbush | *Portulacaria afra*
This succulent's flowers attract many pollinating bees and butterflies, which help support insect-eating birds. The leaves are a source of food and traditional medicine.

Quiver tree | *Aloidendron dichotomum*
Weaverbirds build their massive communal nests in this slow-growing succulent tree, whose branches were once used to make quivers for arrows. Its tubular, yellow flowers sport orange stamens.

Umbrella thorn acacia | *Vachellia tortilis*
Widespread in the Sahel region, where it forms open woodland, this is an important tree for timber. Tolerant of drought, salinity, and waterlogging, it can also help restore degraded land.

Food wars

Plant defense mechanisms

Giraffes eat a lot of acacia leaves and twigs, despite the defense strategies of these trees and shrubs. The plants' main protection is sharp thorns up to 4 in (10 cm) long, but a giraffe's very long tongue can negotiate its way around these, and its tough lips protect it from being stabbed. An acacia also has another line of resistance: when its leaves are being chewed, it releases foul-tasting tannins. Scientists believe that the tree can even release chemicals to warn other acacias to start producing tannins, too. This keeps the giraffes on their guard—they constantly move on to browse "unsuspecting" trees.

Giraffes carefully negotiate the thorns of acacia trees.

Mopane grows in large groups. It can form tall stands, called "cathedral mopane."

Sausage tree | *Kigelia africana* Many animals, including elephants and baboons, feed on the sausage-shaped fruits of this tree. People use its bark, leaves, fruit, and roots to treat a variety of ailments.

Raisin bush | *Grewia flavescens*
Bright yellow flowers bloom on this shrub or small tree, whose delicate fruits attract hungry birds, baboons, and warthogs. People also eat the berries, and soak them in water to make a tasty drink.

Abal | *Calligonum comosum*
Native to North Africa and able to grow in desert as well as dry savanna, this shrub is valuable in stabilizing sand dunes and warding off desertification. It has medicinal properties and edible flowers, fruits, and young shoots.

Mopane | *Colophospermum mopane*
People eat roasted or dried mopane "worms"—moth caterpillars that feed on the tree's leaves and grow to 4 in (10 cm) long. The wood is an excellent fuel and is resistant to termites, so it is good for buildings.

South Africa
Floral kingdom

△ **The flower heads of the pincushion protea** (*Leucospermum cordifolium*) are carried on long stems.

S outh Africa has large areas of grassland, savanna, and karoo semi-desert, with smaller tracts of coastal forest and true desert. It is also home to the unique fynbos and renosterveld biomes (see right), located at the country's southern tip, which together comprise the Cape Floral Kingdom. South Africa's vegetation zones are determined by geology, modification by people and, above all, by climate. Arid areas have a high proportion of drought-resistant succulents, for example, and much of the most fertile land is now used for farming.

Flowers have crinkly red margins

Impala lily | *Adenium multiflorum*
Adapted for surviving drought, this deciduous succulent shrub bears neither leaves nor flowers for much of the year. It produces spectacular blooms during winter.

Shrubs and trees

Many species are drought-resistant. Others have evolved relationships with ants that help them recover quickly from fire damage, or have showy flowers that attract nectar-seeking bird pollinators.

With multiple stiff, protruding styles, the flower head resembles a pin cushion

Each flower head, or inflorescence, is made up of many small flowers

Nodding pincushion |
Leucospermum cordifolium
Cape sugarbirds and sunbirds visit the flowers of this drought-resistant shrub to feed on its abundant nectar. The plant is pollinated by scarab beetles.

Cape chestnut | *Calodendrum capense*
Each flower has five long, narrow, pink petals. Cape chestnut bark is used as an ingredient of skin ointment, and the crushed seeds are used in the manufacture of soap.

Chinese lantern | *Nymania capensis*
Named for the papery capsules in which its seeds are produced, this shrub lives in dry, rocky habitats. It is frost-tolerant and can also survive extreme heat.

Fire heath | *Erica cerinthoides*
This shrublet produces tubular red flowers on short, wiry branches. It benefits from fire, which keeps its growth healthy and compact, and encourages it to flower more freely.

Golden spiderhead | *Serruria villosa*
Ants store seeds from this small fynbos shrub underground. If fire destroys the plants, the stored seeds germinate and recolonize the land.

Spicy conebush | *Leucadendron tinctum*
Yellow male and maroon female flower heads are carried on separate plants, and both have a spicy scent. The spicy conebush produces nutlike fruits that are dispersed by animals.

> ## "The profuse variety, which Flora has strewn over this, her favored country, inspired me ..."
>
> William **Burchell**
> *Travels in the Interior of Southern Africa*, 1822

Pagoda bush | *Mimetes hirtus*
The bright red-and-yellow flower bracts of the winter-blooming pagoda bush attract sunbirds, its main pollinators. This shrub favors damp, boggy areas.

Pompom tree | *Dais cotinifolia*
For a few weeks in November and December, the pompom bears inflorescences of tightly packed pink flowers. When hardened, its cup-shaped bracts are used as decorations.

Arid pincushion | *Leucospermum calligerum*
Ants feed on the plant's seeds, but eat only the fleshy skin. Fire may destroy parent plants, but the buried seeds produce new plants.

Pink mallow | *Anisodontea scabrosa*
The tar-like aroma and sticky leaves of this perennial shrub deter grazing animals. The sand rose grows on coastal sands and disturbed ground, and flowers all year round.

River indigo | *Indigofera jucunda*
Spikes of pink or white flowers grow on this shrub, which can be up to 13 ft (4 m) tall, from December to April. The seeds are borne in cylindrical pods from May to July.

Proteas and daisies

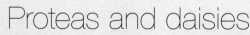

Cape Floral Kingdom

The smallest of the world's six floral kingdoms, the Cape Floral Kingdom lies entirely within South Africa. Of its two biomes, the ultra-diverse fynbos is dominated by proteas and the renosterveld by daisies. More than two thirds of its 9,000 plant species do not occur naturally anywhere else. Many are very localized and at risk of extinction. Fire has a major influence on the fynbos: its vegetation must burn regularly to maintain species diversity.

Myrtle-leaf milkwort (*Polygala myrtifolia*), a fynbos shrub, flowers all year round, peaking in spring.

The king protea (*Protea cynaroides*) is the largest and most spectacular of the proteas, with huge blooms up to 12 in (30 cm) across.

The oleander-leaf sugar bush (*Protea neriifolia*) has narrow, almost tubular, flower heads.

The queen protea (*Protea magnifica*) is one of the most impressive proteas; only the king protea has larger blooms.

Colorful, nectar-rich flowers attract pollinators—and also raiders, such as this Chacma baboon (*Papio ursinus*).

Sunbirds are key pollinators of proteas and pincushions (*Leucospermum* spp.), close relatives of proteas.

Proteas

Sugar bush spectacle

Proteas, known as sugar bushes, are almost all unique to South Africa. Apart from two species that are widespread across Africa, 92 percent of proteas are found only in the Cape Floristic Region of this one country. Their scientific name refers to the Greek god Proteus, who, according to myth, could change his appearance at will, adopting any shape he chose. It is an apt name for these extraordinarily diverse plants, which evolved when Africa was part of the ancient supercontinent Gondwana. Changes to the landscape following Gondwana's break up led to groups of plants becoming isolated and eventually developing into many separate species.

Proteas have composite flowers, consisting of many small florets crowded into large, colorful heads that stand out amid the evergreen foliage. The flowers produce large amounts of nectar, providing an abundant source of food for sunbirds and sugarbirds, which pollinate the blooms as they forage from plant to plant.

At around 300 million years old, proteas are among the oldest flowers.

Essential flames

Fire as a reproductive trigger

Proteas have evolved to endure and even benefit from wildfires. Many can survive fires, because they have dormant buds hidden in an underground root, called a lignotuber. When the growth above ground is burned off, the lignotuber sends up new shoots. In some species, their seeds are only shed after fire. The charred flower head releases seeds that fall into the soil, which is newly enriched with nutrients from the ashes. The seeds then germinate after it has rained.

This scorched protea flower head will release its seeds into the ash. Fires help replenish nutrient levels in the soil.

Madagascar
Unique plant life

△ **Flamboyant** (*Delonix regia*) has flowers with four large orange-red petals and one upright "standard" petal.

Madagascar's long isolation from the African and Indian landmasses is responsible for its high levels of endemism—more than 80 percent of its vascular plants do not grow naturally anywhere else on Earth. They include around 200 types of palm, six different baobabs, and many other trees and shrubs that have adapted to survive drought and fire. Madagascar's unique flora also includes rainforest species that grow in the wetter eastern part of the island.

Trees and shrubs

Baobabs are the ultimate drought-resistant trees, able to store large quantities of water in their massive trunks through the dry season. Other adaptations of Madagascan trees and shrubs to drought include fire-resistant bark and tough, waxy, water-retaining leaves.

Fan-shaped, silver-green leaves grow to 4 ft (1.2 m) across

Bismarck palm | *Bismarckia nobilis*
A fire-resistant species, the Bismarck is often the only palm in areas subject to frequent fires. It develops a stout trunk that may eventually grow to around 60 ft (18 m).

Octopus tree | *Didierea madagascariensis* Growing up to 30 ft (9 m) tall in spiny forest, this sparsely branched tree shows similarities to unrelated New World cacti and African euphorbias. As such, it is an example of convergent evolution.

A mutual benefit

Pollination by lemurs

Using their nimble fingers, black-and-white ruffed lemurs (*Varecia variegata*) pull open the tough bracts of traveler's trees (see opposite page) to reach the energy-rich flower nectar. As a lemur sticks its long tongue into the flower, pollen rubs off onto its snout and is transferred to the next flower the animal visits, making these lemurs the world's largest pollinators. As well as receiving food in the form of nectar, there are future benefits for the ruffed lemurs, as they will also be able to eat the fruit that results from pollination.

The black-and-white ruffed lemur—the main pollinator of the traveler's palm—is a critically endangered species.

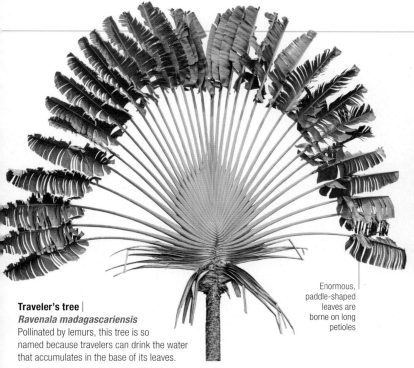

Traveler's tree |
Ravenala madagascariensis
Pollinated by lemurs, this tree is so
named because travelers can drink the water
that accumulates in the base of its leaves.

Enormous,
paddle-shaped
leaves are
borne on long
petioles

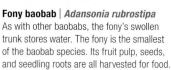

Fony baobab | *Adansonia rubrostipa*
As with other baobabs, the fony's swollen
trunk stores water. The fony is the smallest
of the baobab species. Its fruit pulp, seeds,
and seedling roots are all harvested for food.

Za baobab | *Adansonia za*
The most widely distributed of Madagascar's
baobabs, this deciduous giant can grow to
98 ft (30 m) tall. It flowers soon after the
leaves emerge at the start of the wet season.

Vahondrandra | *Aloe helenae*
With a maximum height of 13 ft (4 m),
vahondrandra is a succulent plant of
spiny forests and sand dunes. It produces
hundreds of red flowers on erect stalks.

Tahina palm | *Tahina spectabilis*
The natural range of this large palm is limited
to a mere 12 acres (5 hectares) of northwest
Madagascar. It flowers just once, when it is
between 30 and 50 years old, and then dies.

"Madagascar is a curious wonderland."
Sir David **Attenborough**
Broadcaster, writer, naturalist

Spectacular blooms give
flamboyant its alternative
name of flame tree

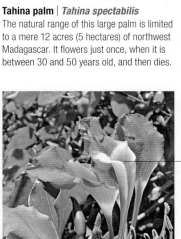

The flowers
appear in late
spring to early
summer

Tapia | *Uapaca bojeri*
Important for many local communities,
this tree bears edible fruits and hosts moths
whose cocoons are harvested for their silk.
The thick bark of the tapia is fire resistant.

Bauhinia | *Bauhinia madagascariensis*
A deciduous shrub or tree of seasonally dry
forest, bauhinia has flowers with five scarlet
and yellow petals. The fibers of bauhinia's
bark are used in the manufacture of rope.

Flamboyant | *Delonix regia*
A tree of dry deciduous forest,
especially in areas with limestone
bedrock, flamboyant is pollinated by
sunbirds and grows to 50 ft (15 m) tall.

Baobab

The African tree of life

Baobab trees, species of *Adansonia*, are African icons. Growing to about 66 ft (20 m) tall, and with enormous swollen trunks, they are immediately recognizable. They are adapted to cope with dry seasons, storing water in their trunk, and losing their leaves to withstand drought. The trunk swells during the wet season as it accumulates valuable water. As a result, it is not possible to use dendrochronology to find out how old they are, although radiocarbon dating has revealed that they can live for more than 1,000 years.

Seeds in the oval fruits

Flowers appear in early summer, hanging from the shoots. These open in the evening and last for only one night. Fruit bats pollinate the flowers, while insectivorous bats prey on visiting moths. Up to six months after flowering, large, pendulous, oval fruits mature. People make porridge and soup from these. Monkeys eat the fruits in the tree and other animals consume them when they fall to the ground, spreading the seeds. These germinate quickly, but young trees may take more than 20 years to flower.

Sudden decline

A threatened icon

Baobab trees live for centuries, but they are not invincible. In the 21st century, many mature trees have died for no obvious reason. The animals that depend on baobabs—including some lemurs—have therefore become increasingly isolated on and around the surviving trees. Together with the expansion of farmland, this threatens the survival of these dependent species. Rising temperatures and reduced rainfall may be factors in the baobabs' sudden decline.

Encroaching farmland further isolates baobabs, the numbers of which are already declining for other reasons.

Grandidier's baobab (*Adansonia grandidieri*) is native to Madagascar, where this avenue of 98-ft (30-m) trees is famous.

ANNUALS AND PERENNIALS

These soft-stemmed plants are hugely diverse in form and play a vital role in ecosystems. Some have a brief life cycle, but others can live for decades.

Northern latitudes
Living on the tundra

△ **Bunchberry** (*Cornus canadensis*) produces round, fleshy berries that provide food for small mammals and birds.

The climate of the northern tundra is harsh. The average winter temperature can fall to −29.2°F (−34°C), and even in summer it barely reaches 54°F (12°C). Plants typically grow low and compact to endure the chill winds, have shallow roots due to the permafrost below the soil surface, and develop waxy leaves to retain moisture when the ground water is frozen. Some have hairs (trichomes) for insulation, or cup-shaped buds to catch sunlight, while others can dry out and then regrow.

Mountain avens | *Dryas integrifolia*
Probably the most widespread of all tundra plants on Arctic islands, its pale flowers follow the sun as it moves across the sky. It forms dense mats that help bind the soil.

Summer blooming

For 6–10 weeks during summer, the thaw comes, winter darkness ends, and sunlight floods the landscape for nearly 24 hours a day, allowing up to 400 flower species to briefly bloom.

Purple-blue flowers form conical clusters

Bunchberry | *Cornus canadensis*
The low-growing, creeping, carpet-forming bunchberry spreads by underground rhizomes. White flowers appear in spring, followed by clusters of bright red berries in summer.

Mountain lupine | *Lupinus arcticus*
Native to northwestern North America, this perennial produces several stems covered with silky hairs. It bears pealike flowers.

The purple blooms typically appear on south-facing slopes

**Pasqueflower |
*Pulsatilla patens***
Diminutive pasqueflowers are covered in fine hairs for insulation. Indigenous people use the plant for healing, but touching it can cause severe allergic reactions.

Glacier buttercup | *Ranunculus glacialis*
Flourishing by icy mountain streams, the glacier buttercup grows at higher altitudes than almost any other flower. Climate change is threatening its fragile habitat.

Moss campion | *Silene acaulis*
This plant forms ground-hugging cushions to retain warmth. Small leaves minimize exposure to the dehydrating wind.

Cotton grass | *Eriophorum vaginatum*
Preferring moist, acidic soils, this plant produces dense, cotton-like inflorescences that Inuit people use for lamp wicks.

Coastal plains in Alaska can burst into gorgeous purple fields of mountain lupine in early summer, especially around Cook Inlet.

"Keep reindeer moss in the dark, freeze it, dry it to a crisp, it won't die."

Helen **Macdonald**
H is for Hawk, 2015

Snow gentian | *Gentiana nivalis*
This annual grows quickly but blooms for only a short time in early summer. It is one of the national flowers of Switzerland and Austria.

Alpine forget-me-not | *Myosotis asiatica*
Alaska's state flower, this low, branching perennial produces small blue flowers in early summer. Its leaves and stems are hairy.

Winter grazing

Reindeer lichen

Like other lichens, reindeer lichen (*Cladonia rangiferina*) is not a plant but a symbiosis between a fungus and an alga. As its common name "reindeer moss" suggests, this lichen forms thick carpets, often covering immense areas on the floor of boreal forests and across the tundra. These swathes of lichen provide winter pasture for reindeer, moose, caribou, and musk oxen, when other food is scarce. Although extremely cold-hardy, it also grows slowly and may take decades to recover if overgrazed. The name reindeer moss is also used for a similar but different species, *Cladonia portentosa*.

Bushy reindeer lichen has an upright, branching form, with each branch further subdividing. It can reach 3 in (8 cm) high.

Purple mountain saxifrage | *Saxifraga oppositifolia*
One of the earliest-blooming flowers, purple mountain saxifrage grows in low mats with stoloniferous (horizontal) stems. Its flowers form a tight cushion that helps reduce heat loss.

Cotton grass (*Eriophorum vaginatum*) is the most abundant plant in the tundra. It helps insulate and warm the soil.

Tundra plants
Treeless plains of the far north

Stretching right around the world in the far north, beyond the vast expanse of coniferous boreal forest, lies the open, almost entirely treeless tundra. Bordering the Arctic Ocean, the tundra covers almost a fifth of the world's land surface.

Tundra winters are long and dark, with thick snow that lasts until spring. Not far below the soil's surface is the permafrost—soil that remains permanently frozen, even in the brief summer. Global warming, however, is melting large areas of permafrost, releasing the trapped greenhouse gas methane.

There are 400 flower species on the tundra, but the stark landscape is mostly carpeted by low-growing shrubs, sedges, grasses, liverworts, and lichens. All tundra plants have shallow roots to avoid the permafrost, and lichens and mosses can survive on bare rock with little moisture. Tundra plants also tend to grow close together, hugging the ground for shelter. Their small leaves minimize water loss, and a fuzzy, hairy coating shields many species from the cold and wind.

"Tundra is a huge, forever frozen wetland covering the entire coast of the Arctic Ocean."

Palmer **Cox** Canadian author and illustrator

Fighting for attention
Tundra pollination

Around 14 bee species live in the Arctic, although pollination is mostly carried out by tiny flies that feed on nectar. During the short flowering season, plants compete to attract pollinators. Competition is intensifying, however, as climate change warms the tundra, causing more plants to flower at the same time. Some prosper at the expense of others, for example, moss campion (*Silene acaulis*) is losing out to mountain avens (*Dryas integrifolia*).

Frigid bumble bees (*Bombus frigidus*) have evolved to survive Arctic conditions.

Foxglove | *Digitalis purpurea* The leaves and blooms of this perennial contain a toxin, small doses of which can be used to treat heart complaints.

Deciduous forests
Woodland wonders

△ **Honeysuckles** (*Lonicera* spp.) are arching shrubs or vines that climb trees for support.

Deciduous woodlands are remarkably rich habitats, with a wide mix of trees and shrubs, climbers, perennial flowers and herbs, bulbs, grasses, sedges, mosses, and lichens. Woodland plants must cope with cold winters, when water is in short supply, and warmer, wetter summers. Because of the thick summer leaf cover, many flowers bloom early in spring, when trees are still in bud, allowing plenty of light through—there are summer and fall flowers in the wood, too.

Dog's mercury |
Mercurialis perennis
This perennial grows on the floor of ancient woodlands, especially in beech, oak, ash, and elm woods, where it often forms dense, unpleasant-smelling masses.

Leaves are highly toxic

Perennials

Many perennials (plants that die back in the fall) flourish in the dappled shade beneath deciduous trees. They usually flower before the leafy canopy overhead is fully formed.

Leaves resemble stinging nettles, but do not sting

Wood sorrel | *Oxalis acetosella*
Clumps of wood sorrel grow in woodlands and shady hedgerows. It has cloverlike leaves and delicate, white flowers with pink or purple veining.

White dead-nettle | *Lamium album*
Flowering all through summer, white dead-nettle is a favorite food plant of woolly bear caterpillars, which metamorphose into garden tiger moths.

Enchanter's nightshade | *Circaea lutetiana*
This herbaceous perennial gets its species name from Circe, the sorceress of Ancient Greek myths, because it was thought to have magical, protective powers.

Primrose flowers are an important early nectar source for butterflies

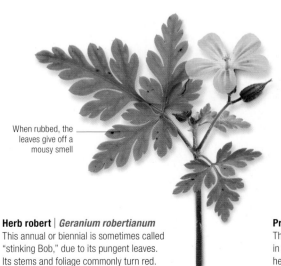

When rubbed, the leaves give off a mousy smell

Pinkish-red flowers have five deeply lobed petals

Red campion | *Silene dioica*
A tall perennial or biennial with a downy stem, this plant produces a riot of pink flowers. The first part of its Latin name refers to Silenus, the drunken Greek god of woodland.

Herb robert | *Geranium robertianum*
This annual or biennial is sometimes called "stinking Bob," due to its pungent leaves. Its stems and foliage commonly turn red.

Primrose | *Primula vulgaris*
The delicate yellow blooms of this perennial appear in early March. It is often seen as a herald of spring, hence its common name of "prime" (first) rose.

Bulbs

Many plants survive the seasonal extremes that occur within deciduous woodlands by storing nutrients in underground organs, known as bulbs. This allows the plant to die back and resprout the following year.

Dog tooth's violet | *Erythronium dens-canis*
Native to woods in southern Europe, this woodland flower gets its name from the toothlike shape of its bulb. It is not related to other violets.

Yellow starburst blooms appear in early spring, a few months after the glossy leaves

Lesser celandine | *Ficaria verna*
Though it prefers the damp soil of hedge and stream banks and moist woodland, lesser celandine may also grow in lawns, where it is considered a weed.

Pale yellow petals surround a darker yellow trumpet

Trumpet daffodil | *Narcissus pseudonarcissus* subsp. *narcissus*
Often seen growing as brightly flowered clumps in spring, wild daffodils are shorter than many of their garden relatives.

Umbel may contain hundreds of individual flowers

Drumstick-shaped flower head sits atop a slender stalk

Round-headed leek | *Allium sphaerocephalon*
Growing wild across Europe, except for the northwest, the round-headed leek is valued by gardeners for its distinctive umbels of deep pink flowers.

Bell-shaped flower is formed from both the sepals and the petals

English bluebell | *Hyacinthoides non-scripta*
The bluebell spreads quickly and carpets woodland floors in late spring. The powerful, distinctive scent of its flowers attracts bee pollinators.

Each nodding, white flower is carried on its own stem

Snowdrop | *Galanthus nivalis*
Among the first spring blooms to appear, snowdrops decorate woodland floors with drifts of striking, white flowers. The seeds are attractive to ants, which carry them off, aiding dispersal.

> "Coy anemone that ne'er uncloses Her lips until they're blown on by the wind."
>
> Horace **Smith** *Amarynthus, the Nympholept*, 1821

When crushed, the leaves smell like garlic

Garlic mustard |
Alliaria petiolata
This is one of the oldest of all culinary herbs, used in Europe for the tangy flavor of its leaves for more than 6,000 years.

The flowers, which have five to nine petal-shaped sepals, close up in cloudy weather

Wood anemone | *Anemone nemorosa*
In spring, wood anemones bloom like a galaxy of stars across the forest floor. They also grow where woodland used to be, so they are sometimes known as "woodland ghosts."

Wild garlic | *Allium ursinum*
Also known as ramsons, wild garlic plants grow rapidly in shady places during spring, filling the air with the pungent smell of their edible leaves.

Corms, tubers, and rhizomes

Corms are underground stems with papery outer layers. Tubers form from a stem or root. Rhizomes grow horizontally beneath the ground, sending roots down and shoots up.

Solomon's seal |
Polygonatum × multiflorum
Solomon's seal is related to lily of the valley, with similar bell-like white flowers, but it grows from much larger rhizomes.

White, sweetly scented flowers appear in early summer

Dutch crocus | *Crocus vernus*
Growing from a corm, the crocus is a spring wildflower in Eastern Europe and Western Russia. Widely grown in cultivation, it is related to *C. sativum*, the source of saffron.

Lily of the valley | *Convallaria majalis*
Spreading underground through rhizomes, lily of the valley can form large colonies. It thrives in shade, producing lush, green leaves and fragrant, bell-shaped flowers.

Oases of light

Woodland clearings

Once full leaf cover grows over in summer, woodland floors can be dark. That is why small clearings can be so important ecologically. Whether they occur naturally, where an old tree falls, or are created artificially, they open up new opportunities for both plants and animals. Bluebells, wood anemones, brambles, wood sorrel, primroses, grasses, and ferns all thrive in the extra light of clearings. These plants are a rich food source for insects, birds, and other animals.

Woodland floor plants are at their most diverse in clearings.

Flowers have six vivid yellow sepals

All parts of the plant are poisonous to humans

Winter aconite |
Eranthis hyemalis
Related to the buttercup, the winter aconite is a perennial of chalky woodlands. It flowers early in spring, then dies back to its underground tubers.

Woodland ferns
Unfurling fronds

△ **Bracken** (*Pteridium aquilinum*), common almost worldwide, sprouts furled fronds, popularly known as "fiddlesticks."

There are more than 10,500 different species of fern, varying from tiny plants ½ in (1 cm) in height to some as tall as trees. Unlike plants that grow from seeds, ferns do not need to be pollinated. Instead, they reproduce from microscopic spores made in "sporangia" on the underside of the fern's leaflike fronds. Spread by the wind, spores germinate independently, then develop through various stages to create new ferns. Fern rhizomes may also sprout underground and, in a few species, fronds develop bulbils (mini-bulbs) that fall off and take root.

All shapes and sizes

Most of today's ferns belong to the Polypodiales order, which first colonized new forests of flowering plants 140 million years ago. The greatest variety is now found in the warm, moist conditions of tropical cloud forests, where thousands of species can grow in a small area.

Tonguelike fronds within a clump unfurl upward

Hart's tongue fern | *Asplenium scolopendrium* Named for its furling fronds' similarity to a deer's tongue, this fern unusually has glossy, green, arching blades rather than divided fronds. Its spores are stored in horizontal structures, called sori, on the underside of its leaves.

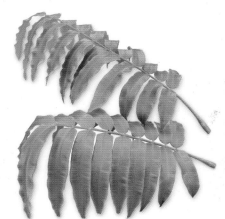

Fertile hard fern fronds grow upright

Hard fern |
Blechnum spicant
Native to much of the northern hemisphere, hard ferns have two types of fronds: flat, sterile fronds with slightly wavy edges, and narrow, upright, fertile fronds (see right).

King fern | *Angiopteris evecta*
The king fern, or elephant fern, native to Southeast Asia and Oceania, is one of the largest and most ancient ferns. It has a thick, trunklike rhizome and fronds up to 30 ft (9 m) long.

Ostrich fern | *Matteuccia struthiopteris*
Native to temperate regions north of the Equator, this lovely fern has large, feathery fronds, resembling ostrich feathers. It is deciduous, and the new fronds unfurl soft and green in spring.

Its hairlike stipes (stalks) gave it the name maidenhair

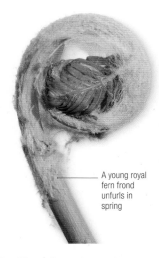

A young royal fern frond unfurls in spring

Royal fern | *Osmunda regalis*
This large fern, native to Europe and western Asia, grows in damp woodland and around streams. It has spreading sterile fronds and shorter fertile, erect fronds.

Fern evolution

Ancient plant pioneers

Earth's plant life on land began with mosses and liverworts (bryophytes)—nonvascular plants, lacking veins to transport nutrients and water. Lycophytes were the first vascular plants that could draw on Earth's resources and so survive harsh conditions. Related ferns, known from fossils, first appeared more than 360 million years ago in the Devonian period and, together with bryophytes and gymnosperms, they dominated plant life for millions of years until flowering plants took over.

The fossil of a prehistoric fern frond shows how closely these ancient plants resemble the many different species of fern found in the world today.

Certain ferns produce billions of spores annually, some of which may travel thousands of miles.

Southern maidenhair fern | *Adiantum capillus-veneris*
Native to tropical and temperate regions, this low-growing deciduous fern grows in soil and on rock faces in a variety of moist habitats.

Chinese brake | *Pteris vittata*
First recorded in the 18th century in China by Swedish explorer and naturalist Pehr Osbeck, this fern grows in tropical and subtropical climates around the world.

Bracken |
Pteridium aquilinum
Bracken may well be the most common plant in the world. It grows on all continents except Antarctica, and is so prolific that it is considered invasive in some areas.

The fronds are triangular, and have triangular leaflets

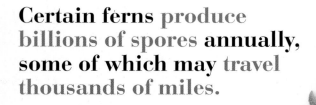

Fronds turn a red-brown in the fall but may then die back

Soft shield fern | *Polystichum setiferum*
This evergreen or semievergreen fern, native to Europe, grows in woodland. Its umbrella-shaped fronds, up to 39 in (1 m) in height, have bright green, divided leaves.

Staghorn fern | *Platycerium bifurcatum*
Native to Indonesia and Australia, the staghorn is an epiphyte (grows on other plants). It has heart-shaped, sterile fronds and gray-green, arching, fertile fronds.

Glades of tree ferns like these have been a feature of tropical forests for hundreds of millions of years.

Tree ferns
Plants that time forgot

Tree ferns are one of the world's most ancient plants. In the Carboniferous period, which ended around 300 million years ago, there were vast forests of them. When these rotted and were buried, they contributed to the formation of coal beds. Most tree ferns today belong to the *Cyatheaceae* and *Dicksoniaceae* families, which became common later, during the Jurassic period.

Tree ferns grow in humid tropical forests around the world. Like other ferns, they spread via spores, but the populations of many species are localized and are found in isolated habitats such as on mountaintops or islands. With a plume of foliage on top of a stem, tree ferns look rather like trees, but the stem, or caudex, is not made of wood and does not form rings. It is composed of rhizomes, which grow vertically and are supported by a tangle of aerial roots. The caudex grows thicker with age as more roots coat its surface. The fronds spray out from the "crown" at its top, and as they grow, the stem becomes taller.

Tree ferns grow very slowly, but can live for hundreds of years.

Fossil ferns

Psaronius

The forests of the Late Carboniferous and Early Permian periods were dominated by a now-extinct tree fern called *Psaronius*. It had a very thin trunk and could grow up to 33–50 ft (10–15 m) tall. The spreading leaves of its crown were usually those of the genus *Pecopteris*, which are among the most common fossils from this period. The term "*Psaronius*" originally referred to just the stem. The leaves and stem have different Latin names because many fossils are classified by their form.

***Pecopteris* leaves** take their name from the Greek word for "comb."

Grasslands and scrub
Blooming fields

△ **Sainfoin** (*Onobrychis viciifolia*) bears pink flowers in erect, conical racemes.

Open to plentiful sunshine, grasslands and scrub are key habitats for plants—filled with grasses and carpeted in summer with the colorful blooms of herbaceous perennials. Some grasslands, such as prairies and alpine meadows, occur naturally where conditions are too dry or exposed for trees. Others are fields left uncultivated but mowed for hay (unlike pastures, which are used for grazing). These farm grasslands are threatened by changes in agriculture.

Vetches

Members of the pea family, vetches are often sown in meadows. They are excellent nitrogen fixers and they can be plowed back into the soil as green manure to increase fertility. They are also good for forage.

Branched tendrils curl around other plants, giving bush-vetch a climbing habit

Bush-vetch | *Vicia sepium*
The habitats of bush-vetch are woodland edges, grasslands, hedgerows, roadsides, and rough ground. It grows fast, making it popular as a fodder crop in tough years.

Bird's-foot trefoil | *Lotus corniculatus*
This perennial gets its name from its seed pods, which are shaped like a bird's foot. A native of Eurasia, it has become an invasive species in North America and Australia.

Red clover |
Trifolium pratense
Native to Europe, red clover has a deep tap root, which makes it tolerant of drought. As a result, it is now used globally as a fodder crop and for green manure.

An extract from the flowers is used to soothe the skin

Each leaf is composed of three leaflets

Sainfoin | *Onobrychis viciifolia* Sainfoin flowers twice a year, in spring and fall. It is easily digested by livestock and acts as a natural worm-control in ruminants.

Daisies

The *Asteraceae*, or daisy family, is one of the largest and most varied of all flower families, containing more than 23,000 species. When most people talk of daisies they mean the ox-eye, the Shasta, and the English daisies.

Ox-eye daisy | *Leucanthemum vulgare*
Native to European meadows, this large daisy now often colonizes newly cleared ground worldwide, via shallow, creeping rhizomes.

Greater knapweed | *Centaurea scabiosa*
Important for bees and butterflies, this thistlelike species lives in lime-rich soil. It grows in hedgerows and dry grasslands, and on cliffs.

Crown of flowers

Floral tradition reinvigorated

Since the 2014 revolution in Ukraine, the country's folk traditions have seen a resurgence, including the *vinok*—the wreath of flowers and ribbons worn by girls and unmarried young women. The *vinok* is woven with grasses and colorful meadow flowers, such as red poppies, white daisies, black-eyed Susans, and blue cornflowers. Each flower has a meaning: roses are for love, cornflowers represent simplicity and modesty, bellflowers signify gratitude, and so on.

The *vinok* was traditionally worn on festive occasions and holy days. Today, it is increasingly worn in daily life.

More meadow flowers

Vetches and daisies are prevalent in meadows but these habitats are also host to hundreds of different annual and perennial plant species. Each offers different growing conditions, so each meadow is a unique mix of species.

Meadow cranesbill | *Geranium pratense*
A Central Asian native, this pretty, mauve flower became common in hay meadows worldwide. It is now largely restricted to road shoulders.

Cup-shaped, yellow flowers grow in nodding clusters on tall stalks

Cowslip | *Primula veris*
Once widespread in Eurasian meadows, this dainty flower has suffered a decline due to changes in farming practices. It was long popular in salads and for making cowslip wine.

Small flowers are particularly attractive to hoverflies

The lacy leaves have a licorice-like aroma

Yarrow | *Achillea millefolium*
Yarrow reaches about 3 ft (1 m) in height, bearing flat-topped or domed flower clusters. A Northern Hemisphere native, it spreads readily by rhizomes and can tolerate disturbance.

Yellow flowers are followed by papery seedpods that rattle when the seeds are ripe

Yellow rattle | *Rhinanthus minor*
Yellow rattle, an annual, is often used to restore or create wildflower meadows. It pushes out dominant grasses, and so maintains species diversity.

Pale lilac-blue flower heads are carried on wiry stems

Field scabious | *Knautia arvensis*
Common on shoulders, especially in chalkland, field scabious was used to treat skin complaints, including scabies and bubonic plague sores.

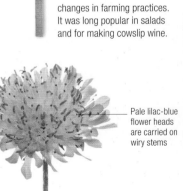

Snakeshead fritillary | *Fritillaria meleagris*
The name "snakeshead" perhaps derives from the scalelike pattern on the purple flowers. It was once known as the leper lily, because its blooms were thought to resemble the warning bells of lepers.

Fine, feathery leaves give the plant a soft, fernlike appearance

Grassland fungi
Rings, rotters, rarities

△ **Parasol** (*Macrolepiota procera*) starts off with an ovoid cap that becomes flatter and broader.

About 20 percent of Earth's land surface is grassland, which supports a huge variety of fungi. The species of fungi present in any grassland vary depending on several factors: the local climate; whether the soil is acidic or chalky (calcareous); and the extent to which it has been altered by plowing and reseeding with fast-growing grass species, or had inorganic fertilizer added. Natural grasslands, such as flower-rich hay meadows, old lawns, and graveyards contain the rarest and most interesting species.

Cap up to 10 in (25 cm) across; gills white or pale cream

Parasol |
Macrolepiota procera
Common and widespread in Europe and eastern North America, this decomposer fruits summer and fall in grassland, woodland clearings, and stable sand dunes.

Field fungi

Many fungi are common and widespread in grassland, thriving as decomposers or associated with plant roots.

Field mushroom |
Agaricus campestris
The cap of this fungus varies from smooth and white to rough with brown scales. Its gills start pink, and then turn dark brown.

St. George's mushroom |
Calocybe gambosa
This species, which has a stout stalk and a smooth, domed cap, grows on grassland and heathland. It fruits in spring, hence its name (St. George's Day is April 23).

Cap up to 2½ in (6 cm) across; gills white, then grayish-pink

Fool's funnel | *Clitocybe rivulosa*
Widespread in Europe and North America, this deadly poisonous fungus often appears in rings in unfertilized grasslands and sand dunes from summer to early winter.

Field blewit | *Lepista saeva*
This decomposer often forms fairy rings in fall and early winter. It is fairly common and widespread in chalk or limestone grassland in Europe and North America.

Giant puffball | *Calvatia gigantea* Widespread in Europe and North America, it favors phosphate-rich soils, and may grow to 31 in (80 cm) in diameter. It is usually found in small groups, but also sometimes in fairy rings, in summer and fall.

Giant funnel | *Leucopaxillus giganteus*
A decomposer fungus of grassy shoulders near hedges and in woodland clearings, this species fruits in late summer and fall. It is widespread in Europe.

Waxcaps, clubs, and corals

Unfertile grassland that has a diversity of clavarioid (club- or coral-shaped) fungi, waxcaps, and earth tongues—collectively known as CHEGD fungi— is called "waxcap grassland."

Longitudinal furrows are often produced

Pale pink or lilac domed cap that usually splits

Pink waxcap |
Porpolomopsis calyptriformis
Sometimes growing in small groups on unimproved grassland, it is named for its pink cap, which is up to 3 in (8 cm) across.

Meadow coral |
Clavulinopsis corniculata
This decomposer is common in unfertilized grassland. Its fruit bodies are usually branched and appear in summer and fall.

Yellow club |
Clavulinopsis helvola
Widespread and common in unfertilized grassland in temperate Europe, this fungus fruits from late summer to early winter.

Blue edge pinkgill |
Entoloma serrulatum
An uncommon decomposer with an unusual blue-black cap that becomes scaly at the center, it fruits from summer to late fall.

Parrot waxcap | *Gliophorus psittacina*
Found in non-fertilized grassland, roadside shoulders, and woodland clearings from summer to late fall, this may have a mutualistic relationship with mosses.

Spores are produced on thick, waxy gills beneath the cap

Violet coral | *Clavaria zollingeri*
This species is widely distributed, but rare in Europe, and is vulnerable at a global level. It produces branching lilac fruit bodies in summer to late fall.

Meadow waxcap |
Cuphophyllus pratensis
Widespread in non-fertilized grassland in temperate regions, it has a stout stem and pale orange gills.

Stalk grows up to 3 in (8 cm) tall

Fairy rings

Spreading, radial mycelia

The fairy ring mushroom (*Marasmius oreades*) is one of the species that forms "fairy rings." Clues to its presence are rings of dead grass where the fungus has killed the roots, lush grass resulting from fungal nutrient release, a circle of fruit bodies, or all three. The rings grow wider with age, and the biggest are hundreds of yards across. Some are thought to be 2,000 years old. Those near Laramie Airport, Wyoming, in the United States are large enough to be seen on Google Earth.

Fairy ring mushrooms originate from an individual mycelium that grows outward at a rate of up to 2 ft (60 cm) a year.

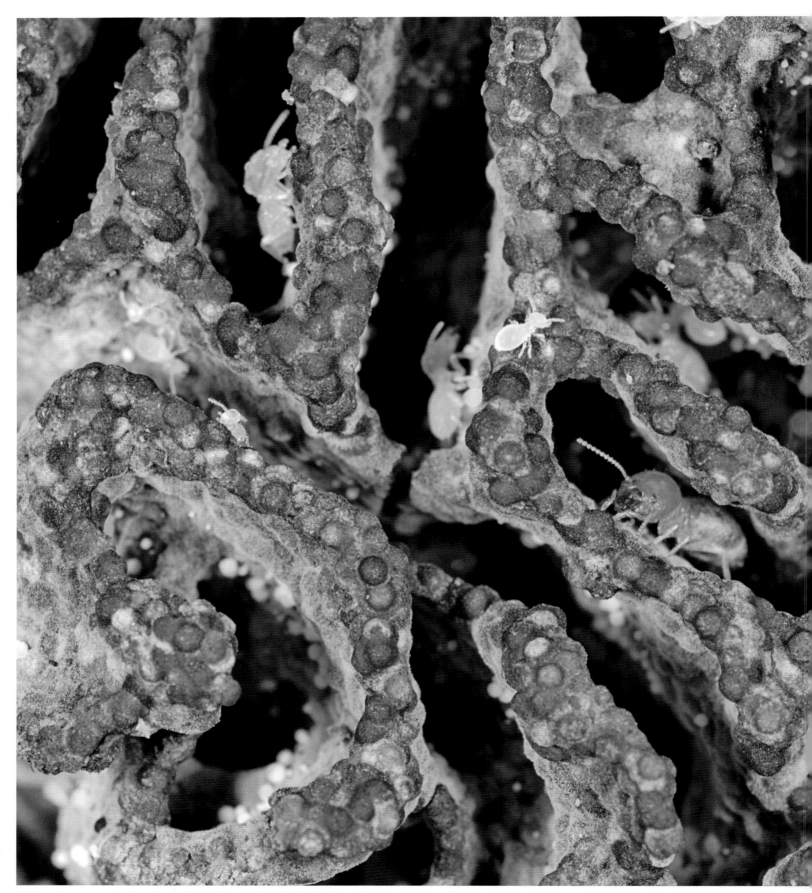

White, newly emerged termites feed on the spherical, white fungal nodules inside a termite nest.

Termite mounds are effectively cooling chimneys that help maintain the underground nest at an appropriate temperature.

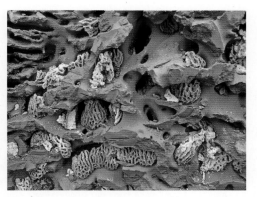

Termitomyces **fungus combs** are formed in spaces in the underground part of a termite nest.

The fruit bodies of a *Termitomyces reticulatus* fungus emerging from a termite mound in Africa.

The termite–fungus relationship is part of a broader food chain, including termite-eating tamanduas (*Tamandua* spp.).

Fungal agriculture
Fungus-farming termites

Many insects need the help of fungi to digest their food. More than 30 million years ago, one of these feeding partnerships evolved between *Macrotermes* termites and *Termitomyces* fungi in Central African rainforests. Assisting each other, these termites and fungi later spread into African savanna grasslands and then into Asia. The termites forage for plant debris, which they take back to their underground nest. Here, young worker termites eat the plant fragments, then excrete them, only partially digested. Fungi living in the termite nest in fungus gardens, or "combs"—porous structures made out of previously excreted plant matter—eat these droppings. The fungi digest the droppings and form highly nutritious spherical nodules, which the termites then eat. This relationship has been described as the first form of agriculture, because the insects effectively "farm" the fungi to obtain their food. However, both partners benefit, because the fungi are also making servants of the insects.

A feeding partnership that mutually benefits termites and fungi.

Largest edible fungus

Termitomyces titanicus

Like other fungi in its genus, *Termitomyces titanicus* breaks down plant material and provides nutrition for *Macrotermes* termites. Found in parts of tropical Africa, including Zambia and DR Congo, its fruit bodies can grow very large. Its parasol-like cap can reach 3 ft (1 m) across, with a stalk up to 20 in (50 cm) tall. The fungus has been sold as food in local markets for generations, but was not described by mycologists until 1980.

Termitomyces titanicus fruit body.

Temperate orchids
Global and diverse

△ **Pink lady's slipper** (*Cypripedium acaule*) is native to eastern North America. It is also called the moccasin flower.

Orchids are one of the largest and most diverse groups of flowering plants. The orchid family includes more than 30,000 individual species, with native representatives on every continent except Antarctica. Genetic sequencing indicates that orchids first appeared 76 to 84 million years ago, if not earlier. They vary greatly in appearance, even within species, which makes identification tricky. Most are pollinated by insects, which they attract by their shape, color, and scent.

Orchids in cool climates

Orchids love warm, damp climates, which is why tropical Ecuador has 4,200 orchid species compared to 55 in the temperate United Kingdom. Despite this, some orchid species grow as far north as Baffin Island.

Helleborine flowers produce nectar that can intoxicate pollinating wasps

Lower lip has shallow furrows

White egret orchid |
Pecteilis radiata
Native to China, Japan, and East Asia, this orchid grows on damp slopes. The shape of its flowers bears a remarkable resemblance to a flying white egret. It is now in decline in the wild.

Chinese ground orchid |
Bletilla striata
Grassy slopes in Japan and mountains in China are the native habitats of this species. The plant's root is boiled to make a glue for coating the silk strings of Chinese instruments.

White flower spike rises about 12 in (30 cm) above the leaves

Netlike leaf veins resemble rattlesnake skin

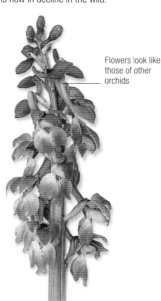

Flowers look like those of other orchids

Tiny flower stems rarely exceed 6 in (15 cm) in height, so they are often overlooked

Purple-tinged, slightly drooping flowers

Rattlesnake plantain |
Goodyera oblongifolia
This plant resembles the plantain, but it is actually an orchid. It is native to much of North America, where it is mainly found in mountain forests.

Early purple orchid | *Orchis mascula*
This orchid is common across Europe, the Middle East, and North Africa. It has no nectar itself, but it attracts bee and wasp pollinators by resembling other orchids that do.

Heart leaved twayblade |
Neottia cordata
This is one of the most widespread orchids in cooler regions of Europe, Asia, and North America. "Twayblade" refers to each stem having two leaves.

Common helleborine |
Epipactis helleborine
The common helleborine is widespread in Eurasia and north Africa. It is now naturalized in North America, where it often colonizes parks.

Pink lady's slipper | *Cypripedium acaule* The pink, pouch-shaped flowers of this orchid look like a medieval lady's slipper.

Naked man orchid |
Orchis italica
Folklore has it that consuming this Mediterranean orchid's flowers aids virility, as the blooms have a labellum (lobed lip) that resembles a naked male figure.

Dense flower head of pale to dark pink blooms

Blooms are butterfly shaped

Spike of whitish to pink flowers can grow to 2 ft (60 cm) tall

Greater butterfly orchid |
Platanthera chlorantha
Broad, white blooms on this widespread Eurasian orchid attract moths for pollination, because their pale color shows up well after dark.

Common spotted orchid |
Dactylorhiza fuchsii
Preferring damp habitats, this may be the most common orchid in northern Eurasia. The Latin name ("finger root") alludes to the finger-shaped rhizomes.

A helping hand

Associations with mycorrhizal fungi

Orchids have tiny seeds with no food-storing endosperm. To germinate they must link with a fungus partner that supplies what they need for growth. These partners are often wood decayers, such as species of *Marasmius* and *Trametes*, or fungal plant pathogens. Most orchids photosynthesize when older, giving the fungus sugars in return for nutrients and water. However, more than 200 species lack chlorophyll, so do not photosynthesize, and are effectively parasitic on the fungus.

Porcelain orchids (*Chloraea magellanica*) form associations with *Tulasnella* spp. fungi.

The striking sawfly orchid (*Ophrys tenthredinifera*), an insect-like Mediterranean species pollinated by sawflies (*Tenthredo* spp.), copies female sawfly pheromones to attract the male.

The bee orchid (*Ophrys apifera*) is one of many *Ophrys* species designed by nature to resemble its pollinator.

The yellow bee orchid (*Ophrys lutea*) from the southern Mediterranean attracts male *Andrena* bees.

The hybrid *Ophrys sphegodes* x *O. holosericea*, created by the species' common wasp pollinator, occurs naturally in Europe.

Pollinated by bees, *Ophrys incubacea* subsp. *atrata* is a subspecies of *O. sphegodes* from southern Europe.

Bee orchids
False love

The bee orchid (*Ophrys apifera*) is one of nature's most accomplished mimics—all in its quest for pollination. With its purple, petal-like sepals and hairy, abdomen-like, lobed lip (labellum), the orchid looks just like a female bee on a flower, and even copies and emits her pheromones to try to ensnare males. Fooled by this, a male bee will attempt to mate, swooping into the velvet-textured lip of the flower, where it becomes smothered in pollen. The bee transfers the pollen to other orchids but gains nothing, for this is a one-sided deal, which is quite rare, as most partnerships in nature are mutually beneficial. The bee has to look elsewhere for a mate.

Ophrys apifera has a native range that stretches from northern Europe to the Mediterranean, and east to northern Iran, while other species within the genus are found in Eurasia and North Africa. Each has slightly metallic-colored petals, and the center of their blooms resembles some kind of insect. Those of fly orchids (*O. insectifera*), for example, look like flies, and those of spider orchids (*O. sphegodes*) look like spiders, but the former uses its pheromones to attract male wasps and the latter to lure male bees.

Orchids are top tricksters when it comes to pollination.

Self-pollinating
In the absence of its bee

In Britain, where the perennial bee orchid flowers in June and July on chalky downland, the long-horned bees (*Eucera* spp.) that pollinate it are rare. In their absence, the plant self-pollinates, transferring its pollen to its stigma to fertilize the flower. Some other *Ophrys* species also self-pollinate, but the spider orchid cannot do this and is pollinated only by the miner bee. If raising such orchids outside the range of their pollinators, horticulturalists may pollinate by hand.

A self-pollinating bee orchid

Purple coneflower | *Echinacea purpurea* A once-abundant mid-season bloomer, the purple coneflower is popular both in herbal remedies and as a garden flower.

North American prairies
Gracing the grasslands

△ **A blanketflower** (*Gaillardia aristata*) bloom turning to seed; the ray florets have already fallen off.

The prairies are flat, temperate grasslands found in parts of North America where temperatures and rainfall are moderate, and there are few trees. The vegetation mostly consists of grasses and flowering wild perennials, which come into bloom in late summer or early fall. In the 1800s, vast areas of the Great Plains were prairies; by the 1930s, most prairie land had gone under the plow, and the unprotected soil became a dust bowl when drought struck. More prairie has since been lost to agriculture and urban development.

Bright yellow-and-red, daisylike flowers

Blanketflower | *Gaillardia aristata*
The blanketflower is one of the most widely cultivated prairie flowers. It fills its native prairies with blankets of midsummer color.

Tallgrass prairie

This type of prairie, which occurs in the wetter, more easterly regions, once covered 150 million acres (60 million hectares) of North America. Today, an estimated 4–13 percent remains intact, most of it in the Kansas Flint Hills.

Panicles of tiny yellow flowers are borne from late summer to fall

Fluffy, thistlelike, rose-purple flowers

Meadow blazing star | *Liatris ligulistylis*
Growing up to 5 ft (1.5 m) tall, this flower is a magnet for butterflies, as well as bees and hummingbirds. The plant is a host for the bleeding flower moth (*Schinia sanguinea*).

Compass plant | *Silphium laciniatum*
This plant derives its common name for the way the tips of its large leaves point north or south, and the surfaces of the leaf blades face east or west.

Prairie crocus | *Pulsatilla patens*
Also known as the eastern pasqueflower, the prairie crocus blooms early, like the woodland crocus, but the two are not related. Its deep root system helps it survive prairie droughts.

Canada goldenrod | *Solidago canadensis*
This plant colonizes disturbed land early by seeding heavily and spreading by rhizomes. Wasps and bumblebees depend on its nectar.

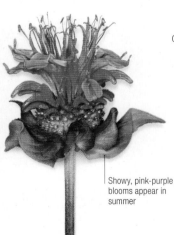

Showy, pink-purple blooms appear in summer

Purple prairie clover | *Dalea purpurea*
This mid-season bloomer is a key prairie plant, found in both tallgrass and midgrass prairies. It thrives after prairie fires.

Wild bergamot | *Monarda fistulosa*
Used medicinally by Indigenous peoples, this plant is "Number Six" to the Oneida people, as it was the sixth medicine given by the Creator.

Composite blooms have yellow ray florets around a darker center of disk florets

Maximilian sunflower |
Helianthus maximiliani
This late bloomer provides seeds for birds, cover for small animals, and food for grazers.

Short- to midgrass prairie

In the central region of the Great Plains, which is drier than the eastern side, sod-forming grasses and bunchgrasses populate midgrass prairie. Farther west is the driest prairie, shortgrass, which is dominated by buffalo grass and grama grasses.

"Nothing could be more lonely ... more beautiful than the view at nightfall across the prairies."

Theodore **Roosevelt**
26th President of the United States

Dense flower sprays are produced from late summer to early fall

The rays of the yellow-centered flowers are usually white, but can be blue or pink

Heath aster | *Symphyotrichum ericoides*
Popular worldwide in cultivated forms, this pretty perennial of the daisy family is now classified as vulnerable in much of its native habitat.

Terminal spike carries groups of tiny purple flowers with yellow stamens

Leadplant | *Amorpha canescens*
Also called prairie shoestring, leadplant is one of the most conspicuous plants of upland prairies. Its foliage typically has a leaden or silvery tinge.

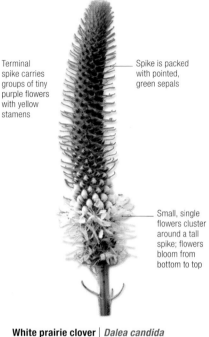

Spike is packed with pointed, green sepals

Small, single flowers cluster around a tall spike; flowers bloom from bottom to top

White prairie clover | *Dalea candida*
This perennial plant produces white flower spikes in midsummer. It is a legume and naturally improves soil fertility by fixing nitrogen from the air.

Dotted gayfeather *Liatris punctata*
A mauve-flowered, perennial herb, dotted gayfeather belongs to the daisy family. Many animals rely on it for food, including elk, white-tailed deer, and pronghorn.

Western ragweed | *Ambrosia psilostachya*
Blooming in late summer, this tall, weedy-looking plant is widespread across North America. It is notorious for triggering hay fever in sufferers.

Prairie grasses

The long roots of prairie grasses extend far underground, helping the plants survive drought, fire, and the attentions of grazing animals. Deep roots also hold the soil in place, keeping erosion to a minimum. When they die, the roots enrich the soil by releasing vast amounts of organic matter.

Curling stigmas of female flowers

Bracts protect clusters of small female flowers; each plant has male or female flowers

Female flower stems are relatively short; male stems are much taller

Big bluestem grass | *Andropogon gerardii*
Reaching up to 8 ft (2.4 m) in height on tallgrass prairies, big bluestem is a "bunchgrass"—it grows in clumps. As it matures, the bases of its stems turn blue or purple.

Blue grama grass | *Bouteloua gracilis*
One of the dominant species of shortgrass prairies and an important forage plant, blue grama is highly resistant to drought. It is a sod-forming grass that creates thick mats.

Buffalo grass | *Bouteloua dactyloides*
Another key shortgrass-prairie species, buffalo grass does not bunch, but spreads out with its roots and shoots to form dense sods. Early settlers used the sods to build dwellings.

Little bluestem grass | *Schizachyrium scoparium*
Like its bigger cousin (above), little bluestem is a bunchgrass native to tallgrass prairies. In the fall, this species turns coppery or orange, with hints of purple.

Dropseed | *Sporobolus heterolepis*
This is one of the shorter bunchgrasses growing on tallgrass prairies. In midsummer, it produces graceful, airy, pink and brown flower heads that fade to silver.

Prairie cordgrass | *Spartina pectinata*
This tallgrass prairie bunchgrass can grow almost as tall as big bluestem (above left). It is tolerant of damp conditions and often grows in marshes.

Mediterranean
Avoiding summer's heat

△ **Sea rocket** (*Cakile maritima*) flowers rapidly turn to pods as seed is set.

The climate of the Mediterranean—with its wet winters and long, hot, dry summers—favors quick-growing plants. Mediterranean annuals and biennials compress their entire life cycle into a few months, germinating in the fall, growing through winter, and then flowering in spring. A few continue on into early summer, but by the time the last rains have finished and the heat begins to build, most have already set seed for the next generation. Changing weather patterns caused by global warming are reducing the time available for these plants to complete their growing cycles.

Flowering frenzy

Despite their brief lives, Mediterranean annuals and biennials have a startling impact when they bloom. In spring and early summer, their flowers create vivid splashes of color in the landscape, before their hues are lost to the heat.

Plants in a hurry

In a rush to reproduce

The need to grow, flower, and produce seed quickly—to ensure the next generation—is not unique to plants of the Mediterranean. It is a survival technique employed by many species that grow in habitats where the conditions favorable for growth are brief due to heat, drought, extreme cold, or waterlogging. Seeds can remain dormant in the soil for years. When growth is finally triggered, many plant species can complete their life cycle in a matter of weeks.

Annual flower seeds primed for dispersal.

Whorls of soft leaves are vulnerable to strong sunlight

Blue woodruff | *Asperula arvensis*
Germinating in the bare soil of wheat fields after cultivation, blue woodruff blooms while the wheat is short, yet still tall enough to give the plant's narrow stems protection.

Pheasant's eye | *Adonis annua*
An early-flowering spring annual, pheasant's eye typically blooms among grasses and other wildflowers. This plant produces characteristic feathery foliage and bright red flowers.

The natural species has purple flowers; modern cultivars produce blooms in a range of colors

Sweet pea | *Lathyrus odoratus*
Widely cultivated as a garden plant, sweet pea is a fast-growing annual climber. Tendrils on the leaf shoots grip onto shrubs and other supports.

Small flowers are surrounded by yellowish bracts that attract pollinators

Sun spurge | *Euphorbia helioscopia*
Like all spurges, sun spurge contains a toxic milky sap to deter grazing animals. This small plant is often seen growing along roadsides during spring.

In early spring, fields and hillsides in the Mediterranean are ablaze with all kinds of annual flowers that attract pollinators.

Common centaury |
Centaurium erythraea
Several forms of this variable species are found around the Mediterranean. A winter rosette of leaves produces stems with large, pink flowers.

Large, yellow daisy heads are produced in succession over several months

Crown daisy |
Glebionis coronaria
The crown daisy can dominate Mediterranean meadows. Feathery foliage grows over winter and large flowers are produced throughout summer.

Flowers are held in a loose spike between narrow leaves

Lesser snapdragon |
Misopates orontium
This widespread species grows among other short plants. The pink flowers are soon replaced by oval seed pods

Love-in-a-mist | *Nigella arvensis*
A member of the buttercup family, love-in-a-mist is a plant of meadows and cornfields. It boasts pale blue flowers that give way to large, inflated seed pods. Seeds shake free of their pods in the wind.

Sea rocket | *Cakile maritima*
An annual plant of coastal areas, the hairless sea rocket can tolerate salt spray. Flowering begins early in spring and continues into midsummer.

False bishop weed | *Ammi majus*
A large annual species, false bishop weed stands up to 3 ft (1 m) tall. It has characteristic feathery foliage and produces large domed heads (umbels) of small white flowers.

Yellow ray florets surround brown disk florets in a compact head

Lush foliage sustains the plant until it is killed by the heat

Field marigold | *Calendula arvensis*
This smaller relative of pot marigold is a common sight in the Mediterranean. It grows and flowers over winter and spring, sometimes even flowering in the fall.

Purple flowers project from between the protective bracts

Honeywort | *Cerinthe major*
Found across the region, honeywort has hairless, blue-green leaves. Dense flower heads with purplish bracts curl over until the flowers open.

Oleander (*Nerium oleander*) grows wild and is also widely cultivated, blooming all year round across the Mediterranean.

Yellow horned poppy (*Glaucium flavum*) flourishes on the seashore. It has a horn-shaped seed capsule.

Mediterranean basin
Diversity across the sea

The Mediterranean basin formed over millions of years, as the Earth's tectonic plates shifted the landmasses of Europe, Africa, and Asia. The water flooding between them was left dotted with islands, where many plant species evolved in isolation, giving rise to a huge diversity. Even where one species is recognized scientifically, numerous unidentified subspecies may exist, potentially a different one on each island.

The orange flowers of silver ragwort (*Jacobaea maritima*)

Diversity is particularly high in bulbous species, including crocuses and snowdrops, and in annuals, whose yearly seeds produce genetically different plants. Because many orchids are designed to attract a single insect pollinator, their flowers are also highly diverse, fueling scientific debate about which are individual species and which are subspecies of others.

Some studies find 350 species of orchid in the Mediterranean basin.

Globe thistle (*Echinops ritro*) is a widespread perennial with broad, prickly leaves that flowers in late summer.

Hollyhock (*Alcea rosea*) is self-seeding and grows wild across the Mediterranean area, but it is native to Türkiye.

Squirting cucumber

Explosive seed dispersal

The squirting cucumber (*Ecballium elaterium*), native to the Canary Islands and the Mediterranean, is a common, yellow-flowering, annual creeper that produces hairy, oval, green fruits. As the fruits ripen, water is drawn in, and pressure builds up in the sap of their cell tissue, eventually forcing each fruit off its stalk. As a fruit drops, its seeds shoot out in a mass of green, gluey liquid. This explosive form of dispersal can shoot out seeds to a distance of up to 20 ft (6 m) from the plant.

The seeds are forced out through a tiny rupture in the fruit that opens up when it breaks away from the stem.

Giant fennel (*Ferula communis*)—a perennial up to 13 ft (4 m) tall—produces clusters of flowers in early summer.

Mediterranean
Safe underground

△ **Portuguese squill** (*Scilla peruviana*) bears cone-shaped flower heads.

T he **Mediterranean climate favors plants** either with very short life cycles (see pp.180–181) or those with the ability to survive the hot, dry summers. Several species of plant use underground storage organs to achieve this. These storage organs not only hold water and nutrient reserves to sustain life, but also shield the plant from the summer heat and intense light while it is dormant. Unrelated species have developed various types of bulb, corm, and tuber in response to the challenging climate.

Starry flowers open from the base of the head first

Portuguese squill | *Scilla peruviana*
A plant of the western Mediterranean, *S. peruviana* is one of the largest squills. Leaves grow in the fall and are joined by large, blue flower heads in spring.

Bulbs

Bulbs are formed underground from concentric swollen leaf bases that grow from a short stem. The examples here, from several Monocotyledon plant families, are fairly widespread across the Mediterranean region.

Sweetly scented flowers are held in a dense spike

Tall flowers have six stamens (unlike crocus blooms, which have three)

Flowers are held on thin stems 4 in (10 cm) tall

Star-of-Bethlehem |
Ornithogalum divergens
This widespread species grows throughout the Mediterranean. A rosette of narrow leaves appears in winter, followed by the head of white flowers in spring.

Meadow saffron |
Colchicum autumnale
Found in all but the extreme east of the region, this is a fall-flowering species. It grows large leaves in winter after flowering has finished.

Autumn snowdrop |
Galanthus reginae-olgae
Unlike most snowdrops, this native Greek species flowers in the fall, before its leaves grow, attracting late-flying bees to pollinate its blooms.

Large flowers are followed by strap-like leaves that grow through winter

Drooping white flowers have a green stripe down the center of each petal

Hyacinth |
Hyacinthus orientalis
Native to the eastern Mediterranean, this species is the ancestor of many garden varieties. It grows in mountainous areas, where the summer heat is less intense.

Sea daffodil |
Pancratium maritimum
A plant of coastal sand, sea daffodil often establishes itself on beaches if it is undisturbed. White flowers appear over several weeks in early fall.

Three-cornered leek |
Allium triquetrum
Originating from Iberia to Italy but now naturalized in many other places, this plant has tall, three-sided flower stems that support umbels of showy blooms.

Yellow Star-of-Bethlehem |
Gagea lutea
This short member of the lily family grows in shady sites across Europe and western Asia. A small leaf rosette gives rise to yellow flowers in early spring.

204. Tulipa Oculus solis St. Amans.

Sun's eye tulip | *Tulipa agenensis* This brightly colored tulip is found in low-lying areas around the Aegean Sea. Short stems support the bright red flowers amid the foliage.

Corms and tubers

Several unrelated Mediterranean plants have developed underground corms (short vertical stems) or tubers (horizontal stems) to survive the summer. The examples here show the range of forms and flowers that have evolved in response to a similar need.

Mouse plant | *Arisarum proboscideum*
Growing from a small tuber, the mouse plant has flowers beneath its foliage. The flowers are enclosed by an elongated spathe shaped like a mouse. Insects lured into the spathe by scent pollinate the flowers as they struggle to escape.

Large cuckoo pint | *Arum italicum*
A relative of the northern European cuckoo pint, this species has leaves marked with a network of white veins. When the white flowers mature, they form heads of bright red berries.

Flowers have funereal black "fall" (drooping) petals, which give the plant its common name

Widow iris | *Hermodactylus tuberosus*
During winter, widow iris produces long, narrow leaves from a small tuber. The plant's spring flowers are very short-lived, each lasting only three or four days.

Flowers feature a hooded spathe, which protects the spadix inside

Friar's cowl | *Arisarum vulgare*
A very common species that emerges immediately after the first rains, friar's cowl produces a succession of leaves and flowers during fall and spring.

> "**The flora of the Mediterranean countries has an indescribable magic.**"
>
> Christopher **Grey-Wilson**
> *Mediterranean Wild Flowers*, 1993

Self-defense

Protection while dormant

Plants with water-retaining storage organs are vulnerable when they lie dormant underground during summer. Food and water are in short supply for animals at this time, so bulbs, corms, and tubers are much sought after by creatures able to dig into the soil. As an evolutionary response, many unrelated plants contain toxins that protect their storage organs. The genera *Anemone*, *Arum*, *Colchicum*, *Crocus*, *Cyclamen*, *Dracunculus*, and *Narcissus* are all poisonous if eaten.

Red squirrels (*Sciurus vulgaris*) are deterred from eating many bulbs, corms, and tubers by their unpleasant taste.

Greek cyclamen | *Cyclamen graecum* This species is found in the eastern Mediterranean, not only in Greece. It flowers in the fall after rain, from tubers growing up to 1 ft (30 cm) deep.

Each flower has numerous narrow petals and yellow stamens

Smooth crocus | *Crocus laevigatus*
Blooming between fall and early spring, this Greek crocus has flowers with prominent purple veins on the outside. Bee pollinators visit as blooms open in the warm sun.

Dragon arum | *Dracunculus vulgaris*
This very large species grows to a height of 3 ft (1 m). Its divided leaves and speckled stems are topped by a large maroon spathe that emits a carrion scent to attract flies.

Grecian windflower | *Anemone blanda*
Growing from a small tuber, the Grecian windflower forms clusters of divided leaves in early spring. The leaves are soon joined by multi-petaled, purple-blue flowers.

Sand crocus | *Romulea tempskyana*
Although it is very small and has extremely narrow, almost needlelike leaves, the sand crocus produces relatively large purple flowers in mid-winter.

Large pink flowers grow on a two-sided spike

Saffron crocus | *Crocus sativus*
The source of the spice saffron, this species originated in the eastern Mediterranean. It has been cultivated for its stigmas for thousands of years.

Iris-like mauve flowers open only in the afternoon

Flowers can be pink, red, or mauve

Barbary nut | *Moraea sisyrinchium*
This relative of irises grows a rosette of narrow leaves over winter. The leaves are followed by a tall stem that produces a succession of flowers during spring.

Field gladiolus | *Gladiolus italicus*
A delicate species, the field gladiolus occurs throughout the Mediterranean. Its narrow, ribbed leaves are topped by a tall, loose head of flowers that bloom in succession.

Crown anemone | *Anemone coronaria*
The leaves of the crown anemone grow over winter, while the soil is damp. Large, variable flowers appear in early spring, turning into fluffy seed heads when they mature.

Desert annuals
Waiting for rain

△ **Mariposa lily** (*Calochortus splendens*) has large mauve blooms that earn it the nickname "Splendid" mariposa.

Many desert plants are annuals, which means they only live for one season. Their seeds may lie dormant for years during long, dry spells. When rain finally comes, the seeds are quick to sprout. Plants grow, bloom, produce new seeds, and wither in a short span of time, sometimes just a few days. After a downpour soaks the arid landscape, the desert can turn into a wonderland of flowers almost overnight. Although the moisture is soon gone, desert plants are highly tolerant of water shortages and salty conditions during their brief lives.

Sprouting policy

The seeds of most desert annuals will only sprout if there is significant rainfall—anything less does not trigger germination. Even then, not all the seeds sprout. This evolutionary insurance policy ensures that some viable seeds always remain in the soil for future years.

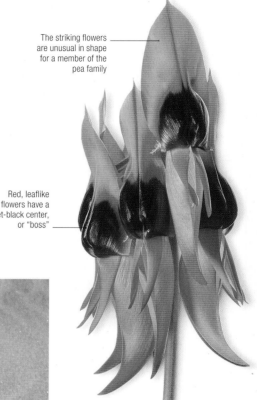

The striking flowers are unusual in shape for a member of the pea family

Red, leaflike flowers have a jet-black center, or "boss"

Sturt's desert pea | *Swainsona formosa*
Native to the dry center, south, and west, this is one of Australia's best-loved flowers, famous for its striking, blood-red color.

Chilean bell flower I *Nolana* **sp.** One of the annuals of Chile's super-dry Atacama Desert, Chilean bell flowers bloom after rains that only occur every seven years or so, transforming the landscape into a sea of color.

Desert evening primrose |
Oenothera primiveris
Yellow flowers are produced amid a dense leaf rosette in winter. This species grows in many flat, dry parts of the southwestern US.

The leaves are full of salty water

Prickly saltwort | *Salsola kali*
Tolerant of dry, salty conditions, this plant is native to Europe and Asia but is now found in many arid and semi-arid regions.

Devil's claw | *Proboscidea parviflora*
This plant produces pale pink flowers that have an unpleasant scent. It also has very sticky foliage that traps small insects.

Arizona lupine | *Lupinus arizonicus*
This plant displays tall, vivid purple blooms in the Mojave and Sonoran deserts, and especially around Joshua Tree National Park and Death Valley National Park in California.

"[the desert pea's] a striking sight in the wild: a blazing sea of red."

Holly **Ringland**
The Lost Flowers of Alice Hart, 2018

Judean viper's bugloss | *Echium judaeum*
The flowers of this species have a forked, serpent-tongue look. It is a key food source for honeybees in Cyprus, Syria, and Israel.

Mariposa lily | *Calochortus splendens*
This lily of California and northwest Mexico produces large, open blooms in late spring. It grows in coastal ranges and valleys.

Bigelow's tickseed | *Coreopsis bigelovii*
The seeds of this daisy resemble bedbugs or ticks. The plant grows in southwestern US ranges and the Mojave and Colorado deserts.

Owl's clover | *Castilleja exserta*
California's owl's clover is actually a kind of paintbrush flower that grows in clusters in open fields. It is a crucial host for the (San Francisco) Bay checkerspot butterfly.

Desert chia | *Salvia columbariae*
This mint-family plant of southwestern North America has fragrant leaves and tall stalks bearing blue flower clusters. Indigenous peoples used its seed as food and medicine.

Desert pioneers

Desert lichen and fungi

Lichens and fungi are vital in desert ecosystems. *Teloschistes capensis* is a shrubby lichen that forms a carpet. Growing alongside other forms of lichen that help bind the loose surface—as well as yeasts and micro fungi—they collectively form the basis of an organic "soil." Lichens survive extreme temperatures and low nutrient availability, and can absorb moisture from air humidity. Some desert fungi partner with plant roots, or feed on dead plant material.

Fruit bodies of the desert shaggy mane fungus (*Podaxis pistillaris*) develop from underground mycelium after rainfall.

Pale evening primroses (*Oenothera pallida*) bloom in profusion in July and August in the deserts of the US Southwest.

Desert blooms
Brief abundance

Some deserts appear so barren and devoid of vegetation that it is hard to believe they could ever look colorful. But some plants are adapted to lie dormant as seeds, rhizomes, or tubers, for years or even decades. When there is a burst of desert rain, they race to germinate, shoot up through the surface, and burst into bloom in a glorious carpet of color. Such desert blooms are brief but truly spectacular and bring with them a proliferation of insects in search of nectar—and birds and small lizards in search of an insect meal. The plants set seed before returning to dormancy when drought returns.

Some plants that appear only occasionally are annuals. They exist as seeds for most of the time, germinating and flowering when there is rain. After they are pollinated, the plants die—apart from their seeds, which are dispersed by wind, animals, or even the flash floods that may accompany the rain.

Plants called geophytes adopt another strategy for surviving drought. They remain buried underground as tubers, rhizomes, or bulbs. These storage organs can survive long periods of drought and spring into life—producing shoots, flowers, and seeds—only when rain falls.

With the right balance of temperature and rainfall, Atacama blooms.

Atacama glory

El Niño gift

Perhaps the most spectacular desert blooms of all flower in the Atacama Desert in Chile. This is one of the driest places on Earth, and there are many years when no rain falls at all. But the periodic El Niño climate pattern, occurring every five to seven years in the southern hemisphere, sometimes brings very heavy rain. That happened in October 2022, creating an astonishing display of flowers that drew photographers from far and wide to capture the spectacle.

Rock purslane (*Cistanthe grandiflora*) comes into flower following rain, creating a carpet of nectar-rich flowers.

Bat flower | *Tacca integrifolia* Native to tropical Asia, it has striking white, purple-veined bracts above its flower clusters and threadlike bracts that look like the ribs of an umbrella.

Tropical plants
Taste of the tropics

△ **The colorful bracts** of beehive ginger (*Zingiber spectabile*) often darken to orange-red with age.

The tropics contain a vast diversity of herbaceous plants, many of them brightly colored. These regions experience little temperature variation during the year and—unless deserts—have wet and dry seasons of varying length. In rainforests, plants develop quickly and grow year round, thriving on soil enriched by fungi and bacteria, which decompose organic matter faster in a wet, tropical climate. In tropical desert habitats, dormant plants grow rapidly after rain.

Tropical Asia

Though under pressure from human activities, rainforests rich in plant life still extend from the mountains to the seashores of India and Sri Lanka, and east to Southeast Asia, southern China, Indonesia, and the Philippines.

Japanese banana | *Musa basjoo*
Despite its name, this plant is native to southern China. Its fibers are used to create textiles (*bashofu*) for carpets, blankets, and clothing, such as kimonos. It is also used to make paper.

Flowers are up to 7 in (18 cm) long

Beehive ginger | *Zingiber spectabile*
Native to Thailand and Malaysia, this plant has purple and white flowers that emerge from yellow-orange, beehive-like bracts. Its leaves are used in traditional medicine.

Easter lily | *Lilium longiflorum*
Now widely cultivated as a fragrant cut flower and garden perennial, this bulb-forming species is native to the subtropical southern islands of Japan and Taiwan.

Cone-like inflorescence

Basket plant | *Aeschynanthus speciosus*
The glamorous, red-and-yellow-flowered basket plant is an epiphyte, native to wet, tropical areas from Thailand south to the Malay peninsula, Indonesia, and Borneo.

Petals are pink, mauve, or blue

Laurel clock vine | *Thunbergia laurifolia*
This flowering vine is native to a region from northeast India to Malaysia. Its leaves are used in Thailand in an herbal tea and valued for their medicinal properties.

Large, petallike bracts hide smaller bracts and tiny flowers

Torch ginger | *Etlingera elatior*
This plant from Indonesia and Southeast Asia, is cherished for its spectacular red flowers. Its flower stems can be up to 16½ ft (5 m) tall.

Red spider lily | *Lycoris radiata*
Bearing bright red flowers in late summer, this perennial is native to subtropical regions from Nepal to Japan and often found on river banks. Its bulbs contain a toxic alkaloid.

Lipstick plant | *Aeschynanthus pulcher*
Native to the mainland and islands of Southeast Asia, this evergreen climber has bright blooms up to 3 in (7.6 cm) long.

Africa

Bright, tropical flowers bloom in the rainforests of West and Central Africa and areas of East and Southeast Africa. South Africa has its own striking, subtropical native plants—some unique to the area.

Flame lily | *Gloriosa superba*
This climbing, bulb-forming perennial has bright orange and yellow flowers in summer. It grows wild in many regions in tropical Africa and in parts of southern Asia.

Bird of paradise | *Strelitzia reginae*
Bright flowers open from the beaklike bracts of this exotic plant, native to South Africa. The "reginae" of its Latin name honors Queen Charlotte, wife of the British king George III.

Cape primrose | *Streptocarpus* spp.
The genus *Streptocarpus* includes more than 150 species of plants with blooms that slightly resemble primroses. They grow on mountains in tropical southern Africa.

Siam tulip | *Curcuma alismatifolia* This pink or purple flowering plant, native to Vietnam, Laos, Thailand, and Cambodia, is not a tulip (*Tulipa*), but a member of the ginger family (*Zingiberaceae*).

Lianas

Climbing in search of sun

Woody vines, known as lianas, are a key feature of tropical forests. From ground roots, their flexible stems twist and climb up more rigid species in a bid to reach light and bear leaves and flowers in the canopy. Because they often form a tangle of vegetation that can strangle a supporting plant or tree, they are known as structural parasites. Lianas belong to many different plant families. Some species grow up to 541 ft (165 m) long, while the stems of others are almost 16 in (40 cm) thick.

A young female drill (*Mandrillus leucophaeus*) straddles a liana stem in Pandrillus Drill Sanctuary, Nigeria.

South America

Most of South America is tropical, and the region includes the world's largest rainforest. More than 14,000 species of seed plant have been identified in the Amazon basin alone.

Scarlet milkweed |
Asclepias curassavica
Widespread in Central and South America, this evergreen plant bears bright flowers that attract bees, butterflies, and hummingbirds.

Scarlet sage | *Salvia splendens*
Growing at altitudes of up to 9,800 ft (3,000 m) in warm, moist Brazilian cloud forests, this evergreen plant can reach a height of 4¼ ft (1.3 m).

Asteranthera ovata
This evergreen vine with vivid red flowers twists its stems over tree trunks in clearings of cool, moist forest in southern Argentina and central and southern Chile.

Magic flower | *Achimenes longiflora*
Also known as Cupid's bow, this plant has a native range from Mexico to Colombia. Its long, trumpet-shaped, violet flowers make it a popular, ornamental houseplant.

Kohleria warszewiczii
This plant, native to Colombia, has rich purple, trumpet-shaped flowers that have a furry surface. It grows from rhizomes in warm, moist habitats.

Goldfish plant |
Nematanthus gregarius
This Brazilian, evergreen climber is named for its small, orange flowers, which look a little like shoals of goldfish.

GLOXINIA SPECIOSA
Voie lactée. (Van Houtte.)

Gloxinia | *Sinningia speciosa* Native to Brazil, this has striking, trumpet-shaped, purple, red, or white flowers. Despite its common name, it is unrelated to plants of the *Gloxinia* genus.

Jade vine has a unique turquoise flower coloration, which is produced by a combination of two chemicals—malvin and saponarin.

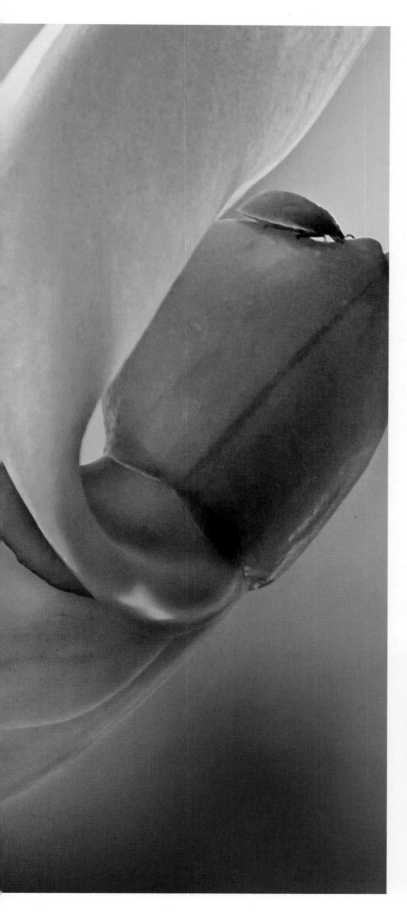

Jade vine

A color like no other

The jade vine (*Strongylodon macrobotrys*) is named for its bright blue-green flowers, which hang in clusters of 75 or more beneath its pale green leaves. In dimly lit rainforests, the luminous, cup-shaped flowers are clearly visible to bats, which visit them at dusk to drink nectar. In fact, the vine depends on bats for pollination. As a bat hangs upside down to feed from each flower, pollen is deposited on the fur on its head, while pollen from other flowers brushes off. This relationship between the species is an example of coevolution.

Jade vine is a woody liana that climbs up the trunks of trees to 66 ft (20 m) above the forest floor to reach the light. In its native Philippines, deforestation now threatens the species with extinction, so its future may depend on cultivation.

Cluster of jade vine flowers

When **pollination** is successful, a **melon-size** fruit develops.

When grown in cultivation, jade vine has to be pollinated by hand.

Asian bamboos
Giant grasses

△ **Common bamboo** (*Bambusa vulgaris*), one of the largest-growing species, thrives in rainy, tropical and subtropical regions.

Bamboos comprise more than 1,400 species of tall, grasslike plants in the family *Poaceae*. Most are native to South and Southeast Asia, with a few species in the Americas. Their typically hollow, woody-ringed stems (culms) are strong and light, which—combined with their speed of growth—make them versatile and sustainable materials. Tropical bamboos are the thickest, tallest, and strongest; some can grow up to 39 in (1 m) in a day.

Bamboo builders

Of the dozen or so key species of bamboo used in construction, each has its own qualities and uses. Most, including the giant dragon bamboo (*Dendrocalamus sinicus*)—the world's tallest, growing up to 151 ft (46 m)—are native to tropical areas of Southeast Asia.

Burmese weavers' bamboo |
Bambusa burmanica
Used for thatching and construction, this large-leaved bamboo, with a native range from India to China, grows up to 62 ft (19 m) tall.

Bengal bamboo | *Bambusa tulda*
This species, native to South and Southeast Asia, has a high tensile strength and is widely used for making paper pulp and also for construction and scaffolding.

Golden bamboo | *Phyllostachys aurea*
While somewhat invasive, this bamboo can be used both ornamentally and to create living fences and make furniture.

Female bamboo | *Bambusa balcooa*
The high yield and drought-resistance of this tall species have encouraged its cultivation for construction in South Africa as well as Asia.

The stems of this bamboo grow in erect clumps up to 66 ft (20 m) tall

Its leaves are lance-shaped with a rough edge

Common bamboo |
Bambusa vulgaris
Native to areas from Indochina to China's Yunnan province, this large species is grown widely for basketry, fuel, paper pulp, and light construction.

Dragon bamboo |
Dendrocalamus giganteus
Growing up to 98 ft (30 m) or more in height, this species is used for scaffolding, boat masts, water pipes, and house construction.

Giant bamboo | *Dendrocalamus asper*
Native to several regions in Asia, this strong bamboo grows up to 98 in (30 m) tall. Its stems, up to 8 in (20 cm) thick, are used to build houses and bridges.

Ecological importance
Helping to save the planet

A key feature of ecosystems in and near the tropics, bamboo is a staple food for pandas, gorillas, and other creatures. The fast-growing plant can also help combat global warming. Just 2½ acres (1 ha) absorbs 18.7 tons (17 metric tons) of carbon annually, a third more than rainforests. Bamboo thrives on problem soils, and its spreading, shallow roots help prevent erosion. Long used to fuel fires by those who lack other energy sources, it also has potential to be a sustainable biofuel.

A gorilla munches on bamboo in Volcanoes National Park, Rwanda. Gorillas consume the shoots and leaves.

Colombian timber bamboo |
Guadua angustifolia
Said to be the strongest of all bamboos, this tropical species, native to Trinidad and South America, is widely used in construction.

Burmese bamboo | *Bambusa polymorpha*
This densely tufted species, with a range from Bangladesh to China, is used to make paper, mats, and in construction.

Indian thorny bamboo | *Bambusa bambos* One of the fastest-growing bamboos, this thorny species has edible shoots when it is young. As it grows hard and woody, its stems are used for house construction, scaffolding, thatching, and fencing.

Enset

The tree
against hunger

For 20 million people in southern Ethiopia, a member of the banana family (*Musaceae*) is a vital, staple crop. Known locally as "the tree against hunger," the enset (*Ensete ventricosum*), which is relatively drought and disease tolerant, supplies life-saving nourishment when other crops fail. Although it is commonly referred as a tree, the enset—like other banana family species—is an herbaceous perennial. It has a trunklike pseudostem up to 33 ft (10 m) tall that develops from an underground corm. Although it bears pear-shaped fruits filled with pulpy flesh and large, black seeds, they are inedible. Instead, people eat the plant's corm and pseudostem, which is cut back each year to encourage growth. The fresh corm and stem may be chopped or grated, then boiled or baked. Both parts are also scraped into a starchy pulp, which is left to ferment in a pit for a year or more, before it is processed to make a bread called *kocho*. Enset cultivation is currently limited to Ethiopia's southwestern highlands, but researchers believe it could be grown much more widely. Because just 15 ensets could feed one person for a year, the plant has the potential to become a major food crop.

The leaf is used as cattle fodder

Panama disease

A fungal banana foe

Dessert bananas lack seeds and are propagated from the rhizomes of existing plants. Being identical clones, the plants are all prone to the same pathogens. In the late 1950s, Panama disease, caused by the soil fungus *Fusarium oxysporum,* wiped out a key banana variety. Today, the most widely grown banana, "Cavendish," is under threat from a new fungicide-resistant strain of the fungus, Tropical Race 4. Scientists are urgently seeking ways to improve the plants' disease-resistance.

A cut banana stem shows how panama disease discolors and blocks stem tissues.

Enset leaves have a central pink rib and can reach a length of over 16 ft (5 m) and a width of 5 ft (1.5 m).

Enset (*E. ventricosum*) is a key food crop, and unused parts are used as mulch to improve the soil and prevent erosion.

The flowers grow in clusters up to 10 ft (3 m) long, enclosed by purple bracts, at the top of the plant's pseudostem.

Ethiopian women scrape the enset stems, which together with leaves are fermented, then used to make kocho bread.

Kocho bread has a dense texture and a sour taste. Served with stews, it can be stored underground for up to a year.

Tropical aroids
Ace of spathes

△ **Taro** (*Colocasia esculenta*) is known mainly for its edible corm, which is also used medicinally and has ritual importance in Hawaii.

The aroids are members of ***Araceae***, a major family of varied, mainly tropical plants that includes more than 140 genera and at least 4,000 species, as new aroids are frequently discovered and recorded. One unifying feature is their spikes of tiny flower (spadices), each one initially enclosed in a large bract (spathe). Many aroids are climbers and epiphytic, while others have roots or are free-floating aquatics.

Ancient family

The *Araceae* plant family dates back more than 130 million years. Most of its genera are native to Asia, with others spread across Africa, the Pacific, and the New World. The largest species is *Amorphophallus titanum*, named corpse flower for its foul-smelling blooms (see pp.204–205).

Generating heat

Aroid flower power

The inflorescences of many aroids are thermogenic, that is, they produce heat, possibly to attract pollinating insects or to survive colder weather. The heat of one *Philodendron* spadix (spike) was recorded at as much as 115°F (46°C) above the ambient temperature. In most thermogenic aroids, the spadix draws on underground reserves of carbohydrates for energy. *Philodendron* species use a more potent source—lipids (fats) stored in sterile male flowers.

The split-leaf philodendron (see opposite) can increase the temperature of its spadix to 95°F (35°C).

Taro | *Colocasia esculenta*
Originally from southeastern Asia, this philodendron spread across the Pacific islands. Its bulbous underground corm is one of the oldest and most widely used staple foods.

It grows to a height of more than 39 in (1 m)

ZZ plant | *Zamioculcas zamiifolia*
The only species of its genus, this semievergreen native of East Africa with glossy, upright foliage is used locally in traditional medicine and widely cultivated elsewhere.

Voodoo lily | *Sauromatum venosum*
A native of tropical Asia and Africa, this is a heat-generating aroid. Its common name may stem from its inflorescence, which smells like rotting flesh to attract insect pollinators.

All parts of the plant are toxic and can irritate

Flamingo flower | *Anthurium andraeanum*
This popular aroid, native to Ecuador and Columbia, has white and yellow spadices rising out of striking, red, heart-shaped spathes.

Elephant foot yam | *Amorphophallus paeoniifolius*
With a native range from tropical and subtropical Asia to north Australia, this heat-generating aroid has a dark red inflorescence that smells like rotten flesh. Its large corm is widely used in Asian cuisines.

Rodent tuber | *Typhonium flagelliforme*
A perennial geophyte, growing from an underground tuber, this *Typhonium* species is native to tropical and subtropical areas from India eastwards to China, and south to northern Australia.

Giant calla lily | *Zantedeschia aethiopica* A native of South Africa with large, fluted, white flowers bracts, it is now commonly grown in gardens.

Big and showy

The 41 genera of aroids native to the Americas are diverse, frequently spectacular, and on average three times larger than Asian aroids. Many are epiphytic, growing high up on larger plants in a bid for sunlight

Split-leaf philodendron |
Thaumatophyllum bipinnatifidum
Although it is often classified as a philodendron, some experts now consider *Thaumatophyllum* a genus in its own right. The popular plant is native to South America.

The big glossy leaves have splits reminiscent of Swiss cheese

The heart of the leaf is often blood red

Its split leaves are similar to those of the better-known Swiss cheese plant

Stems rise high from a treelike "trunk" at its base

Swiss cheese plant | *Monstera deliciosa*
Native to Central America, this aroid has fruits that taste like a mixture of coconut, pineapple, and banana. Taking months to ripen, they are edible when their scales fall off.

Heart of Jesus | *Caladium bicolor*
This native of New World tropical forests is popular as a houseplant for its striking leaves, but every part of the plant contains toxic calcium oxalate crystals.

The tall spadix, its lower portion enclosed in the spathe, emerges directly from the titan arum's underground corm.

The furrowed spathe opens only for two to three days, revealing its deep maroon color within.

Tiny flowers on the base of the titan arum's tall spadix (flower spike) are protected by the surrounding spathe, a modified leaf.

Titan arum

Blooming foul

The titan arum (*Amorphophallus titanum*), which grows wild only on the rainforest slopes of Sumatra, is called the "corpse flower" because it emits a foul smell of rotting flesh when it blooms. The odor lures in pollinators such as flies and carrion beetles, which normally feed or lay their eggs on dead flesh.

The huge plant grows from a corm and produces a single, compound leaf. It may produce leaves for seven years or more before flowering for the first time. Its tall, phallic spadix (flower spike) grows rapidly and can reach a height of more than 13 ft (4 m) in the wild. The flowers are small and located at the base of the spadix, hidden by the enclosing sheath of the spathe. Like other aroids (members of the *Araceae* family of plants), the titan arum is thermogenic (produces heat). The tip of its spadix can reach a temperature of 100°F (38°C) when the plant blooms. Scientists believe that the heat is designed to help disperse the odor of the flowers. It can take up to ten years for the plant to flower again.

"The flowering is brief ... but the bloom is nothing if not memorable."
Paul **Cooper**
Agricultural Experiment Station, Cornell University

A huge corpse flower, 14¹/₂ ft (4.40 m) tall, was recorded on Sumatra in 2022.

Tropical orchids
Floral flamboyance

△ **Pansy orchids** (*Miltoniopsis* spp.) grow at medium altitudes in the northern Andes Mountains.

There are some 28,000 known species of orchid, most of which grow in the tropics. Many are epiphytes and live on other plants rather than in the ground. The richest tropical orchid habitats are montane cloud forests; the mountains of Colombia alone are home to more than 4,000 species. Tropical orchids display an extraordinary variety of structure, color, and size; the world's largest—the tiger orchid, *Grammatophyllum speciosum*—can be found from Southeast Asia to Papua New Guinea.

Flowers emit a strong citrus scent

Moth orchid | *Phalaenopsis bellina*
Native to the hot, steamy riverine forests of Borneo, this epiphytic plant typically grows on tree branch points, where it thrives in the shady conditions and high humidity.

Up in the air

In the tropics, most orchid species live in the forest canopy and do not need soil. Instead, they colonize branches high above the ground, with their green roots hanging down.

Dancing-lady orchid | *Oncidium* spp.
There are about 300 species of dancing-lady orchids. Native to South and Central America, they bear large sprays of flowers made up of many smaller blooms.

Flowers resemble a dancing figure wearing a skirt

Flowers lose their scent as the day becomes warmer

Pansy orchid | *Miltoniopsis* spp.
Miltoniopsis is a small genus of epiphytic orchids native to the tropical cloud forests of central and northern South America. The flowers resemble annual garden pansies and have a roselike scent.

Noble rock orchid | *Dendrobium nobile* This flower grows in lowland and mountain forests in China and Indochina. It is one of the 50 fundamental herbs used in traditional Chinese medicine.

The seed pods of some orchid species can contain more than 3 million tiny seeds.

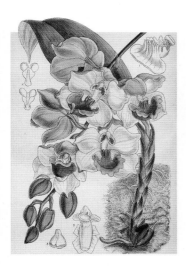

Aganisia | *Aganisia cyanea*
This orchid of wet forests in the Amazon may be submerged for several weeks with no apparent harm. Unusually for an orchid, it may produce blue flowers in cultivation.

Flowers are 3–5 in (8–12 cm) in diameter

Waling-waling | *Vanda sanderiana*
The epiphytic waling-waling is highly valued in its native Philippines. It is known elsewhere as Sander's vanda after the Victorian orchid collector Henry Sander.

Living in the trees

Epiphytic orchids

Most orchids are either epiphytes or terrestrials, though some—lithophytes— grow on rocks. Nearly all tropical orchids are epiphytes that prefer to grow on trees with rough bark, where there are cracks and crevices. Most of them grow on the inner branches of large, mature trees, in light shade—but they are not parasites. Their dangling aerial roots quickly absorb falling rain and nutrients from organic matter that washes down around them. They can survive dry periods due to their large, succulent stems, known as pseudobulbs.

Aerides odorata is a forest-dwelling orchid native to Asia. Growing on trees, it absorbs moisture and nutrients via its aerial roots.

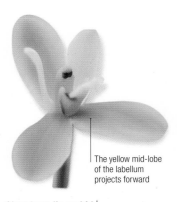

The yellow mid-lobe of the labellum projects forward

Giant boat-lip orchid | *Cymbidium madidum*
A rainforest orchid from northeast Australia, it grows in large clumps near paperbark trees in damp, shady woods, often on fallen tree trunks.

Crimson cattleya | *Cattleya labiata*
First described scientifically in 1818, the beautiful Brazilian *Cattleya* orchid genus kick-started the popularity of cultivated orchids. They remain the archetypal florists' orchid to this day.

Waxy, white and pink flowers have a red-spotted labellum

White nun | *Lycaste skinneri*
This orchid is the highly valued national flower of Guatemala. It is known as the white nun or *monja blanca* because its white blooms resemble nuns' cowls.

Bluish-purple blooms last longer than those of most orchids

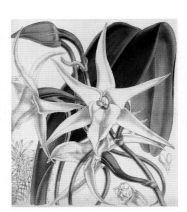

Darwin's orchid | *Angraecum sesquipedale*
In 1862, Charles Darwin predicted that this Madagascan orchid was pollinated by an insect with a very long proboscis. He was right: the insect is a hawkmoth.

Slipper orchid | *Paphiopedilum superbiens*
This strikingly patterned orchid has a shoe-shaped lip and grows in leaf litter in the mountains of Sumatra, Indonesia.

Narrow boat-lipped orchid | *Cymbidium canaliculatum*
Growing in the forks or hollows of trees, this Australian orchid's fragrant, waxy flowers may be brown, purple, or reddish black.

Blue vanda orchid | *Vanda coerulea*
In traditional medicine, sap from the flowers of this northeast Indian orchid are used to treat glaucoma and cataracts.

Panamanian coryanthes (*Coryanthes panamensis*), a species of bucket orchid in Panama, lures a male orchid bee with its sweet scent.

Bucket orchids
The orchid and the bee

Bucket orchids (*Coryanthes* spp.) are epiphytes that grow in tropical forests in Central and South America. They have a special relationship with euglossine bees, commonly known as orchid bees. The orchids and bees have evolved together, and are so specialized that neither can reproduce without the other.

In order to attract a female, the male orchid bee needs a certain perfume, which the bucket orchid provides. This oily scent oozes from the top of the orchid's flower and drips into its bucket-shaped lip below. While trying to reach the scent, the bee slips on the waxy walls and falls into the bucket. There is only one way out for him: a tunnel that he must squeeze through. In doing so, he first brushes past the stigma of the flower, which—if he is carrying pollen from another orchid of the same species—is thus fertilized. As the bee struggles forward, the orchid's pollen sticks to him. Only an orchid bee is exactly the right size for this tunnel. He is big enough for the orchid to deposit its pollen on him, but small enough to be able to finally escape.

> "... **male bees in a state of great agitation swarm around ...**"
> Eric **Hansen,** *Orchid Fever*, 2000

Bucket orchids are intricately designed to trap and release orchid bees.

Cycads

Imperiled palms

The 375 surviving cycad species have an ancient ancestry, dating back around 280 million years to an age long before the dinosaurs. These ancient cycads reached their peak around 150 million years ago, declined, then thrived and diversified 5 to 12 million years ago, when most of today's species evolved. DNA evidence reveals how today's cycads still share similar traits with their ancestors, including the appearance of their leaves. Some cycads, such as those in the *Cycas* genus, can reach 40 ft (12 m) in height and look like a cross between a palm tree and a fern, although they are unrelated. Like conifers, cycads are gymnosperms—plants that produce naked seeds protected by a cone. Cycads bear either male or female cones in the center of a crown of fronds attached to a thick, cylindrical stem. Uniquely among seed plants, a cycad's male cones produce pollen with moving sperm, each with thousands of tiny tails (flagella) to help them swim through a special fluid in female cones to reach and fertilize an egg.

Today, despite their long history, cycads are under threat. Only small native populations remain in tropical and subtropical areas around the globe, because humans have plundered and destroyed their habitats. One species, *Encephalartos woodii*, is now extinct in the wild, and others are critically endangered. Trade in cycads is controlled by an international convention, but it is difficult to enforce—especially when the most valuable specimens change hands illegally for millions of dollars.

Food or foe

Careful handling

The stems, roots, or seeds of a number of cycad species have long been used in southern Asia, Africa, and the Pacific to make a nutritious flour or sago, a food starch. But all parts of cycad plants are harmful if eaten raw, because they contain neurotoxins that can nausea, vomiting, and even death in humans and animals. To render them edible, cycad plant parts must be soaked or boiled to remove the toxins, then dried and ground into a fine or coarse powder.

Encephalartos lebomboensis, native to South Africa, produces red seeds with edible flesh but a toxic kernel.

New leaf fronds unfurl annually in a starlike formation from the crown of a sago palm (*Cycas revoluta*).

It can take 15 years or more for a sago palm to mature and produce a female cone (above) or a male cone.

The male sago palm cone can reach up to 24 in (60 cm) in length and is slimmer than the female cone.

The trunklike stem of this African *Encephalartos* species has a soft, woody exterior enclosing a starchy pith.

A rounded female cone forms at the center of the crown of leaf fronds on a sago palm (*Cycas revoluta*). These cycads are native to Japan and China.

South African perennials
Wildflower heathlands

△ **Lion's ear** (*Leonotis leonurus*) has whorls of tubular, two-lipped orange flowers encircling its square stems.

hanks to its mild climate, South Africa is one of the world's most diverse plant habitats. An astonishing 20,000–25,000 plant species—around 10 percent of all plants found on Earth—grow there. Unthreatened by extremes of weather, perennial plants, which live for several years, thrive in this environment. South Africa is known for its spectacular and colorful wildflower displays, which are triggered by the brief wet season from November to March, or by summer fires in the fynbos regions in the mountains.

Lilylike flowers have six bright red to orange tepals and six long stamens

Flame lily | *Gloriosa superba*
Native to southern Africa and southern Asia, this is Zimbabwe's national flower. It is also called the creeping lily, since it is a vine that uses tendrils to creep over other plants.

Flowers of the fynbos

Fynbos is a type of heathland in South Africa's Western Cape that has wet winters and dry summers. From a distance, it looks barren, but close up, it proves to be one of the world's richest flower habitats.

Leaves have medicinal value and are used in the manufacture of heart drugs

Lion's ear | *Leonotis leonurus*
A type of mint, also known as wild dagga, lion's ear is a tall perennial with striking orange flowers. It grows to a height of around 6 ft (2 m).

Red fall flowers are arrayed like a candelabra

Candelabra lily | *Brunsvigia josephinae*
Growing in very dry regions, the candelabra lily dies back to one of the world's biggest bulbs, typically over 8 in (20 cm) across. Pollination is by nectar-feeding sugarbirds.

Heartleaf ice plant |
Mesembryanthemum cordifolium
This is one of South Africa's "vygie" plants—succulents with fruiting caps resembling tiny figs. The leaves sparkle, icelike, in the sun.

Pajama flower |
Androcymbium melanthioides
This species nestles in dry, stony ground. A crowded flower head cupped by striped bracts earns it the nickname "little-men-in-a-boat."

Blooming in adversity

Fire and the fynbos

The fynbos owes some of its staggering plant diversity to the fires that scorch the land every 10–15 years. Fires return minerals to the nutrient-poor fynbos soil, destroy invasive species, and stimulate the growth of native plants, proteas being the best known-example. In some proteas, fire triggers seed release, while a few can resprout, after the fire, from beneath their flameproof bark. Others have buds that remain inactive below ground, then emerge to bloom after a blaze.

Fire rages across the fynbos, destroying plant growth, which soon recovers.

African lily | *Agapanthus praecox* Often called agapanthus, this is one of South Africa's most common and best-known flowers, now grown in gardens with a mild climate worldwide.

> **"South Africa is the most beautiful place on Earth ... we have been blessed with a truly wonderful land."**
>
> Nelson **Mandela** Former President of South Africa, 1994–1999

The bloom is a composite, with a central flower disk surrounded by ray florets —

Cape bugle lily | *Watsonia borbonica*
One of the first plants to recolonize an area after devastation by fire, this species is a key food source for animals. Spikes of up to 20 showy, typically pink flowers form in spring.

Red hot poker | *Kniphofia uvaria*
The blooms of this tall perennial plant's flower spikes begin scarlet, then turn yellow from the bottom up. It is an invasive species in Australia.

Treasure flower | *Gazania rigens*
Sometimes called the African daisy, this species is among the most attractive of South Africa's many daisies, with vivid yellow flowers and grayish-white leaves.

Angel's fishing rod | *Dierama pulcherrimum*
This pretty wildflower grows as a clump of grasslike stems from a corm, and blooms from early to late summer. It bears nodding, bell-shaped flowers on arching stems.

Alpine flowers
Living the high life

△ **Cobweb houseleek** (*Sempervivum arachnoideum*) grows as a tight rosette of leaves linked by hairs.

Alpine plants get their name from the European Alps, but they occur in the high mountains of other continents, too. Mountaintop plants must survive in thin, stony soils, low temperatures, desiccating winds, and intense UV light. Alpines show common adaptations to these conditions: cushion- or mat-forming habits, a protective covering of dense hairs, and large root systems to anchor themselves and to find sufficient water and nutrients. Flowers lose more water than leaves, so blooms are often small, with almost nonexistent stems that keep them close to the ground.

Bertoloni columbine |
Aquilegia bertolonii
This plant grows in southern France and Italy. Large, blue flowers are carried on short stems among the blue-green, fernlike leaves.

European Alps

The Alps stretch from France in the west to Slovenia in the east. Like other alpines, European species are small, hardy plants that tend to grow at altitudes where conditions are too harsh for larger species.

Alpine rock jasmine | *Androsace alpina*
This species grows as dense rosettes on acid rocks throughout the Alpine region. Tiny leaves and very low-growing flowers minimize exposure to the harsh conditions.

Tufted horned rampion |
Physoplexis comosa
Fused petal lobes and a protruding style form the "tuft" of each flower tip. This species is found in limestone and dolomite landscapes.

Alpine forget-me-not | *Eritrichium nanum* This cushion-forming forget-me-not grows on scree slopes and in crevices. In spring, vibrant blue flowers draw pollinators from far and wide.

Fairy foxglove | *Erinus alpinus*
In spring, short stems of lipped flowers rise from the rosettes of this small perennial. Fairy foxglove produces many seeds, which are scattered around the parent plant.

Golden cinquefoil | *Potentilla aurea*
Mats of golden cinquefoil grow in places sheltered from the strongest winds, where they spread across rock crevices. Relatively large, yellow flowers appear in early summer.

Cobweb houseleek |
Sempervivum arachnoideum
Succulent leaves and dense hairs keep water loss to a minimum. In summer it produces rose-pink flowers on tall stems.

Allion's primrose | *Primula allionii*
Native to limestone cliffs and crevices, this very small primrose grows dense rosettes of leathery, hairy leaves. Pink-to-purple, wavy-edged, stemless flowers appear in spring.

Trumpet gentian | *Gentiana acaulis*
This mat-forming species grows as a low rosette on grassy slopes. Trumpet gentian produces large, bright blue flowers as the last snow melts.

Single, upward-facing blooms sit almost on top of the leaf rosettes

Mountain tassel-flower |
Soldanella montana
The rounded leaves survive under snow in winter. Tall flower stems release heat to melt the snow as the flowers develop in spring.

White-flowered saxifrage |
Saxifraga burseriana
A limy crust on the minute leaves acts as sunscreen and aids moisture retention. The early spring flowers have short stems.

Lady of the snow | *Pulsatilla vernalis*
The dense coating of hairs on the leaves, stems, and flowers of this plant reduce water loss and deflect bright sunlight. The large flowers attract bumblebees.

Alpine toadflax | *Linaria alpina*
A perennial species that grows mats of prostrate stems, alpine toadflax has waxy, blue-green leaves that reflect sunlight. Its flowers are borne on short stems.

Keep your head down

Adapting to high-mountain life

In the winter, high mountain slopes are cold, lashed by winds, and often under deep snow. In summer, the slopes dry out as water drains away. Alpines hug the ground to avoid drying winds, and their tightly packed leaves create still air around the plant. Silvery hairs or limy deposits protect the leaves from sunburn, insulate them against cold, and reduce moisture loss. The limy deposits form when water rich in calcium carbonate is secreted by leaf glands and then evaporates.

Hairs on the buds of pasqueflowers (*Pulsatilla* spp.) protect them from the damaging effects of the sun and wind.

South America

The Andes mountains run for 4,300 miles (7,000 km) along the western edge of South America. Plant adaptations include dense, small-leaved foliage to limit water loss, and underground rhizomes to avoid winter cold.

Whitecup | *Nierembergia repens*
This alpine grows near streams, where temperatures are slightly higher. The blooms resemble bellflowers (*Campanula* spp.), but whitecup is actually part of the potato family.

Andean violet | *Viola montagnei*
Looking completely unlike its northern hemisphere cousins, this violet grows as a tight rosette of succulent leaves. The small, almost black, flowers appear in spring.

Cauliflower-like head of ivory-white flowers is studded with leaf spines

Armadillo's tail | *Nassauvia cumingii*
Silvery, toothed leaves reflect intense sunlight. Each leaf ends with a long, sharp spine, which also projects through the flower head, to deter grazers.

Silver shamrock | *Oxalis adenophylla*
During winter, the silver shamrock survives underground as a bulblike ball of swollen leaf bases. In spring, a rosette of leaves appears, alongside large, pink-to-purple flowers.

Flower-bearing stems can be up to 8 in (20 cm) tall

Mountain foxglove | *Ourisia alpina*
A perennial of Argentina and Chile, this plant is often found near streams or in moist, peaty soils. Red or pink flowers are borne on hairy stems and pollinated by bees and hoverflies.

Around 400 plant species naturally grow wild only in the Drakensberg range.

South Africa

Alpine plants have adapted to live in the cold, windswept mountains of South Africa, such as the Drakensberg range. Some, such as the terra-cotta gazania, have larger lowland relatives (see p.213).

Relatively large, star-shaped, pink flowers appear during summer

Red star | *Rhodohypoxis baurii*
Emerging after winter from a rhizome, this species has a small rosette of narrow, hairy leaves. Leathery bracts protect the flower buds from predators.

Yellow ice-plant | *Delosperma nubigenum*
Succulent, fleshy leaves help this mat-forming species retain water, an adaptation to life in rock crevices. The yellow flowers look like daisies, but they lack a central disk.

Terra-cotta gazania | *Gazania krebsiana*
This *Gazania* species forms a rosette of thick, leathery foliage. The undersides of the leaves roll inward, reducing water loss by trapping still air below them.

Mountain euryops | *Euryops acraeus*
This species forms a dwarf shrub, a mere 12 in (30 cm) high and wide. A profusion of evergreen silver leaves reflects intense light and reduces wind around the plant.

Large, colorful petals advertise the flowers to pollinators

Showy flowers open only in strong sunlight

Guernsey lily | *Nerine sarniensis* Growing from an underground bulb, this species flowers in the fall, before the leaves appear. Tall flower heads ensure pollinators find the blooms easily.

Pioneer plants
First in line

△ **Dandelion** (*Taraxacum officinale*) flower tufts become spheres ("clocks") of white-tufted seeds.

From time to time, fires, floods, and other events ravage a plant community. When this happens, tough pioneer species are ready to take advantage of the new opportunity, and establish themselves quickly. Some pioneers grow from seeds that have lain dormant in the soil, often for many years, until an opportunity arises. Others grow from seeds and spores blown in on the wind.

Leaves develop two blunt corners on either side

Danish scurvy grass | *Cochlearia danica*
Danish scurvy grass is a halophyte (salt-loving) plant of coastal sand dunes. Salting of icy roads has enabled it to spread far inland along roadside verges.

Tough weeds

Pioneers are hardy, drought-tolerant plants that germinate, grow, and reproduce quickly. They are often regarded as weeds, but they are vital for helping many other plants gain a foothold.

Eastern red columbine | *Aquilegia canadensis*
Native to eastern US states and southern Canada, this plant grows in rocky woods, on north-facing slopes, cliffs, ledges, and roadside banks. It flowers in late spring.

Long blooms attract insects and hummingbirds with long tongues

Stonecrops are often used to create green roofs

Stonecrops | *Sedum* spp.
With their tough, succulent leaves, stonecrops can survive on very little water and often spread low across the ground, making them perfect colonizers. The genus contains more than 400 species.

Houseleeks | *Sempervivum* spp.
These hardy succulents are real survivors, able to exist with little soil and virtually no water. The scientific name *Sempervivum* means "live forever."

Five slightly overlapping purple petals surround a white center

Fritillary butterflies lay their eggs on the heart-shaped leaves

The blue flowers are flat, star-shaped, and have five lobes

Clusters of small, yellow flowers sit on little woolly cushions

Kidney vetch |
Anthyllis vulneraria
Kidney vetch spreads rapidly over bare ground. Also known as woundwort, it was used in traditional medicine to help heal injuries and cure stomach problems.

Tall bellflower |
Campanula americana
Like many pioneers, the bellflower is self-seeding, short-lived, and spreads rapidly over bare soil. Many insects visit the flowers for nectar and pollen.

Common dog violet |
Viola riviniana
The common dog violet self-seeds freely. Its purple sprays of flowers often appear in urban nooks and crannies, as well as in woodlands, grasslands, and hedgerows.

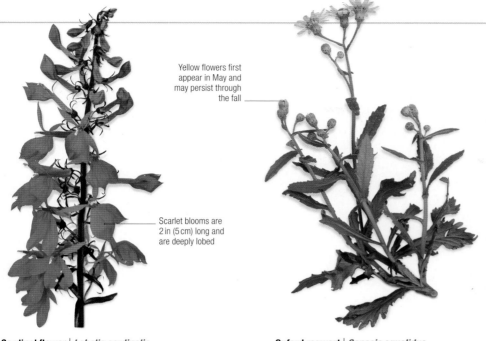

Yellow flowers first appear in May and may persist through the fall

Scarlet blooms are 2 in (5 cm) long and are deeply lobed

Cardinal flower | *Lobelia cardinalis*
This shallow-rooted, herbaceous perennial dies back in the fall and regrows in spring. It thrives in damp, bare ground, especially near ponds and river banks.

Oxford ragwort | *Senecio squalidus*
Originally introduced to Britain from Sicily, this extraordinarily vigorous pioneer spread along the early railroads in the 19th century. It grows in track ballast, on rock piles, and on stone walls.

War flower

Remembrance Day poppy

The common poppy (*Papaver rhoeas*) thrives in disturbed soil, and would quickly emerge in newly plowed fields until herbicides became widely used. No ground is more disturbed than a battlefield, where the poppy flourished in Europe during World War I. After the conflict, it became a symbol of remembrance in many countries—worn as a badge to commemorate the fallen. Money raised by selling the poppy pin is still used to support veterans and their families.

The poppy became the symbol of the World War I armistice.

Dandelion seeds can travel up to 60 miles on the wind.

Upper two petals are broader than lower two

Rose-purple flowers grow on spikes up to 6 ft (2 m) tall

Fireweed |
Chamaenerion angustifolium
Also known as "bombweed," fireweed quickly colonized bombsites during World War II. It was also the first plant to grow on Mount St. Helens after the US volcano erupted in 1980.

Lancelike leaves spiral up the plant's stem

Dandelion | *Taraxacum officinale* This perennial plant spreads rapidly on bare ground. Its seeds can remain viable in the soil for up to nine years.

Mosses colonize bare rocks and provide a foothold for more complex plants.

Moss pioneers
Paving the way

With no roots, flowers, or vascular system, mosses are extremely simple plants, yet they have been giving bare rocks a deep, green, velvety coating for 350 million years. They are one of the world's great pioneers—among the first to appear on land, and even today some of the first to colonize areas laid bare by catastrophes. They can grow in a variety of habitats and survive in harsh conditions. Mosses release acids that break down rocks and contribute to soil formation. More than 90 percent of their cells are dead, but these soak up a huge amount of moisture. This helps the mosses survive and reproduce, and creates new organic layers. The mossy carpets that clothe bare rocks provide microhabitats for a rich variety of invertebrate life, from fly larvae, slugs, and snails to mites and spiders. In damp places, mosses form a nurturing sponge that supports the seedlings of flowering plant pioneers, such as fireweed (*Chamaenerion angustifolium*).

Fireweed

Mosses can absorb up to 25 times their own weight in water.

Mosses can grow on surfaces, such as this old car, that cannot support plants with roots.

SPECIALIZED PLANTS

Over time, some plants and fungi have evolved in extraordinary ways to enable them to survive in the world's most challenging and inhospitable habitats.

Desert succulents
Fleshy and swollen

△ **The tall flower heads** of sea lettuce (*Dudleya caespitosa*) attract pollinators such as hummingbirds and bees.

Several unrelated plant families have adapted to survive in deserts. The often intense sunlight, and lack of regular rainfall, dries plants out unless they are able to capture and retain as much water as possible. Developing swollen leaves, stems, or underground tubers are all methods of storing water and nutrients while times are hard in these arid environments. When conditions improve, these plants, called succulents, are able to produce flowers quickly so they can attract pollinators and set seed before the harshest conditions return.

Tiny flowers grow on branched stems

Alabaster towers | *Crassula deceptor*
Minuscule white hairs cover the swollen leaves of this southern African succulent. The hairs shield the plant's water-storing leaves from sunlight, preventing them from scorching and drying out.

Survival tactics

Despite evolving on separate continents, many plants have adapted in similar ways to survive desert conditions. Fleshy stems or leaves retain water, while toxic sap; a spiny covering; or tough, leathery skin keeps grazers at bay.

The star-shaped flowers consist of five pointed petals

Chihuahua flower | *Graptopetalum bellum*
This mountain dweller from Mexico forms a dense rosette of succulent leaves. In spring, heads of brightly colored flowers appear.

Large red petals attract pollinators

Namibian aloe | *Aloe namibensis*
This large succulent grows in rocky places on the edge of the Namib Desert. It stores water in its long, upward-pointing leaves and sports tall spikes of coral-red flowers in winter.

Baseball plant | *Euphorbia obesa*
The green, ball-shaped stem of this South African native stores water and carries out photosynthesis, just as in cacti. It becomes more cylindrical with age. Tiny green flowers appear in summer.

Ribbed stems contain poisonous, milky sap

Indian corn-cob | *Euphorbia mammillaris*
A native of South Africa, the Indian corn-cob looks like a cactus, with the dead flower spikes along its club-shaped stems acting as spines. The plant's milky sap is an irritant to eyes and skin.

Mexican snowball | *Echeveria elegans*
The hairless, blue-green leaves have a waxy coating to reduce water loss, which also protects against strong sunlight. This rosette-forming species bears pink, yellow-tipped flowers on long stalks.

Fairy elephant's feet | *Frithia pulchra*
This plant has translucent "windows" at the tip of each leaf, allowing light to enter and photosynthesis to occur. It normally grows buried in sand with just the leaf tips visible.

Split-rock lithops | *Pleiospilos nelii*
Each stem grows only two or four paired, semi-hemispherical leaves, minimizing water loss. Large yellow flowers appear from between the youngest pair in the fall.

Sea lettuce | *Dudleya caespitosa* This species is native to the southern coast of California. Water is stored in thick, fleshy leaves, while starry yellow flowers with pointed tips are borne on tall stems.

Ocotillo | *Fouquieria splendens*
Storing water in tall, woody stems, ocotillo has annual leaves that emerge after rain, and red, bird-pollinated flowers. It is native to southern US states and northern Mexico.

Desert candle | *Euphorbia abyssinica*
This cactus-like species of eastern Africa has poisonous sap that deters herbivores. Over time it develops side branches, becoming candelabra shaped, and reaches up to 33 ft (10 m) in height.

Queen Victoria agave |
Agave victoriae-reginae
Although one of the smaller agaves, this species is characteristic of the genus, with a dense rosette of succulent leaves, each armed with a long spine.

Converging forms

Storing water in times of drought

Succulents and cacti are good examples of "convergent evolution," where unrelated species develop similar characteristics in order to grow in particular habitats. Despite their varied forms, from ground-hugging lithops to the towering saguaro (see p.229), these fleshy desert-dwellers have all evolved similar mechanisms with which to survive little rainfall, intense heat and sunlight, and extreme fluctuations between day and nighttime temperatures.

The varied forms of cacti and succulents demonstrate how they have all evolved to conserve moisture, and in many cases, to defend themselves from predators.

The flat-tipped leaves of *Lithops* look like desert pebbles, escaping the notice of grazing mammals.

Living stones

Flowering pebbles

"Living stones" of the genus *Lithops* grow in the deserts of southern Africa. They endure harsh sunlight and UV radiation, strong winds, and a lack of water. To combat these extreme conditions, the plants have adapted to a mostly hidden existence. Each shoot consists of two blunt-tipped, swollen leaves. Resembling pebbles, these are these are hard to distinguish among the desert stones. The plants are partially buried in gravel, so only the leaf tips, with their mottled patterns, are visible. Following rain, a new pair of leaves develops between the old ones, which then wither. A single white or yellow bloom then appears between the new leaves. This is relatively large, an adaptation to attract pollinators to the well-camouflaged plants. Over several years, some species form a clump of leaf pairs, creating a spectacular display of flowers.

Lithops fulviceps var. *aurea*

Living stones cannot self-pollinate and need insects to pollinate them.

Hidden photosynthesis

Receiving light below ground

Several dozen species of "living stones" in the genus *Lithops* live mostly buried in desert gravels. This lifestyle cuts water loss but also reduces the area of leaf able to photosynthesize. However, these plants have evolved translucent leaf windows in the leaf tips, allowing light to penetrate deep into the leaf, where the photosynthesizing chloroplasts are. The leaf windows also contain a kind of "sunscreen" that filters out harmful UV radiation.

Young leaves grow from the slit between the pair of old leaves.

Desert cacti
Water hoarders

△ **Flowers of saguaro** (*Carnegiea gigantea*) appear only on the tips of older mature plants.

Cacti belong to a single plant family, and are native to North and South America. However, they occupy many habitats within these continents, from subtropical forests and scrubland to the very driest deserts. Apart from some primitive species, all cacti have dispensed with leaves to minimize loss of water. Photosynthesis takes place in the stems, which is why they are green. The stems—which they protect against grazers with an array of sharp or irritating spines—also store water that the plants absorb when it rains.

Storing water

To store as much water as possible, many cacti have ribbed stems that expand like an accordion, allowing them to swell without the risk of bursting. A thick skin and waxy coating also help retain the stored water.

Jumping cholla | *Cylindropuntia fulgida*
The stem segments of this plant break off easily when their hooked spines catch on fur or clothing. They "jump" onto the passing animal or person, drop, and then form new plants.

Arizona hedgehog cactus | *Echinocereus arizonicus*
Found in the Chihuahuan Desert of northern Mexico and the southwestern US, this cactus produces large flowers in spring. Its pollinators include bees and hummingbirds.

Teddy-bear cholla | *Cylindropuntia bigelovii*
Named for its woolly appearance, this species is native to Southeastern California, western Arizona, and northwestern Mexico. When mature, it develop distinctive trunks.

Extreme modification

Multi-purpose spines

To protect their moisture-filled stems from animals, cacti have cushion-like shoots called areoles, from which highly modified leaves develop in the form of spines. As well as offering protection, the spines trap water from fog and dew, and direct it down to the ground. They also reflect sunlight and slow the passage of air around the plant, reducing water loss. Cactus flowers, which also grow from areoles, are often big and flamboyant, and project beyond the spines so they are accessible to pollinators.

Sharp cactus spines deter animals from feeding on the fleshy, thirst-quenching stem.

Mexican giant cactus | *Pachycereus pringlei*
One of the tallest cacti, this branching, slow-growing species can reach a height of 62 ft (19 m) and weigh several tons. Once tall enough, it produces white flowers at the stem tips.

Saguaro | *Carnegiea gigantea* This ribbed cactus can exceed 40 ft (12 m) in height and 150 years in age, taking 75 years to grow side arms. Flowers develop at its shoot tips and attract bats.

Saguaro grow for 50 years before first flowering, and can live for 250 years.

Chenille prickly pear | *Opuntia aciculata*
Despite having relatively short spines, this species is formidably armed. Barbed hairs grow with each spine, and if they catch in skin, they are extremely difficult to remove.

Red-orange or yellowish flowers are followed by spiny, fleshy fruits

Each flat, pad-like stem segment grows during a single season

Creeping devil | *Stenocereus eruca*
The long stems of the creeping devil grow along the surface of the soil, rooting at intervals in order to secure the plant and obtain more water.

Golden barrel cactus | *Echinocactus grusonii*
Native to northern Mexico, the golden barrel has yellow spines that ward off herbivores and also help to shade the stem from intense sunlight.

Artichoke cactus | *Obregonia denegrii*
A short-spined species, this cactus has a thick tuft of hairs to protect the growing tip of the stem from the sun. It produces small pink flowers in spring.

Peyote | *Lophophora williamsii*
This small, almost spineless cactus of Texas and northern Mexico contains alkaloids to deter grazers. A dense covering of hairs acts as a sunscreen.

The greenish cones (strobili) of a female plant are larger than those of a male.

Welwitschia
Desert veteran

Unique in many ways, this shrub lives in the coastal belt of southern Africa's Namib Desert, where rainfall is rare but fog is frequent. *Welwitschia* consists of just two permanent leaves, a low woody stem, and a tap root. It gets most of its moisture from fog, which condenses on the leaves and is absorbed through stomata. The tap root grows long enough to reach deep groundwater.

Although the largest *Welwitschia* plants grow only 5 ft (1.5 m) tall, their broad, flat leaves may be enormous, resting on the desert sand. The original leaves produced by a *Welwitschia* seedling are retained and continue to grow through the plant's lifetime. This is even more remarkable because many plants are more than 1,000 years old, and some may be twice that age.

Welwitschia is a dioecious gymnosperm: the male and female reproductive structures—cone-like strobili—grow on separate plants. These produce nectar, which attracts pollinating insects, especially flies. Reptiles shelter from the desert sun under the leaves, which are sometimes eaten by thirsty mammals at times of extreme drought.

"I could do nothing but kneel and gaze at it."
Friedrich **Welwitsch** Austrian botanist

This plant's two leaves often split into long, tattered strips.

Carnivorous plants
Pitfall predators

△ **The flowers of the purple pitcher plant** (*Sarracenia purpurea*) develop in spring, well before the traps become active in summer.

Several carnivorous plant groups have developed pitfall traps. These traps capture insects, or sometimes larger prey, in a liquid-filled cup known as a pitcher, which is developed from a highly modified leaf. A slippery entrance lip (the peristome) makes insects attracted by nectar or the color of the pitcher tumble into the cup. Downward-facing hairs and a waxy surface prevent the insects from escaping, so they drown at the bottom. They are slowly digested by enzymes in the watery fluid, releasing nutrients that the plant absorbs.

Flowers develop on separate stems from the plant's carnivorous pitchers

Purple pitcher plant |
Sarracenia purpurea
The short, pouch-like pitchers of this North American species have a purplish coloring that attracts flies.

Deadly pitchers

In Asian and Australian pitcher plants, the traps are carried on tendrils that extend from the midribs of leaves. In contrast, those from North and South America are formed from the entire leaf.

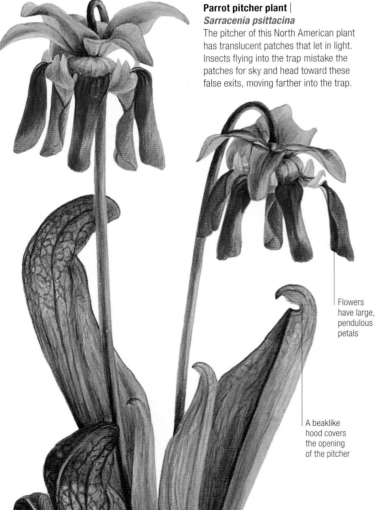

Parrot pitcher plant |
Sarracenia psittacina
The pitcher of this North American plant has translucent patches that let in light. Insects flying into the trap mistake the patches for sky and head toward these false exits, moving farther into the trap.

Flowers have large, pendulous petals

A beaklike hood covers the opening of the pitcher

Lesser sun pitcher |
Heliamphora minor
Instead of a lid, marsh pitcher plants have a small, spoon-shaped cap that secretes nectar as a lure. This Venezuelan native is one of the smallest species of marsh pitcher.

Albany pitcher plant |
Cephalotus follicularis
Widespread in the far southwest of Australia, the Albany has tiny pitchers that grow close to the ground. Ribs on the pitchers carry nectar glands that attract ants.

Yellow pitcher plant | *Sarracenia flava*
This is one of the tallest North American pitcher plants, growing to about 3 ft (1 m). The top of the rolled-leaf trap forms a lid to prevent rainwater from filling the pitcher and diluting the digestive enzymes.

Red pitcher plant | *Sarracenia rubra*
The red color of this North American pitcher attracts flies, and the veined pattern guides them into the trap's mouth. It produces a single dark red flower on a leafless stalk in spring.

Nodding sun pitcher | *Heliamphora nutans*
Like other marsh pitchers, the traps of this species consist of rolled leaves. Many different *Heliamphora* species have evolved on isolated table mountains in northeast South America.

California pitcher plant |
Darlingtonia californica
Native to California and Oregon, the pitchers resemble rearing cobras and have a curved hood with an entrance underneath.

White trumpet pitcher plant |
Sarracenia leucophylla
The slender, fluted, white-lidded pitchers have prominent red veins that guide prey toward the trap. It grows in sandy bogs and pine savannas in some US Gulf States.

Nepenthes aristolochioides
This climbing Sumatran plant produces long pitchers, each with a prominent ring of waxy ridges round the entrance. Spikes under the rim prevent prey from escaping. This species is endangered in the wild.

Each pitcher develops slowly from an extension of a leaf's midrib

Once the pitcher is mature, the lid opens to reveal the trap below

Nepenthes ampullaria
A Southeast Asian species with flask-shaped pitchers, *N. ampullaria* scrambles through forest undergrowth. It is only partly carnivorous, as it obtains the majority of it nutrients from falling leaf litter that collects in its pitchers.

Nepenthes sanguinea
Growing in tropical forests in Southeast Asia, this species is a climber and develops pitchers at the tips of some leaves. It grows as an epiphyte in some regions. Its pitchers can reach up to 12 in (30 cm) long.

Nepenthes inermis
The pitchers of this Asian climber are wide open and, uniquely, have no lip, so are always full of water. Insects drown and dissolve in the bath of enzyme-rich liquid. The pitchers reach up to 3½ in (9 cm) long.

Nutrients from animals

Why some plants are carnivorous

Carnivorous plants live in places such as marshes and bogs, where the soil is poor. These soils are low in nitrogen, which is vital for growth. Carnivorous plants overcome this deficiency by obtaining the nitrogen they need from animals. They have evolved various methods to capture prey, such as pitfalls and active traps (see pp.236–237). Proteins in the bodies of their prey are broken down, and the plants reuse the nitrogen that they contain to help them grow.

Attracted by the colorful pitcher, a fly is tempted to explore deeper but risks falling into the digestive fluids within.

The Mount Kinabalu pitcher plant (*Nepenthes × kinabaluensis*) has a mutually beneficial relationship with the Bornean smooth-tailed tree shrew (*Dendrogale melanura*).

Kinabalu pitcher plant
A potty-trained shrew

The Mount Kinabalu pitcher plant (*Nepenthes × kinabaluensis*) grows in the forests of Borneo, where it has evolved a special relationship with the Bornean smooth-tailed tree shrew (*Dendrogale melanura*), which is native to the forests of South and Southeast Asia. These omnivorous mammals eat fruit, berries, and seeds, as well as a large quantity of invertebrates; a high-protein diet that makes their feces rich in nitrogen.

The Kinabalu pitcher plant has bypassed the need to catch insects for itself by providing food and a toilet for the tree shrew. The animal drinks sweet nectar produced by the plant, which is secreted from a gland above the pitcher bowl, into which it defecates while it feeds. Its feces are digested within the pitcher as if they were insect bodies, although the tree shrew has done much of the digestive work already, making the process much quicker for the pitcher plant. This discreet arrangement has an added benefit for the tree shrews, by preventing predators tracking them down via their feces.

This pitcher plant was discovered in 1914, but not named until 1976.

The pitcher plant provides the tree shrew with a concealed and safer place to relieve itself.

Pitchers trail on the ground, making them easily accessible to tree shrews as they forage for food.

The tree shrew supplies the pitcher plant with nutrients in a form that it can quickly digest.

Carnivorous fungi

Nematode-trapping fungi

Hundreds of species of fungi growing in nutrient-poor environments prey on nematodes to supplement their nutrition. Some immobilize them with a toxin, while others produce microscopic snares to catch their prey. These traps range from sticky knobs or loops, to constricting rings or hook-shaped spores that stick in the nematodes' throats. Fungal hyphae (tiny threads) then grow from the trapping structure into the nematode's body, feeding on it until it is consumed.

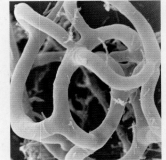

Arthrobotrys oligospora is a fungus that creates loops that it uses to trap nematodes, before eating them.

Carnivorous plants
Spring-loaded traps

△ **The spoon-shaped leaves** of the common sundew (*Drosera rotundifolia*) curl inward and wrap around their prey.

Not all carnivorous plants use pitfall traps (see pp.232–235). Some have glandular hairs that ensnare insects; among these, several—sundews and butterworts—have leaves that curl around their prey after they have been trapped. Other carnivorous plants have triggered mechanisms with moving parts, such as the underwater traps of bladderworts and waterwheel plants, while the Venus flytrap has hinged leaf flaps that snap together rapidly when activated. In each case, enzymes digest the prey, releasing nutrients that the plant absorbs.

Active traps

Plants with active traps have sensitive hairs that detect motion and trigger a response, such as closing around their prey or releasing digestive fluids. Many species feed on flying insects, but several specialize in small aquatic or soil-dwelling invertebrates.

Bladderwort |
Utricularia reniformis
This plant lives in waterlogged soil and uses underground, bag-like traps called "bladders" to catch small insects and worms. It has colorful flowers and kidney-shaped leaves.

Colorful flowers attract pollinating insects

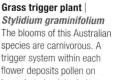

Flower stalks, up to 16 in (40 cm) high, rise from a clump of grasslike leaves

Grass trigger plant |
Stylidium graminifolium
The blooms of this Australian species are carnivorous. A trigger system within each flower deposits pollen on bees, but glandular hairs trap and digest smaller insects.

Sundews produce flowers above their leaves to avoid devouring their pollinators

Common sundew | *Drosera rotundifolia* Widespread in Europe, this species grows in damp marshes and bogs. The hairs on its leaves have glands at their tips that exude a sticky, glistening "dew." Visiting insects become stuck and are gradually digested.

Sanderson's bladderwort |
Utricularia sandersonii
This Brazilian species traps soil-dwelling invertebrates in tiny underground bladders. It has small leaves and pale flowers.

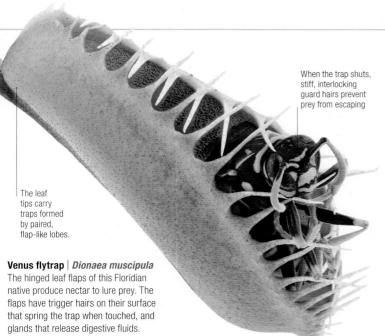

When the trap shuts, stiff, interlocking guard hairs prevent prey from escaping

The leaf tips carry traps formed by paired, flap-like lobes.

Venus flytrap | *Dionaea muscipula*
The hinged leaf flaps of this Floridian native produce nectar to lure prey. The flaps have trigger hairs on their surface that spring the trap when touched, and glands that release digestive fluids.

Moving in for the kill

How traps work

In butterworts and sundews, the cells farthest from the prey fill with water, slowly curving the leaf around the victim. The Venus flytrap closes in a similar way, but much faster. Waterwheel plant traps, in contrast, are pre-tensed, ready to snap shut instantly. Bladderworts pump water from their bladders, creating a partial vacuum. When triggered, a "door" opens and the bladder rapidly expands, sucking in water and prey.

Waterwheel plants (*Aldrovanda vesiculosa*) have underwater snap traps.

Common butterwort |
Pinguicula vulgaris
A rosette of flat glandular leaves traps insects and partly enfolds them in leaf depressions.

Yellow butterwort | *Pinguicula lutea*
Native to North America, this plant captures insects on its flat leaves. The large flowers grow on tall stems, away from the leaves.

Rainbow plant | *Byblis gigantea*
Named for the way that its leaves reflect light, this Australian species traps small insects using sticky, tentacle-like leaves.

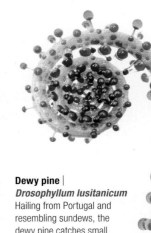

Dewy pine |
Drosophyllum lusitanicum
Hailing from Portugal and resembling sundews, the dewy pine catches small flies. Prey is trapped by the sticky drops, where it is digested.

Gluey mucilage from the stalked glands traps flies, which become increasingly ensnared as they try to struggle free

The red color of the glandular hairs attracts small flies

Common bladderwort |
Utricularia vulgaris
This water plant grows in acid bog pools. Small aquatic organisms are sucked into its submerged bladders when triggered.

Northern dewstick |
Roridula dentata
This South African plant traps insects with its sticky leaves. It feeds on the droppings left by beetles that eat the trapped insects.

Airy shaw |
Triphyophyllum peltatum
This rare West African forest-dweller has large, flat leaves for photosynthesis and narrow glandular ones to catch insects.

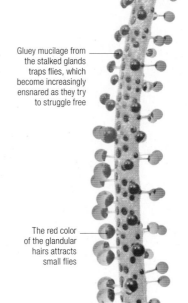

Parasitic plants
Nutrient thieves

△ **Evergreen European mistletoe** (*Viscum album*) is hemiparasitic on woody hosts and has white berries that birds disperse.

Parasitic plants obtain some or all of their nutritional requirements from other living plants. About one percent of flowering plants are thought to be parasites. Although they show great variety, most have a specialized, rootlike organ called a haustorium, which they use to penetrate a host plant. Obligate parasites cannot complete their life cycle without a host, whereas facultative species can but also use their haustoria to derive nutrients from a nearby host.

Tubular flowers bloom between bright red bracts

Giant red paintbrush | *Castilleja miniata*
Valued for its medicinal properties by Indigenous peoples in North America, this parasitic species grows in wet mountain meadows. Its flowers attract hummingbirds.

Hemiparasites

Hemiparasites derive nutrients and water from their host but remain photosynthetic. Depending on where they attach to their host, they may be root parasites or stem parasites.

Red bartsia | *Odontites vernus*
Thriving in nutrient-poor soils, red bartsia's flower spikes grow to a height of 20 in (50 cm). Its flowers supply nectar for a variety of insects.

Bees and wasps visit red bartsia's pinkish flowers

Yellowbeak owl's-clover | *Triphysaria versicolor*
A facultative root hemiparasite, this North American plant can use its haustoria to take nutrients from a host's roots.

Johnny tuck | *Triphysaria eriantha*
Native to California and Oregon, this root parasite has hairy, purplish stems and flowers with a narrow purple upper lip and three bright yellow or pinkish-white pouches.

Love vine | *Cassytha filiformis*
Shoots from this parasitic tropical vine attach to a host and extract its nutrients and water, often killing it. The love vine's stems and juice are used in traditional medicine.

Lodgepole pine dwarf mistletoe | *Arceuthobium americanum*
The fruits of lodgepole pine, a stem parasite, generate heat (thermogenesis) to trigger the explosive dispersal of their seeds.

Indian sandalwood | *Santalum album*
Sandalwood oil from the heartwood of this tropical Asian tree is used in perfumes and to flavor food. It is a root parasite but can survive alone in its early stages.

Moodjar | *Nuytsia floribunda*
The bright orange flowers of this Australian root hemiparasite bloom around Christmas, hence its alternative name of Western Australian Christmas tree.

European mistletoe | *Viscum album* This plant commonly grows in the crowns of broadleaved trees, traditionally symbolizes fertility, vitality, and romance.

Specialized structures

The haustorium

Most parasitic plants have rootlike structures called haustoria, which grow into the xylem (less frequently the phloem) of host plants. They help anchor the parasite, as well as acting as conduits to absorb water and nutrients from the host. These materials may pass from host to parasite through straw-like intrusions in the vascular tissues or may be absorbed directly through cell walls.

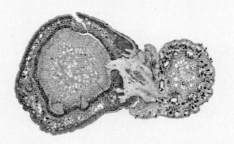

Micrograph showing a haustorium (right) invading a host.

By restricting the growth of invasive species, parasitic plants can encourage biodiversity.

Yellow rattle | *Rhinanthus minor*
Named for the sound of its seeds in their pods, this plant can weaken vigorous meadow grasses, thus enabling wild flowers to thrive.

Witchweed | *Striga hermonthica*
A parasitic plant widespread in Africa, witchweed feeds on cereal crops and can significantly reduce yields in some areas of the world.

Desert quandong | *Santalum lanceolatum*
The olive-like fruits of this root parasite are produced after rain and ripen to a rich, red-purple color.

Field cow-wheat | *Melampyrum arvense* This European root parasite has striking purple flower spikes. Its seeds are dispersed by ants, which feed on them.

Holoparasites

Holoparasites get their fixed carbon from a host plant. Lacking chlorophyll, they do not practice photosynthesis. Some—called mycoheterotrophs—tap into mycorrhizal fungi in the soil that have a symbiotic relationship with other plants, in effect "stealing" these plants' nutrients.

Snow plant | *Sarcodes sanguinea*
The snow plant—named for its emergence just after the winter's snow melts—derives its nutrition from tree roots via mycorrhizal fungi (mycoheterotrophy).

Ghost plant | *Monotropa uniflora*
Because it does not photosynthesize, this waxy white plant can grow on dark forest floors. It takes nutrients from fungi that live in close association with beech trees.

Woodland pinedrops |
Pterospora andromedea
Generally existing only as a mass of roots, it may also produce a flower spike 39 in (1 m) high. Lacking chlorophyll, it takes nutrients from mycorrhizal fungi and pine roots.

The dense spikes of reddish to white flowers appear from early to mid-summer

Greater dodder | *Cuscuta europaea*
This herbaceous dodder parasitizes a wide range of species, including the stinging nettle (*Urtica dioica*). It has pink flower corollas and long, thin, yellow or red stems.

Bird's-nest orchid | *Neottia nidus-avis*
Camouflaged against shaded leaf litter, this honey-colored, mycoheterotrophic orchid can be difficult to spot. It often grows around beech trees in shady woodland.

One-flowered broomrape |
Orobanche uniflora
Lacking leaves and chlorophyll, this species takes nutrients from the root systems of plants including goldenrods and saxifrages.

Jackal food | *Hydnora africana*
Only visible when its fungus-like, reddish-orange flowers appear above the ground, this parasite has roots that attach to those of host *Euphorbia* plants.

Branched broomrape |
Orobanche ramosa
In North America, the branched broomrape is considered a serious pest, because it damages potato, tomato, and tobacco crops.

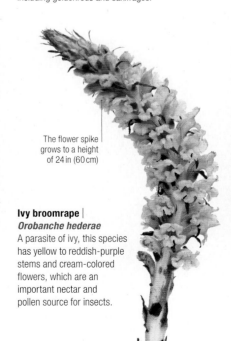

The flower spike grows to a height of 24 in (60 cm)

Ivy broomrape |
Orobanche hederae
A parasite of ivy, this species has yellow to reddish-purple stems and cream-colored flowers, which are an important nectar and pollen source for insects.

Five enormous lobes surround a cuplike structure, within which lie the male anthers or female styles.

Rafflesia

Epic and unearthly

For most of its life in the forests of Borneo and Sumatra, a corpse flower (*Rafflesia arnoldii*) remains invisible. This holoparasite has no leaves, stem, or roots, just a network of threadlike tissues living within the tissues of *Tetrastigma* vines. It absorbs nutrients from the host plant until it produces a bud growing on the vine. The brownish bud grows until it bursts open to produce a flower weighing up to 24 lb (11 kg). Its five blood-red lobes are dappled with white spots.

If the flower is pollinated, seed-filled berries develop. These are eaten, defecated, and dispersed, by small mammals, including tree shrews. If some of the tiny seeds manage to invade the tissue of other vines, the *Rafflesia* life cycle begins again.

Rafflesia flowers can reach 4 ft (1.2 m) across.

Rafflesia blooms into the single **biggest individual flower in the world.**

Foul odor

Pollination

When a corpse flower opens, it emits an aroma similar to rotting flesh. The flower also produces warmth, which helps spread the smell. The odor attracts carrion flies seeking a place to lay their eggs. A male flower's thick, sticky pollen attaches to the flies, which then carry it to the next plant. Since *Rafflesia* flowers are either male or female, one of each must be flowering at the same time—and not far from each other—for fertilization to be successful.

Flies are attracted to the flower.

Epiphytes
Living on air

△ **The urn plant** (*Aechmea nudicaulis*) produces spikes of small flowers with bright red bracts.

Epiphytes grow on other plants, but they are not parasites. Rather, they absorb moisture and nutrients from rain and water vapor via their leaves and aerial roots. They also gather nutrients from the debris that collects on their host plant. Epiphytes growing high on canopy trees have advantages over plants rooted in the soil below—they can access sunlight more easily and are less likely to be eaten by herbivorous animals. Many epiphytes hold reservoirs of water between their leaves, and these provide homes for amphibians and invertebrates.

Orchids, ferns, and cacti

Epiphytes are not limited to angiosperms (flowering plants). Although nine out of every ten species belong to the group—including orchids, bromeliads, and cacti—about one-third of all ferns are epiphytic. Many mosses and liverworts are also epiphytes.

Between 10–25 flowers may bloom on each stem

Moon orchid | *Phalaenopsis amabilis*
One of the national flowers of Indonesia, the moon orchid produces long-lasting, white flowers. It grows on rainforest trees and is pollinated by carpenter bees.

Mistletoe cactus | *Rhipsalis baccifera*
The only cactus native to the Old World—perhaps initially carried there by migrating birds—this epiphyte forms a mass of slender, trailing stems.

Urn plant | *Aechmea nudicaulis* This Neotropical epiphyte is a tank bromeliad—the base of its leaves forms a small water reservoir.

Bird's nest fern | *Asplenium nidus*
Growing on palms or directly on rock, this fern collects water and humus in its leaf rosette. It is used as a stir-fry vegetable.

Curled odontoglossum |
Odontoglossum crispum
Found on large trees in Colombia's montane
forests, this species' striking flowers made it
a focus of "orchid mania" in the 19th century.

Cardinal air plant | *Tillandsia fasciculata*
Growing up to 3 ft (1 m) across in rainforests
and seasonally dry forests, this plant stores
water in a "tank" with several chambers,
and produces brightly colored flowers.

Faham | *Jumellea fragrans*
Native to the Indian Ocean islands of
Mauritius and Reunion, this white, fragrant,
night-flowering epiphytic orchid is pollinated
primarily by hawk-moths.

Each panicle
(branched flower
head) may carry
dozens or even
hundreds of
flowers

Yellow flowers
have maroon,
dark red, or
brown spots

Air plant | *Tillandsia stricta*
The leaves of this South American air plant
form thick rosettes about 4 in (10 cm) across.
Small, short-lived, blue flowers are enclosed
within magenta or pink floral bracts.

Brazilian bromeliad |
Billbergia distachya
A Brazilian native with green, blue-tipped
flowers and pink bracts, this bromeliad is
pollinated by one species of hummingbird.

Staghorn fern | *Platycerium bifurcatum*
The fertile fronds of this epiphyte—native
to rainforests in Australia, New Guinea, and
Indonesia—are shaped like antlers and
grow up to 20 in (50 cm) in length.

Tiger orchid |
Grammatophyllum speciosum
The world's largest orchid, it can exceed
23 ft (7 m) in height, encircle large tree
trunks, and live for over a century.

Coconut orchid | *Maxillaria tenuifolia*
A single, coconut-scented, red flower grows
from each flower stem of this epiphytic
orchid, which is native to Central America.

Spanish moss | *Tillandsia usneoides*
Often growing in dense clumps on trees, this
is not a moss but a flowering epiphyte. Its
slender stems bear many thin, curly leaves.

Water from the air
How epiphytes obtain moisture

Unable to draw water from the soil,
epiphytes have other ways to obtain
and retain moisture. They are covered
with tiny, hairlike structures called
trichomes, whose cells absorb
moisture directly from the air. The
leaves of some epiphytes—tank
bromeliads—form receptacles where
rainwater and moisture from fog
collects and is absorbed by the plant.
Epiphytic cacti and other succulents
are good at retaining moisture during
periods when even the air is bone dry.

Trichomes (shown on a *Tillandsia* spp.)
are modified hairs that obtain water and
nutrients directly from the humid air.

Bryophytes
Primitive plants

△ **Umbrella liverwort** *(Marchantia polymorpha)* quickly colonizes fire-ravaged land, helping to prevent soil erosion.

Bryophytes are small and rootless. They use photosynthesis to feed themselves, but do not have a vascular system to transport water and nutrients, which limits their size. They reproduce with spores, alternating between a dominant gametophyte stage (creating male and female organs) and a sporophyte stage (making spores). Bryophytes include hornworts, liverworts, and mosses, and are an ancient plant form, evolving almost directly from algae.

Hornworts

Members of this bryophyte group, which grow in damp areas all around the world, have hornlike spore-producing structures. There are estimated to be around 215 species.

Liverworts

There are up to 9,000 species of liverwort, named for its lobed, liver-shaped thallus (body). Leafy liverworts have leaflike appendages, while thalloid liverworts are flat and branching.

Umbrella liverwort | *Marchantia polymorpha*
This widespread thalloid liverwort grows in soil and on rocks in wet, shaded areas. At the gametophyte stage, its male and female thalli grow protruding umbrellalike branches.

Dendroceros spp.
Seen here on tree bark, *Dendroceros* hornwort species grow in warm regions and can tolerate dry conditions. Their vegetative tissue (thallus) resembles leaves on vascular plants.

Common pouchwort | *Calypogeia fissa*
This tiny, leafy liverwort is one of the most common. It grows on acidic soil, peat, soft rock, and rotting logs, or may appear in more straggly lobes growing through sphagnum moss.

Snakeskin liverwort | *Conocephalum salebrosum*
First described in 2004, this largish, holarctic liverwort, with thalli over ½ in (1 cm) wide, grows in moist, chalky habitats. It gets its common name from the shiny polygons of its thalli.

Field hornwort | *Anthoceros agrestis*
Horned sporophytes rising from a dark green thallus distinguish the field hornwort, which grows on moist soil in ditches and arable fields in Europe and North America.

Floating crystalwort | *Riccia fluitans*
Typically starting life as spores floating on the surface of water, this thalloid liverwort develops clumps of short threads. It may be aquatic or terrestrial.

Greater whipwort | *Bazzania trilobata*
This leafy liverwort grows in mounds of shoots that resemble piles of green caterpillars. It is common in damp woodland in northern temperate regions.

Mosses

Up to 20,000 species of moss grow worldwide in most habitats. Because they have no roots, mosses have evolved varied structures to absorb water and nutrients from the soil, retain moisture, and maximize photosynthesis. Most are tiny, but *Dawsonia superba* can grow to 24 in (60 cm).

Common haircap | *Polytrichum commune*
Growing in tufts, this moss has wiry shoots up to 16 in (40 cm) long and is typically found in damp woodland, by streams, and on open moors.

If moist, the leaves curve away from the stem; if dry they curl around it.

Stem leaves are tapering, oval, and up to ⅛ in (3 mm) long

Mountain fork moss | *Dicranum montanum*
Cushions of this tiny moss grow up to 1¼ in (3 cm) tall around the base of a tree or on logs. When dry, the wavy branchlets fall off and can regrow into new plants asexually.

Stair-step moss | *Hylocomium splendens*
Widely found carpeting boreal forests and on heaths, moors, and tundra in the northern hemisphere, this red-stemmed moss is red-brown or yellow-green in color.

Sphagnum moss | *Sphagnum palustre*
This is one of 300 *Sphagnum* species that grow on moors, bogs, and marshes. Their spongy form retains water, which reduces plant decomposition, encouraging peat formation.

Living at extremes

Ancient survivors

Over 450 million years, mosses have survived vast climatic changes and still grow in some of Earth's most extreme habitats, ranging from hot deserts to dank, cold caves. They cling to a surface with hairlike rhizoids and use these or their absorbent surfaces to take in nutrients. Some mosses can photosynthesize at temperatures as low as 5°F (−15°C) or up to 104°F (40°C) and can withstand cold of −458°F (−272°C) and heat up to 212°F (100°C). At great extremes, some species become dormant.

Bright green summer moss covers Iceland's Maelifell volcano, contrasting with the dark sand around it.

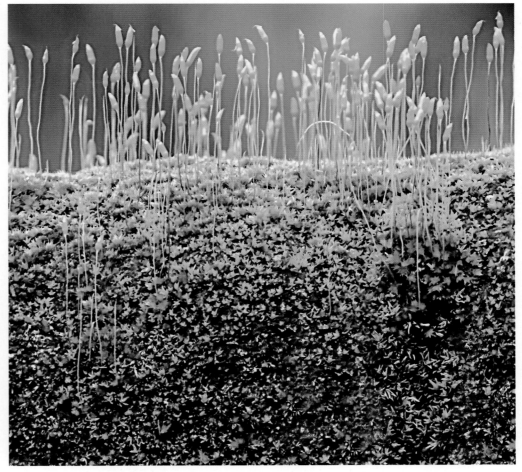

Bonfire moss | *Funaria hygrometrica* This moss forms carpets of shoots and egg-shaped leaves and develops tall sporophytes (spore-bearing stalks). It grows on bonfire sites and in shady, moist soil and damp crevices.

Evolution in isolation
Out on a limb

△ **Fruits of coco de mer** (*Lodoicea maldivica*) take up to 10 years to ripen; their seeds weigh up to 55 lb (25 kg).

Plant species that have evolved in isolation from other members of their family—for example, in populations separated by an ocean or a mountain chain— have evolved adaptations that make them better equipped to thrive in their different environment. This is most obvious on islands far removed from continental land masses, such as Hawaii and Rapa Nui (Easter Island) in the Pacific, St. Helena in the Atlantic, and the islands of the Southern Ocean. Today, many of these unique endemic plants are fighting for survival in the wild.

The pinkish-purple flowers have stems up to 24 in (60 cm) high

Campbell Island daisy |
Pleurophyllum speciosum
Endemic to the Auckland and Campbell islands, the daisy grows in huge rosettes of ribbed leaves up to 4 ft (1.2 m) across.

Succulents and megaherbs

Many island endemics are adapted for life in harsh conditions, including drought, salty air, and persistent wind. Centuries of grazing animals decimated their numbers, but conservation measures have helped bring some species back from the brink of extinction.

The simple, white five-petaled flowers fade to pink

St. Helena ebony |
Trochetiopsis ebenus
Saved from extinction, this shrub—a mallow, rather than an ebony—has been reintroduced at six wild sites on the island.

Toromiro | *Sophora toromiro*
Although extinct in the wild, the small flowering toromiro grows in cultivation, and a program is underway to reintroduce it to its native Rapa Nui (Easter Island).

Campbell Island carrot | *Anisotome latifolia* Growing only on the Auckland and Campbell islands, this megaherb attracts insects that birds such as the New Zealand pipit, above, feed on.

Māmane | *Sophora chrysophylla*
A large shrub or tree up to 50 ft (15 m) tall, this variable plant is endemic to Hawaii. One native bird, the endangered palila, feeds almost exclusively on its seeds.

Macquarie Island cabbage |
Stilbocarpa polaris
This megaherb has yellow or purple flowers, and used to be eaten by castaways, seal hunters, and whalers to prevent scurvy.

Scrubwood | *Commidendrum rugosum*
A drought- and salt-tolerant daisy, scrubwood grows in the wild only on the shrubland and rocky terrain of St. Helena. Its white flowers bloom throughout the year.

Ross lily | *Bulbinella rossii*
The bright, golden-yellow flowers of this perennial lily, which grows on open grassland on the subantarctic Auckland and Campbell islands, appear from October to January.

Socotran fig | *Dorstenia gigas*
A "bottle tree" adapted to survive drought, this woody succulent can grow in desertlike conditions and on sheer rock faces on its native Socotra in the Arabian Sea.

Cucumber tree |
Dendrosicyos socotranus
Endemic to Soqotra, the succulent-stemmed tree grows up to 20 ft (6 m) in height and has a bloated trunk up to 39 in (1 m) thick.

Coco de mer | *Lodoicea maldivica* Endemic to two islands in the Seychelles, this palm is incredibly slow growing, and produces the largest and heaviest seeds in the world.

Olulu | *Brighamia insignis*
Since the extinction of its natural hawkmoth pollinator, the yellow flowers of olulu, a Hawaiian palm now also extinct in the wild, have had to be pollinated artificially.

Going large

Megaherbs

The herbaceous plants of cold regions are mostly small and cushion-like, but species on the subantarctic Auckland, Campbell, and Macquarie islands have evolved different features to survive rain, wind, and cold. Large, dark leaves are thought to help the plants trap more of the area's brief periods of sunlight, enabling them to photosynthesize more efficiently, retain heat, and produce seeds effectively. The leaves may also protect these plants from salt spray and wind damage.

Huge, ribbed leaves help the Campbell Island daisy (*Pleurophyllum speciosum*) survive its cold, wet environment.

Socotra desert rose (*Adenium socotranum*) has a swollen trunk up to 8 ft (2.5 m) in diameter. It blooms after the rainy season, in March and April.

Socotra desert rose (*Adenium socotranum*) bears pink or red flowers in spring while the tree is leafless.

The trunk of the dragon's blood tree (*Dracaena cinnabari*) oozes thick, red resin when cut, which gave rise to its name.

Cucumber tree (*Dendrosicyos socotranus*) is a tree in the gourd family (*Cucurbitaceae*) that even grows on rock faces.

Monolluma socotrana is a succulent whose striking red flowers smell of rotting flesh to attract pollinators.

Socotra archipelago
The islands of diversity

More than a third of the plant species that grow on the four islands of the Socotra archipelago, southeast of Yemen in the Indian Ocean, are found nowhere else on Earth. This high degree of endemism—exceeded only by the islands of the Galápagos, Hawaii, and New Caledonia—is a result of millions of years of isolation from continental Africa and Arabia.

From June to September, the islands are swept by hot, dry, exceedingly strong monsoon winds blowing from Africa, and temperatures can exceed 104°F (40°C). Exposed areas are sparsely vegetated with dry shrubland, and succulents abound. On the plains and limestone plateau of Socotra, by far the largest of the islands, the climate has encouraged drought-resistant plants such as the cucumber tree (*Dendrosicyos socotranus*) and the Socotra desert rose (*Adenium socotranum*), whose bloated trunks store water in the cooler, wetter winter months. The drought-resistant dragon's blood tree (*Dracaena cinnabari*) with its distinctive, umbrella-shaped crown, grows on the island's limestone plateaus and in the Hajhir Mountains.

Socotra also has a great variety of endemic reptiles, including the Socotra chameleon (*Chamaeleo monachus*) and Socotran racer snake (*Hemerophis socotrae*), as well as birds, bats, and several spiders including the Socotra Island blue baboon spider (*Monocentropus balfouri*), a type of tarantula.

"Socotra is ... one of the most biodiversity rich and distinct islands in the world."
UNESCO **World Heritage Convention**

Socotra Island blue baboon spider

Temperate aquatics
Water-loving plants

△ **Flowering rush** (*Butomus umbellatus*) flowers emerge from spherical buds.

Purple loosestrife |
Lythrum salicaria
Native to Europe, where its purple flowers grow in shallow water, this plant became an invasive nuisance in North America after being introduced there.

Aquatic plants grow in water or very wet soil on the margins of lakes and rivers, in ditches and marshes, or on the surface of ponds and slow-flowing rivers. They provide shelter for aquatic animals, add oxygen to their environment through photosynthesis, filter pollutants from water, stabilize riverbanks, and help to recycle nutrients. Floating aquatics may be unattached or have roots attached to the substrate. Emergent aquatics have their roots in water but their stems and leaves above it. Submerged aquatics live totally underwater.

Emergent and floating

A great variety of emergent and floating aquatics thrive in temperate regions, and play a crucial role in many ecosystems. People have used some for traditional medicine or food. When introduced to regions where they are not native, some have become a nuisance.

Numerous stamens and pistils

Bright yellow flowers appear in early spring

Flowering rush | *Butomus umbellatus*
Cup-shaped, rose-pink and white flowers bloom in summer in damp ditches and around the edges of freshwater ponds.

Cattail | *Typha latifolia*
This plant of shallow fresh water has distinctive flower spikes. Its roots and leaves have been used in traditional medicine.

Marsh marigold |
Caltha palustris
The marsh marigold, or kingcup, thrives in many damp places, including wet woodland, ditches, and around the edges of ponds.

Bogbean | *Menyanthes trifoliata*
A characteristic rhizome of bogs in temperate North America, Europe, and Asia, this plant has bright white, star-shaped flowers.

Arrowhead | *Sagittaria sagittifolia*
Named for the distinctive shape of its emergent foliage, it also has oval floating leaves. Its white flowers have purple bases.

Greater spearwort | *Ranunculus lingua*
This tall aquatic buttercup grows to 3 ft (1 m). It bears large, yellow, five-petaled flowers and has long, narrow leaves.

Dense cluster of lilac-pink flowers from July to October

Water mint | *Mentha aquatica*
This plants aromatic leaves can be used to flavor food and drinks. Butterflies, hoverflies, and beetles visit its flowers for nectar.

Photosynthesizing under water

Aquatic adaptations

Plants need sunlight, water, and carbon dioxide (CO_2) in order to carry out photosynthesis. Aquatic plants with leaves above the water do not need special adaptations to photosynthesize, but it is harder for fully submerged plants to obtain the CO_2 they need. Having small leaves without a waxy coating makes it easier to absorb CO_2.

Pondweed has leaves that are only a few cells thick and have no waxy cuticle. This makes photosynthesis easier.

Hornwort | *Ceratophyllum demersum*
A submerged, rootless aquatic plant with whorled leaves, hornwort releases chemicals that suppress the growth of phytoplankton.

Water horsetail | *Equisetum fluviatile*
Growing to 4 ft (1.2 m) tall, water horsetail is a plant of fens and lake edges. It produces tiny, spherical spores rather than seeds.

Large, rounded leaves persist all year

Brooklime | *Veronica beccabunga*
This species has thick, juicy stems and spikes of small, bright blue flowers. It provides shelter for small fish and tadpoles.

Leaves are long, narrow, and swordlike

Yellow flag iris | *Iris pseudacorus*
This marginal aquatic grows to 3 ft (1 m). Its large, bright yellow flower petals fold back on themselves.

White water lily | *Nymphaea alba* It has white and yellow flowers and 1-ft (30-cm) leaves that float on still or slow-flowing water.

The fossil of an ancient horsetail (*Equisetum* sp.) is instantly recognizable from the fanlike rays of branches sprouting from the stem.

Horsetail
Prehistoric plant

Horsetails (*Equisetum* spp.) are miniature descendants of giant plants that thrived in the Carboniferous era. Fossils reveal that horsetails almost 100 ft (30 m) tall were among plants that dominated Earth some 350 million years ago. Their dead plant matter, compressed over time, contributed to the world's coal deposits.

Like ferns, to which they are related, horsetails are widespread in temperate, moist conditions across the Northern hemisphere and reproduce using spores. The plants have hollow, jointed stems and, because their leaves are tiny and scalelike, it is the stems that perform photosynthesis. In some species, such as the field horsetail (*E. arvense*), whorls of needlelike branches sprout from each segment of stem, creating a "horse's tail" shape. In others, such as the rough horsetail (*E. hyemale*), the stems are branchless and topped by a spore-bearing cone.

Field horsetail
(*E. arvense*)

Equisetum may be the oldest surviving genus of vascular plants.

Tiny horsetail leaves appear as scales at the base of each joint of the stem.

Tropical aquatics
Warm water specialists

△ **The seed pod of blue lotus** (*Nymphaea nouchali*) bursts, scattering the seeds, which then sink quickly.

Tropical aquatic plants grow in fresh and brackish water—in lakes and rivers, as well as estuaries, where freshwater meets the sea. While some of these habitats are permanent, others disappear during the dry season, and the plants that live there have adaptations that enable them to thrive. The most important of these environments are the Pantanal and the Amazon basin in South America; the Okavango delta and parts of the Congo basin in Africa; and the Ganges delta and Tonlé Sap in South and Southeast Asia.

Hydrophytes

Plants that live in water (hydrophytes), grow above, below, or on the surface (see right). They are vital in aquatic environments, oxygenating and shading the water, and providing food and habitats for insects and other animals.

Bog moss | *Mayaca fluviatilis*
Native to Central and South America, this plant grows entirely underwater. It produces pink, three-petaled flowers and can regenerate from tiny fragments.

Shiny green leaves float on water

Amazon frogbit | *Limnobium laevigatum*
This floating plant produces small white and yellow flowers. Like many aquatics, it can also reproduce asexually when segments of stolons break off.

Creeping primrose-willow | *Ludwigia repens*
This aquatic member of the evening primrose family (*Onagraceae*) has reddish stems and small yellow flowers that open at dusk. Its growth can form dense floating mats.

Water hyacinth | *Pontederia crassipes*
A free-floating tropical plant with mauve flowers, it is native to South America but has become highly invasive in temperate wetlands around the world, crowding out other aquatic species.

Flowers are held 1 ft (30 cm) above water

Blue lotus | *Nymphaea nouchali*
Blue lotus grows from rhizomes rooted beneath the water, and its leaves float on the surface. It features prominently in early Asian literature and art.

Sweet flag | *Acorus calamus*
The ancient Egyptians made perfumes from the aromatic leaves of sweet flag. Several cultures have used this emergent in traditional medicine.

Sword-shaped leaves grow up to 7 ft (2 m) tall

Spadix bears many tiny greenish-yellow flowers

Guyanese arrowhead |
Sagittaria guayanensis
Named for the shape of its floating leaves, this perennial herb of tropical Central and South America has white flowers. Arrowhead has been used in traditional medicine.

Water hedge |
Alternanthera reineckii
Water hedge grows on riverbanks and in seasonally submerged areas of South America. Its reddish leaves make it a popular ornamental plant.

Papyrus |
Cyperus papyrus
This large emergent has played an important role in the development of human civilization. It has been used to make papyrus paper and in construction.

In hot climates, papyrus is one of the fastest-growing plants on Earth.

Sacred lotus | *Nelumbo nucifera* A symbol of longevity in South and East Asia, it has floating leaves and colorful flowers. Its seeds can remain dormant for long periods in desiccated ponds.

Straight vallisneria | *Vallisneria spiralis*
This plant is pollinated by water. Surface tension creates small dimples around the floating female flowers, into which the tiny male flowers are drawn. It is an invasive nonnative species in New Zealand.

Dwarf hygrophila |
Hygrophila polysperma
Dwarf hygrophila is a hardy aquatic that can form dense mats in fresh water, sometimes occupying the entire water column and shading out all competition.

Types of aquatic plants

Lifestyle adaptations

Aquatic plants are grouped into four categories. Emergent aquatics root into the soil beneath the water, but much—often most—of the plant grows above the surface. Floating-leaved plants also root into the submerged soil, but their leaves float on the water surface. Free-floating species are suspended on the surface of the water and are not attached to the soil by roots. Submerged plants are completely immersed in the water; some have roots attached to the soil, but others have no root system at all.

Healthy aquatic environments support a variety of plants.

A network of small spines covers the underside of giant water lily leaves and stems, protecting them from fish and aquatic mammals that may feed on them.

Amazon water lily
Aquatic monster

The giant water lily's flowers are short-lived and nocturnal, starting to unfurl during late afternoon.

When fully open, a flower—which is white until it is pollinated—may be 16 in (40 cm) in diameter.

The large water lily leaf easily supports the weight of a wattled jacana (*Jacana jacana*), a long-toed wader bird.

One of the world's largest lilies, the Amazon water lily (*Victoria amazonica*) is remarkable for more than its size. It grows in freshwater lakes in the Amazon basin, where water levels fluctuate greatly between the seasons. When the water rises in the wet season, the lily's rhizomes in the mud at the bottom of the lake produce stalks up to 26 ft (8 m) tall that extend to the surface. The stalks develop huge, circular, floating leaves with upturned rims. The leaves can grow to 10 ft (3 m) across and can support the weight of a small child.

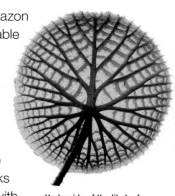

Underside of the lily leaf

The lily's large flowers open at night and generate their own heat—a mechanism known as thermogenesis. This boosts the flowers' production of scent and helps attract certain species of scarab beetle, which pollinate the lily. Once a flower has been pollinated, its stalk contracts, so it remains submerged until the seeds are mature. The seeds then float to the surface using air sacs, drifting away to settle on exposed mud as the dry season approaches and the lake water recedes.

The lily's seeds can be ground into flour, and its stalks are also edible. The Tupi people of Brazil have a legend about the plant's origin, which describes how a chieftain's daughter once leaned over the water to embrace the moon's reflection. She fell in and disappeared, and was transformed into a giant lily flower.

Pretty in pink

Pollination

Amazon water lilies are pollinated by two species of *Cyclocephala* scarab beetle, which are nocturnal. Attracted by the flowers' scent, warmth, and white color, they climb inside. Later in the night, the flowers close shut, trapping the beetles inside, which feed on succulent tissues called staminodes. The next day, the flowers open partially, allowing the beetles to leave by pushing past the stamens, collecting pollen on their bodies in the process.

Once pollinated, the lily flower turns from white to reddish pink.

A single plant can produce up to 50 leaves in one season, completely dominating its aquatic environment.

Marine and coastal plants
Beside the sea

△ **Sea holly** (*Eryngium planum*) has striking, spiny leaves and cone-shaped flowers that make it a popular garden ornamental.

Coasts are very tough places for plants. They are constantly sprayed with salty water and exposed to wind and rain—and there are few footholds in the rock and sand of cliffs and beaches for roots to establish. Yet many plants not only survive but thrive in these challenging habitats, and play a key role in paving the way for other species. They stabilize sand dunes with their roots, and provide shelter and nutrients for insects and other plant life. One type of flowering plant, seagrass, actually grows in the sea—its ancestors having colonized the ocean millions of years ago.

Rock sand-spurrey |
Spergularia rupicola
This sprawling little perennial survives by clinging to sea cliffs or crevices in rocks. It has small, pink or white flowers.

Shifting sands

Coastal habitats are both fragile and dynamic. The land is constantly eroded by the sea, while sediment deposited by rivers creates marshes and mudflats. The plants that grow here are adapted to scant resources, with fleeting opportunities to colonize new ground.

The bright yellow, dandelion-like flowers are self-fertilizing

Golden samphire |
Limbarda crithmoides
This rugged, tufted perennial grows in salt marshes. The name "samphire" comes from "Saint Peter," patron saint of fishermen.

Seaside daisy | *Erigeron glaucus* This is a perennial wildflower of the US west coast, from Oregon to California. It grows on coastal bluffs, forming low, spreading clumps of succulent leaves and dainty, pale-pink flowers.

Marram grass | *Calamagrostis arenaria*
Tough marram grass can colonize even loose sand dunes. It grows in clumps from thick rhizomes, binding the sand grains together and helping to buffer the dunes against erosion.

Sea oats | *Uniola paniculata*
This tall grass is native to the Atlantic coast of the southern US and Mexico. It is a protected species in the US, due to its valuable role in stabilizing sand dunes with its extensive roots.

Sea holly | *Eryngium planum*
A spiky, thistlelike plant with silvery-blue leaves and steel-blue flower heads, sea holly is native to central Europe and east Asia, where it originally grew inland.

The fragrant, showy flowers are pink or white

Sea bindweed | *Calystegia soldanella*
Like other species of bindweed, sea bindweed is a vine with pretty, trumpet-shaped flowers. It grows in beach sand and is native to many coastal regions around the world.

Sea kale | *Crambe maritima*
This salt-tolerant relative of the cabbage has big, wavy-edged leaves and white flowers. It is edible as well as striking, so is cultivated both as an ornamental and for culinary use.

Beach rose | *Rosa rugosa*
This tough, multi-stemmed rose grows in thickets on sandy shores. It has wrinkled leaves and edible rose hips, and is also known as the beach tomato.

California sea pink |
Armeria maritima **subsp.** *californica*
This is the Californian subspecies of sea pink or sea thrift. It is a compact, shrubby perennial with cushions of thin leaves and pink flowers.

Eel grass | *Zostera marina*
Also known as sea wrack, eel grass is one of around 60 species of sea grass. Its range extends from the north Pacific to the Arctic, where it survives ice cover for many months.

Posidonia australis

Ancient marine giant

In 2022, researchers discovered what could be the world's largest individual plant: a specimen of the giant seagrass *Posidonia australis*, growing on the sea bed in Shark Bay, Western Australia. The scientists used genetic markers to analyze samples from across the seagrass meadow—and found that the whole meadow was a single plant. It covers 70 square miles (180 sq km), and is estimated to be 4,500 years old. Since 2010, cyclones and heat waves have killed off part of the meadow.

The seagrass in Shark Bay is unusual in that it is a polyploid—a hybrid with the full genetic material of both its "parents."

Mangrove root systems provide shelter for crustaceans, jellyfish, and spawning fish.

Mangrove trees
On land and sea

Mangrove trees grow in salty coastal or estuarine waters, mostly in tropical and subtropical regions. Two main species are the red mangrove (*Rhizophora mangle*) and the black mangrove (*Avicennia germinans*), but "mangrove" can refer to any tree growing in these aquatic conditions. Mangrove forests provide important habitats for wildlife, and their massive, complex root systems play a key role in preventing coastal erosion, filtering pollutants from water, and storing large quantities of carbon.

Mangroves are halophytes—plants adapted to salty soil or saltwater conditions that would kill most other vegetation. They are usually the first to colonize intertidal zones, but survival in these environments presents great challenges. They have limited fresh water, their roots have little access to oxygen, and they usually grow in soft, unstable mud. Mangroves need special adaptations to stop the salt in their surroundings from sucking water from their cells. Some have roots that filter out most of the salt; others secrete salt through their leaves, or concentrate it in old, soon-to-drop leaves. Mangroves also obtain oxygen from the air via their roots. The arching, stilt-like "prop" roots of many species help stabilize them against the flow of the tides.

Mangroves prefer water that is 50 percent fresh, 50 percent seawater.

How mangroves breathe

Aerial roots

Plants breathe through their leaves, stems, and roots, but there is little oxygen in the waterlogged mud where mangrove trees grow. Two adaptations enable them to overcome this problem. Some species have vertical or cone-shaped roots, called pneumatophores, that stick up out of the mud. Their surface is covered with hundreds of pores (lenticels), so they function like snorkels. Mangrove trees without pneumatophores access oxygen through lenticels on their prop roots.

Most pneumatophores grow 8–20 in (20–50 cm) out of the ground, but the biggest can be up to 10 ft (3 m) tall.

Exploiting harsh environments
Surviving extremes

△ **Norway spruce** (*Picea abies*) has reddish-brown seed cones with diamond-shaped scales.

Plants have evolved many adaptations that help them thrive in the most inhospitable environments. Some have thick bark and waxy, needlelike leaves that protect them from extreme cold, while others have leaves with a thick, waxy cuticle that reduces evaporation in hot climates. Some others have trunks that store water or deep root systems that tap into groundwater. Some turn extreme conditions to their advantage by exploiting the heat of bushfires to release their seeds.

Blue hibiscus |
Alyogyne huegelii
This evergreen shrub with large lilac flowers is tolerant of drought and frost. It thrives in sands and gravels in south and west Australia.

A variety of strategies

The plants featured here use different strategies to cope with extreme heat, cold, temperature range, drought, and salinity, or with regular bushfires or a lack of soil.

Norway spruce | *Picea abies* This is a tall conifer of northern North America and Eurasia that tolerates cold to -40°F (-40°C).

Yerba mansa | *Anemopsis californica*
An aromatic herb with cone-shaped inflorescences and white petals, yerba mansa is a halophyte, tolerant of saline environments such as salt flats.

Marsh samphire | *Salicornia europaea*
Edible cooked or raw, marsh samphire is a small halophyte with bright green stems and tiny scalelike leaves. It grows in temperate, intertidal salt marshes.

Scarlet bottlebrush | *Melaleuca rugulosa*
Named for its bright red "bottlebrush" flowers, this drought-resistant shrub is native to dry scrub in South Australia and Victoria. It has gray, peeling bark and grows to 13 ft (4 m) tall.

Argan tree | *Sideroxylon spinosum*
For centuries, people have used the oil from this desert tree's seeds in beauty products. Its small, leathery leaves are adapted for life in arid conditions in north Africa.

Hyacinth | *Scilla madeirensis*
Endemic to Madeira and the Selvagens Islands, this rare bulbous plant grows on volcanic cliffs with little or no soil. Its flowers grow on a 2-ft (60-cm) stem.

Purple saxifrage | *Saxifraga oppositifolia*
This perennial is one of the hardiest plants on Earth, surviving in the bitterly cold Arctic at 83 degrees north—and at 14,780 ft (4,505 m) in the Swiss Alps.

Acorn banksia | *Banksia prionotes*
Named for the shape of its flower spikes, this plant of dry Australian scrubland releases seeds during bushfires. These later germinate in the ground.

Trumpet-shaped flowers may be orange, red, or yellow

Cape honeysuckle | *Tecoma capensis*
Sunbirds visit this evergreen, drought-resistant South African shrub to feed on the nectar in its clusters of bright flowers. Wind disperses its seeds.

Saguaro cactus | *Carnegiea gigantea*
This stem succulent can live for up to 250 years, and grow to around 50 ft (15 m) tall. Saguaros can survive extreme drought in North American deserts.

Victorian box | *Pittosporum undulatum*
Pollinated by insects, this Australian shrub bears small fruits containing seeds. Birds and flying foxes feed on the fruits and disperse the seeds in their feces.

Tapping into deep water

Phreatophytes

In arid areas, the only constant source of water may be groundwater deep beneath the surface of the ground. Some plants, called phreatophytes, have deep roots to reach it. Examples include mesquite trees (*Prosopis glandulosa*), which have extended taproots up to 82 ft (25 m) deep, *Welwitschia mirabilis*, and argan trees (*Sideroxylon spinosum*). Because they have a constant supply of water, they do not need to store it like cacti and baobab trees do.

Phreatophytes may thrive in inhospitable places with no surface water at all.

Desert holly | *Atriplex hymenelytra* This plant can tolerate the driest and hottest regions of North America, including the Sonoran and Mojave deserts. It can also survive frosts.

'Ōhi'a lehua
Pioneering plant

The 'ōhi'a lehua (*Metrosideros polymorpha*) is the most widespread woody plant on the actively volcanic islands of Hawai'i. It is highly variable in form, ranging from a dwarf shrub to a tall forest tree. Following volcanic eruptions, it is also usually the first plant to colonize lava flows, establishing itself just a few years after the basalt magma has cooled. The plant's ability to close the pores on its leaves when toxic volcanic gases are blown its way give it an advantage over other plants. 'Ōhi'a lehua produces bright red, orange, or yellow powder puff-shaped flowers. These are pollinated by insects, and by birds called honeycreepers, which visit to feed on its nectar. Once its seeds have germinated, they produce slow-growing seedlings that sprout from fissures in the bare rock.

Culturally, 'ōhi'a lehua is one of the most important plants on the Hawaiian archipelago, referenced in traditional songs and stories, and regarded as a physical manifestation of local deities. Every year, 'Ōhi'a Lehua Day is celebrated on April 25. However, in recent years, the plant has been decimated by 'ōhi'a death—a rapidly spreading disease caused by a species of *Ceratocystis* fungus.

Since 2010, disease has killed more than 1 million of these plants.

Lava flows frequently reshape the landscape—and vegetation—of the Hawaiian islands.

'Ōhi'a lehua seedlings establish themselves first in small fissures in pahoehoe (smoothly undulating) lava flows.

Plant invaders
Beautiful aliens

△ **The flower spikes of common cattail** (*Typha latifolia*) burst when mature and release tens of thousands of seeds.

A great many naturalized, nonnative plants present no problems for their adopted environment. A minority, however, outcompete native plants and may threaten not just these plants but entire ecosystems. When they smother agricultural crops, their impact is economic as well as environmental. These invasive nonnatives are often successful because there are no natural controls, such as herbivores, or because they spread rapidly, or a combination of these factors.

Common lantana | *Lantana camara*
Native to Central and South America, this shrub colonizes farmland and forests in many other regions, including tiger habitats in India.

Migrant species

Many invasive plants were introduced to new regions because of their attractive appearance, before people understood the consequences. Others arrived by accident, perhaps as seeds among imported goods. Once established in their new homes, many have proved hard to control.

Large trusses of flowers are produced from spring to early summer

Rhododendron | *Rhododendron ponticum*
This shrub was introduced to many areas for its bright, violet-purple flowers. It spreads rapidly, however, crowding out native plants and even poisoning some species of bee.

Pearl wattle | *Leucaena leucocephala*
A small, fast-growing tree from Mexico and Central America, pearl wattle is invasive in many regions, outcompeting local species.

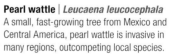

Prickly pear | *Opuntia* spp.
Known for its sweet fruit and large, colorful flowers, prickly pear became a problem weed in Australia soon after it was introduced from the Americas (see box, opposite).

Hiptage | *Hiptage benghalensis*
In some parts of the world where it has been introduced for its flowers, this liana or shrub climbs over native plants and smothers them.

Himalayan balsam |
Impatiens glandulifera
Out-competing native riverbank species, this quick-growing annual plant also leaves bare earth when it dies, causing soil erosion.

Heart- or shovel-shaped leaves are borne in a zigzag pattern along the stems

White flower tassels bloom in late summer and early fall

Floating pennywort | *Hydrocotyle ranunculoides* This aquatic plant blankets lakes, starving other plants of light.

Reddish-orange, tulip-like flowers bloom at the ends of branches

Each dense, spherical flower head has about 100 small, mauve-to-pink blooms

After blooming, female flowers form a cylindrical fruiting spike

Japanese knotweed | *Reynoutria japonica*
In temperate regions, this species forms dense colonies that force out other plants. Its deep, spreading roots can even damage buildings.

African tulip tree |
Spathodea campanulata
On many Pacific islands, this African tree has colonized forests, plantations, and farm land.

Catclaw mimosa | *Mimosa pigra*
Due to its fast-growing seedlings, this shrub can rapidly colonize riverbanks and floodplains where it is not native.

Common cattail | *Typha latifolia*
This freshwater reed filters pollutants from water, but it spreads rapidly and often displaces other aquatic plants.

Tamarix | *Tamarix ramosissima*
A hardy Eurasian shrub, tamarix has plumes of showy pink flowers. In southern California, it outcompetes cottonwood and other native species for limited groundwater.

Giant hogweed |
Heracleum mantegazzianum
The sap of this large perennial causes skin burns when exposed to sunlight. Native to the western Caucasus, it has spread widely.

The "green hell"

Prickly pear control

New World prickly pear cacti were first brought to Australia in the late 18th century. Settlers used them as hedging plants and for animal fodder. The plants thrived and spread over vast areas of farmland, some of which had to be abandoned. No treatment was effective until the South American cactus moth (*Cactoblastis cactorum*) was released. Its caterpillars ate the cacti's soft tissues and cleared most of the "green hell" between 1926 and 1933.

Australia's invasive prickly pear issue was headline news in publications at the time.

Kudzu
Running amok

Kudzu (*Pueraria montana*) is a drought-resistant vine native to Asia and Northern Australia, where it has been cultivated for millennia as a food and fiber crop. It produces pink flowers, and in 1876 it was introduced to the United States as an ornamental plant. In the 1930s, during the Great Depression, the US Soil Conservation Service advocated the widespread planting of kudzu for cattle fodder and to control soil erosion, which was a serious problem in the South. Farmers were offered financial support to grow millions of acres of the plant.

Nicknamed "mile-a-minute vine," kudzu is a trailing perennial with tuberous roots. Nodes produce tendrils at regular intervals along its stems and, if the stem is in contact with soil, more roots. More stems grow from these rooting points, spreading in every direction. The roots can become huge, and the stems of a single plant can grow up to 1 ft (30 cm) a day. By the 1950s kudzu was becoming a problem in the US, because plantings that had been left unattended were overwhelming shrubs, trees, telephone poles, fences, and small buildings. In 1970, the US Department of Agriculture listed kudzu as a weed, and in 1997 it was declared a Federal Noxious Weed, but by this time the damage had been done.

The vine is so vigorous that it can bring down power lines and block rights of way, and its control has proved to be extremely expensive.

Kudzu tubers

Dubbed "The vine that ate the South," kudzu is estimated to cover 7.4 million acres (3 million hectares) of land in the US.

The leaves of kudzu are compound, with three rounded, heart-shaped leaflets.

Kudzu flowers are usually purple, magenta, or red, and exude the scent of grapes.

Kudzu is a legume, producing seed pods containing kidney-bean-shaped seeds.

Kudzu thrives in open, sunny ground, quickly smothering shrubs and trees on abandoned land and at forest edges.

Fungal invaders

Unwelcome arrivals

People have inadvertently moved animals, plants, and fungi from place to place on a small scale for thousands of years. However, in the last 150 years, an explosion in international travel and trade has resulted in the movement of organisms on an unprecedented scale, often to the detriment of native species. When organisms arrive in a new region, some colonize only a very limited area, and many fail to become established at all. Others become invasive and can have a major impact on the resident species.

Invasive fungi can visibly change entire landscapes if they cause disease in plants; but many other less noticeable fungi that rot wood or partner with plants (mycorrhizal fungi) can be equally invasive. More than 200 species of mycorrhizal fungi have been introduced to the Southern Hemisphere in new tree plantations. These fungi partner with plant roots (see pp.52–53) and can help their host plant flourish and spread. In some areas, for example, exotic pines are spreading from plantations into the wider landscape.

The death cap fungus (*Amanita phalloides*), which is native to Europe, is now resident in the US. On the east coast it is not invasive, but on the west coast it is beginning to dominate. It was introduced into the San Francisco Bay area of California in the mid-20th century, and it has colonized some areas to such an extent that almost 20 percent of plant root tips are now partnered with this fungus rather than with native fungi.

Invasive species often reduce the diversity of native fungi.

Death cap (*Amanita phalloides*), a highly toxic species, has a mutualistic relationship with oaks (*Quercus* species).

Slippery Jack (*Suillus luteus*) is invasive in Africa and North and South America, having been imported on nonnative trees.

Red cage fungus (*Clathrus ruber*) is spreading north in Europe, and along the coasts of North America.

Devil's fingers (*Clathrus archeri*) has long, red arms with dark, slimy patches containing spores.

Devil's fingers (*Clathrus archeri*) emerging from its protective "egg." This wood decomposer is invasive in much of Europe and parts of North America.

BENEFICIAL PLANTS

Throughout history, people have depended on plants for food, materials to build their homes, and transportation, and to make healing lotions and medicines.

Drupes
Stony fruits

△ **Olives** (*Olea europaea*) can be harvested at any stage, from green and unripe to fully ripe and black.

A **drupe, or stone fruit,** is a fruit with a fleshy layer around a shell—the stone or pit—containing a seed. Many drupes evolved in tandem with animals that disperse the seeds by eating the fleshy part of the fruit, and then swallowing and defecating the stone. Some small drupes grow as clumps called aggregates. Raspberries, blackberries, and dewberries are really aggregates, not berries.

Purple-to-black drupelets have a waxy bloom

Dewberry | *Rubus caesius*
There are several dewberry species. The aggregates of these plants are coated with a thin layer, or "dew," of waxy deposits. They are often less "seedy" than blackberries.

Rubus

The fruit of *Rubus* species, including raspberries, produce small fruits, known as drupelets, that are clustered together to form an "aggregate." Each drupelet contains a tiny stone.

The conical torus remains on the plant when the fruit is picked, creating a hollow core

Each "bump" on the blackberry is a tiny drupe containing a single seed

Raspberry | *Rubus idaeus*
One of the most widely used of all aggregates, raspberry's dietary fiber content (6 percent) is among the highest of any fruit.

Blackberry | *Rubus fruticosus*
This aggregate grows wild in many European countries. Blackberries are important for moths, which feed on shoots and leaves as caterpillars, and over-ripe fruits as adults.

Prunus

Prunus is a huge genus of trees and shrubs known for their spring blossom and tasty fruits, such as plums, cherries, and apricots. The *Rubus* genus includes aggregate-bearing brambles and cane fruits.

Ripe plums can be purple, red, green, or yellow

Plum | *Prunus domestica*
Stones found at sites in Ukraine dating back 8,000 years hint that plums might have been the first fruit to be domesticated. They are related to damsons and gages.

Sloe | *Prunus spinosa*
The sloe is the fruit of the blackthorn tree—a food plant for the larvae of many moth and butterfly species. The small, blue-black fruits measure about ½ in (1 cm) across.

Seed dispersal

Chiropterochory

Encouraging animals to eat fruits and thereby spread seeds is a key survival strategy employed by plants. Birds often perform this service, depositing seeds far and wide, but they are not alone. In the tropics, flying foxes and other large bats feed on fruit growing in the forest canopy, such as guavas, mangoes, breadfruit, carob, and figs. These fruits may not all be bright in color but they do have a potent smell to entice the bats. Spreading seeds via bats is called chiropterochory.

The Pemba flying fox, one of the largest fruit bats, emerges at dusk to forage for figs, mangoes, and breadfruit.

Sour cherry | *Prunus cerasus*
This tree is one of a large group of *Prunus* species known as "true cherries." They are native to the whole Northern Hemisphere, and are especially varied in East Asia.

Peach | *Prunus persica*
Peach trees have been cultivated in China since Neolithic times. The ripe fruit has a downy skin, whereas the skin of the closely related nectarine is smooth.

Apricot | *Prunus armeniaca* The most extensively cultivated species of apricot tree, *Prunus armeniaca* probably originated in Central Asia.

Fruit drupes

Many plant species produce drupes, with flesh surrounding a hard stone. In some cases, it is the flesh that is eaten, such as mangoes. For others, it is the stone, such as with almonds. These are commonly regarded as "nuts," which is incorrect.

Oblong, silvery-green leaves were used in traditional medicine

Mango | *Mangifera indica*
Indigenous to southern Asia, the mango has sweet, soft flesh that clings to its big stone. This encourages large animals, such as elephants, to swallow the stone, aiding seed dispersal.

Mango fruits of different cultivars range in size— the smallest are plum-sized

Ripe olive fruits (with the stone removed) consist of 20–30 percent oil

Olive | *Olea europaea*
The olive is one of the oldest of all drupes, first appearing around 40 million years ago. It has been used by humans for at least 100,000 years.

The hard fruits measure 2.5 cm (1 in) across

Amla | *Phyllanthus emblica*
Also known as the Indian gooseberry, the flesh of the amla has a sour, bitter taste, and is valued in South Asian cuisine. Cherished by Buddhists, it is known by them as myrobalan.

Loquat | *Eriobotrya japonica*
Widely grown in China, the loquat is loved for its sweet taste. It is seen as a symbol of wealth and happiness because of its golden color.

White sapote | *Casimiroa edulis*
A tropical fruiting tree of Mexico and Central America, the white sapote has thin-skinned drupes with an edible pulp. The seeds are said to cause drowsiness.

Soft seed fruits

△ **Citrus flowers** commonly have a rich, sweet scent.

Berries are soft, round, often edible fruits, typically containing seeds, but never stones. An avocado "stone" is actually a seed, so the avocado is a berry. Conversely, strawberries and raspberries are commonly thought of as berries, but botanically they are drupes (see pp.276–277). Berries are fruits that grow from the ovary of a single flower, with the outer layer of the ovary wall developing into the edible flesh.

The sweet, tangy, fragrant fruits, are best eaten when slightly overripe and softened

Persimmon | *Diospyros kaki*
The persimmon was cultivated in China around 2,000 years ago, and later introduced to Japan, where it is called *kaki*. Trees do not bear fruit for the first few years, but then crop for decades.

Valuable fruits

Berries are a key part of the human diet, and have been so since earliest days of *Homo sapiens*. Today, some berries are crops of vital economic significance. About 125 million people worldwide, for example, depend on coffee for their livelihoods.

Coffee leaves, berries, and seeds contain caffeine, which is thought to deter herbivores

The sweet berries (sometimes called "coffee cherries") are edible

Greenish-brown, edible skin

Kiwi fruit | *Actinidia deliciosa*
This confusingly named fruit naturally grows as a vine in the mountains of China (it is also known as Chinese gooseberry). It was introduced to New Zealand only in the 20th century.

Coffee | *Coffea arabica*
The "beans" roasted for drinks are the seeds of coffee berries. Native to East Africa but widely cultivated, *C. arabica* accounts for around 65 percent of global coffee production.

Yellow-orange flesh contains a cavity filled with numerous black seeds

Papaya | *Carica papaya*
Native to Central America, the papaya, or pawpaw, is now widely grown in the tropics and subtropics. Fruits form large clusters on the palmlike trees. Each fruit can weigh as much as 25 lb (11 kg).

American cranberry |
Vaccinium macrocarpon
Cranberries are widespread in the cooler parts of the northern hemisphere. The American cranberry is the species from northern North America.

There are more than 10,000 known varieties of grape; 1,368 are grown in cultivation—eaten fresh or dried, or used in the production of wine.

Blueberries are rich in antioxidants as well as vitamin C and fiber

Highbush blueberry |
Vaccinium corymbosum
Native to eastern North America,
the highbush blueberry is a deciduous
shrub that grows in dense thickets.

Avocado |
Persea americana
This evergreen tree or
shrub is native to Mexico,
and Central and South
America. Its fruits can be
cooked but are commonly
used raw in salads, drinks,
and desserts.

The lingonberry
has the highest
antioxidant content
of any berry

Lingonberry | *Vaccinium vitis-idaea*
The lingonberry is a small, acid-loving European
shrub native to the northern reaches of Europe,
Asia, and North America. Its tart red berries are
made into jams, sauces, preserves, and syrups.

Common grape | *Vitis vinifera*
The grapevine is a fast-growing liana, native
to a region that extends from the Mediterranean
to Central Asia. Wine grapes need long, dry,
warm-to-hot summers and cool winters.

Citrus

Tangy and acidic, citrus fruits originated in the
Himalayan foothills and were cultivated in the
Mediterranean more than 3,000 years ago. Many
citrus fruits we know are cultivated hybrids of
three wild plants: mandarin, pummelo, and citron.

Glossy double
(two-part)
leaves

Makrut lime |
Citrus hystrix
The fruits of the makrut lime,
although sour, are edible and
can be used like limes. The
leaves and the zest from the
knobbly rind are key flavoring
ingredients in Thai cuisine.

Mandarin leaves are
waxy and evergreen

Mandarin orange | *Citrus reticulata*
Originating in South China, the mandarin is one
of the key citrus fruits. The earliest mandarins
were quite bitter, but modern hybrids are sweet,
and they are renowned for being easy to peel.

Pummelo | *Citrus maxima*
Native to Southeast Asia,
the pummelo is the largest
citrus. It is the ancestor of
the grapefruit, but sweeter.
The orange is a hybrid of
pummelo and mandarin.

Citron | *Citrus medica*
Citrons are yellow-green
citrus fruits that resemble
large, knobbly lemons. Their
rind is so thick that they have
almost no juice, but they are
used for making candied peel.

The global grape

Viticulture

The earliest evidence of growing grapes to make wine,
known as viticulture, is from Georgia and dates back
at least 8,000 years. The Ancient Greeks spread
viticulture to Spain, and later the Romans took it
to France and Germany. When the Roman empire
collapsed, monasteries helped develop Europe's great
wine-making regions. Portuguese and Spanish
colonists introduced grapes to the Americas as early
as the mid-1500s. Today, viticulture is global, and wine
is made wherever there is a mild climate, including in
California, South Africa, and Australia.

Workers tread grapes in this 2nd-century mosaic
scene, discovered at a Roman villa in Mérida, Spain.

Pomes
Apple and relatives

△ **Apple blossoms** appear in spring, at the same time as the leaves.

Pomes are fruits of the *Malinae*—the shrubs and small trees that form the apple subgroup of the *Rosaceae* family. Pomes are "accessory" fruits, which means that their edible flesh does not develop from the ovary but from other (accessory) parts of the flower. The hypanthium, the flower tube at the base of the petals, fuses around the ovaries, and then swells to create a mass of solid, juicy flesh. Inside, the pericarp (ovary wall) containing the seeds forms an inedible core.

Apple size, shape, sweetness, and acidity depends on the variety

Apple | *Malus domestica*
The apple is the most widely grown pome, with more than 7,000 varieties worldwide and global production of around 88 million tons. Trees are propagated mostly by grafting.

The apple subgroup

There are around 1,100 *Malinae* species; all produce pomes, but only a few of them are eaten. Typically, *Malinae* blossom in spring, and the fruits develop through summer to ripen in the fall.

Wild apples have a rougher skin than domestic varieties

Wild apple | *Malus sieversii*
The wild ancestor of the domestic apple has long been celebrated in Central Asia, especially in Kazakhstan and the Tien Shan mountains. It is now considered at risk of extinction.

Common pear | *Pyrus communis*
Apples and pears are the most economically important pomes. The common pear, the source of most varieties, was cultivated in the Middle East and Europe thousands of years ago.

Although tiny and bitter, crab apples make delicious jelly

Crab apple | *Malus sylvestris*
The crab apple tree is so-named because it resembles a "crabbed" (gnarled and twisted) version of the apple tree. Crab apple trees are often covered in lichen and mistletoe.

The large, open calyx earns the medlar the nickname "monkey's bottom"

The fruit looks like a golden-yellow pear; when immature, it is covered in down

Medlar | *Mespilus germanica*
Medlar is an apple-like fruit cultivated since Roman times. It is too bitter to eat even when fully ripe, so it is left to over-ripen, or "blet." It develops an apple scent and honey-like flavor.

Quince | *Cydonia oblonga*
The fruit of the quince tree is hard and tart-tasting, even when ripe. However, once cooked with sugar, it makes sweet and citrusy marmalade, jam, and *dulce de membrillo* paste.

Asian pear | *Pyrus pyrifolia*
This type of pear is smaller, rounder, crisper, and sweeter than its European cousin. Following spring blossoms, the fruit takes four to seven months to fully ripen.

Leaves are green on top, white underneath

Small fruits turn vivid red in the fall

Tiny, apple-like fruits, or haws, are dense and dry

Leaflets have corrugated (rugose) edges

Reddish fruits, or hips, look like cherry tomatoes

Common whitebeam | *Sorbus aria*

The common whitebeam is native to Europe, where it is often planted as an ornamental in parks. Its small, hard fruits, which are popular with birds, are sometimes made into jam.

Common hawthorn | *Crataegus monogyna*

Also known as the mayflower (and the "faerie tree" in Ireland), the hawthorn forms the bulk of hedgerows across the UK, where its froth of white flowers scents the air in late spring.

Japanese rose | *Rosa rugosa*

One of several plants known as Japanese rose, *R. rugosa* is a hardy native of coastal sand dunes in eastern Asia. Used as an ornamental, it is now invasive in Europe and the Americas.

Fruits, called sorbs, are astringent and gritty

Common service tree | *Sorbus domestica*

This tree also goes by the name of sorb-apple. It is native to southern and central Europe, especially the Balkans. It is related to both rowans and the wild service tree (right).

Pinnate leaf, made up of numerous leaflets along a central stem

Wild service tree | *Sorbus torminalis*

Native to Europe, northern Africa, and southwestern Asia, this tree belongs to the same genus as rowan (*S. aucuparia*). Its fruit is seldom eaten, as it is not palatable until over-ripened.

Father of apples

Tracing the apple's ancestry

In the early 20th century, Russian botanist Nikolai Vavilov traced the apple's ancestry to a single grove near Kazakhstan's largest city, Almaty (its former name, *Alma-Ata*, means "father of apples"). Vavilov found apples growing wild, densely tangled, in the nearby Tien-Shan mountains. The locally popular aport apple developed from these. In Soviet times, many orchards were destroyed, but there are now efforts to restore them.

Toyon | *Heteromeles arbutifolia*

Sometimes called the Christmas berry or California holly, this California native is prized for its pretty white flowers, which are borne in early summer, and its deep red clusters of fall fruit.

Toyon fruit is edible, but the pips are poisonous

Medieval illustration of apple-picking

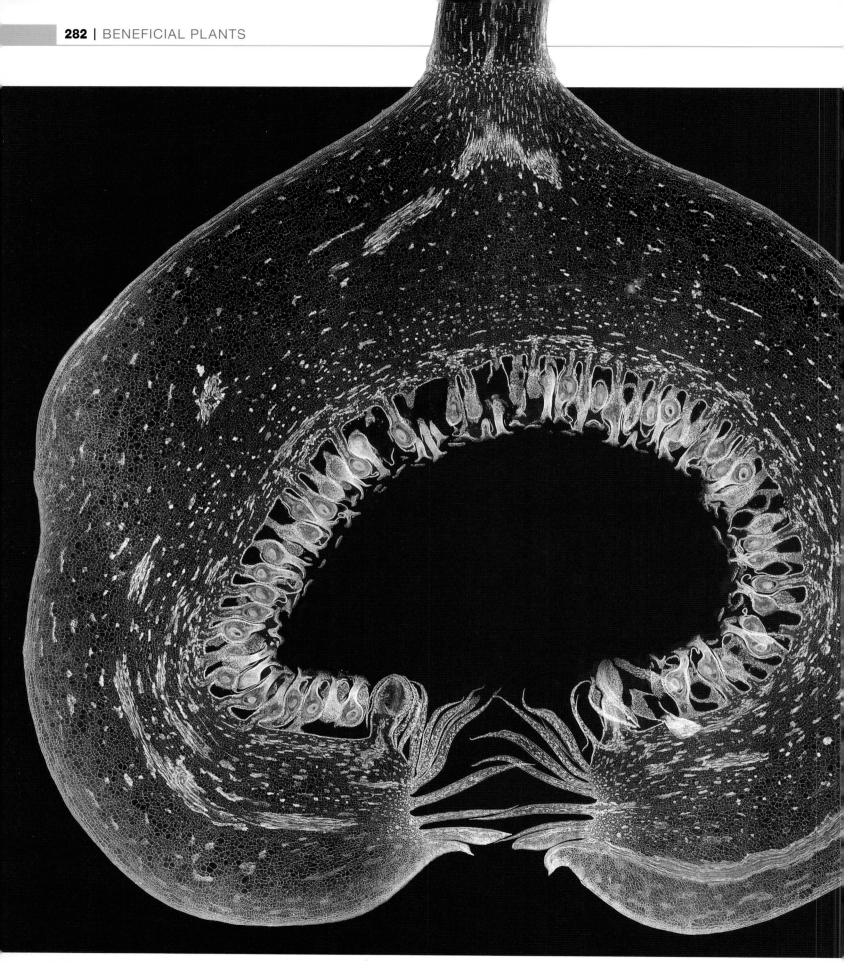

A micrograph of a fig tree's syconium reveals its fleshy interior, lined with flowers, and the tiny ostiole (opening), fringed with bracts, which will be the entry point for a female wasp.

FIG | 283

Fig

The fruit with extra crunch

A ripe fig from the tree *Ficus carica*, native from the eastern Mediterranean to Central Asia, is not strictly a fruit but an inflorescence—a fleshy, bulbous stem (syconium) that encloses clusters of flowers. Such an arrangement could make pollination tricky, so most cultivated fig trees are propagated from cuttings—a practice that scientists believe began in the Near East up to 11,400 years ago. However, the cultivated Smyrna and San Pedro varieties, plus some 850 wild *Ficus* species (many with inedible fruits) each have their own unique tiny wasp pollinator.

In a remarkable tale of coevolution dating back 70 million years, *Ficus* plants developed a special relationship with wasps from the family *Agaonidae*. When the fig's female flowers require pollination, the fig tree sends out an aromatic signal that attracts a queen fig wasp, which squeezes into the syconium through a tiny opening (ostiole). The female deposits pollen, collected from the syconium in which she developed, and lays eggs on the tiny flowers that will feed her progeny as they develop. The female then dies in the fig. Wingless male wasps hatch first and mate with emerging females. Males may chew an escape route out of the fig for the females, but then also die, while the females leave, fly to other figs and repeat the cycle.

A fig (*Ficus carica*) leaf

Young green buds on a fig tree branch signal the beginning of the syconium's development.

The syconium develops and swells as flowers begin to form on the fleshy interior.

A queen fig wasp, pregnant with eggs and bearing pollen, is attracted to a ripening syconium.

The ostiole on the base of each fig loosens temporarily to admit a wasp when the fig is ready for pollination.

Historians believe that the fruit eaten by Eve in the Garden of Eden, was a fig, not an apple.

Tomato family
Essential ingredient

△ **Eggplant flowers** are self-pollinating, containing both pollen-producing anthers and pollen-receiving pistils.

The plants we know as tomatoes belong to a group of more than 2,300 species that make up the *Solanum* genus. These plants, which all tend to grow as vines or shrubs, have interesting chemistry and poisonous leaves. However, their fruits and tubers also provide us with some of the world's most important foods, including eggplants and potatoes, as well as tomatoes. *Solanum* is the largest genus in the nightshade family, the *Solanaceae*—which is also sometimes, confusingly, referred to as the Solanum family.

Fruits ripen into a variety of colors, including red, orange, yellow, and purple

Tomato | *Solanum lycopersicum*
Though largely considered a vegetable, in botanical terms the tomato is a fruit—a kind of berry. *S. lycopersicum* is the domesticated form of the wild tomato, and a key ingredient of cuisines throughout the world.

Tomatoes

Tomatoes originated in the South American Andes and were used by the Aztecs at the time of the conquest by Spain. The Spanish brought them to Europe, and European colonizers spread them around the world.

Orange-yellow flesh surrounds the pulp and small seeds

Naranjilla | *Solanum quitoense*
A delicate, tomato-like fruit that grows in shady places in northwestern South America, the naranjilla has a citrus flavor. The hairy, brown coat that protects the fruits is easily rubbed off when they are ripe, revealing the orange skin.

Tamarillo | *Solanum betaceum*
Originating in the Andes, the tamarillo, or tomato tree, is now grown worldwide. It has egg-shaped fruits that turn red when ripe. The skin is bitter, but the flesh is juicy, with a sweet-sour taste. Unripe fruits are slightly toxic.

African eggplant | *Solanum aethiopicum*
Also known as the bitter tomato, this relative of the tomato is a traditional vegetable used in many African countries, including Uganda and Nigeria. The nutritious leaves are also eaten as a leafy vegetable.

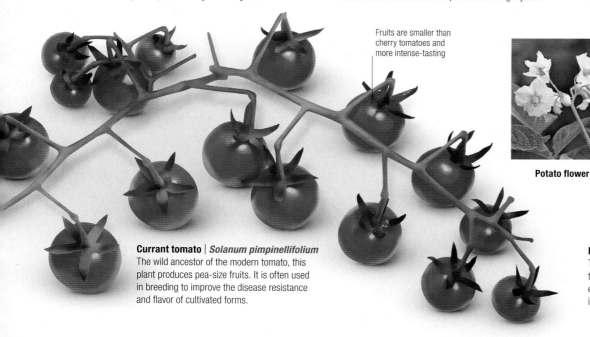

Fruits are smaller than cherry tomatoes and more intense-tasting

Currant tomato | *Solanum pimpinellifolium*
The wild ancestor of the modern tomato, this plant produces pea-size fruits. It is often used in breeding to improve the disease resistance and flavor of cultivated forms.

Skin varies from light brown to purple

Potato flower

Potato | *Solanum tuberosum*
The potato is one of the world's major food crops. Like the tomato, it originated in the Andes, but the key part for eating is the underground tuber, not the fruit. Being rich in starch, potatoes are a good source of carbohydrates.

> ## "What I say is that, if a fellow really likes potatoes, he must be a pretty decent sort of fellow."
>
> A. A. **Milne** British author, 1926

Wolf-apple flowers

Wolf-apple | *Solanum lycocarpum*
A South American food crop, the wolf-apple is so-named because it is widely eaten by the maned wolf of the Cerrado—the Brazilian savanna.

Wolf-apple fruits measure up to 5 in (13 cm) in diameter

Turkey berries are roughly pea-size

The fruit is a large berry with a glossy surface

Turkey berry | *Solanum torvum*
Usually consisting of a single stem, this spiky shrub gives clusters of berries which, though yellowish when fully ripe, are harvested for use while still green.

Eggplant | *Solanum melongena*
Native to Southeast Asia, the fruit of this plant is used in many Mediterranean and Middle Eastern dishes, such as moussaka.

Peppers

Peppers, or capsicums, are a genus of about 30 species of flowering plants in the nightshade family that are native to the tropical Americas. Some are widely grown for their fleshy or pungently flavored fruits.

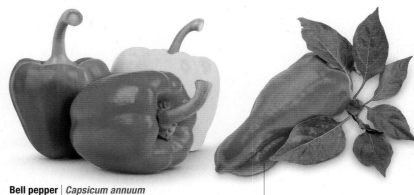

Bell pepper | *Capsicum annuum*
Originating in tropical America, bell peppers produce fleshy fruits that are used in salads and cooked dishes. Cultivars produce fruit in a range of colors, including candy-striped forms.

Fruit is mild-tasting and slightly sweet

Chile pepper | *Capsicum spp.*
Known as chile peppers, some cultivars of *C. annuum*, including jalapeño, bear pungent fruits that are used to add "heat" to foods. *C. chinense* is a capsicum species that produces super-hot varieties, such as habanero.

Chile pepper flower

Flesh of chile peppers contains capsaicin—the chemical that gives chiles their "heat"

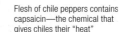

Murder and magic

Noxious nightshades

Many plants in the *Solanaceae*, or nightshade family, contain potent alkaloid chemicals, such as the tropanes in mandrake (*Mandragora officinarum*), belladonna (*Atropa belladonna*), and black henbane/ stinking nightshade (*Hyoscyamus niger*). Tropanes can be poisonous and also hallucinogenic, and these plants have become deeply intertwined with witchcraft, magic, and murder— as well as, in the modern age, the design of many therapeutic drugs.

Black henbane may have been what Viking warriors took to send them "berserk" before going into battle.

Melepego Indicus flauus
cum semine suo aperto
ubi conspiciuntur semina.

Melon vines have strong, scrambling stems, large palmate leaves, typically yellow flowers, and clinging tendrils.

Melons and squashes

Firm and fleshy

△ **The flowers of the cucumber** (*Cucumis sativus*) emerge between large leaves that shield young fruits.

Melons, squashes, and watermelons belong to the family *Cucurbitaceae*, comprising some 975 species. Known as cucurbits or gourds, many have been cultivated for more than 11,000 years for their edible fruits—botanically "pepos," a type of berry. Most species have white or yellow flowers and are fast-growing vines that trail or climb. The majority prefer warm climates; only a few, such as cucumbers and summer squashes, can tolerate the cold.

Melons and cucumbers

Many gherkins, melons, and cucumbers belong to the *Cucumis* genus, native to Africa and southern Asia. The plants have tendrils and are creepers or climbers with fleshy, edible fruits that are mostly eaten raw or may be pickled.

The cucumber's surface is covered with spines

Maroon cucumber | *Cucumis anguria*
Native to southwest Africa, this plant is naturalized in the New World, where its fruit is often pickled. It is the only *Cucumis* species with prickly stems and leaf stalks.

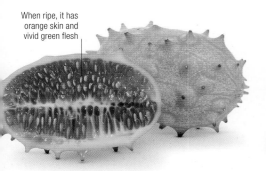

When ripe, it has orange skin and vivid green flesh

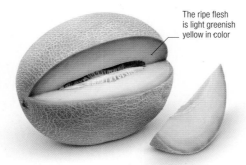

The ripe flesh is light greenish yellow in color

Bees pollinate the bright yellow flowers

Horned melon | *Cucumis metuliferus*
Sometimes known as kiwano, the horned melon fruit is a traditional food in its native Africa. Sweet when ripe, it has edible seeds, and its green flesh is said to taste like a mixture of melon, banana, and lime.

Honeydew melon | *Cucumis melo*
Oval-shaped with a smooth skin, the honeydew is one of many cultivated melon varieties that share the same *C. melo* species name. Türkiye and China are the biggest producers.

Cucumber | *Cucumis sativus*
The plant is a creeping vine, which in different varieties produces small gherkins (often pickled) and larger salad cucumbers. The long, green fruits are more than 90 percent water.

The mottled or striped green shell encloses red, pink, or yellow flesh

Ribbed skin identifies the European cantaloupe

The seeds, though used in Ayurvedic medicine, are not considered edible

Watermelon | *Citrullus lanatus*
This species is native to Africa's eastern Sahara Desert, where archaeologists have found related seeds dating back 6,000 years. The fruits can weigh 4–44 lb (2–20 kg).

Cantaloupe | *Cucumis melo* var. *cantalupensis*
This name generally refers to orange-fleshed melons cultivated in Europe, but is sometimes inaccurately used for American muskmelons (*C. melo* var. *reticulatus*), which have musky, netted skins.

Bitter melon | *Momordica charantia*
Native to tropical and subtropical areas of the Old World, bitter melon—harvested before it is fully ripe—is widely used in Asian and Chinese dishes, and in traditional medicine.

Squashes

Cultivated up to 10,000 years ago, fruits of the *Cucurbita* genus of New World plants include summer squashes, such as zucchini, and winter squashes, such as pumpkins.

Summer squash | *Cucurbita pepo*
Cultivars of *C. pepo* produce both winter squashes and smaller, summer zucchini, harvested while immature and known as courgettes in the UK.

When ripe, this squash can weigh up to 20 lb (9 kg)

Cushaw squash | *Cucurbita argyrosperma*
Native to Central and South America, this winter squash is mainly cultivated for its oil-rich seeds, although the fruit and flowers are also eaten.

Winter squash | *Cucurbita* spp.
The term "winter squash" is applied to several species and named cultivars of *Cucurbita* that can be stored during winter, including the common pumpkin, *C. pepo*.

Under its tough skin, the flesh is white.

Asian pumpkin | *Cucurbita ficifolia*
The perennial climber that produces this melon-shaped squash is native to South America. The fruit is eaten raw and cooked, and its seeds are often roasted.

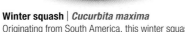
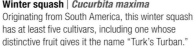

This squash is ripe if it sounds hollow when tapped

Winter squash | *Cucurbita maxima*
Originating from South America, this winter squash has at least five cultivars, including one whose distinctive fruit gives it the name "Turk's Turban."

Pattypan squash | *Cucurbita pepo* var. *clypeata*
This flattish, round summer squash with scalloped edges has a nutty flavor and is at its most tender if harvested when 2–4 in (5–10 cm) in diameter.

Spaghetti squash | *Cucurbita pepo* subsp. *pepo*
When cooked, the flesh of this orange, carotene-rich *C. pepo* subspecies falls away in spaghetti-like ribbons or strands—hence its common name.

In 2023, a record pumpkin in the US weighed in at 2,749 lb (1,247 kg).

Hundreds of pumpkins (*Cucurbita pepo*) ripening in the US, where farmers in the top six pumpkin-growing states produced more than 2,232,142 tons (2,267,961 metric tons) in 2022.

Butternut squash | *Cucurbita moschata*
This winter squash species, a scrambling vine native to Central and South America, produces heavy, long, pear-shaped fruits, enjoyed in a variety of savory dishes.

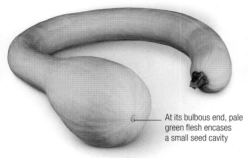

At its bulbous end, pale green flesh encases a small seed cavity

Tromboncino squash | *Cucurbita moschata*
This heirloom species, cultivated over generations in Liguria, Italy, is a climbing vine with long, hanging fruits. It is one of a few winter squashes also harvested in summer.

Gourds

The fruits of some members of the *Cucurbitaceae* family have particularly hard, strong shells known as gourds, which have long been used to make spoons, bowls, jewelery, and even musical instruments.

Wax gourd | *Benincasa hispida*
The fruit of the wax gourd, a trailing vine native to islands of the southwest Pacific, has a thick, waxy skin that gives it a long shelf life. Its flesh is used in soups and curries.

Bottle gourd | *Lagenaria siceraria*
With a native range of western tropical Africa to Ethiopia and Tanzania, this vine is grown for its edible, hard-shelled fruits that are traditionally used as bowls and utensils.

Luffa gourd | *Luffa aegyptiaca*
While the young fruit of this vine is edible, the mature fruit is tough and is best known for its fibrous interior; when dried it can be used as a bath sponge or scrubbing brush.

Cucamelon | *Melothria scabra*
Named for its tiny fruit's watermelon appearance and cucumber taste, this newly popular species has long been cultivated in its native Mexico and Central America.

The long, slim fruits can reach more than 5 ft (1.5 m) in length

Snake gourd | *Trichosanthes cucumerina*
Native to southern and eastern Asia, and northern Australia, this vine bears snakelike fruits, picked when young. The red pulp is cooked as a tomato substitute.

Calabash

Music-making gourds

Two species popularly named "calabash"—the bottle gourd (*Lagenaria siceraria*) and the calabash tree (*Crescentia cujete*) from the Americas—bear similar round or oval fruits. The hard shells of these fruits have long been used to create traditional musical instruments, from the kora—a West African harp-lute—to Indian stringed instruments, such as the sitar, surbahar, and tanpura.

The calabash tree grows in wet, tropical areas.

Wild date palm | *Phoenix sylvestris* This wild species is native to South Asia. *Phoenix dactylifera*, its close relative, is the main cultivated species of date palm.

Palm fruit

Tropical delights

△ **Chilean wine palm fruits** resemble miniature coconuts and taste similar.

Palms comprise **2,600 species** of perennial flowering plants in the family *Arecaceae*. Most are native to tropical and subtropical regions, where they naturally grow in moist, humid forests. Although they are often described as trees, botanically, a palm is a woody herbaceous plant like bamboo or banana. Palms produce various edible fruits, the best-known being coconuts and dates.

Useful palms

Most palm fruits are drupes (see pp.276–277), and many are edible. Some palm fruits contain useful oil, while others are harvested for their heart of palm—the pale, white, inner core of the palm.

Peach palm | *Bactris gasipaes*
The peach palm is a long-lived perennial tree native to Central and South America. The small, tough fruits are highly nutritious, but must be stewed for hours to be edible.

Betel fruits turn from green to yellowish-red as they ripen

Ripe açaí berries have a sharp, earthy taste, with hints of dark chocolate and blackberry

Salak fruits are sweet and acidic, with a taste like pineapple

Betel nut palm | *Areca catechu*
Native to the Philippines, the betel nut palm is cultivated widely. In many Asian and Pacific countries, people chew its "nuts" (seeds) for their stimulant effect.

Açaí palm | *Euterpe oleracea*
This South American palm is cultivated for both its fruit and its edible heart. Although it bears large clusters of fruit all year, they are not harvested during the rainy season.

Salak palm | *Salacca zalacca*
A short-stemmed, massive-leaved palm of Indonesia, the salak has fig-size fruits. The "snakeskin" peel surrounds garlic-like lobes that are used in soups or pickled.

Jelly palm | *Butia capitata*
Native to Brazil, Uruguay, and Argentina, the fruits of this palm have bright orange, fragrant flesh. It is used to make juices, alcoholic drinks, jellies, and ice cream.

Chilean wine palm |
Jubaea chilensis
This Chilean palm has edible fruit, and its sap is made into the syrup *miel de palma* (palm honey) or palm wine.

Oil palm | *Elaeis guineensis*
The fruit of this palm yields oil that is used in many food products. Swathes of forest are felled to create palm oil plantations, raising serious environmental concerns.

Desert food source

Date palms

Sometimes called the desert palm, the date palm (*Phoenix dactylifera*) can be cultivated in arid regions where few other crops are able to grow. Date palms are highly valued because they make it possible to live in places such as deserts and oases, where there would otherwise be little food. The palms grow very tall, sometimes reaching more than 100 ft (30 m), and bear fruit throughout the year. They can survive long periods of drought and extremely high temperatures.

Date palms provide food for animals as well as people, as seen in this Roman mosaic from 2nd-century Lebanon.

Coconuts can drift for thousands of miles at sea. Germination is slow, and the thick husk helps stop the shoot from growing before the coconut reaches land.

Coconuts are grown throughout the tropics, where they can take up to 20 years to reach peak production.

The outer husk of the coconut is green when young, maturing to brown. Young fruits are harvested for coconut milk.

Harvesting is done by hand, either by climbing the trees or using a cherry picker. The trees can reach 98 ft (30 m) tall.

Coconut fiber, or coir, is an important commercial product. The biggest producers are India, Sri Lanka, and Vietnam.

Coconut
The ocean wanderer

The coconut palm (*Cocos nucifera*) is well known for its fruit, which has a delicious flavor. The edible white flesh is encased in a hard, hairy shell, while the hollow center contains a tasty liquid known as coconut milk. The nuts have a remarkable capacity for dispersal, because they float easily in their thick outer husks, and can survive at sea for 120 days and still take root when they reach land. Coconuts were domesticated thousands of years ago by people in Southeast Asia, and were later introduced by Europeans to the Americas. But opinion is divided as to where the species originated—and whether, in fact, the nuts could have floated naturally all the way across the Pacific.

The inside of a coconut is hollow.

A **single palm can** produce around 180 coconuts a year.

Palm fiber

Woven armor

Between the thick outer husk and the hard inner shell of a coconut is a layer of fiber called coir. "Brown coir," from ripe coconuts, is highly resistant to salt water and is used to make products such as ropes, mats, baskets, and brooms. "White coir," from unripe nuts, is used for finer brushes, string, and fishing nets. Today, coir is also used for potting medium, as an alternative to peat. In the 19th century, the warriors of the Gilbert Islands, in the Pacific Ocean, even made armor out of woven coir.

Gilbert Islands warriors in armor.

Nuts
Hard shells

△ **Almond blossoms** (*Prunus amygdalus*) appear before the leaves in early spring.

A nut is a fruit with a tough shell and a kernel inside that is usually edible. While most nuts are also seeds, not all seeds are nuts. Botanically, true nuts are fruits with a hard outer shell that does not crack open naturally, but in general usage, nuts are any edible kernel with a shell. Some of the foods we call "nuts," such as almonds, pistachios, walnuts, and pecans, are really drupes, like plums and peaches. Coconuts are "dry drupes."

True nuts

In most true nuts, the edible portion is the plant embryo, which stores protein and fat to nourish the young seedling plant. The nutshell protects the kernel from contamination.

Hazelnut | *Corylus avellana*
Hazel trees are a traditional feature of British hedgerows. Their yellow male catkins and red-centered, female flowers appear on the same tree in late winter to early spring.

The nut of the hazel tree is called a cob

Macadamia nuts have the hardest shell of any nut.

Single nut in a spiny case

Sweet chestnut | *Castanea sativa*
The nuts of this native of southern Europe and Asia Minor have been used in cooking since ancient times. Sweet chestnut trees are very long-lived: the Hundred Horse chestnut in Sicily is maybe 4,000 years old.

Glossy, brown nut has a pale attachment scar, or hilum, at one end

Chinese chestnut | *Castanea mollissima*
This chestnut is native to China, Taiwan, and Korea. It is an important food source for wildlife and a key ingredient in Asian cuisine. A spiny cupule protects two or three nuts.

Legume "nuts"

Despite the name, peanuts are not botanically nuts, but legumes, like peas. They produce multiple seeds in a pod, which do not grow on trees, like true nuts.

Peanuts have a high oil content

Peanut | *Arachis hypogaea*
While the peanut, or groundnut, plant flowers above the soil surface, its nuts form underground. Peanuts are farmed in huge quantities in the tropics and subtropics. They are usually sold with their shells removed, or are processed for oil.

Troubling trend

Nut allergies

Nuts are a highly nutritious food, eaten by humans since prehistory. But some people, especially children, have a serious allergic reaction to them, and the incidence of nut allergies seems to be on the rise. Nut allergy is one of the most dangerous food allergies because it can cause severe and even fatal reactions (anaphylaxis). As well as the nuts themselves, nut oils and butters can trigger allergic reactions. More than six million Americans of all ages are allergic to peanuts and nearly four million are allergic to tree nuts. For many sufferers, the allergy lasts their whole lifetime.

Certain proteins in peanuts trigger reactions in people with peanut allergy. Some people allergic to peanuts are also allergic to tree nuts.

Tree nuts and seeds

The seeds of some fruit-bearing trees are called tree nuts. They typically have a very hard shell and leathery "meat" inside. Like peanuts, these nuts can provoke dangerous allergic reactions.

Up to 24 nuts grow like orange segments inside a hard pod

Three-sided nutshell is very hard

Bunches of up to 20 nuts form on the trees

Brazil nut | *Bertholletia excelsa*
The Brazil nut, or *castanha-do-pará*, is not usually cultivated but harvested from stands of wild trees that grow in the Amazon forest, causing significant environmental damage.

Macadamia | *Macadamia integrifolia*
Australia's most popular nut grows on small to medium-size trees that are native to the Queensland rainforests. Most macadamia nuts eaten in the US are grown in Hawaii.

Kola nut | *Cola nitida/acuminata*
The evergreen kola nut tree of West African rainforests is now cultivated widely. The bitter nuts contain caffeine. They are chewed as stimulants and used to make cola drinks.

Drupes

Some nuts are fruit drupes with no flesh, just a hard case with an edible seed inside. Cashews are drupes, not legumes like peanuts, and, like all drupes, they grow on trees.

Tough hull encloses the edible kernel

The hull of the pecan starts off green but gradually dries and turns brown

Two-part kernel

Fruits are surrounded by a thick, leathery, gray-green hull

Common walnut | *Juglans regia*
Today, China is the leading producer of the walnut, which originated in Iran. Trees usually fruit five years after being planted. Walnut wood is prized for furniture-making.

Candlenut | *Aleurites moluccanus*
The candlenut, a Southeast Asian species, is widely used in Indonesian and Malaysian cuisine. In Hawaii, candlenuts, or *kukui*, were traditionally burned to give light

Pecan | *Carya illinoinensis*
The pecan is a species of hickory native to the southern US and northern Mexico. With a rich, buttery, slightly sweet taste, pecans are often used in desserts such as pecan pie.

Almond | *Prunus amygdalus*
The almond tree is native to Iran and the Eastern Mediterranean region. It was one of the earliest domesticated fruit trees, because it is easy to grow from seed.

Pistachio | *Pistacia vera*
A small tree of the cashew family, the pistachio is thought to originate from Iran. Its nuts are used in baklava, ice cream, and other desserts, and added to sweet foods to give yellow-green coloring.

The fruits grow on the pistachio tree in clusters

Each leaf is made of up to five pairs of broad, leathery leaflets

The case splits to reveal a greenish nut coated with a thin, reddish skin

Wild Fruit. 40.

Kajoo

Anacardium occidentale

Cashew nut.

Draw 9 N. 27 P. 140

The cashew tree (*Anacardium occidentale*) bears oblong leaves with a notched tip, delicate pink and white flowers, and fruits attached to oblong "pseudofruits" called cashew apples.

41. Gumiferous Tree.

Draw 9 No 6
_PP. 62. 63_

Sahlphul.
बल्लफल
Baswellia serrata
or thurifera.
Cdstanka Aniek
Scale of Inches Res. No 9 h
— Page 376.

Cashew nut
Nutty apple

Cashews, with their sweet crunch and buttery texture, are among the most popular of all edible nuts. In Western countries, they are eaten as protein-rich snacks, while in South and Southeast Asia, they are a much-used ingredient in many dishes. Cashew trees (_Anacardium occidentale_) originated in Brazil and were carried to Africa and India by Portuguese missionaries in the 16th century. The evergreen trees, which grow to 40 ft (12 m) tall, are now widely cultivated in South and Southeast Asia, West and East Africa, and South America.

The cashew is usually described as a nut, but it is not quite what it seems. The cashew tree yields what appear to be apple-shaped fruits, called cashew apples. However, the cashew apple is not a fruit, but an enlarged stem, called a hypocarp, that can be eaten fresh or cooked, or fermented to produce vinegar. The true fruit emerges from the lower end of the cashew apple and looks a little like a kidney bean. It is a drupe—a fleshy fruit containing a central kernel—the cashew "nut." The nut is enclosed in two layers—a thin, smooth, greenish-brown coat and a hard shell, both of which must be removed before the nut can be eaten.

The drupe and the larger hypocarp

Dangerous cover

Toxic hazard

In Western stores, cashews are usually sold as the kernel alone, with the outer layers removed. There is a good reason for this: between the two outer layers sits an oil resin (cashew nut shell liquid, CNSL) so toxic that it can blister skin. When harvested, cashew apples are picked by hand, then the drupes are detached and laid in the sun for the resin to dry out, or roasted until the drupes crack open and the resin catches fire. CNSL has a variety of industrial applications.

After being harvested, the true fruits are separated from the orange or red cashew apples and dried in the sun.

Lettuce | *Lactuca sativa* Originally farmed by the ancient Egyptians, lettuce is now widely used for salads, in a huge variety of forms.

Leafy greens
Edible leaves

△ **Watercress** has a peppery, slightly bitter taste and is a source of iron; calcium; and vitamins A, C, and E.

The large, green leaves of many vegetables are eaten for their taste and health benefits, either raw as salad or cooked (typically boiled or stir-fried). While there are around 1,000 species of vegetable with edible leaves, not counting their cultivars, the average supermarket rarely stocks more than a handful of different types. Leafy greens are typically low in fat, high in fiber, and rich in vitamins C and especially K. However, the leaves may lose much of their vitamin content if they are not eaten soon after cutting, and some leafy greens have relatively short shelf lives.

Spinach | *Spinacia oleracea*
A native of Persia, this versatile leaf is eaten raw or cooked. It is famed for its high levels of iron and vitamins A and C, and as the source of strength of the cartoon character Popeye.

Cool climates

Leafy greens in cool climates tend to have more tender leaves than those in warm climates, because they do not need to be so tough to reduce water loss. Many belong to the large cabbage and mustard family, the brassicas.

Bok choy | *Brassica rapa* subsp. *chinensis*
Also called pak choi, this large leafy vegetable belonging to the mustard family is widely used in Chinese cooking. It has green, ruffled leaves and smooth, white, juicy stems.

Watercress leaves are eaten when still young

Brussels sprouts |
Brassica oleracea var. *gemmifera*
These mini-cabbages of Mediterranean origin have long been grown in northern Europe, especially Belgium (hence the common name).

Watercress | *Nasturtium officinale*
Native to Europe but naturalized elsewhere in streams, pools, and ditches, watercress is a hardy, creeping perennial. It may be one of the earliest leaves eaten by humans.

Garden orache | *Atriplex hortensis*
Orache is a hardy annual, saltier but very similar in taste and texture to spinach. It was part of the Mediterranean diet in ancient times and is growing in popularity today.

The outermost leaves go darkest green

There are many colorful cultivars of chard

Cabbage | *Brassica oleracea* var. *capitata*
Cabbages are large, densely packed heads of leaves formed by some cultivars of the European wild cabbage, *Brassica oleracea*. They are typically white-green or red-purple.

Sorrel | *Rumex acetosa*
A native of Eurasian grasslands, sorrel still commonly grows wild. Its tangy leaves can be cooked like spinach, added to salads to give a zesty kick, or used as a culinary herb.

Kale | *Brassica oleracea* var. *acephala*
Like cabbages, kale and its acephala cousins are descended from wild cabbage, but they lack a central head of leaves (*acephala* means "without a head").

Chard | *Beta vulgaris* subsp. *cicla*
Young chard leaves are eaten raw in salads, while older leaves are fried or sautéed to remove the slightly bitter taste. Chard leaves do not travel well once harvested.

Warm climates

A much wider variety of green leaves is eaten in the tropics, although the leaves tend to be smaller and chewier than those of the brassicas grown in cooler regions. As long as they are well watered, many of these leafy greens can be harvested year-round.

The leaves are a key ingredient in Burmese salads

The leaves are widely used in Southeast Asian dishes

Gotu kola | *Centella asiatica*
The swamp-growing gotu kola, also called Asian pennywort, is a popular ingredient of dishes in Southeast Asia and Oceania. It is also valued for its wound-healing properties.

Water spinach | *Ipomoea aquatica*
Flourishing freely in waterways, this Southeast Asian creeping vine can grow up to 4 in (10 cm) per day and is considered an invasive species in some places.

Flowers are individually small but form showy pompom clusters

Mimosoid leaves are easily digested by livestock

Soft, pungent leaves

Ulam raja | *Cosmos caudatus*
A plant of Mexico and tropical South America, this plant is naturalized in other tropical zones. Called *ulam raja* ("king's salad") in Malaysia, it is often eaten dipped in shrimp and chile paste.

Caigua | *Cyclanthera pedata*
This vine has long been cultivated in the Andes for its fruit, which is cooked stuffed with other ingredients, and for its young leaves, which are eaten raw or cooked.

As well as being vitamin-rich, aibika leaves are high in protein

The leaves have an unpleasant odor that is eliminated by cooking

Mimosoid |
Leucaena leucocephala
Young mimosoid leaves are eaten in salads and soups or cooked as a vegetable. Originally a native tree of Mexico and Central America, it is now widely grown in tropical regions to provide fodder for livestock.

The flowers give pods eaten as *phak krathin* in Southeast Asia and *guaje* in Mexico

Aibika | *Abelmoschus manihot*
Leaves of aibika, or sunset hibiscus, are used in salads and in the Filipino dishes *pinangat*, *tinola*, and *sinigang*. Aibika is native to tropical and subtropical Asia and northeast Australia.

Climbing wattle | *Senegalia pennata*
In Southeast Asia and parts of India, the leaves of the vine-like climbing wattle are used in omelets, curries, stir-fries, and soups. The leaves also have medicinal uses.

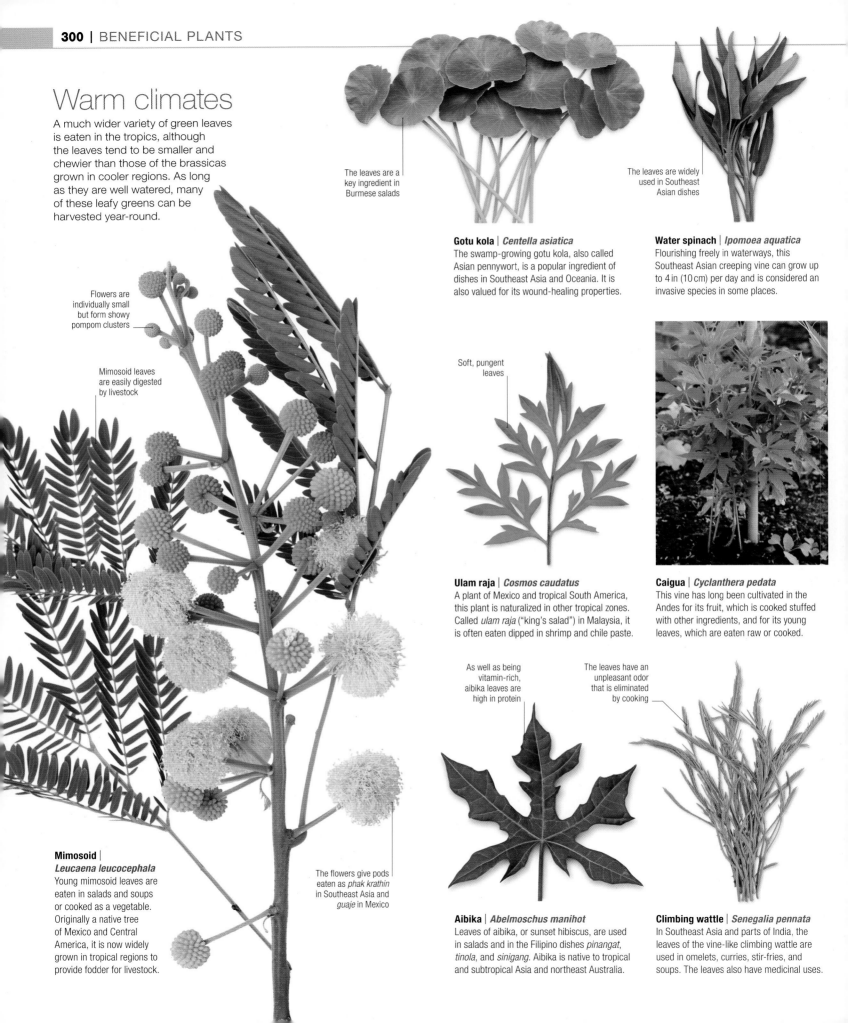

Deeply veined, leaves are up to 6 in (15 cm) long

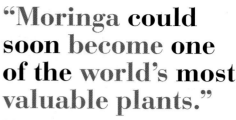

"**Moringa could soon become one of the world's most valuable plants.**"
Noel **Vietmeyer**
US National Academy of Sciences

Mauka | *Mirabilis expansa*
This was a key root and leaf vegetable for the Incas of ancient South America. Mauka is still valued today in Ecuador and Peru, because it grows at high altitudes in the Andes.

Green amaranth | *Amaranthus viridis*
This annual is widely used in *saag* dishes in India and Bangladesh, rather than spinach. Red amaranth was popular with the Aztecs of ancient Mexico.

The vitamin- and mineral-rich leaves are used fresh or ground into a powder and added to dishes

Leaves can be vivid pink as well as green

Chaya | *Cnidoscolus aconitifolius*
Probably originating in the Yucatán Peninsula, Mexico, this fast-growing tree or shrub was cultivated by the Mayans. In Central America, it is used as an alternative to spinach.

Lagos spinach |
Celosia argentea var. *argentea*
This colorful plant is widely eaten as boiled greens in West Africa, but it is considered a troublesome weed in parts of southern Asia.

Like the rest of the drumstick tree, its flowers are edible

Moringa | *Moringa oleifera*
This native Indian tree is now grown as a crop in warm places around the world. Its leaves, roots, and immature pods are consumed as vegetables; the edible seeds also yield oil.

The bitter leaves taste mildly sweet and nutty when cooked

African cabbage | *Cleome gynandra*
Cleome gynandra of Africa is now widespread in the tropics. Its leaves are dried and mixed with milk or butter in sub-Saharan Africa, and pickled with rice water in Southeast Asia.

Melinjo | *Gnetum gnemon*
This Southeast Asian plant is a relative of conifers. It is called melinjo in Indonesia, where it is used in the cherished vegetable curry of the Aceh region, *kuah pliek*.

Living off the land

Bush food

For tens of thousands of years, Indigenous Australians ate "bush food" growing wild or cultivated at low intensity. Nutritious and sustainable, bush food included leaves such as river mint (*Mentha australis*), New Zealand spinach (*Tetragonia tetragonioides*), and mountain pepper (*Tasmannia lanceolata*). The arrival of Europeans had a devastating effect on the availability of bush food, as wild land was lost to agriculture and settlement, and nonnative foods were introduced. Today, people once again value bush food as an important resource.

Young shoots of New Zealand spinach (*Tetragonia tetragonioides*).

Edible flowers and stems
Floral flavors

△ **Unless harvested,** leeks (*Allium ampeloprasum*) produce pink or white flowers.

With most plants, it is the seeds, fruit, leaves, and roots that we eat, but some kinds of flower, bud, stem, and stalk are also edible. Edible blooms such as nasturtiums are easy to identify as flowers, but others, such as capers (unopened flower buds), have less obvious flowering structures. Stems include bulbs, which are underground leaf shoots with modified scales or buds. For example, the edible bulbs of onions are among the world's most important culinary crops.

The edible leaves have a stronger flavor than the stalks

Celery | *Apium graveolens*
A native of the Mediterranean and Middle East, celery has crunchy, edible stalks that are eaten raw or added to dishes such as soups and stews.

Stems, stalks, and bulbs

Grocery stores typically stock a range of edible stems, stalks, and bulbs, including garlic, onion, and celery. Some other bulbs, including grape hyacinth, can also be eaten, although they are not necessarily especially tasty.

Each garlic bulb consists of several segments, or cloves, covered by papery skin

Asparagus has almost no leaves, just small scales

Onion | *Allium cepa*
Originating in southwest Asia, the onion is not particularly nutritious, but is used in cooking worldwide because its strong flavor enhances many dishes.

Asparagus | *Asparagus officinalis*
In spring, the young asparagus stems, or "spears," that appear above ground are cut for eating while still soft and tender. *A. officinalis*, garden asparagus, is the main edible species.

Rhubarb | *Rheum rhabarbarum*
The tart-tasting red stalk of rhubarb that is stewed to fill pies and crumbles looks like a stem, but it is actually a large leaf stalk, or petiole.

The white and light green parts are the tenderest and most flavorful

Eye-watering vegetable

Why onions make you cry

Like all alliums, onions absorb sulfur from the soil. The sulfur links to amino acids in the plant's cells to form compounds called sulfoxides. When onions are chopped and their cells are ruptured, they release enzymes that break down the sulfoxides, first to form sulfenic acid, and then an acrid gas called syn-propanethial-S-oxide. It is this gas that irritates eyes, although the effect is short-lived.

Dicing onions makes eyes weep.

Garlic | *Allium sativum*
Though native to Central Asia, garlic is now grown globally for use as a pungent seasoning in cooking, as well as for its medicinal properties.

Leek | *Allium ampeloprasum*
Despite its appearance, the fleshy part of leeks that we eat is a tightly folded bundle of leaf sheaths, not a stem. Leeks have a mild onion taste.

Flowers and buds

Besides the chunky florets of cauliflower and broccoli, a surprisingly large range of garden flowers can be eaten, including nasturtium, rose, marigold, geranium, primrose, sweet violet, and hibiscus.

Onions have been cultivated for more than 5,000 years, making them one of the world's oldest crops.

Chives produce soft, dense, purple umbels (flower clusters)

Funnel-shaped flowers taste similar to watercress

Nasturtium | *Tropaeolum majus*
The leaves and flowers of nasturtium add a peppery freshness to salads, while the young, green seed pods can be also pickled.

Globe artichoke |
Cynara cardunculus
Scolymus Group
The thistlelike flower buds of globe artichoke have thick outer scales that encase the edible "heart" within.

Chives | *Allium schoenoprasum*
Like onion and leek, chives belong to the *Allium* genus. Its green leaf stalks are diced for use as seasoning, and its soft flower heads can be added to salads.

Green stalks, as well as unopened flower buds, are used for flavoring

Each floret within the curd is a mass of tiny flower buds

Broccoli | *Brassica oleracea* var. *italica*
Related to cauliflowers, broccoli has dense clusters, or florets, of green flower buds. The florets are edible if they are cropped before they turn tough and begin to bloom.

Cauliflower |
Brassica oleracea (Botrytis Group)
A highly modified type of cabbage, its tightly packed florets form a dense, mounded flower head called the "curd."

Grains
Energy foods

△ **Wheat grains,** like other cereals, are a type of grass seed.

Grains are the small, hard, dry fruits of cereal crops. Ground up to make flour, they are the chief ingredient of bread and other bakery products. Grains can be stored for long periods and transported easily in bulk, so they have become the world's basic, or staple, foods. The greatest source of grain is cereal crops—annual grasses, such as wheat and oats, that yield a single crop each year.

The big four (human staples)

Grains provide almost half of human food energy, the bulk of which comes from the "big four" cereal crops: wheat, rice, oats, and corn. These four versatile grains can be grown almost anywhere.

The grain-bearing tips of cereal stems are known as ears

Wheat comes from an ear, or spikelet, made up of florets

Common wheat | *Triticum aestivum*
Wheat, the most widely grown food, covers 780,000 sq miles (2 million sq km) and yields 860 million tons of grain per year.

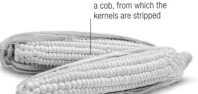

Corn has a solid ear called a cob, from which the kernels are stripped

Corn | *Zea mays*
Although not covering such a large area as wheat, corn is even more heavily produced, yielding 1.3 billion tons annually.

Outside of each oat floret is called a glume

Common oat | *Avena sativa*
Oats are widely grown in cooler, wetter regions and thrive in poor soil. They are often used for animal feed.

The grain's protective husk is removed to leave only the seeds—a process called winnowing

Rice | *Oryza sativa*
For more than half of the world's population, especially in southern and eastern Asia, rice provides the basic staple food.

Wheat does best where there is regular rainfall and temperatures are warm but not too hot.

Other major grains

While the big four grains are humanity's primary food sources, other cereals are also grown for brewing beer, animal fodder, and for use in industrial products. Some are better suited to marginal conditions than the big four.

All cereal crops begin life green, then ripen yellow and gold in the sun

Stalks and leaves are coated with a white wax

Rye grains are used chiefly for bread and for rye whiskey

Sorghum |
Sorghum bicolor
This grain is grown widely in Africa, where it is a major food crop, because it is more drought and heat resistant than other cereals.

Barley | *Hordeum vulgare*
Produced in vast quantities, about 70 percent of all barley is used as fodder and much of the rest for brewing.

Rye | *Secale cereale*
This fares better than other cereal crops in heavy clay, and in sandy, infertile, or drought-affected soils.

Pearl millet | *Cenchrus americanus*
Also called bajra, pearl millet does well in less fertile, dry soils. It is a popular food crop in India and Africa.

High-yielding hybrids

The Green Revolution

In 1943, agronomist Norman Borlaug developed wheat hybrids with shorter stems. Boosted with fertilizers and water, these fast-growing dwarf hybrids gave a huge yield, since less energy went into the stem. Such hybrids dramatically increased global wheat production, in what was called the Green Revolution. But this way of growing is demanding of water resources and requires intense inputs of pesticides and fertilizers. The hybrid seeds are also infertile, so farmers must buy new seeds every year.

Punjab was the first Indian state to adopt the dwarf hybrids, but intensive farming is lowering the water table.

Ancient grains

Grains, such as common wheat, are much modified from their wild ancestors. Other, less altered grains, dubbed "ancient grains," are more nutritious and have remained largely unchanged over the last several hundred years.

Ancient farmers selected seeds from the firmest heads to plant

Einkorn wheat |
Triticum boeoticum
Einkorn was perhaps one of the first wheats to be domesticated, 10,000 years ago in southern Türkiye.

Emmer wheat |
Triticum turgidum subsp. *dicoccoides*
Like einkorn, emmer was domesticated by selectively planting varieties that kept their head intact, rather than scattering seed loosely.

Spelt wheat | *Triticum spelta*
An important staple in Europe from the Bronze Age to the Middle Ages, spelt can do well in damp conditions that other wheats won't tolerate.

Terraced rice fields have been cultivated for centuries by Vietnam's H'mong people, who make up 95 percent of the mountain population in the country's northwest.

Rice
Food for billions

For more than half the world's population, rice is a staple food, with almost 513.5 million tons (521 million metric tons) of milled rice produced annually. Rice grains are the fruits of the grass *Oryza sativa*, first domesticated 9,000 years ago in China's Yangtze valley and now grown in thousands of varieties around the world. China, India, Bangladesh, Indonesia, and Vietnam are the top five producers; South and Southeast Asian countries are the main consumers.

Husked, polished rice

Traditional rice cultivation is both labor and water intensive. Farmers raise seedlings in nursery beds and, after a month, transplant them to paddy fields. These flooded fields, enclosed by banks, retain water up to 4 in (10 cm) deep and are drained before harvesting. In hilly areas, paddies are built into terraces. To help conserve increasingly scarce fresh water resources, more sustainable cultivation techniques are being encouraged, and new technologies used to assess crop needs.

Cultivating rice requires 24–30 percent of the world's total fresh water.

Asian rice (*Oryza sativa*) growing in Japan, where "Koshihikari" is the most popular cultivar.

Fungal diseases of crops
Going to rot

△ **Late blight** (*Phytophthora infestans*) affects the skin and flesh of potato tubers, leaving them inedible.

Feeding Earth's human population, which could number nine billion by 2050, relies on agricultural crops. Pests and diseases reduce yields by more than 50 percent, almost half of this through disease, of which about two thirds is due to fungi and fungus-like oomycetes (water molds). The five most devastating diseases are wheat leaf rust, rice blast, corn smut, soybean rust, and potato late blight. Together, these destroy crops that would have fed between 600 million and 4 billion people.

Foliage and stems quickly die in cool, damp weather

Late blight | *Phytophthora infestans*
This oomycete (water mold) kills potato and tomato plants, and rots the tubers and fruits in the field or during storage.

Natural defenses

Most plants are resistant to most fungal diseases much of the time. They have a range of physical and chemical defenses, and if a fungus does manage to get inside a plant, it activates an immune response.

Tumorlike galls, or smuts, caused by the fungus

Uninfected kernels

The fungus enters through wounds in the skin

Corn smut | *Ustilago maydis*
This fungus creates galls that contain plant tissue, fungal hyphae, and blue-black spores. They are eaten as a delicacy in Mexico, known as *huitlacoche*.

Soy bean rust | *Phakopsora pachyrhizi*
Causing rust-colored lesions on leaves, premature leaf loss, and fewer beans, this basidiomycete is a widespread problem on soy beans and other legumes.

Powdery mildew | *Erysiphales* spp.
This order of ascomycete fungi remove water and nutrients from the cells on the upper surface of leaves, causing as much as a 40 percent loss of productivity.

Brown rot | *Monilinia* spp.
This fungus enters the skin of apples, pears, plums, and other fruit via wounds. It then spreads rapidly, killing cells, and making the fruit turn brown.

Frosty pod | *Moniliophthora roreri*
This disease causes cocoa pods to ripen early and decay. It can reduce harvests by 40 percent or more, and is spreading in South and Central America.

Wheat leaf rust | *Puccinia triticina* One of the most common causes of wheat rust disease, it can reduce yields considerably.

Infected leaf is orange-red, crumpled, and thickened

Peach leaf curl | *Taphrina deformans*
Overwintering in the buds of peach and almond trees, this fungus penetrates the leaf tissue when the buds open, and makes the leaves fall prematurely.

Gray mold | *Botrytis cinerea*
Damaging soft fruit, such as strawberries and gooseberries, this fungus can also cause noble rot in grapes, which can then be used to create fine, sweet dessert wines.

Patches of white mycelium on underside of leaf

Downy mildew | *Sclerospora* spp.
An oomycete disease, it spreads between leaves and plants by airborne spores, especially in wet weather. Most species have a narrow range of host plants.

Rice blast | *Magnaporthe grisea*
This is one of the most devastating fungal diseases of rice. It occurs in about 80 countries, and causes global crop losses of up to 30 percent.

Panama disease | *Fusarium oxysporum*
This fungus wiped out the Gros Michel banana variety by 1960, and a new variant is now threatening the more resistant Cavendish banana variety.

Changing history

Potato late blight

Phytophthora species—more closely related to brown algae than to fungi—cause devastating plant diseases. *Phytophthora infestans* changed the course of history by destroying most of Ireland's potato crop in mid-1800s. More than one million people died of starvation and more than a further million emigrated to North America. *Phytophthora ramorum* has killed huge areas of oak (*Quercus*) in the United States, and is currently killing larch trees (*Larix*) in the UK.

Between 1845–1852, Ireland suffered the Great Famine, which resulted from recurrent episodes of potato blight.

Legumes
Protein packed

△ **Garden peas** (*Pisum sativum*) are eaten while still young, before they start to harden.

egumes are the pea family (*Fabaceae*), one of the largest families of flowering plants. They provide foods rich in protein and fiber. Most legumes have long, narrow fruits called pods that contain seeds arranged in a line. The pods typically split to release their seeds. It is usually only the seeds that are edible, but with some legumes the entire pod may be eaten when young and green. Soft, fresh seeds are called peas or beans; when dry and hard, they are known as pulses or grain legumes.

Trees

Most legumes are sprawling vines and shrubs, but a few grow as trees, including mesquite, tamarind, and carob, which can grow to 49 ft (15 m) tall.

Mesquite |
Prosopis juliflora
The mesquite tree produces peas that are traditionally used for bread flour in Mexico. They are now finding new uses as starch in gluten-free products.

Mesquite pods are a favorite food of cattle

Hard, brown seeds are surrounded by edible pulp

Carob | *Ceratonia siliqua*
The pods of the carob tree, a native of the eastern Mediterranean, can be dried and ground into a powder similar to cocoa.

Pods, which do not split, have seeds set in soft pulp; in the wild, animals eat the pods and disperse the seeds

Tamarind | *Tamarindus indica*
Originating in tropical Africa, tamarind is now also grown in southern Asia, Mexico, and Central America. Its pod pulp is made into a paste that adds a tart flavor to foods.

Peas

There is a variety of pea-producing legumes. Peas are usually small and round—unlike beans, which are typically flatter and longer. Pea plants also have hollow stems, whereas bean stems are more solid.

Alfalfa |
Medicago sativa
Alfalfa leaves and stems are fed to livestock as hay, while its sprouted seeds are eaten in salads. Alfalfa's long roots enable it to survive dry conditions.

Leaves look a little like clover

Flowers are white, lilac, or violet

Chickpea | *Cicer arietinum*
After soy, the protein-dense chickpea is the most widely grown pulse. Mashed-up chickpeas are the main ingredient of hummus and falafel.

Garden pea |
Pisum sativum
Garden peas are the legumes most often grown in cooler climates. They are eaten fresh, either cooked or raw, or dried and used as ingredients in soups.

Pods bear up to 10 peas

Lentil | *Lens culinaris*
Used in curries, soups, and stews, this lens-shaped pea is dried or cooked and canned after ripening. Lentils can be ground into flour for bread and cakes.

Beans

More varied in color and shape than peas, beans are usually grown for seeds that are eaten dry, or processed, rather than fresh. Beans are a staple food in many countries.

Adzukis are also called red beans

Adzuki bean | *Vigna angularis*
A key food in Japan, Korea, and China, adzuki beans are often boiled and mashed to make red bean paste, an ingredient of many East Asian dishes.

Mung bean | *Vigna radiata*
A fast-growing species of the Indian subcontinent, the mung bean is used in dal and curries. Like all beans, it helps to improve soil fertility by fixing nitrogen.

King of beans

The rise of soy

Soy is often called the "King of Beans," because it has so many uses. It is not only a major animal fodder crop and an important staple food for many people the world over, it also yields soybean oil for cooking and it can be made into biodiesel fuel. Such versatility means that soy is in ever-increasing demand. The steep rise in soy farming has led to deforestation and the loss of key ecological sites. It is also displacing Indigenous peoples and small farmers from the land.

The soy bean harvest yields around 440 million tons each year, the majority of which is fed to animals.

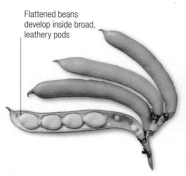

Lima beans have fine ridges radiating from the eye

Flattened beans develop inside broad, leathery pods

Immature soy beans cooked while still in their pods are known as edamame

Lima bean | *Phaseolus lunatus*
The lima bean is native to Central America. Large, fat, yellow varieties are also known as butterbeans.

Fava bean | *Vicia faba*
Important in Europe, this is one of the few beans eaten fresh. Though easy to grow, fava beans do not tolerate hot weather.

Soybean | *Glycine max*
Nutritious soy is used to make soy milk; tofu; meat and dairy substitutes; and, when fermented, tempeh and soy sauce.

Runner bean | *Phaseolus coccineus*
The whole pod is sometimes eaten when green and fresh. The beans themselves have long been part of Central American cuisine.

Kidney bean | *Phaseolus vulgaris*
The kidney bean is a variety of *P. vulgaris*. Other varieties include pinto, black, and navy beans (the beans used for canned baked beans).

Kidney beans come in a range of colors and may also be speckled

The pod is lined with kidney-shaped beans

India consumes the most beans globally, around 5,700,000 tons per year.

Root vegetables
Carbohydrate stores

△ **Beets** (*Beta vulgaris*) are a versatile vegetable, used in salads, savory and sweet dishes, and also for pickling.

Root vegetables are edible, underground parts of plants that are good sources of carbohydrates. They are mostly storage organs, in which the plant builds up its supply of starches and sugars. However, "root vegetable" is not a botanical term, and what we commonly describe as root vegetables includes bulbs, rhizomes, corms, and stems as well as true roots. The potato, for example, is a tuber. In cool climates, though, most root vegetables are indeed true roots.

Kohlrabi |
Brassica oleracea
(Gongylodes Group)
This is the stem of a biennial cabbage cultivar, probably originating in the Middle East.

Cool roots

True roots, such as radishes, carrots, turnips, and beets are important crops in cooler climates. These cold-hardy staples help fill gaps in the diet during months when little else will grow.

Sugar is made in the rosette of leaves and stored in the root

The root is about 20 percent sugar

Taproot is fleshy and edible in its first year, but becomes woody in its second growing season

Sugar beet | *Beta vulgaris* subsp. *vulgaris*
This is the plump, white, sucrose-rich root of a beet plant cultivar. It provides about 30 percent of the world's sugar—the rest comes from cane, which only grows in warm climates.

Wild parsnip | *Pastinaca sativa*
Originating from Eurasia, the parsnip is a biennial root vegetable that is harvested annually. It was the main source of sugar until beets and cane were developed.

The red color comes from water-soluble pigments called betalains

Leaves are removed if the roots are to be stored

Once lifted, the long, white roots can be stored for weeks if kept cool

Beet | *Beta vulgaris*
A cousin of sugar beet, beets have been a culinary ingredient since Roman times, most notably in the Eastern European dish borscht. Its pigments make it useful as food coloring.

Daikon | *Raphanus sativus* subsp. *sativus*
This is a fast-growing Eastern Mediterranean winter radish. It was taken to China and Japan in around 500 BCE, before being reintroduced as a crop to Europe in the mid-16th century.

Rutabaga |
Brassica napus **(Napobrassica Group)**
Probably a hybrid of cabbage and turnip, this root vegetable is native to Scandinavia and Russia. It is also known as swede and Swedish turnip.

Radish | *Raphanus sativus* The small, red, peppery orbs grown as summer radishes have crisp flesh. They mature quickly, which makes them a popular crop to grow.

Costly crop

Sugar beet and topsoil loss

The global annual sugar beet harvest is more than 298 million tons (270 million metric tons). It is well known that excess sugar in the diet poses a health risk, triggering obesity, diabetes, and heart disease. But growing sugar beet also damages the soil. Although some is recovered, it is estimated that in the UK around 551,000 tons (500,000 metric tons) of topsoil is lost each year as it is taken up along with the vegetable harvest.

Sugar beet is processed to extract the sugar, and then the remaining pulp is pressed and fed to livestock.

Inedible dark brown or black "skin" (the cork layer) is removed before eating

White turnips have a smooth outer skin

Arracacha root has a high starch content

Celeriac is a corm with an earthy, slightly sweet, celery-like taste

Black salsify | *Scorzonera hispanica*
Originating in Southern Europe, this root crop is tolerant of poor soil. Also called the oyster plant for the taste of its long taproot, it has edible flowers and leaf shoots, too.

White turnip | *Brassica rapa* subsp. *rapa*
Turnip is the taproot of a biennial plant of the mustard family. It can be mashed or eaten in stews, or used for animal fodder. Turnip was a key crop in the US before the Civil War.

Arracacha | *Arracacia xanthorrhiza*
Native to the Andes, this is a popular root in South America, often grown alongside crops such as corn, beans, and coffee. It is typically used in soups, purees, and especially stews.

Celeriac |
Apium graveolens var. *rapaceum*
Celeriac originated in the Mediterranean, and is now widely grown across Europe, northern Asia, and north America.

> **"You ask me what life is. That's like asking what a carrot is. A carrot is a carrot and there's nothing more to know."**
>
> Anton **Chekhov** Russian playwright

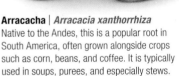

Carrot |
Daucus carota subsp. *sativus*
Domesticated more than 1,100 years ago in Central Asia, more than 44 million tons (40 million metric tons) of carrots are grown globally each year. Orange carrots were first cultivated in the 16th century; before that, carrots were purple or yellow.

Arrowroot | *Maranta arundinacea* Valued for its thick corm, arrowroot was one of the first plants domesticated in South America, some 10,000 years ago.

Warm climates

In warm climates, most root vegetables are not true roots but tuberous roots, rhizomes, and corms. They are such an important source of energy in tropical regions that they are often the staple foods, rather than grains.

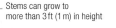
Stems can grow to more than 3 ft (1 m) in height

Ginseng | *Panax ginseng*
Asian ginseng, native to northeast China and Korea, has a gnarled root or rhizome that looks a bit like a human figure. It has long been a key ingredient in Chinese traditional medicine. Slow-growing, the roots take five years to reach maturity.

Juvenile shoot emerging

Ginseng has been used in traditional Chinese medicine for more than 2,000 years.

Ginger has a thick, branched rhizome with a brown outer layer and yellow center

Ginger | *Zingiber officinale*
A perennial plant, ginger is probably native to Southeast Asia. Its pungent rhizome has long been used as a flavoring and for its supposed health benefits.

Konjac | *Amorphophallus konjac*
The Southeast Asian konjac has a dramatic lily flower. Its large, starchy corm is popular in Japan, China, and Korea for making a jellylike dish, known as *konnyaku*.

Rhizomes form branching mats

Turmeric | *Curcuma longa*
Native to India and Indonesia, the turmeric plant has branching, yellow rhizomes that are boiled and dried to make a powder used for coloring and flavor in Indian food.

Leaf cuttings (or root sprouts) can be used for propagation

Abundant blue or purple flowers appear in summer

Breadroot | *Psoralea esculenta*
The breadroot, or prairie turnip, is an herbaceous perennial plant with a tuberous root that was highly valued as a staple food, foraged by Indigenous peoples of North America.

Cassava | *Manihot esculenta*
Possibly domesticated by the Maya, cassava, or manioc root, is the main source of carbohydrate in the tropics after rice and corn. It is usually eaten as tapioca: starch extracted from cassava is turned into flour.

Yam | *Dioscorea* spp.
The tuberous roots of vines called yams are an important staple food in tropical regions. They are cherished with rituals among the people of Nigeria and Benin.

Sweet potato |
Ipomoea batatas
Although sometimes called yams, sweet potatoes are not related to true yams or even potatoes. They are the tuberous root of a vine belonging to the morning glory family.

Yacón roots are sweet and crunchy when eaten fresh

Yacón | *Smallanthus sonchifolius*
Long grown by farmers on the slopes of the Andes in Peru and Colombia, this daisylike flower with its edible, tuberous roots is now grown in regions with a mild climate.

Commercially harvested fungi
Tasty and nutritious

△ **Straw mushroom** (*Volvariella volvacea*) is rich in protein and is highly prized globally.

Humans have eaten mushrooms for 12,000 years, and they appear on Egyptian hieroglyphs from more than 6,500 years ago. Jelly ear fungi (*Auricularia cornea*) were cultivated in China around 2,200 BCE, and the ancient Greeks cultivated velvet pioppini (*Clitocybe aegerita*) on animal dung about 200 years later. White button mushrooms (*Agaricus bisporus*) were grown in the gardens of Versailles, France, in the 17th century, and later in Paris catacombs and quarries.

Shop mushrooms

Edible fungal fruit bodies are highly nutritious, and those featured here are sold commercially. Decomposer fungi can be cultivated on dead organic materials, but mycorrhizal species are mostly collected from the field.

Spores are formed on veins or wrinkles rather than gills

Chanterelle |
Cantharellus cibarius
As expensive to buy as they are difficult to cultivate, chanterelles are usually collected from coniferous and broadleaved forests from late summer to late fall.

Shiitake | *Lentinula edodes*
Cultivated on logs in Southeast Asia for food and traditional medicine for centuries, shiitake is now one of the mostly widely grown mushrooms worldwide. It is rich in B vitamins and dietary fiber.

Growing here on a bed of inoculated grain

Cap grows to 6 in (15 cm) in diameter

Commercial varieties come in several different colors

Oyster mushroom | *Pleurotus ostreatus*
Grown commercially on an industrial scale, and also popular to grow at home on logs of broadleaved trees or pasteurized straw in plastic bags, some say that the oyster mushroom tastes similar to its bivalve namesake.

Black truffle | *Tuber melanosporum*
Truffles are the underground fruit bodies of ascomycete fungi that grow in a mutualistic relationship with various trees, including oak (*Quercus* spp.) and hazel (*Corylus avellana*). Traditionally, people use dogs to sniff them out.

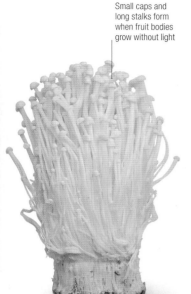

Small caps and long stalks form when fruit bodies grow without light

Enoki | *Flammulina filiformis*
Cultivated in Japan and China for centuries, the enoki mushroom is now widely popular for its slightly sweet taste. It is usually grown in the dark.

Straw mushroom (*Volvariella volvacea*) is grown throughout East and Southeast Asia on beds of rice straw. These mushrooms are usually harvested when they are at the immature, button stage.

Straw mushroom | *Volvariella volvacea*
The third most widely eaten mushroom globally, they are sold fresh in the regions where they are cultivated. Elsewhere, they are usually available dried or canned.

Mature, fully developed cap

Portobello | *Agaricus bisporus*
Portobello, white button, Roman brown, or cremini mushrooms are different stages of fruit body development or color varieties of the same species.

The cap is convex on young fruit bodies; it later flattens

Matsutake | *Tricholoma matsutake*
Commonly growing with Japanese red pine, (*Pinus densiflora*), it has been harvested from natural forests, and is now recorded as a threatened species.

Dangerous look-alikes

Fungal toxicity

Some poisonous fungi look very similar to edible ones. The very poisonous Jack-o-lantern (*Omphalotus olearius*), with its orange-yellow-brown cap, can be mistaken for a chanterelle, while the deadly poisonous death cap (*Amanita phalloides*) is sometimes confused with the edible straw mushroom. Wild fungi must never be eaten unless they have been identified as edible with 100 percent certainty.

Shimeji | *Lyophyllum shimeji*
Several species of shimeji mushrooms are native to East Asia. Some feed on decaying matter, so can be cultivated, but *Lyophyllum shimeji* is a mycorrhizal fungus.

Multiple cups on central stalk

Morel | *Morchella esculenta*
Growing in well-drained woodland, morel fruit in spring. A highly prized edible mushroom when cooked, it is poisonous when raw.

Lion's mane | *Hericium erinaceus*
Common in some countries but rare in Europe—and illegal to pick in the UK—the fungus can be cultivated on inoculated wood.

Death cap is deadly poisonous, it must not be eaten.

Culinary herbs
Aromatic leaves

△ **Mint** (*Mentha* x *piperita*) is a vigorous, easy-to-grow plant that does well in most soil types.

Culinary herbs are leaves or leafy twigs of aromatic plants that are used to give flavor to dishes. Some herbs can be used dried; others are best used fresh because they lose their volatile aroma compounds when heated. Most herbs are perennial, but by growing new plants continually, leaves and stems can be kept soft and palatable. Much of the flavor of herbs comes from the essential oils they contain. These oils can be extracted for use in perfumes, cosmetics, toiletries, lotions, hair products, toothpastes, and soaps, and also added to food products.

Herbs

Although many plants are used to flavor food around the world, a small number of herbs are commonly used in a wide range of different cuisines. For some herbs, such as mint and basil, there are many cultivated varieties, each with distinctive flavors.

Thyme leaves can be used either fresh or dried

Flowers are borne from mid to late summer

Leaves retain their flavor for years if dried and stored carefully

Slender stems are tender and have a similar taste to the leaves

Cilantro | *Coriandrum sativum*
Popular in Asian and Mexican cuisine, cilantro is easily grown from seed. Its leaves, stems, and seeds (called coriander) are used in cooking, and it also has edible flowers.

Common thyme | *Thymus vulgaris*
The leaves of this low-growing, evergreen shrub can be picked year-round, though spring or summer sprigs taste best. Its nectar-rich flowers are loved by insects.

Sage | *Salvia officinalis*
Long used for stuffings and sausages, this native Mediterranean herb is traditionally said to enhance wisdom. Some research suggests it may help boost memory.

Sage has downy, slightly rough, leaves

French favorites

Herbs in French cuisine

Fine French cooking uses distinctive herb combinations. The most delicate *fines herbes*—tarragon, parsley, chervil, and chives—are added at the end of cooking. *Herbes de Provence*, namely marjoram, rosemary, thyme, oregano, and lavender, are used in the robust stews and dishes of meat, fowl, and fish in southern France. A *bouquet garni* consists of sage, parsley, thyme, bay leaf, and peppercorns tied with string or wrapped in cheesecloth. It is added to soups and stocks for flavoring, but not eaten.

Herb bundles have been used in French cooking for centuries—the first known use of "bouquet garni" was c. 1833.

Delicate, feathery leaves grow in clusters

Dill | *Anethum graveolens*
The fine leaves of dill are a key ingredient in many Scandinavian and eastern European recipes. Dill is used raw and chopped, because it quickly loses its flavor when dried.

Parsley | *Petroselinum crispum*
Tangy parsley is added to sauces, soups, and butters, or used as a garnish. Its crisp texture goes well with potatoes. Curly-leaved parsley is milder than the flat-leaved varieties.

Basil leaves are frost-sensitive, so the plant does not thrive in colder climates

Basil | *Ocimum basilicum*
There are many types of basil, from pungent sweet basil to Thai basil, with its hint of licorice. Fresh sweet basil leaves are used to make pesto and added to salads and tomato-based sauces.

Leaves contain oil that is known to repel some insect pests

Mint | *Mentha x piperita*
Peppermint is a hybrid of spearmint and water mint, and the most widely used of the 25 types of mint. It is added to sweet and savory dishes and made into herbal tea.

Leaves tend to be more flavorful before the plant flowers

Lemongrass | *Cymbopogon citratus*
Growing in dense clumps, the leaves have a fresh, lemony aroma that makes it a favorite in Southeast Asian cooking. Its woody stalks can be used whole or chopped and pounded to a paste.

Dark green, glossy leaves can be picked and used all year round

Bay laurel | *Laurus nobilis*
The leaves of the bay laurel are not eaten but added to slow-cooked dishes such as stews, casseroles, and soups to infuse flavor. They are used as whole leaves, either fresh or dried.

Oregano | *Origanum vulgare*
This small, evergreen Mediterranean shrub is central to Italian and Greek cooking. It is closely related to the sweeter-tasting marjoram.

Oregano grows as clumps and sends up attractive heads of pink or white summer blooms

Spices
Adding flavor

△ **Fragrant saffron** (*Crocus sativus*) is one of the most ancient and highly prized of all spices.

Derived from parts of plants, typically in a dry form, spices are mainly used to flavor food, but they are also used in medicines and cosmetics. Whereas herbs tend to come from the leaves of nonwoody plants, spices are derived from parts of woody plants such as roots, rhizomes, bark, fruit, and seeds. Most originated in tropical Asia; only three are from the Americas—allspice, capsicum peppers, and vanilla. In the 18th century, such was the demand for Asian spices in Europe that many spice-yielding plants were grown on tropical islands to boost the supply.

Sumac | *Rhus coriaria*
The fruits are dried and ground to make tangy, red sumac spice, a key flavor in Middle Eastern dishes. Sumac is also used in traditional medicine and as a dye.

From rhizomes to seeds

Popular spices illustrate the range of plant parts used. Ginger and turmeric come from rhizomes. Cinnamon comes from bark and star anise from fruit, while cardamom and nutmeg are seeds, often ground into a fine powder.

The peeled bark is sliced, rolled, and then dried

Both seeds and pods are dried and used

Star anise | *Illicium verum*
The distinctively star-shaped pericarps of *Illicium verum* are harvested, dried, and used whole or ground. The spice has a similar flavor to unrelated aniseed.

Aniseed | *Pimpinella anisum*
The fragrant and aromatic seeds of this flowering plant, native to the Mediterranean and Middle East, are especially popular for flavoring alcoholic drinks.

Cinnamon | *Cinnamomum verum*
A spice once worth more than gold, cinnamon is produced from the inner bark of a small evergreen tree in the laurel family, native to Sri Lanka, India, and Myanmar.

Cinnamon sticks are used whole or ground to a powder

Saffron | *Crocus sativus* The purple saffron crocus, flowering here in Ukraine, is in decline in the wild. Saffron is made from its stigmas.

Fenugreek | *Trigonella foenum-graecum*
A member of the pea family, fenugreek is native to the eastern Mediterranean, southern Europe, and western Asia. Its dried seeds have been valued as a spice since ancient times.

Nutmeg | *Myristica fragrans*
Native to the Moluccas (Spice Islands), nutmeg became a popular and costly spice in the 17th century. Similarly flavored mace comes from its reddish seed covering.

Golden spice
Aromatic crocus flowers

Saffron, highly valued for millennia and native to the Mediterranean area and southwestern Asia, is the most expensive of all spices. To make just 1 g of saffron requires the stigmas of some 150 *Crocus sativus* flowers. These are picked by hand and their stigmas carefully removed, then dried. More than 363 tons (400 metric tons) of the spice is produced worldwide each year. The flowers are grown in India and southern Europe, but around 90 percent of all saffron comes from Iran.

Picking saffron for its medicinal properties is illustrated in a medieval Austrian health manual.

Vanilla | *Vanilla planifolia*
Probably originating in Mexico and Central America, vanilla is produced from the fragrant pods or "beans"' of the vanilla orchid, a popular flavoring in desserts.

Peppercorns grow in bunches on the vine

Black pepper | *Piper nigrum*
The world's most traded spice, black pepper is the dried fruit of *Piper nigrum*, a native of the Malabar coast of India. White pepper is the inner seed or berry.

The fruit, a green capsule, contains 15–20 dark seeds

Cardamom | *Elettaria cardamomum*
A perennial native to the moist forests of southern India produces the cardamom fruit and seeds often used in South Asian dishes and Scandinavian pastries.

Seeds of white mustard are ground into a yellow powder

White mustard | *Sinapis alba*
The ground seeds of *Sinapis alba* or those of brown mustard (*Brassica juncea*), both members of the *Brassicaceae* family, are used to create mustard.

Cumin "seeds" are actually dry fruits in a form known as schizocarps

Cumin | *Cuminum cyminum*
The seedlike fruits of an herbaceous annual of the parsley family, cumin is native to an area from Iraq to Afghanistan but now more widely cultivated, especially in India.

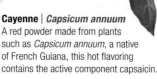

A clove is made up of the long calyx and unopened sepals and petals of a dried clove bud

Clove | *Syzygium aromaticum*
The aromatic flower buds of trees native to the Maluku Islands of Indonesia, cloves add a pungent flavor to foods and are also used in medicinal and cosmetic products.

C. annuum leaves add a pungent flavor to garnishes and stir-fries

Cayenne | *Capsicum annuum*
A red powder made from plants such as *Capsicum annuum*, a native of French Guiana, this hot flavoring contains the active component capsaicin.

Nutmeg
Highly prized for centuries

Native to the Indonesian Banda islands, the tropical, evergreen nutmeg tree (*Myristica fragrans*) produces a round, edible, apricot-like fruit with a dark-brown seed (nutmeg), encased in a red, fleshy membrane (mace)—both used as spices. The tree, which can reach up to 65 ft (20 m) in height, yields fruit after five to eight years and lives for up to 70 years, producing as many as 1,000 fruits annually when it is fully grown.

For centuries, nutmeg was highly prized in Europe. A rare delicacy in ancient Greece and Rome, it was ground to powder and used for incense and to flavor alcoholic drinks. Later, Arabian and Venetian traders brought nutmeg and other spices from the Far East, making them a sought-after luxury, enjoyed by the European elite and used copiously to flavor food at medieval banquets. From the 15th to the 17th centuries, European nations battled to dominate the lucrative spice trade. In 1667, the Dutch gained full control of the Indonesian Spice Islands, but the French and English acquired nutmeg cuttings and seeds, planting them on islands they had colonized in the Indian Ocean and West Indies, where the spice trees still grow.

Dried nutmeg enclosed in mace

While nutmeg is best known as a spice, its oil has long been used topically to ease arthritis pain and ingested to treat gastrointestinal problems. In large doses, it was once falsely claimed to induce abortion, but can produce hallucinogenic effects. However, consuming too much nutmeg can cause severe nausea, and heart and nerve damage.

In 1667, England ceded a nutmeg-growing island to the Dutch in exchange for a swampy Manhattan.

A 19th-century illustration shows the fruit of the nutmeg tree (*Myristica fragrans*). In Indonesia, it is eaten as a snack, crystallized in sugar with the nutmeg seed and red mace casing removed.

Oils

Oil producers

△ **Opium poppy** (*Papaver somniferum*) flowers have four petals and may be red, white, pink, or mauve.

Many plants are grown for the oils they contain. Some plant or "vegetable" oils are edible and are used for baking, frying, or dressing salads. Others are ingredients of fuels, lubricants, protective coatings, candles, soaps, cosmetics, and much more. Plant oils are obtained mostly by crushing the plant, usually the seeds. Essential oils are organic compounds derived from aromatic plant sources, and they are extracted by distillation. Oils can also be obtained by maceration, which involves soaking plant material with a solvent.

The seeds have a hard shell

Black mustard | *Brassica nigra*
The oil from pressed seeds is sometimes used in cooking but is mostly avoided because it contains erucic acid. The seeds can also be distilled for an essential oil.

Pure and refined

Plant oils can come from vegetables, nuts, seeds, fruits, and cereal grains. Most oils for consumption are refined chemically or with heat to make them palatable or to extend their shelf-life.

Some, but not all, flowers produce olives

Olive flesh, contains 20–30 percent oil

Olive tree | *Olea europaea*
For thousands of years, people in the Mediterranean region have pressed the fruit of olive trees for their oil, which is used for cooking and dressing food.

Seed kernels are crushed to obtain the oil

Fibers protect the seeds

Cotton | *Gossypium hirsutum*
Once only thought of as a byproduct of the cotton industry, cottonseed oil was developed to create margarine and is now a popular cooking oil.

Oil is extracted from the seeds with chemical solvents or by pressing

Sunflower seeds

Sunflower | *Helianthus annuus*
Native to the Americas but now cultivated throughout the world, sunflowers are one of the main sources of oil for cooking.

Seeds are held in a long green capsule, like a pea pod

Sesame | *Sesamum indicum*
This perennial crop was cultivated in parts of South Asia before 2000 BCE. Oil from its seeds has always been used in cooking, baking, and cosmetics.

Peanut | *Arachis hypogaea*
Also known as groundnuts, peanuts grow underground. Their oil is considered healthy for cooking because it is high in monounsaturated fat.

Corn | *Zea mays*
The mild flavor of corn oil makes it popular for frying and in margarine. It is also used in the production of biofuel.

Seeds are crushed at a low temperature to produce oil

Canola | *Brassica napus napus*
Also, known as rapeseed, canola is one of the three major sources of vegetable oil internationally, along with palm oil and soybean oil.

The cost of plant oils

Climate change

Oilseed production is rising rapidly as people move to higher-protein diets and as more is needed for cosmetics and biofuels. The demand is driving a massive increase in land devoted to growing oil palms and soybeans. Much of this has led to the destruction of tropical rainforests and savannas—habitats with high carbon stocks—which is fueling global warming and having a devastating effect on wildlife and people's way of life.

Harvesting sunflowers for vegetable oil, production of which has risen dramatically in recent years.

Flowers may be orange, yellow, red, or white

Red and yellow dyes can be made from the flower petals

Safflower | *Carthamus tinctorius*
This thistlelike plant is the source of colorless seed oil, which is valued in cooking because of its high proportion of polyunsaturated fats.

Leaflets are lanceolate, tapering to a point, with serrated margins

Hemp seeds are pressed to extract their oil

Hemp | *Cannabis sativa* cultivars
The hemp plants grown for hemp oil contain almost no psychoactive ingredients. The refined oil is used in cosmetics.

Upward-facing, sky-blue flowers have five petals

Walnuts are single-seed stone fruits

English walnut | *Juglans regia*
Medical scientists are researching walnut oil because its high linoleic acid content may give it anti-inflammatory qualities.

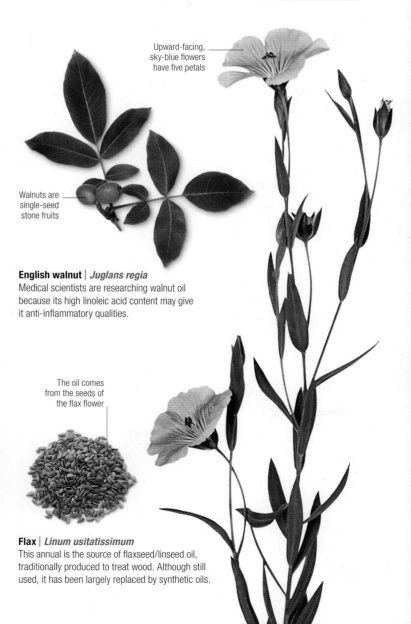

Tiny seeds are held inside a pod, which gradually hardens and dries

Opium poppy | *Papaver somniferum*
Poppy seeds are widely used whole in baking. Artists use the oil extracted from crushed seeds for binding pigments in oil paints.

Soybean | *Glycine max*
This oil is the second most widely consumed vegetable oil after palm oil. China, the US, Brazil, and Argentina are the world's leading producers.

The oil comes from the seeds of the flax flower

Flax | *Linum usitatissimum*
This annual is the source of flaxseed/linseed oil, traditionally produced to treat wood. Although still used, it has been largely replaced by synthetic oils.

Oil palm plantations in Indonesia cover more than 34 million acres (14 million hectares).

Palm fruits grow in bunches that can weigh as much as 66 lb (30 kg) and are harvested by hand.

The fruits are ready to harvest when they turn from black to red-orange. Each fruit contains around 25 percent oil.

A five-fold increase in oil palm production in Indonesia since 2000 has led to a vast expansion of plantations.

Oil palms, here in a Malaysian plantation, take four to five years to produce their first fruit, but can remain productive for 30 years.

Palm oil
A vast industry

The fruits of the oil palm tree (*Elaeis guineensis*), native to tropical Africa, yield two oils so widely used that the global market is worth more than $64 billion. Dark red oil from the fruit pulp is used in Asian and African cooking, but most of this oil is further refined to remove its color and taste, then added to processed foods from cookies to ice cream. Palm kernel oil is mainly used in the manufacture of cosmetics, detergents, and soaps. Malaysia and Indonesia, where the trees were first planted as ornamentals in 1848, today produce around 85 percent of all palm oil. Such expansion has caused vast deforestation, yet the oil palm fruit is a highly efficient crop. While satisfying 40 percent of global demand, oil palms take up only 6 percent of all land used to produce vegetable oils. The World Wildlife Fund (WWF) argues for more sustainable palm oil production that balances economic and environmental needs.

Ripened palm oil fruit

Oil palm trees are highly productive; each tree can yield 14 bunches of up to 3,000 fruits annually.

Plight of orangutans

At risk of extinction

Expanding palm oil plantations are a threat to the orangutans of Borneo and the Indonesian island of Sumatra. As a result of habitat loss, the primates stray onto plantations in search of food and are often shot as pests. Others die trying to protect their young, frequently targeted for the illegal pet trade. As many as 5,000 orangutans are killed each year. Of a total of 230,000 orangutans a century ago, 57,000 are left in Borneo and 13,800 on Sumatra.

The Sumatran orangutan (*Pongo abelii*) is one of three orangutan species, two of which live on Sumatra.

Beverages
Steeped infusions

△ **Dog roses** (*Rosa canina*) adorn hedgerows in early summer, with the hips appearing in the fall.

Most of our drinks, especially hot beverages such as tea and coffee, are made from plants. Leaves and flowers, in particular, can be steeped in hot water to make a wide range of teas, but teas can be made from bark and fruits, too. Many beverages are drunk for the stimulating, refreshing effect of their small caffeine content. South American guarana has the highest caffeine content, at up to 5.8 percent—nearly three times more caffeine than is found in coffee. Japanese matcha green tea almost equals guarana for its caffeine hit.

Teas

Legend says tea-drinking began in China around 4,700 years ago. Nowadays, tea is either China tea, made from the leaves of *Camellia sinensis*, or any drink or infusion made from leaves, fruits, or flowers steeped in hot water.

Rose hip | *Rosa canina*
All roses yield drupes called hips in late summer or fall, but the hips of the climbing dog rose, *R. canina*, are especially good for teas that are said to relieve pain in the joints of arthritis sufferers.

Rose hips can be eaten raw or made into jams and jellies, as well as tea

Cocoa | *Theobroma cacao*
Both chocolate and cocoa are made from the seeds (often called "beans") of the cacao tree, an evergreen native to the lowlands of the tropical Americas and now also widely grown in Africa.

Sakurayu | *Prunus cerasus*
Japan has hundreds of cherry cultivars. The cherry blossom is pickled in salt and plum vinegar and then dried. When infused in hot water, the dried leaves make *sakurayu* tea—a traditional drink served at Japanese weddings.

The aromatic leaves grow on distinctive square stems

Spearmint | *Mentha spicata*
Strong and fragrant, mint is grown as a tea and culinary herb. Moroccan mint tea is at the center of social life in the Maghreb region of North Africa.

Compact, yellow, fragrant flowers grow along the stem

Mountain tea |
Sideritis syriaca
Mountain tea, or *dag cayi*, is made from flowers of the ironwort plant, which grows on damp, high pastures in the mountains of the Eastern Mediterranean.

"The mere chink of cups and saucers tunes the mind to happy repose."
George **Gissing** *The Private Papers of Henry Ryecroft*, 1903

Coffee seeds (or "beans") are dried and roasted; the ground beans are then "brewed" with hot water

Coffee fruits are small, fleshy berries

Coffee | *Coffea arabica*
The majority of the world's coffee is made from *Coffea arabica* (commonly called arabica) and most of the rest comes from *C. canephora* (known as robusta). Arabica produces a sweeter drink than robusta, but robusta has a higher caffeine content.

Fermenting and distilling

Alcoholic beverages

People have long used plants to make alcoholic beverages for their relaxing, intoxicating effects. In wine and cider making, the alcohol is formed by letting the sugars in grapes and apples ferment naturally. With beer, starch in grain must first be turned to sugars by adding malt or yeast. Distilling makes stronger spirits, such as whiskey, from grains or potatoes, rum from sugar cane, and brandies from wine or from fruits such as apricots, peaches, cherries, plums, and blackberries.

Dandelion wine, like other wines made from wild plants, is made in a similar way to wine made from grapes.

Rooibos blooms are vivid yellow, like those of broom

Green tea leaves are exposed to the scent of jasmine flowers

Blooms grow in clusters

Chamomile can flower two or three times a year

Rooibos | *Aspalathus linearis*
An earthy tea is made from the leaves of a small shrub that grows in the scrubland of South Africa's Cederberg mountains. Rooibos is caffeine-free, low in tannins, and rich in antioxidants.

Jasmine tea | *Jasminum officinale*
This climbing plant is native to the Caucasus and Central Asia. For 2,000 years, jasmine has been grown in the mountains of China for its white blooms, which add fragrance to green tea.

Yerba mate | *Ilex paraguariensis*
Mate is an infusion made with the leaves of the yerba mate tree, a holly species native to the mountains of South America. The drink is traditionally served in a cup made from a calabash gourd.

Chamomile | *Matricaria chamomilla*
This plant has long been used in folk and traditional medicine. Its flowers are infused to make a calming herbal tea. Native to southern and eastern Europe, and western Asia, chamomile is now grown worldwide.

Flower calyces are boiled in water to make hibiscus tea

The leaves have three to five lobes

Pegaga | *Centella asiatica*
Also called Indian pennywort, pegaga has long been used as a medicinal tea. It is popular in Southeast Asia, but its health benefits are not proven.

Hibiscus | *Hibiscus sabdariffa*
Native to Africa, this hibiscus was introduced to Asia and the Caribbean and is now naturalized in many places. The flower calyces are used to make a cranberry-tasting tea that has been shown to help lower blood pressure.

Tea trees, here in a vast plantation in the Malaysian highlands, are pruned to restrict their height and encourage the growth of new, vigorous, leafy branches.

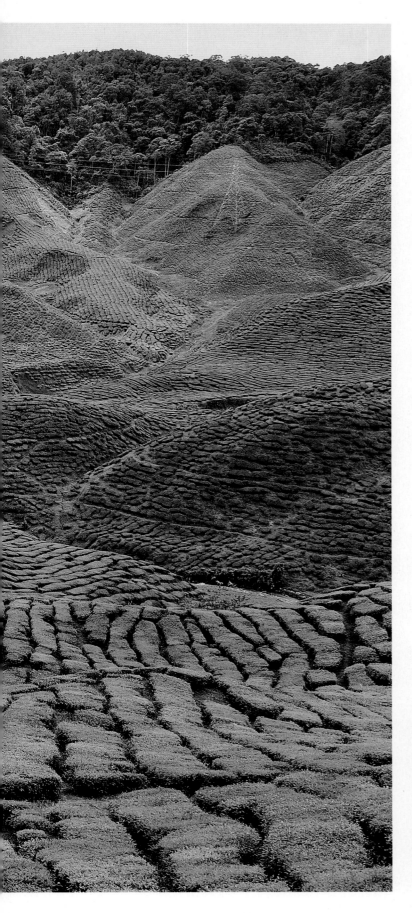

Tea

An ancient beverage

Tea tree leaves before processing

All species of tea grown today are hybrids of *Camellia sinensis*, the original tea tree, first cultivated in southwest China 5,000 years ago. The two main types are now *C. sinensis* var. *sinensis* and its ancient, larger-leafed relative, *C. sinensis* var. *assamica*, native to an area from northeast India to China. According to legend, Chinese emperor Shennong discovered tea around 2700 BCE, when some tea leaves dropped by chance into the boiled water he was sipping. He liked the drink's taste and its stimulative effect, and his influence popularized tea across his empire.

Tea arrived in Europe and the US in the mid-1600s, but was initially an expensive luxury and heavily taxed in Britain. In the late 1700s, the tax was slashed, and in 1837 the British East India Company began to cultivate tea in Assam. Tea became cheaper and is now many countries' favorite beverage.

Around the world, more than 5 billion cups of tea are consumed each day.

Tea is poured as people prepare for a feast in this scene from a 1,000-year-old Chinese mural.

Traditional medicines
Age-old remedies

△ **Witch-hazel** (*Hamamelis virginiana*) bark, twigs, and leaves are all used in herbal medicine.

Plants have been used since ancient times for traditional and herbal medicine. "Herbals" (books describing the medical uses of herbs) were the go-to guides for medicines for many hundreds of years. Thousands of different plants have featured in traditional medicine over the millennia. Science has not always been able to prove or disprove their efficacy, though a few have been analyzed chemically to provide the basis for pharmaceutical products.

Common mullein |
Verbascum thapsus
This biennial is native to Europe, North Africa, and Asia. Powders, infusions, and poultices made from its roots, leaves, and flowers provide herbal remedies for a range of illnesses.

Medicinal plants

Although they offer "natural" benefits, medicinal plants should be used with caution. Unlike manufactured medicines, their potency varies from plant to plant.

Some flowers have a bright yellow patch to guide pollinating bees

Leaves were often made into a poultice and applied to the skin

Leaves are used in a warm compress or drunk as tea

The name ribwort comes from the prominent veins on the leaves

Yellow, saucer-shaped flowers yield oil for use in herbal medicine

Thickleaf yerba santa |
Eriodictyon crassifolium
The Chumash people took "sacred herb" to keep the airways open for proper breathing.

Eyebright | ***Euphrasia* spp.**
Plants in this large genus of alpine or subalpine flowers are used to alleviate eye ailments, such as conjunctivitis.

Ribwort plantain | ***Plantago lanceolata***
Also called ribwort, plantain's leaves and roots are said to combat problems ranging from coughs and fever to constipation, and to treat wounds and stings.

The heartwood contains an essential oil that is used medicinally

Flowers change color as they mature, so pink and blue flowers may be seen at the same time

Indian sandalwood | ***Santalum album***
This small tree is a parasite on the roots of other trees. Oil extracted from the tree has long been used in ayurvedic medicine for treating skin conditions.

Common witch-hazel |
Hamamelis virginiana
Witch-hazel distillation is a treatment for skin irritation. Hamamelitannin chemicals in the plant may have some effect on colon cancer.

Lungwort | ***Pulmonaria officinalis***
In traditional medicine, lungwort is a remedy for breathing disorders. Its large leaves are mottled with white spots and were said to resemble lungs.

All parts of the plant can be eaten

Primrose-like flowers open late afternoon, hence the plant's common name

Evening primrose | *Oenothera biennis*
As a tea or salve, evening primrose was used by the Americas' Indigenous peoples to remedy bruises, muscle pains, and boils. The seeds give oil, which is taken as a supplement.

The leaves can be made into a paste to relieve swelling

Turmeric | *Curcuma longa*
This spice contains curcumin, which is an anti-inflammatory. The orange rhizomes (underground stems) are cooked, dried, and then powdered for use in medicines.

Purple coneflower | *Echinacea purpurea*
A summer-flowering perennial, purple coneflower yields echinacea oil, which is popular as a natural medicine for alleviating the symptoms of colds and coughs.

Feverfew | *Tanacetum parthenium*
A member of the daisy family and native to Eurasia, especially the Balkans, feverfew is traditionally used to treat fever and headaches.

Flowers can be pinkish-red or white

Tea tree | *Melaleuca alternifolia*
The leaves of this small tree provide an oil used by Indigenous Australians to treat coughs and skin ailments. The tea tree is native to eastern Australia.

Dioscorides

De Materia Medica

Folk healers traditionally passed on lore concerning the curative properties of herbs by word of mouth. During Greek and Roman times, physicians, such as Celsus, began writing this knowledge down. Dioscorides, a Greek military surgeon with the Roman army in the first century CE, produced a compendium of all known medical treatments. He did not restrict himself to plants, but also included remedies involving animal and mineral ingredients. His influential *De Materia Medica* (On Medical Material) remained the leading pharmacological text until the 18th century.

Depiction of Dioscorides c. 1300, discussing the properties of mandrake, a medicinal plant, with a student.

Flowers, stems, and leaves are all used in medicinal preparations

Flowers appear around the summer solstice, close to June 24—the feast day of St. John the Baptist

St. John's wort | *Hypericum perforatum*
This plant grows wild across Eurasia, but it may be a hybrid. St. John's wort contains psychoactive chemicals and is used traditionally for treating depression.

Pharmaceutical plants
Modern medicines

△ **Belladonna** (*Atropa belladonna*) has five green sepals where the black fruit is attached to the plant.

Plants have long been used for traditional herbal remedies (see pp.332–33) but many now play an important role in the development of modern medicines. Increasingly, the pharmaceutical industry is breaking down the chemicals that these plants contain to create the basis of mass-produced medicinal drugs. Many of these chemicals can be synthesized in laboratories, but growing the plants that produce them on a large scale can be much cheaper.

Getting the right plant

Growers screen many plants to select the exact species or cultivar that yields the right bioactive compounds. To get high levels of galantamine, which is used to treat Alzheimer's disease, for example, growers select the narcissus cultivar 'Carlton'.

Because leaves are tiny, photosynthesis mostly occurs in the stems

Female flowers produce red fruits, which enclose a black seed

Ma huang |
Ephedra sinica
Ma huang is a shrub native to northeast China, Russia, and Mongolia. It yields the drug ephedrine, which physicians use to raise blood pressure and to treat asthma.

Pods are collected with the leaflets, then dried and separated

Dried seed pod

Senna | *Senna alexandrina*
The laxative drug senna is derived from the dried leaflets or fruit pods of this plant, which is native to northeast Africa and Arabia. The active chemical components are glycosides called sennosides.

Opium poppy | *Papaver somniferum*
The opium poppy, which now grows across much of Eurasia, is the source of three powerful alkaloids used as drugs: morphine, codeine, and papaverine. Morphine remains the most powerful relief for severe pain.

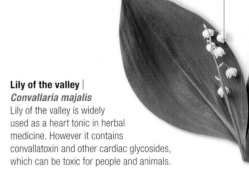

Six tepals fused at base to form bell-shaped flowers

Lily of the valley |
Convallaria majalis
Lily of the valley is widely used as a heart tonic in herbal medicine. However it contains convallatoxin and other cardiac glycosides, which can be toxic for people and animals.

Coca | *Erythroxylum coca*
The leaves of the coca plant, which is native to South America, contain the cocaine alkaloid. When chewed, they act as a mild stimulant, suppressing pain, hunger, and fatigue, but they are also the source of the psychoactive drug cocaine.

Pacific yew | *Taxus brevifolia*
This tree is the source of the therapeutic element paclitaxel, one of the most effective natural-sourced treatments for breast, lung, and ovarian cancer, as well as Kaposi's sarcoma.

Fine hairs cover the leaves giving them a pale appearance

Leaves contain only small traces of salicin

Finely chipped bark

White, pink, and red flowers grow in whorls, and fruits are very small

Flower spikes grow to 5 ft (1.5 m) tall

Portion of dried root

Bell-shaped, dull purple flowers are faintly scented

White willow | *Salix alba*
The bark of white willow is one of the most ancient painkilling remedies. It contains salicin, the basis of the synthetic drug aspirin (acetylsalicylic acid).

Belladonna | *Atropa belladonna*
The leaves and berries of this plant, also called deadly nightshade, are poisonous, but a source of the nerve agent atropine and anticholinergics (drugs that control muscle movements).

Indian snakeroot | *Rauvolfia serpentina*
This is an evergreen shrub native to South and East Asia. The roots are a source of reserpine, one of the first major drugs used to treat high blood pressure.

Aloe is a succulent from dry regions of Africa, Eurasia, Europe, and the Americas

Quill of dried bark

Aloe | *Aloe vera*
Traditionally, aloe vera has been used to treat and heal wounds. It is believed that bioactive agents such as aloe-emodin are responsible, but the plant's efficacy is not yet proven.

Madagascar periwinkle |
Catharanthus roseus
This pretty flower yields two drugs: vincristine has increased childhood leukemia survival rates; and vinblastine treats Hodgkin's disease.

Cinchona | *Cinchona pubescens*
The cinchona is a fast-growing evergreen tree native to the Andes. Its bark has long been used as a source of quinine, used to treat malaria.

Foxglove | *Digitalis purpurea*
This biennial plant is a source of the long-used heart medication, digoxin. However, its leaves, flowers, and seeds are toxic to humans in anything other than the smallest doses.

Tube-shaped, pinkish-purple flowers have spots on the lower lip

The discovery of aspirin

Medical research

In 1763, English vicar Edward Stone noticed that willow bark tastes bitter, like cinchona. He tried the bark on ague (fever) sufferers, who soon felt better. In 1853, it was discovered that the pain-relieving ingredient is salicylic acid, but this attacks the stomach. Then, in the 1890s, scientists found salicylin, a less damaging form of the acid, and made Aspirin powder—the first commercially available painkiller.

The German pharmaceutical company Bayer began production of Aspirin in 1899; it is still sold worldwide.

" **Cultivating cinchona is the solution for reclaiming the malarial region.** "

Huang **Riguang** Chinese agriculturalist

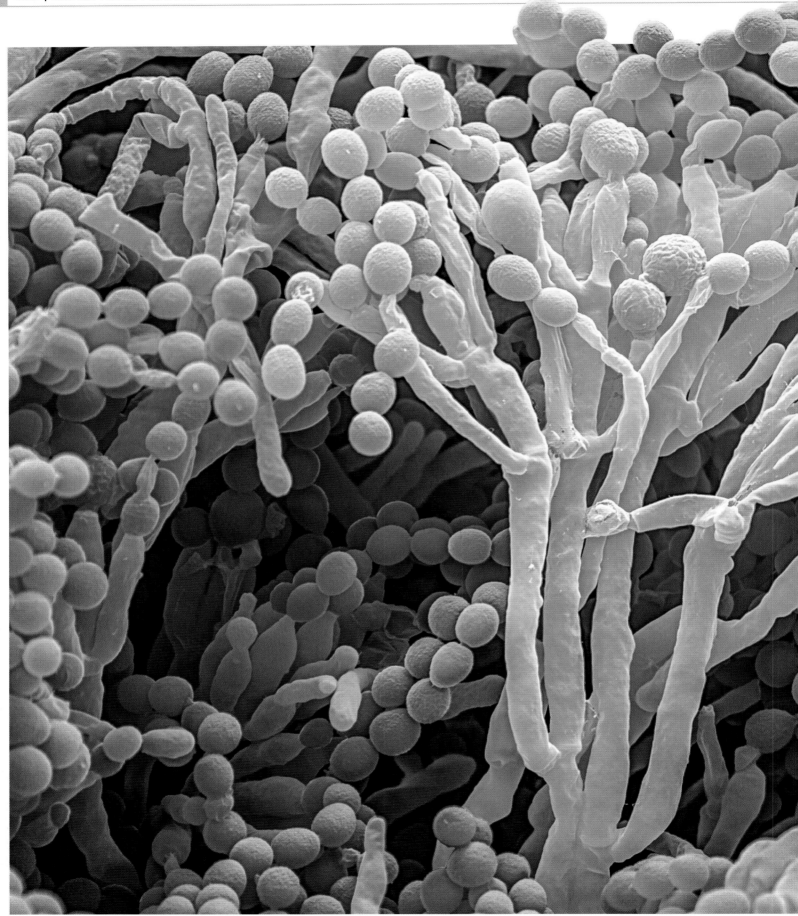

Penicillium rubens produces prolific numbers of asexual spores, which form in chains at the ends of hyphae with many branches.

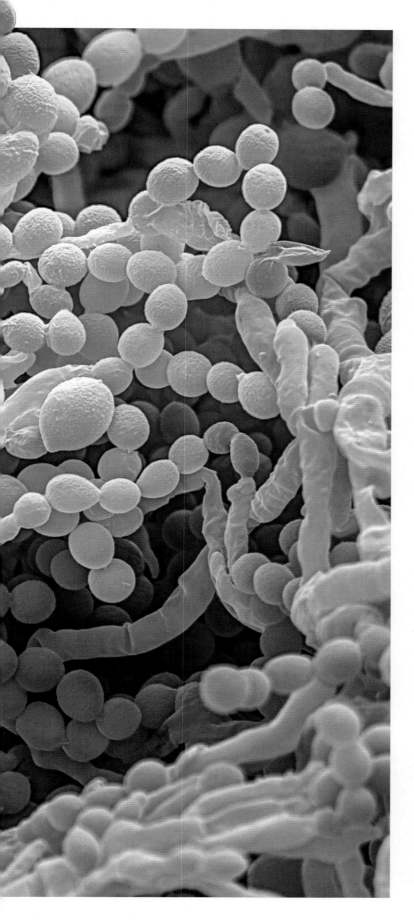

Pharmaceutical fungi
Life savers and health preservers

Penicillin is probably the best-known medicine derived from fungi. It was discovered in 1928 by Alexander Fleming. Returning from vacation, he noticed that the Petri dishes on which he had been growing bacteria for his research had been contaminated with a fungus, now known as *Penicillium rubens*, that had killed the bacteria around it. Howard Florey and Ernst Chain pioneered a method to mass-produce the bacteria-destroying chemical in the fungus—penicillin—in 1939, and in 1945, Dorothy Hodgkin confirmed the chemical structure of this revolutionary antibiotic. Other antibiotics subsequently derived from fungi include griseofulvin and cephalosporin.

Antibiotics are not the only important medicines that come from fungi. The soil fungus *Tolypocladium inflatum* was found to produce a chemical—cyclosporine—that suppresses part of the human immune system. Transplant patients are given cyclosporine to prevent their bodies from rejecting their new organs. Statins, which lower blood cholesterol and lessen the risk of heart disease, were also discovered in fungi. The first statin identified, mevastatin in *Penicillium citrinum*, was never marketed, but lovastatin, found in *Aspergillus terreus*, is used globally by more than 200 million people. *Claviceps purpurea*, which causes ergot in rye, produces alkaloids similar in structure to human neurotransmitters, such as serotonin. These chemicals are used to manage Parkinson's disease and severe migraine. Ephedrine for treating asthma is derived from yeast species.

Penicillium fruiting on an orange

Penicillin has saved the lives of millions of people and extended human life by an average of 23 years.

Fibers
Natural fibers

△ **Kenaf** (*Hibiscus cannabinus*) bears yellow, white, or purple flowers.

Ramie | *Boehmeria nivea*
This is a nettle native to China. Its fibers are soft but strong and are used for products as varied as industrial sewing thread and fabrics for household furniture and clothing.

People have cultivated plants for their fibers for 10,000 years or more. Fibers are long strands of cellulose cells held together with gums and pectins and can be spun into thread for making cloth, pulped to make paper, or used for many other things. The three main types of fiber are bast (the stems of dicotyledonous plants such as flax and hemp), leaf (the leaves of monocotyledonous plants such as sisal), and seed-hairs (such as cotton and kapok). Fibers also come from wood grass (such as bamboo) and fruit (coconut, for example).

Bast fiber

A plant's bast fiber grows between the bark and the inner core. The stalks are harvested by cutting them close to the base, or pulling them up. The fibers are usually then freed from the stalk by retting, or using water and bacteria to dissolve the surrounding pulp.

Jute | *Corchorus* **spp.** Called the "golden fiber," jute is the long, soft, shiny fibers of a few species of the hibiscus and mallow family (*Malvaceae*). It is second in importance only to cotton.

Hemp leaves have a distinctive palm-shape

Industrial hemp | *Cannabis sativa*
Native to Central Asia, this annual plant has long been cultivated for its bast fibers, which are used in agrotextiles, fiberboard, and cottonized for clothing.

Kenaf | *Hibiscus cannabinus*
Ancient Egyptians cultivated this tall annual herbaceous plant for its bast, which they used for ropes and boat sails. Car manufacturers now make car panels from it.

Sunn hemp | *Crotalaria juncea*
Native to South Asia, this annual plant has been cultivated since ancient times. Its bast fiber is used to make ropes, fishing nets, sacking, and canvas.

Flax | *Linum usitatissimum*
This annual provides the fiber to make linen, one of the most ancient fabrics. Linen is stronger than cotton, dries more quickly, and is more resistant to strong sunlight.

> ## "A kind of cloth the making of which, when made of hemp, entails a great waste of hemp."
> Ambrose **Bierce**
> *The Devil's Dictionary*, 1906

Leaf fiber

Some plants produce leaf fiber, which forms in the thick leaves of plants, such as those in the agave family. The leaves are harvested by hand then scraped to release the fibers. This "hard" fiber is used for ropes.

Abacá | *Musa textilis*
Once used for ship's rigging and fishing nets because of its strength and resistance to saltwater, abacá is now being tested as a replacement for fiberglass in cars.

Henequen | *Agave fourcroydes*
This is a fiber plant of the asparagus family (*Asparagaceae*). Native to Mexico and Guatemala, it has been used to produce fiber since pre-Columbian times.

Sisal | *Agave sisalana*
In Central America, people have used this for fiber since pre-Columbian times. It is widely utilized for ropes and is replacing glass fibers in composite materials.

New Zealand flax | *Phormium tenax*
This fiber comes from a plant native to New Zealand in the family *Asphodelaceae*. People have used it since ancient times to make ropes, fabrics, and baskets.

Seed-hair fibers

Many plants produce hairs that are used to help disperse their seeds or to protect them. The hairs of certain plants are an important source of natural fiber, such as milkweed and cotton (see pp.340–341).

Coarse reddish-brown fibers are made of lignin and cellulose

Milkweed | *Asclepias syriaca*
The seedpods of milkweed are mechanically processed to extract the floss—a soft fiber—for use in life jackets and insulation materials.

Coconut | *Cocos nucifera*
Coir is the seed-hair fiber from the outer shell, or husk, of coconuts. Being rich in lignin, it is very strong and is used in the manufacture of ropes, brushes, mattresses, and car seats.

Fabric from fungi

Sustainable materials

Mycelium is tough, waterproof, and sustainable. Cultivated on low-value crop waste, it can be grown in molds of the desired shape and size to create a wide variety of products, such as building materials, packaging, and even fabrics. Its strength, flexibility, and insulation qualities can be controlled by using different fungi species, and varying amounts and types of plant material.

Mycelium leather is being developed as a sustainable alternative to traditional animal and synthetic leathers.

Cotton

The fabric of society

People have used cotton for making fabric for more than 8,000 years. It remains the most popular natural fiber for clothing, because it is light, breathable, durable, easily dyed, and simple to shape into garments. The main centers of early cotton growing were Peru, the Indus Valley (present-day India and Pakistan), and the Kingdom of Kush in the Nile Valley. Industrial production took off in the late 18th century, when enslaved people, forced to work on plantations in the southern US, grew vast quantities of cotton to supply Britain's textile mills.

The seeds of the cotton plant (*Gossypium* species) grow in a fluffy head of soft, white fibers—the boll. The fibers are separated from the seeds, then spun together to make cotton yarn. Separating the seeds and fibers was time-consuming until 1794, when US inventor Eli Whitney patented a mechanical cotton gin that sped up the separation process and massively boosted production. Today, the main centers of cotton production are China and India.

Cotton requires a long growing season, typically maturing in 200 days.

Darwin's cotton (*Gossypium darwinii*) is a cotton species found only on the Galápagos Islands.

Cotton plantations, such as this one, cover more than 2 percent of the world's arable land.

Temperate timber
Managed forests

△ **European white beech** (*Fagus sylvatica*) has pointed, oval leaves that turn orange-brown in the fall.

Wood is an essential component of trees and many other plants. Beneath their bark, young sapwood transports and stores nutrients, while the inner heartwood core provides strong support. Since prehistoric times, humans have used wood for fuel and construction, relying on forests to regenerate and supply this versatile, natural material. However, as human activity increases, forest depletion is causing concern. To preserve a timber supply and enough trees to absorb carbon dioxide effectively, sustainable forest management is now crucially important.

The small, white flowers grow in racemes 2–6 in (6–15 cm) long

Black cherry |
Prunus serotina
Native to eastern North and Central America, the black cherry produces an easily worked, red-brown wood, often used for cabinets and furniture. It is grown in Eurasia as an ornamental.

Hardwood

Although a few evergreens produce hardwood, it comes mainly from broadleaved deciduous trees. These grow more slowly than most softwood species, which makes their timber denser, stronger, and more durable as a result.

An ash tree's compound leaves are each made up of 5–11 leaflets

Collectively, the nuts are called beech mast

European white beech |
Fagus sylvatica
Its large size and the quality of its strong, pliable timber make this tree a popular commercial choice. This species is widespread and can grow to a height of up to 100 ft (30 m).

White birch | *Betula papyrifera*
Native to North America, this species is fast growing for a hardwood tree. Its pale red-brown timber is widely used for firewood, veneers, paper, furniture, and plywood.

White ash | *Fraxinus americana*
This North American species has a timber similar to oak. Valued for its stability and resistance to warp, white ash is frequently used for making furniture and cabinets.

Black walnut |
Juglans nigra
Native to eastern North America, walnut is highly prized for its strength, relatively straight grain, and pale to chocolate-brown color. It is used for furniture, veneers, paneling, and small wooden objects.

Oval leaflets are carried on each side of the stem (pinnate)

European oak | *Quercus robur* One of around 600 oak species, the European oak is native to most of Europe, as well as Asia Minor and North Africa. It can take up to 150 years of growth for the tree to develop its world-renowned hard, durable timber.

Softwood

Softwood timber is obtained mostly from conifers—trees that have needlelike leaves and usually bear cones. Of the 650 species of softwoods throughout the world, around 50 are prized for commercial use.

Pointed, red-brown buds grow between this fir's soft needles

Douglas fir |
Pseudotsuga menziesii
This North American tree, also grown in the UK, New Zealand, and Australia, can reach more than 295 ft (90 m) in height and live for 1,000 years. Its timber's many uses include for flooring, doors, and veneers.

Spalted timber

Stained by fungi

Wood affected by fungal growth is not suitable for load-bearing products, because it can lack strength. However, the staining caused by some fungi creates attractively patterned timber, known as "spalted wood," and has been used decoratively for centuries. The beefsteak fungus (*Fistulina hepatica*) enhances the color of colonized oak wood, for example, producing "brown oak," which is used in the production of veneer. Other fungi species create different stains and patterns.

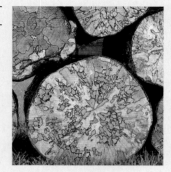

Spalted beech wood is a prized decorative timber and has distinctive dark lines caused by fungal growth.

Needles have two white stripes on their underside

Western hemlock | *Tsuga heterophylla*
Native to North America but introduced to Europe, this tree has shoots densely covered in needles. Its wood is used in roof decking, crates, pallets, and general construction.

Western red cedar | *Thuja plicata*
Not a true cedar, despite its name, this tree is popular for its red-brown wood, which has a straight grain. Its uses include for beams, boxes, boats, and musical instruments.

Scots pine | *Pinus sylvestris*
A beautiful, shapely tree, the Scots pine is one of three British native conifers. Its timber is easily worked and widely used in general joinery and construction.

Common yew | *Taxus baccata*
The long-lived, slow-growing yew is native to Britain and produces a hard timber still used to make longbows, as well as furniture, objects, and veneers.

European larch | *Larix decidua*
This larch is deciduous and produces a tough, durable timber that resists rot. It is valued for doors, window frames, external cladding, and boat-building, among other uses.

Crimson female cones, which produce seeds, develop in spring

This larch's soft needles grow in tufts from short spurs on its branches

About 80 percent of timber used is softwood, because it is easier to work with and cheaper than hardwood.

Cork oak

The tree that is skinned alive

The evergreen cork oak, *Quercus suber*, which grows in woodland around the western Mediterranean, yields a highly versatile material—cork. Used since antiquity, it is light, durable, elastic, and heat and sound proof. While best known from wine bottle stoppers, it has numerous other commercial applications from flooring to thermal insulation in spacecraft.

Wine bottle corks from *Q. suber*

Most trees have a protective outer layer of cork bark, but it is especially thick in the cork oak. It possibly evolved to help the tree resist the wildfires common in its native region. Uniquely, the tree regenerates the layer and suffers no damage if it is expertly harvested in late spring or early summer when the cork separates readily from the trunk. A mature tree must be at least 25 years old before the first cork is stripped off, then around nine years is left between harvests to allow the tree to recover. By the third harvest, the cork is suitable for wine-bottle stoppers. This key use of cork was threatened by a fungal compound that can contaminate cork stoppers, causing the musty taste of "corked" wine. As synthetic stoppers became more popular, some worried that cork woods, an important habitat for endangered wildlife, might disappear. New production methods have eliminated the fungal problem, and sustainable cork production is flourishing.

The cork, stripped from the trees by hand with small axes, is left to dry for at least six months.

Beneath the outer cork layer, the bark of *Quercus suber* is red-brown. In Portugal, the leading cork producer, cork oaks are protected by law and cover almost 1.8 million acres (730,000 ha).

Tropical timber
Threatened forests

△ **Utile** (*Entandrophragma utile*) produces brown-black pods that ripen in December or January and split open to release winged seeds.

Tropical hardwoods are slow-growing and create beautiful, richly colored wood so highly prized that countless trees have been felled. Overexploitation, combined with loss of habitat, has decimated populations of trees such as mahogany and rosewood, and severely damaged tropical forests. In an attempt to control the trade in tropical hardwoods, many species are now listed by international conservation bodies as vulnerable or endangered.

Africa's rainforests

Around 18 percent of the world's rainforests are in Africa, but its deforestation rate is high. It is the world's third largest supplier of tropical hardwood, mostly from the Congo Basin, which is second only to the Amazon rainforest in size.

Iroko | *Milicia excelsa*
This large, deciduous tree from tropical Africa can live for 500 years. However, its teak-like timber is so popular that it is now classified as a vulnerable species.

African mahogany |
Khaya grandifoliola, K. senegalensis
Because it resists termite infestation, *Khaya* is often used for canoes and door frames, but both species are vulnerable.

Hardwood logs dry in the open air in a national park in Gabon, which has logging quotas to help conserve its rainforest.

Utile | *Entandrophragma utile*
Once widespread in tropical Africa, this tall, deciduous tree produces a high-quality red hardwood. Overexploitation has greatly reduced numbers of utile, making it vulnerable.

South America

The Amazon region of South America contains almost a third of the world's tropical rainforests, which are under threat. Logging and ranching reduced the rainforests by 386,102 sq miles (1,000,000 km²) between 1978 and 2021.

Leaves grow in 10–20 alternate pairs of leaflets

Brazilian rosewood | *Dalbergia nigra*
This tree has rose-scented wood, long used for fine furniture and musical instruments, but it is now so vulnerable that most trade in it is banned.

Balsa | *Ochroma pyramidale*
The timber of this fast-growing tree is the lightest and softest hardwood. White to oatmeal in color, it is often used for model-making, buoys, and surfboards.

Honduran mahogany | *Swietenia macrophylla*
Valued for its fine, red-brown wood, but vulnerable in its native range from Mexico south to Brazil and Bolivia, this tree is now naturalized in Southeast Asia and the Pacific.

Trade in tropical hardwoods

Reducing illegal logging

China is the world's largest importer of tropical hardwood, while Papua New Guinea is the lead exporter in a lucrative international trade that has severely depleted rainforest trees. In a bid to safeguard what is left, the International Tropical Timber Organization (ITTO) promotes sustainable management and legal harvesting of wood, and many nations now have laws that have reduced illegal logging. International trade in the timber of highly endangered species, such as Brazilian rosewood (*Dalbergia nigra*), is banned to help ensure the trees survive.

Overexploitation of tropical hardwood has destroyed vast areas of ancient rainforest that took centuries to develop.

Papua New Guinea has cut down almost half of its total rainforest since 2001.

Asia and the Pacific

Tropical Asia has been widely deforested as its population has expanded. From 2000 to 2020, Indonesia lost a third of its old-growth forest to oil palm plantations. China is now creating new hardwood plantations to meet demand.

Ceylon ebony |
Diospyros ebenum
Ebony trees often grow alone. Their dark, near-black heartwood is highly prized and used for inlay, carving, and piano keys.

Teak | *Tectona grandis*
Near waterproof and decay-resistant, teak has long been used for boats and outdoor furniture. Native species are endangered, and most teak is now grown on plantations in Indonesia and Myanmar.

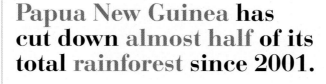

The leaves are large and papery with an often hairy underside

Plantation teak grows faster than teak in the wild

Narra | *Pterocarpus indicus*
Valued for its red-brown wood that can be highly polished, narra's uses include cabinetry and veneers, but it is now classed as endangered.

Compound leaves have up to 11 leaflets attached alternately to the middle vein

Mature Pará rubber trees (*Hevea brasiliensis*), such as these, will have multiple slits from latex harvesting. The trees can be tapped repeatedly for 20 years or more if well managed.

Rubber tree
Tapped for profit

Latex is a sticky emulsion that is part of many plants' defense system. In some tree species, it coagulates when exposed to air to form a rubbery, waterproof substance, long used by Indigenous peoples of the Americas to make balls and containers. By the 19th century, Europeans had begun to realize its potential: when US chemist Charles Goodyear developed a vulcanization process (heating natural rubber with sulfur) that made it more stable, latex tapped from the tall Brazilian Pará rubber tree (*Hevea brasiliensis*) became the major source. Speculators bought up tracts of Amazon rainforest to develop rubber plantations and shipped vast quantities to Europe. In 1875, the British government asked planter Henry Wickham to procure *H. brasiliensis* seeds, and he successfully smuggled out 70,000 seeds to London. Shipped to Sri Lanka, they became the basis of a new, more efficient Asian rubber plantation industry that came to dominate the market. Leaf blight has decimated young rubber trees in the Amazon since 1935, and still limits their cultivation in South America.

Synthetic rubber is now widely produced, but natural rubber is considered superior, and *H. brasiliensis* is still the main source. Once a tree is six years old, its bark is cut diagonally at different levels every few days to drain off latex. This continues for many years until the supply dwindles.

Lumps of raw rubber

A single tree produces 132–330 lb (60–150 kg) of rubber in its lifetime.

Tappers cut shallow, diagonal slits in the bark in the early morning when the water content of the latex is higher.

Latex trickles from a cut in the tree bark, down a gutter, into a cup that is left in place for at least three hours.

A rubber farm worker in India hangs out rolled sheets of latex to dry; it will need further processing before export.

Rubber trees, such as this plantation in Thailand, look like natural woodland, but are often grown on deforested land.

Plant pigments
Creating color

△ **True indigo** (*Indigofera tinctoria*) is a plant in the bean family. The intense blue dye is produced from its leaves.

People began making dyes from plants in prehistoric times. A wide range of materials were used, including lichens, barks, oak galls, berries, nettles, and flowers. These were often crushed, boiled, or fermented to extract their colors. For thousands of years, many dye plants were grown as crops: woad and madder in temperate parts of the world, and stronger-colored dyes, such as sorghum and indigo, in tropical regions. Today, however, most natural plant dyes have been replaced by synthetic alternatives, and the plants are no longer cultivated for this purpose.

Reds and pinks

Since the creation of a synthetic form of the natural dye alizarin, in 1868, red plant dyes have almost disappeared from use. Before that date, people used plants of the madder genus (*Rubia* spp.) and others, such as sorghum and brazilwood, to dye their cloth red.

The edible seeds are also used to create a red dye

The leaves can also be used to produce a dye

The dye is extracted by pulverizing the leaf sheaths

Tannin-rich berries develop from the fluffy, red flower head

Staghorn sumac | *Rhus typhina*
Most species of sumac contain tannins in their leaves, bark, and fruit. This was used for leather-making and as a reddish-brown dye.

Madder is a food plant for caterpillars of the hummingbird hawkmoth

The outer layer of madder root gives red dye, the inner layer saffron-orange

Sorghum | *Sorghum bicolor*
Red sorghum is a variety of *Sorghum bicolor*, which is native to Africa and is widely grown as a food and fodder crop. An extract from red sorghum is traditionally used for dying fabric.

Pussy willow | *Salix caprea*
Willow trees may not appear to be likely sources of pigment, but the bark of several species can be boiled gently to release dyes, such as the pink shade produced by pussy willow.

Sappanwood | *Biancaea sappan*
In medieval Europe, the best red dye came from the heartwood of the Asian sappanwood tree. At the time it was called brazilwood, from the French word *braise*, meaning "embers."

Madder | *Rubia tinctorum*
The roots of some madder species contain alizarin. *Rubia tinctorum*, also known as dyer's madder, was a species especially prized for the vivid color it produces.

Blues and greens

Deep blue dyes from indigo and woad plants were used for millennia. In Europe, woad was largely replaced by indigo when it began to be traded from Asia. In 1883, synthetic indigo was created, and the plant-based industry was rendered obsolete.

Woad has clusters of yellow flowers

Woad leaves contain the same chemical as those of true indigo

The leaves give the most dye

Woad | *Isatis tinctoria*
The woad plant originates from the Asian steppes. In medieval Europe, Toulouse, France, was a prosperous woad-growing region.

Cow parsley | *Anthriscus sylvestris*
The stems, leaves, and flowers of this northern European meadow plant yield a green dye when simmered slowly in water.

True indigo | *Indigofera tinctoria*
Native to dry, tropical regions of Africa, Asia, and the Americas, true indigo is a scrambling shrub that was once widely cultivated for its vivid blue dye.

Fungal pigments

Dyes from fungi

Fungi and lichens produce many pigments that were traditionally used to dye wool and silk. Concerns about the environmental effects of synthetic dyes has led to a revival of interest in fungi as potential alternatives. They offer a broad color spectrum, including reds from *Cortinarius* species, purple from the cinnamon bracket (*Hapalopilus nidulans*), vibrant yellow from the sulfur tuft fungus (*Hypholoma fasciculare*), and blue and green from the scaly hedgehog fungus (*Sarcodon imbricatus*).

Dyer's polypore (*Phaeolus schweinitzii*) yields green, brown, or gold, depending on the material and the dye fixative used.

Yellows and oranges

Yellow hues are the easiest colors to make from plants, and some of these dyes have an ancient tradition. They include saffron, the deep, rich yellow made from the stigmas of the *Crocus sativus* flower, which is cherished in Hinduism and in Irish folklore.

Dyer's tickseed | *Coreopsis tinctoria*
A brightly colored wildflower from the North American prairies, dyer's tickseed contains a wide spectrum of dye chemicals that combine to produce an orange pigment.

Golden chamomile | *Cota tinctoria*
This chamomile is a European native. Its daisylike flowers are dried for a few weeks, then soaked to give a pale yellow, buff, or orange dye.

Myrobalan | *Phyllanthus emblica*
The fruits of India's myrobalan tree are used in cooking, while an extract from the leaves produces a brown dye, used for textiles.

Flowers, seeds, leaves, and stalks all produce yellow dye

Weld | *Reseda luteola*
Like woad and madder, weld was once a traditional dye plant in Europe. It is now mainly found growing wild on wasteland.

> **"... not any person shall dye any wool ... into cloth unless the same wool be perfectly woaded."**
> Act of Parliament
> England 1550

Krishna's attendants show hands decorated with henna in an 18th-century manuscript painting.

Henna

An ancient pigment

Henna is a natural, copper-colored dye. It has been used for coloring hair, skin, nails, and fabrics, especially in South Asia, for at least 5,000 years. It comes principally from the leaves of the henna plant (*Lawsonia inermis*), a small tree native to South Asia, the Arabian Peninsula, and East Africa, which bears small, brown fruits and flowers with white, oval petals. Henna is now cultivated in many warm regions of the world. The dye is made by crushing the leaves, stems, and flowers of the plant into a fine powder and mixing it with water to make a paste. The rich color comes from a pigment in the leaves and stems called lawsone, or hennotannic acid. The stain it makes on skin, hair, and nails is only temporary, but can be made to last longer by adding lemon juice, tea, or essential oils.

Henna fruits, flowers, and leaves

Ancient Egyptians used henna to protect their skin from sunburn.

Mehndi art

Painting with henna

Originating in South Asia, Mehndi is an art form that involves painting elaborate patterns on the skin in henna with a plastic cone, paintbrush, or stick. It is typically used for Hindu, Muslim, and Sikh weddings and religious ceremonies. Although often called a henna tattoo, unlike a tattoo it is only temporary. Sikh and Hindu brides typically have their hands and feet painted, while others may have their hands and other body parts, such as their back and chest, decorated.

Natural pigments such as indigo are sometimes used alongside henna to add contrast to mehndi designs.

Ornamental trees
Cultivated beauty

△ **Black elder** (*Sambucus nigra*) has juicy berries that attract birds, and are used to create drinks and preserves.

Ornamental trees are selected and bred to give pleasure. Since antiquity, some species have been singled out for appealing characteristics such as perfume, striking spring blossoms, aesthetic form, decorative bark or berries, and richly colored fall foliage. Over time, arboriculturalists have developed numerous cultivars of the most popular species, seeking to enhance their most appealing qualities. As a result, many ornamental trees are now very different from their wild ancestors, and, being bred for yards, are often smaller than woodland trees.

Paperbark maple | *Acer griseum*
Native to central China, this is now widely cultivated in the northern temperate zone for its decorative, copper-colored, peeling bark and lovely fall foliage.

Choosing well

As with any plant, what grows where depends on soil type and climate. Lilacs, for instance, thrive in well-drained, fertile, chalky soil, while acers prefer slightly acidic soil. Frost is the enemy of many decorative species.

Common lilac | *Syringa vulgaris*
Native from Southeast to Central Europe, lilac is cherished for its fragrant hanging clusters (panicles) of late spring flowers in shades of purple, pink, and white.

The white flowers are star-shaped

Juneberry | *Amelanchier lamarckii*
Native to North America, the juneberry is popular for its pretty, white spring blossoms, which attract bees; its dark-red summer berries, enjoyed by birds; and its fiery fall foliage.

Common hawthorn |
Crataegus monogyna
Long associated with myths and pagan rites, the trees grow wild across Europe and are popular as ornamentals for their fragrant blossoms and red fall berries.

The Judas tree has clusters of rosy pink or purple flowers in spring

The scent is stronger when it is warm and sunny

Judas tree | *Cercis siliquastrum*
This tree may get its common name, from the apostle who died by suicide after betraying Christ, due to its dark, pendulous seedpods or its widespread cultivation in Israel.

Black elder | *Sambucus nigra*
Native to Eurasia, black elders have striking, dark foliage and clusters of pink-white flowers in spring, often used to make a delicious cordial. Its fall berries are also edible.

Himalayan birch | *Betula utilis*
This hardy, elegant tree is one of many birch species valued for their form and attractive, peeling, silvery bark, used for centuries as paper high in the Himalayas. Sacred Sanskrit texts written on birch bark still survive.

Japanese cherry | *Prunus serrulata* With its beautiful blossoms, this species has many cultivars; 'Kanzan', developed in Japan's Edo period (1603–1868), is one of the most popular.

Maple leaves are palmate (hand-shaped)

The rowan has pretty red clusters of fall berries

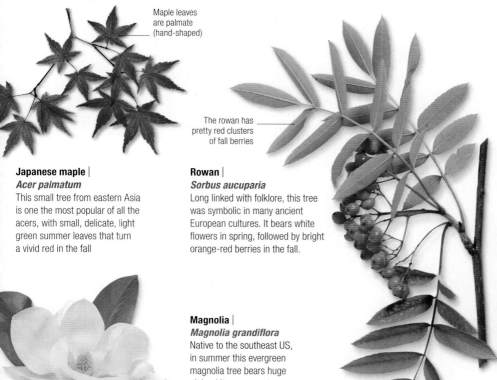

Japanese maple |
Acer palmatum
This small tree from eastern Asia is one the most popular of all the acers, with small, delicate, light green summer leaves that turn a vivid red in the fall

Rowan |
Sorbus aucuparia
Long linked with folklore, this tree was symbolic in many ancient European cultures. It bears white flowers in spring, followed by bright orange-red berries in the fall.

Magnolia |
Magnolia grandiflora
Native to the southeast US, in summer this evergreen magnolia tree bears huge pink-white or magenta, tulip-like flowers that often have a lovely fragrance.

Trees in art

A bid to capture nature

Attracted by the beauty, longevity, and symbolism of trees, artists down the ages have depicted them in every season—blossoming, leafy, autumnal, or skeletal. Among the best-known are works by British artist John Constable, French impressionist Claude Monet, Dutch post-impressionist Vincent van Gogh, and US landscape photographer Ansel Adams.

For Van Gogh, olive trees had a powerful biblical significance.

Cherry blossom
Symbol of spring

When the first cherry trees (*Prunus* spp.) bloom on the subtropical island of Okinawa in mid-January, the Japanese begin to celebrate their beauty in the annual spring festival *hanami* (flower viewing). By the end of May, as many as 600 different varieties will have blossomed in parks and gardens across Japan. Each area stages cherry blossom festivals (*sakura matsuri* in Japanese)—picnics with dancing and music under the trees to coincide with the fortnight of their flowering.

The *hanami* tradition, which began in the Japanese Nara period (710–794 CE), originally celebrated the blossoming of *ume*—Japanese apricot (*Prunus mume*). However, from the Heian period (794–1185) onward, it became associated with the similar-looking cherry tree blossoms, particularly those of the Japanese cherry (*Prunus serrulata*), the Oshima cherry (*P. speciosa*), and their many cultivated varieties. While many other countries now stage cherry blossom festivals, the flowers (*sakura*) have a deeper cultural significance in Japan. People once believed that rice paddy gods who could bring good harvests dwelt in the blossoms, while the brief flowering period symbolizes new life but also its transience.

Jindai-Zakura, Japan's oldest cherry tree, is up to 2,000 years old.

Cherry blossom is celebrated in this 19th-century print by Japanese artist Katsushika Hokusai.

Typical cherry blossoms, like these in the grounds of Himeji Castle, Japan, range in color from white to dark pink, but some cultivated varieties may be yellow or even green.

Poppy | *Papaver rhoeas* Poppies brightened arable fields across Europe before the advent of herbicides. Though fewer now grow wild, they are widely cultivated.

Cultivated ornamentals
A cornucopia of blooms

△ **Love-in-a-mist** (*Nigella damascena*) produces distinctive seedpods after flowering.

Parks and gardens around the world are adorned with an astonishing variety of ornamental plants that look very different from their wild counterparts. Many of them have been cultivated for gardens since antiquity. Over thousands of years, gardeners have picked out a host of wild species for their appealing characteristics and bred them to create cultivars with heightened qualities such as the color, shape, and perfume of their flowers—often altering the plants so much that it is almost impossible to trace their heritage.

Masses of oil-rich seeds develop at the flower's center

Sunflower |
Helianthus annuus
Native to Mexico, this tall annual thrives in summer heat elsewhere, attracting bees to its flowers and small birds to its seeds.

Different environments

Many species may be cultivated to bloom more often and to grow in conditions that differ from those of their native range. Tender plants may become hardier and perennials become annuals.

The flowers have five petals and are up to 2 in (5 cm) in diameter

Love-in-a-mist has threadlike compound leaves

D. purpurea f. *albiflora* is a naturally occurring white-flowered form

Impatiens |
Impatiens walleriana
This prolifically flowering plant is native to East Africa but now popular worldwide as a half-hardy bedding plant.

Love-in-a-mist |
Nigella damascena
Native to the Mediterranean region, this annual was named for its pretty flowers, framed in a mist of feathery bracts.

Foxglove | *Digitalis purpurea*
A biennial or perennial, this attractive plant can grow up to 5 ft (1.5 m) tall. Although all parts are toxic, chemicals from its dried leaves are used in heart medications.

Sweet peas are planted from seed each year

The bell-shaped flowers attract both butterflies and bees

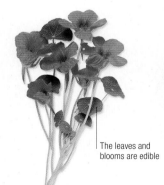

The leaves and blooms are edible

Each long stem has a solitary flower

Viper's bugloss | *Echium vulgare*
Native to western Eurasia, this plant's snake name may come from its spotted stem and "bugloss" (Greek for "ox-tongue") from its leaves.

Garden nasturtium | *Tropaeolum majus*
This trailing plant with vivid orange-red, funnel-shaped blooms has no known wild ancestor and was cultivated from a hybrid first grown in Peru.

Zinnia | *Zinnia elegans*
Cultivars of this widely naturalized plant with showy flowers enjoy a sunny position, reflecting zinnia's native range from Mexico to Nicaragua.

Sweet pea | *Lathyrus odoratus*
Native to southern Italy and Sicily, this popular climbing annual is cultivated for its delicate, sweet-smelling, purple or pink flowers.

Clematis | *Clematis patens*
The name of this spring-flowering climber, native to eastern China and southern Japan, is derived from the Greek for "tendril," referring to the leaf tendrils it uses to cling to a support.

Its narrow flower spikes bear masses of tiny yellow flowers

Goldenrod | *Solidago virgaurea*
Also known as woundwort, this tall, prolific garden perennial was once used to heal wounds, and its inflorescence is still a component of some herbal medicines.

Large tubular flowers bloom from spring to early summer

Prairie beardtongue | *Penstemon cobaea*
This plant, which grows wild on American prairies, has tall, showy flowers, typical of its genus, which includes some 280 species.

Bees are greatly attracted to the lupine's colorful flower spikes

"... the duty we owe to our gardens`... is to so use the plants that they shall form beautiful pictures."

Gertrude Jekyll *Color in the Garden,* 1908

Flowers bloom from late summer to late fall

Florists' chrysanthemum | *Chrysanthemum × morifolium*
This popular plant first reached Europe from its native China in the late 17th century. The hybrid has vivid blooms in varieties that include cascades, charms, sprays, and pompoms.

Garden lupine | *Lupinus polyphyllus*
Originating in temperate areas of North America, where it grows by streams and creeks, this popular, tall perennial has many colorful cultivars.

Giant blue hosta |
Hosta sieboldiana var. *elegans*
This variety of *H. sieboldiana*, a hosta native to Japan, has become popular for its giant, sculptural leaves and spikes of trumpet-shaped flowers.

Bleeding heart | *Lamprocapnos spectabilis*
Native to northeast Asia, where it grows in temperate woodland, the bleeding heart is popular for its delicate heart-shaped blooms.

The pendant flowers have pink outer and white inner petals

The white inner petals form a droplet beneath the heart

The leaves can irritate, so wear gloves if handling them

Garden phlox | *Phlox paniculata*
This garden classic originating in the central and eastern US has showy, fragrant flowers that can be pink, purple, lavender, red, or white, and bloom throughout the summer.

Biting stonecrop | *Sedum acre*
In the wild, this stonecrop grows from Greenland to the Mediterranean on sand dunes, shingle, grassland, and roadsides. Gardeners often use it in hanging baskets and containers.

Daylilies are not true lilies (*Lilium* spp.) but have similar flowers

Orange daylily | *Hemerocallis fulva*
A vigorous perennial that grows in clumps, the orange daylily, native to the mountains of east Asia, is a garden favorite for its vivid flowers.

The fragrant flowers are purple, pink, or white

Carnation | *Dianthus caryophyllus*
This popular plant, native to the Balkan peninsula, has been bred into hundreds of varieties, both annual and perennial, since the 1500s.

Lanceleaf tickseed | *Coreopsis lanceolata*
Its deep yellow, daisylike flowers make this plant a popular garden choice. It also grows wild on grassland, in forest glades, and in fields in the US, parts of Canada, and Mexico.

Great Dixter
Spectacular country garden

A life-long passion for horticulturalist and writer Christopher Lloyd (1921–2006), the garden at Great Dixter in East Sussex, UK, was originally planted by his parents, Daisy and Nathaniel, around their centuries-old family home. Its mixed borders abound with exuberant colors. Topiary birds, an exotic garden, a wildflower meadow, and formal ponds add further delights. Dismissing low-maintenance gardening, Lloyd declared "I'm interested in high maintenance," and the garden he created reflects his assiduous, endlessly experimental approach.

The Long Border at Great Dixter is a blaze of color in summer.

The pink or white flowers can be up to 4 in (10 cm) in diameter

Chinese peony | *Paeonia lactiflora*
On cultivars of this peony, native to central and eastern Asia, the large blooms are spectacular and fragrant. Gardeners often use a circular metal frame to support them.

Ornamental bulbs
For color and scent

△ **Tuberose** (*Agave amica*) has fleshy, tuberous underground roots that give the plant its name.

Planting ornamental bulbs is a simple and foolproof way to introduce color and fragrance into a garden. True bulbs, corms, rhizomes, and tubers contain nutrients and moisture to help a plant survive winter cold and summer heat. Most can be stored for at least a season. Popular varieties include tulips (*Tulipa* spp.) daffodils (*Narcissus pseudonarcissus*), and hyacinths (*Hyacinthus orientalis*). The Netherlands, renowned for its tulip fields, exports three billion tulip bulbs annually.

Bulbs

Varying greatly in size, bulbs have layers of fleshy scales around a developing shoot; some also have a papery outer tunic. Roots grow from a basal plate at the bottom of the bulb.

Stems can bear up to 30 flowers and can grow to 6 ft (2 m) tall

Flowers open in a wide range of colors

The bunch of little, oval blooms on its flower spike gives the plant its common name

Turk's cap lily |
Lilium martagon
These tall, striking, crimson flowers are native to Eurasia. They are now grown in gardens across the northern hemisphere, where they prefer slightly dappled shade.

Nerine | *Nerine bowdenii*
Also known as the Bowden lily, this South African perennial plant is hardy in regions with mild winters, where it can form large clumps. It produces heads of pink flowers in the fall.

Grape hyacinth |
Muscari neglectum
Grape hyacinths are Mediterranean perennials grown widely for their dense spikes of usually blue to dark-blue spring flowers.

Hyacinth |
Hyacinthus orientalis
According to myth, the Greek god Apollo created this plant from the spilled blood of his beloved Hyacinth, a Spartan youth killed by a discus.

Garden tulip | *Tulipa gesneriana* Much hybridized, the tulip is perhaps the most popular of all cut flowers.

Black Persian lily |
Fritillaria persica
With its tall, purple-black, towering racemes of up to 30 bell-shaped flowers, the Persian lily adds a touch of drama to a garden.

Tubers, corms, and rhizomes

Some plants sprout from tubers (thick, underground stems), others from squat corms that—unlike true bulbs—have no visible layers, or from rhizomes that grow horizontally below the soil surface.

Ivy-leaved cyclamen |
Cyclamen hederifolium
Native to Türkiye and much of Europe, this is the hardiest cyclamen. It is easily cultivated and grows wild in woods and on scrubland and rocky terrain.

White, waxy flowers are trumpet-shaped

Tuberose | *Agave amica*
Also known as *Polianthes tuberosa*, tuberose is native to central and southern Mexico. In cultivation, it is now hybridized and widely grown as a fragrant garden flower.

Flower color and shape varies greatly according to the variety grown

Dahlia | *Dahlia* spp.
Originally native to Mexico and Central America, dahlias have been extensively cross-bred and hybridized to create thousands of name varieties. They are popular summer-flowering plants.

Tulips and Ottoman culture

Flower power

Native to Central Asia, the tulip was so highly prized by the Ottoman sultan Ahmed III that a period of cultural renaissance during his reign became known as the Tulip Age (1718–1730). Huge quantities of imported bulbs fed the craze, and tulip gardens sprang up across Istanbul, celebrating a bloom long revered in Ottoman culture as the holiest flower.

A tulip motif decorates Iznik lapis tiles in Istanbul's Rustem Pasha mosque, built in 1561, when ceramic production in the Anatolian town of Iznik was at its peak.

Flowers are 2 in (5 cm) long with paler lower petals

Up to 20 deep pink flowers grow on a loose flower spike

Field gladiolus | *Gladiolus italicus*
Grown from corms, the field or Italian gladiolus is a tall, elegant plant from the Mediterranean and Central Asia. It grows wild in fields and on hillsides in its native habitat, flowering in spring.

Flower stems can reach 6½ ft (2 m) tall

Indian shot | *Canna indica*
Native to the tropical and subtropical Americas, this tall, striking ornamental grows from rhizomes and produces racemes of red-orange flowers from summer to early fall.

DIRECTORY

After millions of years of evolution, the plant kingdom has diversified hugely. Botanists classify plants in order to place them in families and understand them better.

The taxonomy of plants

The approach used to classify living organisms, known as taxonomy, was developed by Swedish botanist Carolus Linnaeus (1707–1778), who devised a hierarchical system consisting of classes, orders, genera, and species. Modern scientists constantly review existing classifications that were commonly based on observation, but they do not always agree. This directory of plant orders is based on *A Higher Level Classification of All Living Organisms*, Public Library of Science, 2015.

The cool, moist climate in New Zealand's Fiordland National Park encourages the growth of a wide variety of mosses and liverworts.

Mosses

Among the most ancient of plant forms, mosses are nonflowering and typically form mats or cushion-shaped clumps. Despite their small size, they are remarkably resilient. They are able to grow in a wide range of habitats, from woodland to deserts, and are found on every continent, including Antarctica.

ANDREAEOBRYALES

Family 1 **Genus** 1
Species 1

This order contains a single species, *Andreaeobryum macrosporum*—a small moss with clustered, upright stems that is found in Alaska and western Canada. It grows on rocks rich in iron, magnesium, and calcium, and changes in color from green when young to reddish-brown, and then jet black when it matures.

Native range North America

ANDREAEALES

Family 1 **Genera** 2
Species 101

The mosses of the order Andreaeales include species that form dense cushions on wet rocks and are therefore known as rock mosses. Most species are found in South America and Antarctica, but the order has a global distribution. In tropical regions, species are found only on high mountain tops where conditions are cool.

Native range Every continent

BARTRAMIALES

Family 1 **Genera** 13
Species Around 420

The tuft or cushion mosses of Bartramiales grow worldwide. Species form loose to dense tufts and are usually found on soil, but also sometimes on rocks. In tropical regions, they grow in montane habitats at high altitudes where conditions are cool and moist.

Native range Every continent

Common apple-moss |
Bartramia pomiformis
This mound-forming moss has blue-green leaves and green, globular spore capsules.

△ BRYALES

Families 14 **Genera** 78
Species 1,782

The large Bryales order includes thread mosses, thyme mosses, tree mosses, and hump mosses. The order has a global distribution with species found in a wide range of habitats. They form clumps or patches, some having quite large leaves in opposite rows. Several species reproduce almost exclusively by asexual means.

Native range Every continent

White-tipped moss | *Hedwigia ciliata*
Also known as fringed hoar-moss, this species is often found on stonework, such as walls, stone roof tiles, and gravestones.

◁ HEDWIGIALES

Family 1 **Genera** 6
Species 47

This order of medium to large-size mosses has one family—*Hedwigiaceae*. Its species mainly grow upright or to one side in loose or dense mats, and spread over damp rocks in temperate and subtropical habitats.

Native range Every continent

▽ HOOKERIALES

Families 2 **Genera** 58
Species 818

Species in this order of leafy mosses are mostly found in tropical climates. They are pleurocarpous, that is, they spread in carpets, rather than growing erect. Their leaves are typically green, translucent, quite large for mosses, and asymmetrical. They are usually arranged in flattened rows along the stems.

Native range Every continent

Shining hookeria | *Hookeria lucens* This species, which grows in moist, shaded forest areas around the world, is notable for its bright green leaves, with hexagonal cells visible to the naked eye.

The native range of some moss species extends to just a few square yards.

Umbrella moss | *Hypnodendron kerrii* This member of the *Hypnodendraceae* family is native to New Zealand and is growing here in an ancient forest.

▽ HYPNALES

Families 15 **Genera** 280
Species 3,400

This order includes the feather mosses, so-called because their leaflets grow opposite each other on reclining stems, giving them a feather-like appearance. Hypnales species live on every continent, growing in soil, on rocks, or epiphytically on trees. Some thrive in extreme conditions. The feather-moss *Pleurozium schreberi* is common in the Arctic, while the hook-moss *Sanionia uncinata* is abundant in maritime Antarctica.

Native range Every continent

△ HYPNODENDRALES

Families 4 **Genera** 11
Species 92

Although Hypnodendrales species grow worldwide, most are found in the southern hemisphere. Many of the mosses have an upright, dendroid (treelike) form, and resemble small trees or fern fronds.

Some tropical species are epiphytic, but the majority are ground-dwelling mosses that grow in forests.

Native range Every continent

ORTHOTRICHALES

Families 5 **Genera** 41
Species 919

This order of mosses has a global distribution and includes bristle-mosses, and pincushion mosses, named for their characteristic forms. These plants form loose clumps on rocks and epiphytically on trees. Many are tropical or subtropical.

Native range Every continent

▷ PTYCHOMNIALES

Families 1 **Genera** 11
Species 32

These mosses have small upright stems with densely packed leaves and are found from sea level up into the mountains, mainly in the southern hemisphere. At their main (gametophyte) life stage, they are

dioecious—either male or female, with males sometimes reduced to dwarf plants. Several species are epiphytic on trees.

Native range Asia, Australasia, Europe, North America, South America

Ptychomnion aciculare Widespread in moist forest, this Ptychomniales moss has red-brown sporangia, visible here amid its foliage.

Hypnales is the largest order of mosses, which includes around a third of all species.

Velvet feather moss | *Brachythecium velutinum* With its much-branched stems, this abundant moss forms creeping mats on dead wood and in waterlogged grass. It has a worldwide range.

BUXBAUMIALES

Family 1   **Genera** 4
Species 28

The mosses of this order's only genus—
Buxbaumia—are often microscopic at their
short gametophyte developmental stage.
They grow on tree trunks and logs, mainly
in the northern hemisphere. Unusually,
their sporophyte phase is longer than their
gametophyte stage, and their distinctive,
asymmetrical spore capsules give them
their common name of elf-cap moss.

Native range Asia, Australasia, Europe,
North America, South America

▷ SPLACHNALES

Families 3   **Genera** 16
Species 136

Uniquely among bryophytes, Splachnales
includes coprophilous species—mosses
that grow primarily on animal feces and
also on animal carcasses and bones. A
number of them are also entomophilous,
meaning their spores are dispersed by
insects rather than the wind. Most of these
mosses form dense cushions, and their
prominent sporophytes smell of carrion.

Native range Every continent

▽ RHIZOGONIALES

Families 2   **Genera** 14
Species 27

Most mosses in this order are epiphytic,
growing on branches, tree trunks, or logs
in moist forest, where a dense canopy

Pinkstink dung moss | *Splachnum sphaericum* This moss grows mainly on herbivore dung and produces many red-brown sporangia on red-yellow stems. In Britain, it is found on upland heaths and in bogs, and is the most common species of its genus.

reduces light levels and water loss. The
order includes both dioecious species that
bear either male or female sex organs, and
monoecious mosses that produce both
male and female sex organs.

Native range Every continent
except Antarctica

Ribbed bog moss | *Aulacomnium palustre* This widespread moss of the Rhizogoniales order, grows mainly in bogs or on wet heaths and produces curved spore-bearing capsules (sporangia).

ARCHIDIALES

Family 1   **Genus** 1
Species 34

This order contains only the family
Archidiaceae and one genus, *Archidium*,
but its species grow almost worldwide.
Plants form loose mats of prostrate stems,
creeping over their substrate. They grow
on damp rocks and soil in temperate to
subtropical climates.

Native range Every continent
except Antarctica

BRYOXIPHIALES

Family 1   **Genus** 1
Species 2

Mosses of this order's only genus,
Bryoxiphium, are distinctive species with
narrow shoots that hang downward from
the rock substrates to which they attach,
giving colonies of them a pendulous
appearance. Both *Bryoxiphium* mosses
are very small, with shoots usually less
than 1 in (2.5 cm) long. Species grow
across the northern hemisphere.

Native range Asia, Europe, North America

Dung mosses attract flies to spread their spores. All other mosses rely on the wind.

▷ DICRANALES

Families 11   **Genera** 103
Species 1,538

This order of mosses, which includes the fork and pocket mosses, has species that grow worldwide in a range of habitats. Most are cushion-forming, with numerous, long, upright, unbranched stems that create lax domes or clumps. The leaves often curve to one side as they grow. In some genera, the leaves are held in two opposite ranks, making the stems appear flat.

Native range Every continent

Common pocket moss | *Fissidens taxifolius*
This widespread moss has short, spreading stems bearing two ranks of pointed leaves. It grows on shaded ground and on rocks.

Screw-mosses are named for the spirally twisted teeth on their spore capsules, which must "unscrew" to release the spores.

Wall screw-moss | *Tortula muralis* This moss has tiny, silver hairs that project from the leaf tips, and bears slim, spore-producing capsules on stalks up to ½ in (1.5 cm) high.

Leaves form a cushion ½–¾ in (1.5–2 cm) high

Purple fork moss | *Grimmia pulvinata*
Growing on rocks, roofs, and walls, this widespread moss has leaves that end in long, silvery hairs. Its spore capsules grow on curved stalks.

▽ GRIMMIALES

Families 2   **Genera** 16
Species 365

Mosses in this order form small, domed cushions. Their numerous, upright stems grow close together, creating a dense habit. Their spore-producing structures (sporophytes) are often clearly visible, and may be stemless or have their own stems. Species are mainly found in Arctic, Antarctic, and cool temperate regions, but some also grow in tropical montane habitats.

Native range Every continent

△ POTTIALES

Families 4   **Genera** 103
Species 1,621

One of the largest orders of mosses, species in this group are found in virtually all habitats worldwide. The plants form small, dense or lax cushions, depending on the size of their stems. Many species that grow in harsh environments have adapted, and have smaller stems and form tighter cushions. The matte leaves have pointed or rounded tips.

Native range Every continent

SCOULERIALES

Families 2   **Genera** 3
Species 10

This small order of mosses includes two families that have quite different habits. Plants in the *Drummondiaceae* family are epiphytes that grow on wood, whereas members of the *Scouleriaceae* family are found in permanently wet environments, growing at stream edges or partially submerged—they are known as splash zone mosses. Plants from both families grow to form mats of lax stems and are very dark green to almost black in color.

Native range Every continent

▽ DIPHYSCIALES

Family 1   **Genus** 1
Species 15

This order contains a single genus of moss—*Diphyscium*. The species have very short stems with relatively large, strap-shaped, brownish green leaves that form dense rosettes. They bear spore capsules that barely project above the leaves. These mosses often grow in dark, humid sites, such as shaded gullies.

Native range Every continent

▷ ENCALYPTALES

Families 2   **Genera** 2
Species 47

These mosses form small, dense cushions of erect shoots on soil, rocks, or wood. They are known as extinguisher mosses because their hoodlike spore capsules, borne on reddish stems, resemble a candle snuffer. Some species bear capsules only occasionally, producing brown, threadlike structures in the leaf axils instead.

Native range Every continent

Spiral extinguisher moss |
Encalypta streptocarpa
Favoring lowland sites with chalk or limestone soils, this moss forms loose clumps of leaves and only rarely produces spore capsules.

FUNARIALES

Families 7   **Genera** 35
Species 388

Forming dense mats or tufts on soil, rocks, and tree bark, these plants have short stems with broad leaves, often crowded at the stem tips. Spore capsules are borne on tall, very twisted or curved stems that unwind rapidly when the spores are mature and ready for dispersal. In Latin, *funis* means "rope," so species belonging to the genus *Funaria* are often known as cord mosses.

Native range Every continent

GIGASPERMALES

Family 1   **Genera** 6
Species 9

The majority of mosses in this order are found in the southern hemisphere, where they often grow on volcanic soils. They are almost stemless, forming low mats. The extremely short, erect stalks emerge from fleshy, creeping, underground rhizomes. The leaves are pale green or whitish, and the spherical spore capsules are stemless, forming on the ground.

Native range Every continent except Antarctica

Nut moss | *Diphyscium foliosum* The distinctive spore capsules of this moss look like tiny grains of wheat.

Nut moss capsules shoot out a cloud of spores when they are hit by a drop of rain.

Common hair-cap moss | *Polytrichum commune* This tall, tussock-forming moss is common in damp woodlands and on boggy moorland throughout the northern hemisphere. Its stems are stiff and unbranched, with narrow, pointed leaves.

TIMMIALES

Family 1   **Genus** 1
Species 10

This order contains one genus of mosses, found throughout the northern hemisphere. The plants have stiff stems that may grow as individual stalks or form large, rather lax clumps. They are most often found on rocks and in crevices on cliffs, or growing near streams and bogs.

Native range Africa, Asia, Australasia, Europe, North America

OEDIPODIALES

Family 1   **Genus** 1
Species 1

This order contains one species of moss, found in the cooler regions of Eurasia and North America, but also in southern South America. The plants have translucent, broad, rounded leaves on short stems, resembling leafy liverworts. They often produce buds of tissue (gemmae) in the leaf axils, which detach to form new plants. They also form spherical, spore-producing capsules on thick, erect supporting stems.

Native range Asia, Europe, North America, South America

◁ POLYTRICHALES

Family 1   **Genera** 19
Species 233

Mosses in this order are found worldwide. They are larger than other types of moss, forming substantial, loose clumps of thick, erect stems that grow from an underground rhizome. They have numerous, rather spiky leaves and develop elliptical, buff-brown spore-producing capsules on tall stems.

Native range Every continent

Mosses evolved 450 million years ago, and have survived a range of major climate changes.

Knobbly clusters of
new branches form
at the shoot tips

Blunt-leaved bog moss |
Sphagnum palustre
Like its relatives, this peat-forming moss grows
on wet ground, and holds large amounts of water.

During the First World War, mosses were used as wound dressings.

◁ SPHAGNALES

Family 1   **Genera** 2
Species 306

This order of peat mosses has a global
distribution. Species grow in permanently
saturated bogs, where they form peat over
thousands of years. The plants have a
feathery appearance and can hold up to
20 times their dry weight in water. Their
stems and leaves can be green to red,
and they form short-stemmed, brown,
spore-producing capsules at the stem tips.

Native range Every continent

TAKAKIALES

Family 1   **Genus** 1
Species 2

The members of this order are found in
North America and eastern Asia, where they
grow as a thin mat on rocks. Previously

classified as liverworts, due to the similarity
of their leaves and stems, their spore-
producing structures prove that they are a
primitive form of moss. They are thought to
be some of the oldest living plants on Earth.

Native range Asia, North America

▽ TETRAPHIDALES

Families 2   **Genera** 3
Species 14

These mosses are found throughout
the northern hemisphere growing on
bare rocks, usually in deciduous forests.
They have prostrate stems that cling to their
substrate, with leaves arranged in rows on
opposite sides of the stems. The opening
at the tip of their spore-producing capsules
has four teeth—a feature that separates
these mosses from other moss species.

Native range Asia, Australasia, Europe,
North America

AMBUCHANANIALES

Family 1   **Genus** 1
Species 2

This small order contains only two
species, which are similar to sphagnum
mosses (*Sphagnaceae*) and closely
related to them. *Ambuchanania*

leucobryoides grows in bogs in Tasmania.
It has brown-green stems and forms
spherical, pale yellow, spore-producing
capsules on the stem tips. *Eosphagnum
inretortum* is found in bogs in North
America and Europe.

Native range Australasia, Europe,
North America

Pellucid four-tooth moss | *Tetraphis pellucida* Clusters of leaves on the shoot tips of this moss form tiny cups; these contain buds of reproductive material.

Hornworts

Hornworts are a division within the informal grouping called bryophytes. They are small, easily overlooked, leafy plants found worldwide in damp places, which they are among the first to colonize. Hornworts are named for their tall, narrow sporophytes, which—unlike in other bryophytes—continue to grow throughout their lifetime.

The body of hornworts, such as smooth hornwort (*Phaeoceros laevis*), consists of a flattened, lobed structure, known as a thallus. It lacks roots, stem, leaves, and vascular tissues.

▷ ANTHOCEROTALES

Families 1   **Genera** 3
Species 87

This order of hornworts has a global distribution, though most species are tropical. They are found in aquatic and terrestrial environments, such as wet soil and banks, where the relatively small, flat thallus develops long, erect sporophytes. Like other hornworts, they reproduce sexually and asexually.

Native range Every continent except Antarctica

Field hornwort | *Anthoceros agrestis*
Damp stubble fields, trampled ground, and the sides of ditches are home to this inconspicuous hornwort with distinctive, frilly leaf lobes.

▽ NOTOTHYLADALES

Family 1   **Genera** 4
Species 64

This order of hornworts has a wide distribution throughout the world. These are small plants, with a thallus that lies prostrate on the soil. The sporophytes may be short and grow outward, although some genera have longer, upright sporophytes, as in most hornworts.

Native range Every continent except Antarctica

LEIOSPOROCEROTALES

Family 1   **Genus** 1
Species 1

This order consists of a single species (*Leiosporoceros dussii*), which is both genetically and morphologically distinct from all other hornworts. Its thallus forms liverwort-like mats on soil substrates, and it can become a persistent weed of container-grown plants.

Native range North America, South America

▽ DENDROCEROTALES

Family 1   **Genera** 4
Species 67

These hornworts have a global distribution but are most frequently found in tropical regions of Asia and South America. Several species in this order—especially in the genus *Megaceros*—are among the largest hornworts, with a large gametophyte thallus and particularly long, erect sporophytes, up to 2 in (5 cm) tall.

Native range Africa, Asia, Australasia, North America, South America

PHYMATOCERALES

Family 1   **Genus** 1
Species 2

This order of hornworts contains a single genus (*Phymatoceros*). The two species are found in southwest Europe and North America, where they are fairly uncommon. Plants form a liverwort-like thallus, which produces globular tubers on its lower surface to help survive hostile seasons. Sporophytes are produced shortly after the tubers begin growing.

Native range Europe, North America

Mature spores at the tips of the horns are orange

Carolina hornwort |
Phaeoceros carolinianus
Growing in damp fields and on the sides of ditches, this species has male pits and female sex organs mixed together on a medium-size thallus.

The dark green thallus rosette is 1¼–1½ in (3–4 cm) across

Dendroceros | *Dendroceros* spp.
The ribbonlike lobes of *Dendroceros* gametophytes spread across damp rocks or tree bark in tropical and subtropical forests.

Lycophytes

Although their taxonomy is still under review, lycophytes are considered distinct from other bryophytes, because they have a vascular system connecting the roots and leaves. They include club mosses and quillworts, plants that are closely related to, but distinct from, ferns. Some grow in freshwater as well as terrestrial environments.

Spring quillwort | *Isoetes echinospora*
Quillworts grow in slow-moving streams and ponds. They have densely tufted, hollow leaves, with spore cases hidden in their swollen bases.

△ ISOETALES

Family 1   **Genus** 1
Species 203

The quillworts form a single genus (*Isoetes*) in this order. All are aquatic or semiaquatic plants with a clump of narrow, quill-like leaves growing from a corm at the base. Spores form in separate male and female sporangia at the base of the leaves, and species are distinguished by the structure of these sporangia.

Native range Every continent except Antarctica

▷ LYCOPODIALES

Family 1   **Genera** 16
Species 503

This order of lycophytes is known as the club mosses. They are low-growing plants whose stems creep along the ground and become erect at their ends. Each shoot bears sporangia in a cone-like terminal structure, or strobilus. The latter's resemblance to a battle club gives these plants their common name. The spores are all the same size.

Native range Every continent except Antarctica

▷ SELAGINELLALES

Family 1   **Genus** 1
Species 709

This order consists of a single family and a single genus (*Selaginella*). These fern relatives are distinguished by two rows of sessile leaflets on each side of the stems, making them look relatively flat. They can grow as creeping to erect plants. Most are tropical, but a few species survive in cooler or desert conditions.

Native range Every continent except Antarctica

Strobilus forms at the end of the stem

Interrupted club moss |
Lycopodium annotinum
This is a club moss of moors, mountains, and moist coniferous forests in temperate regions of the northern hemisphere.

Krauss' spike moss | *Selaginella kraussiana* Native to tropical Africa, this plant commonly grows in damp, shady conditions near fresh water, and at the edge of forests. It is long-lived, and has a low, branching, shrubby habit.

Lycophytes first appeared in the Silurian period, approximately 425 million years ago.

Liverworts

Found mainly in damp, shaded habitats, liverworts are thought to be the simplest of all the existing groups of land plants. They come in two distinct forms; some are flat and ribbonlike (thalloid), while others have slender stems flanked by tiny leaves. Related to mosses, liverworts do not produce flowers or seeds, and spread by shedding spores or fragmenting.

Haplomitrium gibbsiae
Named after botanist Lilian Gibbs, this species belongs to the *Haplomitriaceae* family.

The convex leaves are arranged in neat rows on each side of the stem

Great featherwort |
Plagiochila asplenioides
A delicate liverwort with translucent leaves, this species forms spreading, mosslike tufts. It grows on shaded rocks and soil, particularly on chalk and limestone.

△ CALOBRYALES

Family 1　　**Genera** 2
Species 9

These liverworts have a flat (thalloid) form and are considered to be "primitive" species. The body of the plant comprises a single flattened structure, usually lying flat against its substrate but occasionally growing erect. As with other liverworts, it is anchored by a long, tubular structure called a rhizoid.

Native range Asia, Australasia, Europe, North America, South America

TREUBIALES

Families 1　　**Genera** 3
Species 12

This order contains relatively large, leafy liverworts, and is believed to be intermediate between the flattened (thalloid) species and leafy forms. During reproduction, the gametophyte stage (see pp.18–19) has either male or female structures, not both.

Native range Asia, Australasia, Europe, North America, South America

◁ JUNGERMANNIALES

Families 40　　**Genera** 216
Species 3,199

This order consists of leafy liverworts that resemble mosses. Their small leaves are often lobed and are usually arranged in two overlapping rows, one on each side of the stem. Jungermanniales is one of the largest orders of liverworts, and is most widespread in temperate and humid subtropical regions.

Native range Every continent

▽ PORELLALES

Families 7   **Genera** 86
Species 2,944

This large order of liverworts contains both leafy and flat (thalloid) types of plant. Some are small, creeping plants, but there are also more upright leafy forms with branching stems bearing two rows of small leaves. Some species are common in many regions of the world, but others have a very limited natural range and are threatened with extinction.

Native range Every continent except Antarctica

Wall scalewort | *Porella platyphylla*
A common plant on limestone cliffs and boulders in temperate regions, this plant has relatively large, complex leaves.

▷ PTILIDIALES

Families 3   **Genera** 4
Species 7

There are only a few species of leafy liverworts in this very small order. These plants grow as dense mats of feathery stems, resembling mosses. They are found in subarctic and temperate climates, mainly in North America, but some species are found in New Zealand and the extreme south of South America.

Native range Asia, Australasia, Europe, North America, South America

METZGERIALES

Families 2   **Genera** 14
Species 467

The liverworts in this order have a flattened structure, with their branched stems clinging to rocky substrates. They are described as "simple" liverworts because their tissues are thin and relatively undifferentiated—often so thin, in fact, that they are translucent. Metzgeriales liverworts grow throughout the world, but the fragility of their structures means that they can only thrive in environments with high levels of permanent moisture or atmospheric humidity.

Native range Every continent except Antarctica

The oldest known liverwort fossils were found in rocks more than 471 million years old.

PLEUROZIALES

Family 1   **Genus** 1
Species 12

This order—containing just a single family and the single genus Pleurozia—was previously included in Jungermanniales, but is now separated on molecular evidence. Pleuroziales are leafy liverworts, mostly (but not always) growing as epiphytes in tropical montane forests. Studies of purple spoonwort (*Pleurozia purpurea*) suggest that the sac-shaped leaf lobes on the underside of its stems collect tiny invertebrates such as protists as well as water—so this liverwort may be partly carnivorous.

Native range Every continent except Antarctica

Tree fringewort | *Ptilidium pulcherrimum* This species grows on tree bark and has leaf edges with many long, thin teeth.

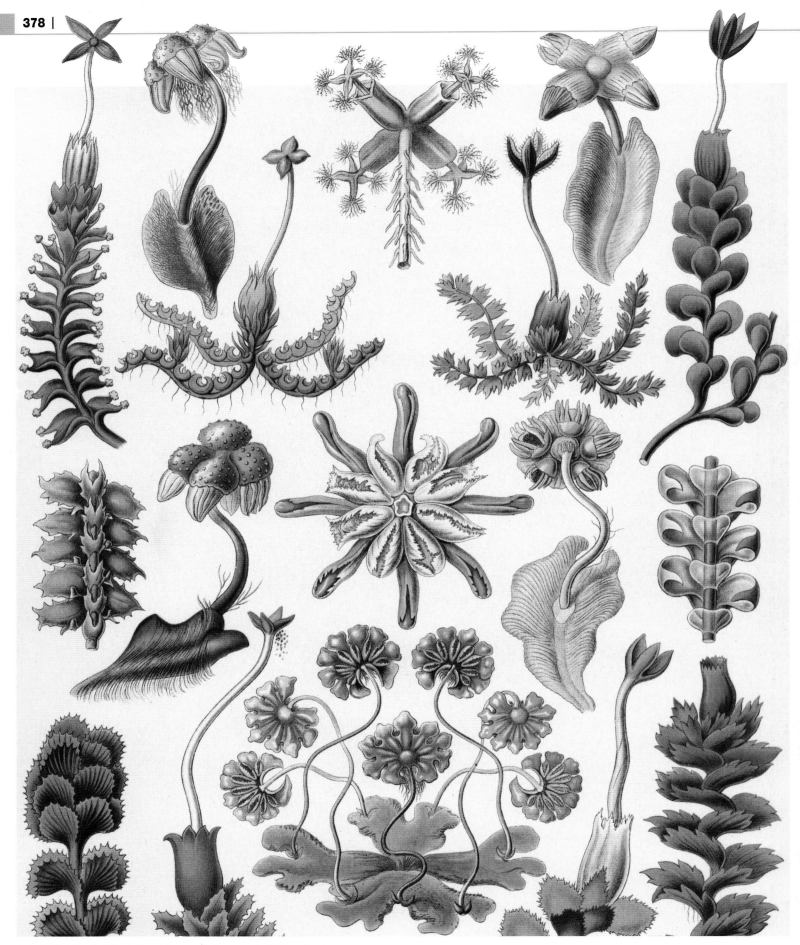

Early 1900s botanical illustration of liverworts by German naturalist Ernst Haeckel.

▷ FOSSOMBRONIALES

Families 5   **Genera** 6
Species 105

The species in this order are small, thalloid liverworts. These plants are confined to damp, often coastal, environments, where they creep across damp rocks and remain prostrate. They are either male or female, with small antheridia (male sex organs) or archegonia (female sex organs) toward the tips of their vegetative body (thallus).

Native range Every continent except Antarctica

PALLAVICINIALES

Families 5   **Genera** 13
Species 78

This order of thalloid liverworts grows around the world. Its members are small creeping plants, which occasionally form clumps. Their structures are thin and often translucent, and they only grow in moist habitats—often the banks of streams.

Native range Every continent except Antarctica

▽ PELLIALES

Families 2   **Genera** 4
Species 15

Of the two families that make up this order, the *Pelliaceae* is confined to the Northern Hemisphere. Its members have a flat, thalloid growth habit, and *Pellia* species are widespread in temperate climates. The other family, *Neterocladaceae*, only occurs in the Southern Hemisphere and contains a single genus of leafy liverworts.

Native range Every continent except Antarctica

Overleaf pellia | *Pellia epiphylla*
Growing on wet peat and rocks, this ribbon-shaped liverwort often forms a tufted mat. It produces black spore capsules.

Acid frillwort | *Fossombronia wondraczekii*
This species produces black capsules, from which spores are released.

▽ BLASIALES

Family 1   **Genera** 3
Species 3

This small order of liverworts was previously considered part of the order Metzgeriales, but molecular evidence separates them. These are flat thalloid liverworts that naturally grow in the Northern Hemisphere. The plants are medium-size and typically creep over damp surfaces and in crevices between rocks.

Native range Asia, Europe, North America

Common kettlewort | *Blasia pusilla* This species has a lobed body and distinctive reproductive cells known as gemmae.

▷ MARCHANTIALES

Families 13   **Genera** 34
Species 494

The Marchantiales order is made up of thalloid liverworts, which have a prostrate thallus that forms branches. In *Riccia* species the thallus becomes a straggly mat of branching shoots. In species of the large genus *Marchantia*, which often grow on recently burned ground, the thallus is shorter but forms dense mats of shoots covering the surface. Male and female plants have stalked, umbrellalike reproductive structures.

Native range Every continent except Antarctica

Liverworts have been used to treat wounds, ease fevers, and help cure many other ailments in traditional medicine.

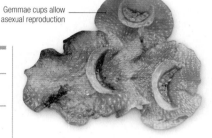

Gemmae cups allow asexual reproduction

Crescent-cup liverwort | *Lunularia cruciata*
Common in gardens, this pale green liverwort has distinctive reproductive structures on its thallus that look like tiny fingernails. The plant's surface is dotted with tiny air pores.

NEOHODGSONIALES

Family 1   **Genus** 1
Species 1

The single species, *Neohodgsonia mirabilis*, is only found in upland forests in New Zealand and on the South Atlantic island of Tristan da Cunha. It has a thalloid growth habit with rounded lobes, gemmae cups on the surface, and distinctive male and female sex structures resembling four-leaf clovers growing from the thallus.

Native range Australasia

SPHAEROCARPALES

Families 3   **Genera** 5
Species 40

This order consists of plants known as bottle liverworts. They have rows of rounded leaves along a very short stem. Their key identifying feature is the flask-shaped envelope (involucre) that surrounds each sex organ, which makes them resemble a cluster of small green bottles. Most species are found in North America.

Native range Australasia, Europe, North America

Ferns and relatives

Most ferns can be recognized by their graceful fronds, which unfurl as they grow. Together with horsetails and whisk ferns, they make up a diverse and ancient group of nonflowering plants that reproduce by means of spores. Ferns grow in a wide variety of habitats, although the majority thrive where there is moisture and shade.

Common horsetail | *Equisetum arvense* This horsetail, which can be invasive, has deep, black, underground rhizomes that sprout hollow shoots, bearing symmetrical whorls of side stems.

△ EQUISETALES

Family 1   **Genus** 1
Species 39

Known as horsetails, the species in this order's only genus, *Equisetum*, are found mostly in temperate climates in the northern hemisphere. All have jointed stems with leaves reduced to scales at the stem nodes. Some species have whorls of side stems, while others are more rushlike. Unbranched, spore-bearing shoots grow separately in spring.

Native range Every continent

MARATTIALES

Family 1   **Genera** 6
Species 132

Considered one of the more primitive orders of ferns, its species are largely tropical or subtropical, although a few occur in Arctic and Antarctic areas. Most are large, ground-dwelling ferns that bear pinnate or bipinnate fronds with spore-bearing sporangia on the undersides. The fronds of *Angiopteris evecta*, a rainforest species, can be up to 30 ft (9 m) long.

Native range Every continent

▷ OPHIOGLOSSALES

Family 1   **Genera** 9
Species 123

The small ferns of this order belong to a single family, *Ophioglossaceae*, with only nine genera. They are generally small and have an underground stem (rhizome) and emergent leaves. Uniquely, each frond has a sterile segment that photosynthesizes and, at its base, a fertile spore-bearing segment branching from it. The sterile section is pinnate, except in the genus *Ophioglossum*—so-called adder's-tongue ferns—where it is single and tonguelike.

Native range Every continent

PSILOTALES

Family 1   **Genera** 2
Species 19

This order includes the most primitive vascular plants living today. These plants, known as whisk ferns, have no roots, but are anchored by a short rhizoid, a thin, horizontal structure from which short shoots develop. Species have no leaves, although those of the genus *Tmesipteris* have leaflike extensions on each side. All Psilotales species have green, globular spore-bearing synangia called enations that grow on the sides of the stems.

Native range Every continent except Antarctica

Sporangium capsules hold hundreds of fern spores

Common moonwort | *Botrychium lunaria* Like other Ophioglossales species, this fern's fronds have a vegetative section and a taller fertile section topped by spore capsules.

▽ CYATHEALES

Families 8   **Genera** 13
Species 744

While some members of this order are small and spreading, many are tree ferns that form a thick, trunklike stem. Some can reach 80 ft (25 m) in height. Typically, at their crown, they develop a large whorl of bipinnate fronds with spore-bearing sporangia on their undersides.

Native range Every continent

Tree fern fronds have a radial symmetry

Sporangia under each frond

Tasmanian tree fern | *Dicksonia antarctica* This stout-stemmed tree fern is widespread in southeast Australia and Tasmania. It needs shade and usually grows among trees.

▽ GLEICHENIALES

Families 3 **Genera** 10
Species 165

These are large, mainly tropical ferns from around the world. They include the forking ferns of the *Gleicheniaceae* family and the umbrella ferns of *Dipteridaceae*. Species of both have large fronds and creeping rhizomes. In *Dipteris* species, the fronds bifurcate, dividing repeatedly in twos to form the umbrellalike shape typical of the family. Spores are borne in ring-shaped sori on the underside of fronds.

Native range Every continent

A crown of narrow fronds radiates horizontally outward above the thin stem

One row of sori lies each side of the midrib on the undersides of the fronds

Umbrella fern | ***Sticherus cunninghamii***
This distinctive fern is native to New Zealand, where it is widespread on damp ground, often in forests, from coastal to montane regions.

▷ HYMENOPHYLLALES

Family 1 **Genera** 9
Species 617

The fronds of the small ferns in this order, sometimes known as filmy ferns, are characteristically translucent. The blades between the veins are usually only one cell thick, which also makes them highly susceptible to drying out. Species tend to grow on damp rocks, beside streams, or as epiphytes in rainforests. Most species are found in moist, tropical or warm temperate regions. These ferns usually have slender, creeping rhizomes.

Native range Every continent except Antarctica

Wilson's filmy fern | ***Hymenophyllum wilsonii*** Typical of its family, this temperate fern has thin, translucent leaves with veins extending to the tips.

▽ OSMUNDALES

Family 1   **Genera** 6
Species 18

These terrestrial ferns, with distinctive upright stems, are often found in damp areas beside streams in tropical and temperate regions. In several genera, particularly *Osmunda*, spore-bearing leaves are found either separate from the sterile, photosynthesizing leaves, or as distinct sections of the same leaf.

Native range Every continent

Royal fern | *Osmunda regalis*
Often cultivated, this stately, mainly European fern has a rosette of spreading fronds with narrower, spore-bearing fronds at its center.

▽ POLYPODIALES

Families 26   **Genera** 257
Species 9,673

This is the largest order of ferns, and includes many common wild and cultivated species. Genera are found all over the world, growing in tropical, semitropical, and temperate zones. Spores are produced in circular sori, in lines on the undersides of the leaves. In some genera, species have separate fertile fronds.

Native range Every continent

Lemon-scented fern |
Thelypteris limbosperma
Found in damp habitats on acid soil, the fronds of this fern release a lemon scent when bruised.

Japanese climbing fern | *Lygodium japonicum* Native to South Asia and the western Pacific, this vine-like fern can be over 90 ft (27 m) long.

▷ SALVINIALES

Families 2   **Genera** 5
Species 74

These are all aquatic or semiaquatic ferns, generally found in tropical to temperate regions. Those of the family *Salviniaceae* are floating ferns, whereas those in the *Marsileaceae* water clover family have a rooted rhizome with emergent or floating leaves. *Salvinia* and *Azolla* species are fast-growing ferns, which can become invasive in freshwater lakes and rivers.

Native range Every continent except Antarctica

Floating fern | *Salvinia natans*
Often forming a dense carpet, this water fern has small, oval leaves covered with water-repellent hairs. It is common in the tropics.

△ SCHIZAEALES

Families 3   **Genera** 4
Species 190

This order of ferns contains three families and four genera. They include climbing ferns in the genus *Lygodium* and small comb ferns of the genus *Schizaea*. Although Schizaeales ferns can look very different, all have dimorphic (fertile and sterile) fronds and sporangia similar in form. They are primitive ferns—some with fossils dating back at least 145 million years.

Native range Africa, Asia, Australasia, North America, South America

Gymnosperms

This group of plants consists of conifers, which evolved 300 million years ago, and the similarly ancient cycads, ginkgos, and gnetophytes. They have little in common, other than unlike flowering plants, they form their seeds on exposed surfaces, typically on specialized scales.

▷ CYCADALES

Families 2 **Genera** 10
Species 355

These are the most primitive living gymnosperms. The plants are mostly tropical trees, often with a single short, thick stem topped by a whorl of long pinnate leaves, but some resemble tree ferns or palms. All species are dioecious (either male or female), and bear large cones produced at the stem apex in alternate years once the plant is mature.

Native range Africa, Asia, Australasia, North America, South America

Maidenhair tree | *Ginkgo biloba*
This distinctive tree is easily recognized by its fan-shaped leaves, which turn bright yellow in the fall. Originally native to southern China, it is now cultivated worldwide.

△ GINKGOALES

Family 1 **Genus** 1
Species 1

Today this order comprises a single species—the large maidenhair tree (*Ginkgo biloba*), whose fan-shaped leaves are widely used in alternative medicine. Fossils of *Ginkgo* species date back more than 200 million years. The order reached its maximum diversity between 145 million to 66 million years ago, then gradually shrank to the one species alive today.

Native range Asia

Burrawang |
Macrozamia communis
Native to Australia's southeast coast, this cycad has large cones with red, fleshy seeds. It often grows in dense stands.

▽ GNETALES

Families 3 **Genera** 3
Species 93

Unlike other gymnosperms, the species of this order all have xylem vessels in their stems—thin tubes that convey water and minerals from the roots to the rest of the plant. The three genera are otherwise quite distinct; *Gnetum* is a genus of small, evergreen trees, *Ephedra* species are shrubs or vines, and the only *Welwitschia* species (*W. mirabilis*) is a desert plant.

Native range Every continent except Antarctica

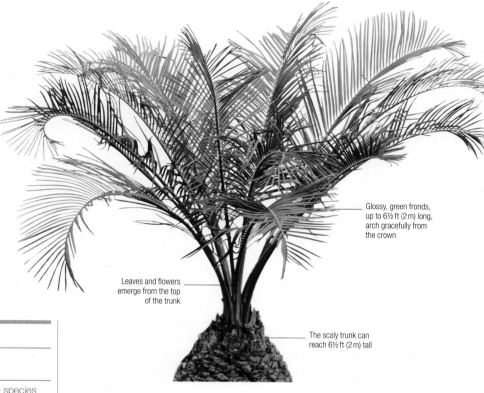

Glossy, green fronds, up to 6½ ft (2 m) long, arch gracefully from the crown

Leaves and flowers emerge from the top of the trunk

The scaly trunk can reach 6½ ft (2 m) tall

The term gymnosperm comes from the Greek word *gymnos* (naked) and *sperma* (seed).

Welwitschia | ***Welwitschia mirabilis*** Endemic to the African Namib Desert, this plant grows one pair of strap-like leaves that split over time. Branching systems growing out of its stem bear pollen and seed cones.

▷ PINALES

Families 8	Genera 70
Species 615	

This is the largest of the gymnosperm orders, and includes all of the trees known as conifers. Most are large, evergreen forest trees, but some are shrubs and a few genera are deciduous. Most are distinguished by the presence of woody female cones, but members of *Taxaceae* and *Podocarpaceae* have individual seeds with a fleshy aril (seed covering).

Native range Every continent except Antarctica

Flat, dark green needles may turn bronze in winter

Japanese umbrella pine |
Sciadopitys verticillata
The only member of its family, this ancient Japanese species is distinct from other conifers in having 20–30 needles clustered in whorls.

Narrow leaves extend horizontally from the branchlets

The fleshy fruits are edible, with a sweet, pine-like flavor

Chinese plum-yew |
Cephalotaxus fortunei
This small, densely branched conifer has fleshy cones, which turn purple-brown when ripe. It grows in mountain forests in China and Myanmar.

Leaves are scalelike, in whorls of three or sometimes pairs

Colorado spruce | ***Picea pungens***
Bright blue-gray leaves, with prickly tips, make this a popular ornamental tree. Native to western North America, it typically grows on mountains.

Western juniper | ***Juniperus occidentalis***
This long-lived tree grows on rocky mountain slopes in western US states. Like other junipers, it produces seeds inside berrylike cones.

Golden larch | ***Pseudolarix amabilis***
Native to eastern China, the golden larch turns brilliant yellow in the fall before losing its leaves. Its cones break up as they scatter their seeds.

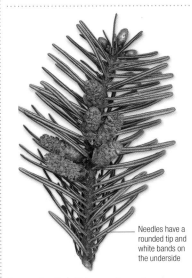

Needles have a rounded tip and white bands on the underside

Caucasian fir | ***Abies nordmanniana***
Originally from mountains in the Black Sea region, this is a popular Christmas tree in Europe because it retains its needles indoors.

California nutmeg | ***Torreya californica***
This rare conifer is restricted to canyons and mountains in California. It is unrelated to the true nutmeg, although it has nutlike seeds.

European silver fir | *Abies alba*
Named after the silver bands on the underside of its leaves, this fir has upright resinous cones. They disintegrate in order to scatter their seeds.

Needles are arranged in double ranks, one rank shorter than the other

Needles radiate in spirals from the twig, more densely on the top side

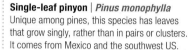

Red fir | *Abies magnifica*
This drought-resistant fir is found on dry mountain slopes in California. It has upcurved leaves and upright cones up to 8 in (20 cm) long.

Single-leaf pinyon | *Pinus monophylla*
Unique among pines, this species has leaves that grow singly, rather than in pairs or clusters. It comes from Mexico and the southwest US.

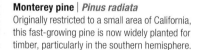

Scalelike leaves lie forward

Cones form on twig tips

Monterey pine | *Pinus radiata*
Originally restricted to a small area of California, this fast-growing pine is now widely planted for timber, particularly in the southern hemisphere.

Swiss stone pine | *Pinus cembra*
This slow-growing European tree produces small cones that fall intact. Birds such as nutcrackers feed on them and disperse the seeds.

Taiwania | *Taiwania cryptomerioides*
One of Asia's largest conifers, this tropical species has a trunk up to 10 ft (3 m) thick. It has spiny-tipped leaves and small, rounded cones.

Japanese cedar | *Cryptomeria japonica*
A cypress rather than a true cedar, this tree has slender leaves and small, rounded cones. It grows on mountains in China and Japan.

Female cones are barrel-shaped, maturing over two years

Gray-green needles are arranged in stiff clusters of 10–20

Atlas cedar |
Cedrus atlantica
This north African cedar has short needles and upright cones. When ripe, the cones slowly break up to release their seeds.

Needles from pine trees can be made into a tea that can fight off scurvy.

Angiosperms

With more than 300,000 species, flowering plants—or angiosperms—are by far the largest group of plants, as well as the most diverse. They play a vital role in most land-based ecosystems, producing food and shelter for animals and many other living things.

Greater masterwort | *Astrantia major*
A plant of alpine meadows and open woods in southern Europe, astrantia has showy pinkish bracts (specialized leaves) beneath its heads of small flowers.

Tiny flowers are arranged in compact umbels

The center of the umbel is tinged, making it look like a single flower

Thin, palmate leaves radiate from nodes on the stem

ICACINALES

Family 2   **Genera** 33
Species 222

This order comprises two families, including *Icacinaceae*, the white pear family. All the plants in this order are tropical evergreen trees or lianas, mostly from the southern hemisphere. They largely have flowers with tiny petals or no petals, and an almost dry drupe fruit. The family was widespread in the Paleocene era, and its oldest member is known from a fossil fruit more than 80 million years old.

Native range Africa, Asia, Australasia, North America, South America

AMBORELLALES

Family 1   **Genus** 1
Species 1

This order of primitive evergreen shrub is considered to be the oldest diverging branch of the angiosperm taxonomic tree. It contains a single family, which has a single genus, with only one species: *Amborella trichopoda*. This scrambling shrub from New Caledonia bears small flowers, with males and females on separate plants. The female flowers develop into red berries, each containing a single seed.

Native range Australasia

◁ APIALES

Families 7   **Genera** 494
Species 5,489

The order Apiales is dominated by the highly distinctive and economically important carrot family (*Apiaceae*, often known by the older name *Umbelliferae*), which has at least 3,500 species. The ginseng family (*Araliaceae*), consisting of ivies and ginseng, is another large family, while the parchment-bark family (*Pittosporaceae*) of evergreen shrubs and trees is medium-size. Four small families, each with fewer than 20 species, complete the order.

Native range Every continent except Antarctica

▽ AQUIFOLIALES

Families 5   **Genera** 21
Species 745

The holly family (*Aquifoliaceae*) is the main representative of the Aquifoliales order, and includes mostly tropical trees and shrubs with toothed leaves. Other members of this small order are: an odd family of twining herbs, the *Cardiopteridaceae*; three Asian shrubs in the *Helwingiaceae*; four South American shrubs and trees in the *Phyllonomaceae*; and a family of tropical trees, the *Stemonuraceae*.

Native range Every continent except Antarctica

Common holly | *Ilex aquifolium*
A woodland understory shrub or small tree from Europe, north Africa, and northwestern Asia, holly develops spiny leaves to discourage grazers.

The first flowering plants evolved 250 million years ago.

▷ ASTERALES

Families 11   **Genera** 1,743
Species 26,870

Eleven families make up the Asterales. The largest is the daisy family (*Asteraceae*), with some 25,000 species. Typically, each flowerlike head (capitula) has many individual flowers, called florets, surrounded by showy rays. Some of the bellflower family (*Campanulaceae*) show similar characteristics. This order also includes the bogbean (*Menyanthaceae*) and fanflower (*Goodeniaceae*) families, in addition to seven smaller families.

Native range Every continent except Antarctica

Garden marigold | *Calendula officinalis*
This species has been cultivated for so long that its origins are unknown. Calendula extract from the flowers is used to treat skin problems.

Leaves and stems are coated in a soft down

Cottonweed | *Otanthus maritimus*
This shrubby, woolly perennial grows in coastal habitats in southern Europe, north Africa, and southwest Asia.

Common ragwort | *Jacobaea vulgaris*
Toxic to farm animals and avoided by rabbits, this native perennial from Europe and western Asia has invaded grasslands almost worldwide.

Deep red flower buds open into white florets

Butterbur | *Petasites hybridus*
Plants of butterbur are either male or female. It grows in wet meadows and beside streams throughout Europe and eastward to Iran.

Leaves are deeply toothed

Nettle-leaved bellflower |
Campanula trachelium
This hairy perennial grows in hedges around Europe, Iran, and north Africa.

Salsify | *Tragopogon porrifolius* A biennial herb of grassy places around the Mediterranean, salsify has lilac or reddish-purple flower heads, surrounded by longer, pointed bracts.

Around 10 percent of all flowering plants belong to the order Asterales.

▽ BORAGINALES

Family 1   **Genera** 148
Species around 2,700

Because of uncertainties over how the forget-me-not family (*Boraginaceae*) relates to other families, a new order, Boraginales, was proposed in 2016, just for this one family of around 2,700 species. They range from small annual herbs to large trees, often with conspicuous hairs and swollen bases on their stems or leaves. Some species are edible, and others are used to produce dyes.

Native range Every continent except Antarctica

The spotted leaves supposedly resemble unhealthy lungs

Common lungwort |
Pulmonaria officinalis
Once thought to be efficacious against tuberculosis, this blotched-leaved perennial grows in shady places throughout central Europe.

BRUNIALES

Family 1   **Genera** 13
Species 74

This Eudicot order contains a single family: *Bruniaceae*. All the members of the order are evergreen shrubs with a heather-like appearance, and are native only to the Cape region of South Africa. They are small plants with thin branches and small flowers, usually in dense flower heads. The stems are clothed in minute, needlelike leaves, often tipped with black. The flower parts are in fives. Some species are cultivated as ornamentals.

Native range Africa

▽ CORNALES

Families 7 **Genera** 41
Species 676

The revised order Cornales contains seven families, five of which are insignificant—one with just a single species of evergreen tree from Africa. The main family is the dogwood family (*Cornaceae*), a loose taxonomic grouping of shrubs and small trees found in temperate zones and on tropical mountains. The hydrangea family (*Hydrangeaceae*) includes several popular garden plants.

Native range Every continent except Antarctica

Dove tree | *Davidia involucrata*
This small flowering tree from China is impressive in bloom, with flower heads ¾ in (2 cm) across, surrounded by creamy bracts.

▽ DIPSACALES

Families 2 **Genera** 46
Species around 1,090

Dipsacales is found mainly in the northern hemisphere. Its members usually have compact heads of small flowers. Of its two families, *Adoxaceae* contains about 200 species and *Caprifoliaceae* almost 900 recorded species.

Native range Every continent except Antarctica

Red berries develop from the flowers in the fall

European cranberry bush | *Viburnum opulus*
Native across Europe and Asia, this hedgerow shrub has flattened flower heads with large, sterile, outer flowers around smaller, fertile ones.

▽ ERICALES

Families 22 **Genera** 367
Species 13,740

The Ericales is a major order. Its largest member is the heather family (*Ericaceae*), with more than 4,000 species of shrubs, mainly in acid soils. It also includes 900 species in the primrose family (*Primulaceae*); 385 species in the phlox family (*Polemoniaceae*); and carnivorous plants in the pitcher plant family (*Sarraceniaceae*).

Native range Every continent

Eyes are yellow at first, turning red as they age

Hairy androsace | *Androsace villosa*
In a genus of arctic-alpines, this perennial of mountains from Europe to the Himalayas has dense white flower heads and silky leaves.

Sweet pepper bush | *Clethra alnifolia*
This deciduous shrub grows in wet forests and bogs in eastern North America. Its leaves turn yellow or orange in the fall.

Creeping jenny | *Lysimachia nummularia*
From Sweden to the Caucasus, the spreading stems of this perennial creep among vegetation in damp shade and on streamsides.

Angiosperms represent approximately 80 percent of all the known green plants now living.

Stems are rigid, holding upright sprays of flowers

Jacob's ladder | *Polemonium caeruleum*
This tall perennial has cup-shaped lavender or white flowers. It grows in rocky and grassy places in Europe and northern Asia.

Tight flower buds open in summer or early fall

Heather | *Calluna vulgaris*
This evergreen shrub, with spikes of pale purple flowers, dominates vast areas of moorland in northern Europe, eastward into Asia.

▷ ESCALLONIALES

Family 1   **Genera** 7
Species 125

This order, in the Eudicots, contains a single family: *Escalloniaceae*. All its members are trees or shrubs, mostly from Australasia and South America, with flower parts in fives. The largest genera are *Escallonia*, members of which are mostly small, evergreen shrubs; and *Polyosma*, which are tropical trees.

Native range Asia, Australasia, North America, South America

▽ GARRYALES

Families 2   **Genera** 3
Species 27

Any classification system raises anomalies, and the order Garryales is one of these. It was once placed in the Cornales, but modern genetic investigation separated out this order of two families and around 20 species. The silky tassel family (*Garryaceae*) includes two genera: *Garrya*, from North America, and *Aucuba*, from eastern Asia. The *Eucommiaceae* family contains just one species: *Eucommia ulmoides*, a tree of mountain forests in central and southern China.

Native range Asia, Europe, North America

Some cultivars have
yellow-blotched
leaves

Spotted laurel | *Aucuba japonica*
Individual examples of this shrub are male or female. Male plants have upright flower spikes; the females have small, clustered flower heads.

Redclaws | *Escallonia rubra* This evergreen shrub loose clusters of tubular, deep pink flowers.

▽ GENTIANALES

Families 5   **Genera** 1,038
Species 22,571

The order name celebrates the gentians of mountains and gardens, but the *Gentianaceae* family has only around 1,600 members. The madder family (*Rubiaceae*) is the largest in the order, with more than 13,000 species, including tropical shrubs such as coffee. The oleander family (*Apocynaceae*), strychnine family (*Loganiaceae*), and jessamine family (*Gelsemiaceae*) complete the order.

Native range All continents except Antarctica

Brightly colored
berries are toxic
if eaten

The angiosperms originated about 250 million years ago.

Bead plant | *Nertera granadensis*
Named for its small, beadlike fruits, this perennial with tiny, green flowers is native to Australia, New Zealand, Pacific islands, and South America.

▷ LAMIALES

Families 25   **Genera** 1,059
Species 23,755

Modern taxonomy has expanded the scope of this order to include 25 families, typically with tubular flowers and unequal petal lobes. The largest families are the mint family (*Lamiaceae*, often known by its older name *Labiatae*) and the figwort family (*Scrophulariaceae*), each with 5,000–6,000 species. Others include the olive family (*Oleaceae*) and plantain family (*Plantaginaceae*).

Native range Every continent except Antarctica

Purple toothwort | *Lathraea clandestina*
This parasitic west European perennial, with no green leaves, taps the roots of trees for food. Its flower heads emerge from underground shoots.

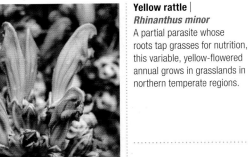

Yellow rattle |
Rhinanthus minor
A partial parasite whose roots tap grasses for nutrition, this variable, yellow-flowered annual grows in grasslands in northern temperate regions.

Shrubby globularia | *Globularia alypum*
Growing in dry regions of the Mediterranean, this poisonous, low, evergreen shrub has globular heads of sweet-scented, blue flowers.

Bracts can last for weeks or months, but the flower itself fades within days

Zebra plant | *Aphelandra squarrosa*
Originating from coastal Brazilian forests, this popular houseplant has pale-veined leaves and yellow flower spikes ringed with yellow bracts.

Elegant, colorful anthers enhance this species' ornamental charm

Wide, flared petals are attractive to butterflies, which pollinate the flowers

Heart-shaped leaves are dark green, with pale undersides

Flaming glorybower |
Clerodendrum splendens
This African vine, with clusters of tubular, red flowers, twines round trees in its native forest habitat, or trellises in gardens.

PARACRYPHIALES

Family 1   **Genera** 3
Species 37

This Eudicot order has just a single family, *Paracryphiaceae*, which prior to recent reclassification contained just a single species. All its members originate from Australasia, the Philippines, and New Caledonia. They are evergreen shrubs or small trees, with axillary or terminal heads of small flowers with parts in fives.

Native range Asia, Australasia

▽ SOLANALES

Families 5   **Genera** 161
Species 4,812

The potato family (*Solanaceae*), an economically important family of up to 4,000 species, dominates this order. Many species contain poisonous alkaloids. The bindweed family (*Convolvulaceae*) includes tropical climbers and low-growing herbs. The three other families in this order are the *Hydrolaceae*, with one genus, found only in the Americas; five African trees in the *Montiniaceae*; and a pantropical herb in the *Sphenocleaceae*.

Native range Every continent except Antarctica

The lanterns change color from green to orange as they mature

Chinese lantern | *Alkekengi officinarum*
Native to Asia and Europe, this perennial bears white summer flowers that are followed by berries contained within papery, lantern-like calyces that turn bright orange in the fall.

▽ AUSTROBAILEYALES

Families 3   **Genera** 5
Species 96

The order Austrobaileyales is made up of only three families. Members of this order are trees, shrubs, and climbers. The flowers of most species are single and have many petals. Perhaps the best-known species is a spice, star anise.

Native range Asia, Australasia, North America

Austrobaileya scandens
The flowers of this rare, primitive climber, found only in rainforests in Queensland, Australia, smell of rotting fish to attract pollinating flies.

▷ BERBERIDOPSIDALES

Families 2   **Genera** 3
Species 4

This order of Eudicots contains two families but only four species. The *Aextoxicaceae*, originating from Chile, are dioecious evergreen trees; the *Berberidopsidaceae*, from Chile and eastern Australia, are evergreen woody scramblers. All species have flower parts in fives and rounded, berrylike fruit.

Native range Australasia, South America

BUXALES

Family 1   **Genera** 7
Species 120

Containing just a single family of around 120 species, the order Buxales is found in temperate, subtropical, and tropical regions. Most of its members are trees or shrubs, with simple, evergreen leaves and separate male and female flowers on the same plant. Many species are grown ornamentally. Box (*Buxus sempervirens*) wood is used for carving.

Native range Africa, Asia, Europe, North America, South America

Coral vine | *Berberidopsis corallina* This is a scrambling shrub with bright red, spherical flowers. It is native to the woodlands of central and southern Chile.

Various members of Solanaceae were implicated in witchcraft practices in medieval Europe, and elsewhere.

▷ CARYOPHYLLALES

Families 39   **Genera** 734
Species 13,418

The Caryophyllales is a diverse order of 39 families of trees, shrubs, climbers, succulents, and herbaceous plants, ranging from carnations to cacti. Many grow in harsh environments but have evolved special adaptations for survival, such as fleshy leaves to store water during drought conditions. Some species have even become carnivorous, and trap and digest insects to obtain extra nutrients.

Native range Every continent

Succulent leaves store water

Hottentot fig | *Carpobrotus edulis*
This sprawling, fleshy South African species has showy flowers and edible fig-like fruits. It grows in open dry habitats, where it can be invasive.

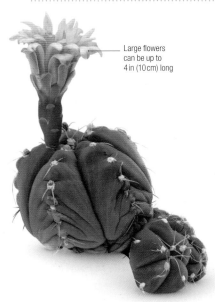

Large flowers can be up to 4 in (10 cm) long

Spider cactus | *Gymnocalycium horstii*
This spherical, clump-forming cactus probably grows wild only in rocky grassland near Rio Grande do Sul in Brazil.

Matucana intertexta
A mountain valley region of Peru is the only home of this clump-forming species with a spherical or short cylindrical stem.

Flowers, produced in spring, are up to 4 in (10 cm) long

Spines are initially white, but become stronger and darker with age

Stems have 14–25 ribs, sometimes spiraling

The leaves are used in traditional medicine to treat inflammation

Four o'clock flower | *Mirabilis jalapa*
From dry open habitats in tropical Central and South America, this species has fragrant flowers that open during the late afternoon.

Turk's cap cactus |
Melocactus salvadorensis
When mature, this Brazilian cactus produces a flower-bearing structure on top of its stem.

The most striking ecological feature of the Caryophyllales order is its dominance in alkaline and arid regions of the globe.

Rigid hornwort |
Ceratophyllum demersum
This is a submerged species with no roots, inhabiting ponds and ditches in non-arctic Europe. It has tiny flowers and whorls of leaves.

△ CERATOPHYLLALES

Family 1 **Genus** 1
Species 5

A single family, the *Ceratophyllaceae*, makes up this order. Called hornworts, these plants are completely unrelated to the nonflowering hornworts. They are free-floating, rootless aquatics with whorls of finely divided leaves, tiny male and female flowers, and spiny fruits.

Native range Every continent except Antarctica

Golden guinea vine | *Hibbertia scandens*
A vigorous climber or scrambler, this evergreen shrub grows near the east coast of Australia and in New Guinea.

△ DILLENIALES

Family 1 **Genera** 11
Species 524

The order Dilleniales contains only the *Dilleniaceae*, a mainly tropical family of around 360 species of trees, shrubs, and climbers. Most species have alternately arranged leaves and bisexual flowers (with male and female parts), with five sepals, five petals, and numerous stamens. Some produce dry fruits that open to shed their seeds, others have berries. A few are grown as ornamentals or for timber used in construction and boat building.

Native range Every continent except Antarctica

ACORALES

Family 1 **Genus** 1
Species 2

Only one genus and up to four species make up the order Acorales. Called sweet flags, these waterside and wetland plants have a fleshy flower spike of small flowers and were once classified as aroids. Botanists now believe they represent the earliest branch of the monocots family tree, and may hold clues to what the first monocots looked like.

Native range Asia, Europe, North America

▽ ALISMATALES

Families 14 **Genera** 180
Species 4,391

This order includes many common aquatic plants as well as the mainly land-based aroid family (*Araceae*). Aroids, which can be dramatic in appearance, have a distinctive reproductive anatomy consisting of a fleshy

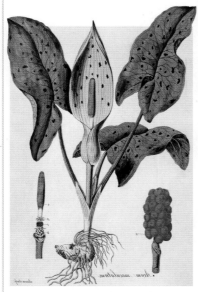

Lord and ladies | *Arum maculatum*
The spadix of this spring-flowering European native heats up to attract pollinating insects. It produces poisonous red berries in the fall.

spike of tiny flowers called a spadix and a leaflike surround called a spathe. The other families in the order include many freshwater species, as well as several families of seagrasses.

Native range Every continent except Antarctica

▷ ARECALES

Families 2 **Genera** 189
Species 2,604

Since 2016, a family of 16 endemic Australian trees has been added to the order Arecales, which is dominated by more than 2,000 species in the palm family. Typically growing from one central bud, palms vary from towering trees to slender climbing rattans (climbing palms). Their huge leaves are either feather-shaped or fanlike. Most live in tropical rainforests.

Native range Africa, Asia, Australasia

Fronds have almost no stalk and grow in a spiral arrangement

Petticoat palm |
Copernicia macroglossa
Native to Cuba, this relatively small palm is named for the skirt of dead leaves that it retains below its crown.

Trunk grows slowly to around 25 ft (8 m) high

Fossils show palms in the Arecales order existed more than 80 million years ago.

▷ ASPARAGALES

Families 14 **Genera** 1,144
Species 39,055

This diverse order of 14 families includes familiar garden flowers such as daffodils and irises, desert-adapted plants such as agaves, and a few trees. Some of its members were previously classified in the order Liliales, but modern genetic techniques have now changed our understanding of these interrelationships. The order also includes the highly specialized orchid family.

Native range Every continent

Mother-in law's tongue |
Dracaena trifasciata
This tropical West African species with stiff patterned leaves is a popular houseplant. It is also grown for its fibers.

Leaves can reach
6 ft (2 m) tall in
wild specimens

Firecracker flower |
Dichelostemma ida-maia
Cultivated for its flowers, this woodland species is native to Oregon and California.

Aphyllanthes | *Aphyllanthes monspeliensis*
When not flowering, this Mediterranean species looks like a clump of rushes, with many slender stems that are almost leafless.

Lesser butterfly orchid | *Platanthera bifolia*
Found in various habitats across temperate Eurasia, this sweetly scented, pale-flowered orchid is pollinated by night-flying moths.

Common asphodel | *Asphodelus aestivus*
This common, narrow-leaved Mediterranean plant produces many pinkish-white flowers on a tall stem.

Stems usually
bear between one
and five flowers

Amaryllis | *Hippeastrum* spp.
This genus of showy, bulb-forming plants is native to warmer parts of the Americas. Many cultivated varieties and hybrids exist.

Flower panicles
can reach 8 ft
(2.5 m) tall

Spanish dagger | *Yucca gloriosa*
Like all yuccas, this coastal species from southeastern regions of the US relies on a specialized yucca moth for pollination.

Wagener's masdevallia |
Masdevallia wageneriana
Typical of its genus, this small, epiphytic orchid from Venezuela has sepals with narrow "tails."

Glossy leaves have
a leathery texture

Natal lily | *Clivia miniata*
Horticulturalists have bred many varieties of this South African woodland plant for its showy flowers and evergreen leaves.

Two lateral
petals flank the
enlarged lip

Each flower has three
sepals, around ¾ in
(2 cm) long

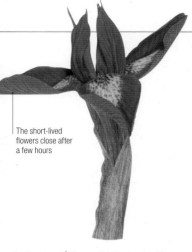

The short-lived flowers close after a few hours

Barbary nut | *Gynandriris sisyrinchium*
This wild Mediterranean iris grows from a corm (a bulblike underground stem), which helps it survive unfavorable conditions.

Most plants in the Asparagales order have straplike leaves.

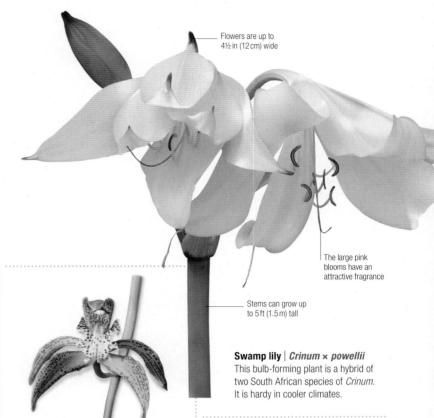

Flowers are up to 4½ in (12 cm) wide

The large pink blooms have an attractive fragrance

Stems can grow up to 5 ft (1.5 m) tall

Swamp lily | *Crinum × powellii*
This bulb-forming plant is a hybrid of two South African species of *Crinum*. It is hardy in cooler climates.

The bright orange color attracts the plant's hummingbird pollinators

The lip is usually marked with darker spots or stripes

Orange guarianthe |
Guarianthe aurantiaca
This tree-living species is native to tropical Central America. Many ornamental varieties and hybrids have been bred by horticulturalists.

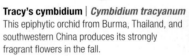

Tracy's cymbidium | *Cymbidium tracyanum*
This epiphytic orchid from Burma, Thailand, and southwestern China produces its strongly fragrant flowers in the fall.

Sterile flowers form a "tassel"

Flower stems grow 8–24 in (20–60 cm) tall

Tassel hyacinth | *Muscari comosum*
The flower heads of this Mediterranean species have fertile and sterile flowers, the latter forming the purplish "tassel" at the top.

Windowsill orchid | *Pleione formosana*
Native to parts of China, this small ground-living orchid dies back during the winter months.

Each flower is 1–2 in (3–5 cm) long

Montbretia | *Crocosmia × crocosmiiflora*
A 19th-century hybrid created from two South African species, this popular garden plant is invasive in some areas.

Leaves have an attractive, purple underside

Tahitian bridal veil |
Gibasis pellucida
This species from Central and South America has thin stems and three-petaled, white flowers.

△ COMMELINALES

Families 5   **Genera** 68
Species 812

This order contains five families, with the majority of species belonging to just one of them—the *Commelinaceae* or spiderwort family. Most are low-growing plants, typically from warmer regions. Many have attractive, three-petaled, blue flowers (reduced to two petals in some species), making them popular as ornamentals.

Native range Africa, Asia, Australasia, North America, South America

▽ DASYPOGONALES

Family 1   **Genera** 4
Species 20

This order is not recognized by all botanists. It comprises a single family (*Dasypogonaceae*), with members found only in Australia. The family used to form part of the *Xanthorrhoeaceae* (grass tree) family, which is also native to Australia. Plants have flower parts in threes, with sepals and petals that look identical and are called tepals.

Native range Australasia

▽ DIOSCOREALES

Families 3   **Genera** 25
Species 860

This order contains just three families. It is dominated by the yams, a family of mainly tropical climbing plants. Several species of yam have been cultivated since ancient times for their edible tubers. The order also includes the small bog asphodel family (*Nartheciaceae*), which is mainly found in northern temperate regions.

Native range Every continent except Antarctica

▷ LILIALES

Families 10   **Genera** 67
Species 1,580

Many plants once considered members of the lily family, including onions and hyacinths, have been moved into the order Asparagales. The ten families in the Liliales include the true lilies and tulips, the sarsaparilla and colchicum families, and the colorful alstroemeria family. Several lily species are toxic to humans and animals.

Native range Every continent except Antarctica

False helleborine | *Veratrum album*
Native to the northern hemisphere, this species belongs to a genus of poisonous plants with branched flower heads of greenish-white blooms.

Stamens are hairy and almost as long as the petals

Bog asphodel | *Narthecium ossifragum*
This European plant lives in nutrient-poor, upland habitats. After fertilization, its seed capsules develop a fiery orange color.

Blue tinsel lily | *Calectasia cyanea* This species from Western Australia forms small clumps of woody stems with narrow leaves. Its star-shaped flowers fade from purplish blue to white as they age.

Liliales are thought to have evolved during the Cretaceous period— 100 million years ago.

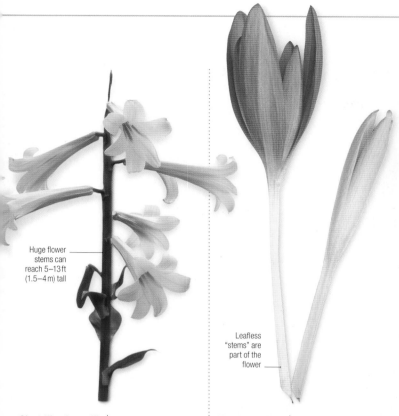

Huge flower stems can reach 5–13 ft (1.5–4 m) tall

Giant Himalayan lily |
Cardiocrinum giganteum
Found from the Himalayas to China, this giant lily grows for several seasons before flowering.

Leafless "stems" are part of the flower

Meadow saffron | *Colchicum autumnale*
The crocus-like flowers of this European native appear in the fall, months before its leaves. Despite being poisonous, it is cultivated widely.

Flowers have gold bands and brown spots

Foliage is slender and grasslike

Flowers have a checkerboard pattern

Golden-rayed lily | *Lilium auratum*
Native to Japan, this bulb produces up to 20, highly fragrant, white flowers on stems that can reach 8 ft (2.5 m) tall. It is widely cultivated.

Snakeshead fritillary | *Fritillaria meleagris*
This bulb-forming European species has flowers with a unique pattern. It grows wild in damp meadows, but is more common in cultivation.

Thatch screw pine | *Pandanus tectorius* No relation of real pines, this tropical, coastal tree has long been a vital source of materials for Pacific Island cultures.

△ PANDANALES

Families 5   **Genera** 36
Species 1,610

Found mainly in tropical regions, the five families in this order include species of trees, shrubs, climbers, and smaller plants. Many look superficially like palms, except that they have simpler, strap-shaped leaves. Often called screw pines, around half of them belong to the genus *Pandanus*.

Native range Africa, Asia, Australasia, South America

PETROSAVIALES

Family 1   **Genera** 2
Species 3

This order has one family (*Petrosaviaceae*), which is native to eastern Asia. *Petrosavia* species live on forest floors and have no chlorophyll. Unable to photosynthesize, they obtain their food by living as parasites on fungi. All plants in the order have similar spikes of small, upward-facing, star-shaped, cream flowers.

Native range Asia

▷ POALES

Families 14   **Genera** 998
Species 23,955

The order Poales includes wind-pollinated families that dominate certain ecosystems, such as the grasses (*Poaceae*) of prairies and savannas, the sedges (*Cyperaceae*) of bogs in the northern hemisphere and the restios (*Restionaceae*) of cool, damp areas in the southern hemisphere. Bromeliads mainly live as epiphytes growing on tropical trees.

Native range Every continent

Inner leaves are tinged pink

Leaves are up to 1 ft (30 cm) long

Blushing bromeliad | *Neoregelia carolinae*
At flowering time, the central leaves of this Brazilian bromeliad turn crimson, and it produces blue or violet flowers.

Clumps of spikelets hold the flowers

Cock's-foot | *Dactylis glomerata*
Native to Eurasia and North Africa, and often grown in hay fields and pastures, this common grass has distinctive tufty flower heads.

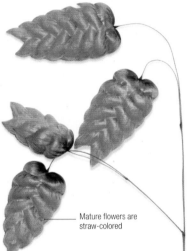

Mature flowers are straw-colored

Large quaking grass | *Briza maxima*
This Mediterranean annual grass gets its name from the way its fine-stalked flower heads shake at the slightest breeze.

Smaller male flowers grow higher up the stem than female flowers

Branched bur-reed | *Sparganium erectum*
Separate ball-shaped clusters of male and female flowers develop on the same flower stalk in this wetland species of the northern hemisphere.

Common reed | *Phragmites australis*
Widespread in both temperate and tropical regions, this shallow-water grass can colonize large areas via its creeping horizontal stems.

A ripe tuber is crisp and sweet

Chinese water chestnut | *Eleocharis dulcis*
Native to Asia, this wetland sedge has clumps of tubular stems. It is cultivated for its edible underwater tubers.

Orange-red bracts enclose this bromeliad's budding white, tubular flowers

Dyer's tillandsia | *Racinaea dyeriana*
This epiphytic bromeliad is endangered in the wild due to the destruction of its native mangrove forests in Ecuador.

Each spikelet bears tufts of bristlelike awns

Three-awned goat grass | *Aegilops neglecta*
A relative of wheat, this low-growing, drought-resistant annual grass is native to the Mediterranean and Middle East.

Citronella | *Cymbopogon nardus*
A type of lemongrass, citronella originates from tropical Asia. It yields an oil used in perfumes and for repelling insects.

Dwarf papyrus sedge | *Cyperus haspan*
Native to damp tropical and subtropical areas, this sedge grows in tufts of green stems, topped by yellow-green florets that turn bronze.

Flowers emerge from scaly bracts

Yellow-eyed grass | *Xyris* spp.
This genus of grasslike plants, widespread in warmer regions of the world, bears small, yellow flowers on slender stems.

Pink quill | *Wallisia cyanea*
Native to Ecuador and Peru, pink quill is an epiphytic perennial that grows on rainforest trees at up to 2,800 ft (850 m) above sea level.

The flower spikes reach 29 in (75 cm) in height

Tiny flowers are yellowish brown

Soft rush | *Juncus effusus*
This widespread rush thrives in damp, infertile soils. Its cylindrical stems are filled with spongy tissue, or pith.

Bird's nest bromeliad | *Nidularium innocentii*
The small, white flowers of this Brazilian plant nestle within red bracts at its center.

Scarlet star | *Guzmania lingulata*
This tree-living bromeliad has a wide native range from Central America to Brazil. It is a popular ornamental species.

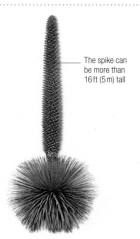

The spike can be more than 16 ft (5 m) tall

Queen of the Andes | *Puya raimondii*
Native to the central Andes, the world's largest bromeliad produces a single colossal flower spike after many years of growth.

Sea barley | *Hordeum marinum*
Native to areas from North Africa and Europe east to Central Asia, this grass has a dense, compact seed head with many bristly awns.

Soft hairs coat the flower heads

Hare's tail | *Lagurus ovatus*
The distinctive, furry, oval flower heads of this mainly coastal Mediterranean grass make it popular in dried flower arrangements.

Crested dog's-tail | *Cynosurus cristatus*
Low-growing, apart from its flower stalks, this grass from Europe and Western Asia is often used for lawns because it resists trampling.

Silver-veined prayer plant |
Maranta leuconeura
This Brazilian forest plant folds its leaves together at night to conserve moisture. Cultivated varieties have strikingly patterned foliage.

△ ZINGIBERALES

Families 8   **Genera** 97
Species 2,810

Many species in this mainly tropical order grow giant leaves at the end of stalks. Although Zingiberales includes no true woody trees, some species—such as the banana plant—grow very large. Many Zingiberales have showy flowers and foliage and have become ornamentals. The ginger family, *Zingiberaceae*, the largest in the order, includes several other important spice plants besides ginger itself, such as tumeric.

Native range Africa, Asia, South America

▽ CANELLALES

Families 2   **Genera** 9
Species 89

The two families of this order—*Canellaceae* and *Winteraceae*—are aromatic trees and shrubs with leathery leaves. The flowers in most Canellales species have both male and female parts and the fruit is a berry. The leaves and bark of some species can be used medicinally.

Native range Africa, Asia, Australasia, South America

Winter's bark | *Drimys winteri*
Native to the coastal rainforest in Chile and Argentina, this tree has fragrant flowers, and aromatic bark and leaves.

The red, pink, or maroon flowers have a fruity scent

The green leaves are large, oval, and aromatic

Carolina allspice |
Calycanthus floridus
Native to woods and the banks of streams in the southeastern US, this plant can reach a height of 10 ft (3 m), with a spread of up to 12 ft (3.6 m).

▽ CHLORANTHALES

Family 1   **Genera** 4
Species 73

Fossil records of *Chloranthaceae*, the only family in the order Chloranthales, date back more than 100 million years. Its members are mainly tropical shrubs and trees with small, stalkless flowers and colorful, fleshy, aromatic fruits. They grow mainly in cool, montane forests (mountain timberline forest)—especially the South American Andes—at altitudes of up to 10,000 ft (3,000 m).

Native range Asia, South America

△ LAURALES

Families 7   **Genera** 97
Species 3,746

The trees, shrubs, and woody vines of the order Laurales grow mainly in tropical and subtropical regions. The largest family—*Lauraceae*—includes more than half the genera and most of the Laurales species. The classification of this order is based on genetic analysis rather than morphological characteristics. Many plants are aromatic and used in cooking and medicine.

Native range Africa, Asia, Australasia, South America

The **fruit of the banana plant is technically a berry. More than 1,000 varieties of banana are cultivated worldwide.**

Sarcandra glabra With a range of medicinal uses, this evergreen shrub of the order Chloranthales inhabits damp ground—especially shady banks of streams—in tropical and subtropical Asia, China, and Japan.

▽ MAGNOLIALES

Families 6   **Genera** 148
Species 3,264

Consisting almost exclusively of trees and shrubs, the Magnoliales are a primitive order, widely distributed in the fossil record. Although very variable, most have simple, alternately arranged leaves and flowers, with both male and female parts. Of the six families in the order, the *Magnoliaceae* is the best known; many are widely cultivated in gardens for their spectacular flowers.

Native range Africa, Asia, Australasia, North America, South America

Thick, knobbly rind covers the sweet pulp

Sweetsop | *Annona squamosa*
Also known as sugar or custard apple, this plant has a native range from Mexico to Colombia, but is now widely grown in India and Pakistan.

▽ PIPERALES

Families 3   **Genera** 18
Species 4,188

The order *Piperales* includes herbaceous plants, trees, and shrubs that are widely distributed in tropical regions. The stems have scattered bundles of vascular tissue, a characteristic of monocots. Members of the *Piperaceae* family have tiny flowers which lack petals and are clustered in spikes. Many species are aromatic.

Native range Every continent except Antarctica

The leaves are glossy and evergreen

Asarabacca |
Asarum europaeum
This creeping species grows in European woodlands. Its large leaves conceal tiny, red to purple flowers.

Gunnera | *Gunnera manicata* Huge leaves and tall flower spikes characterize this species, which grows beside water and is native to southern Brazil.

△ GUNNERALES

Families   **Genera** 2
Species 65

The two families that make up the Gunnerales order were previously classified in separate orders, because they are visually quite different. However, genetic analysis has recently shown that the families are closely related. The family *Gunneraceae* consists of a single genus of large herbaceous plants growing in damp habitats, whereas *Myrothamnaceae* species grow wild in African deserts. *Gunnera* species are often grown in gardens as ornamental plants.

Native range Africa, Australasia, South America

▷ NYMPHAEALES

Families 3   **Genera** 9
Species 101

This primitive order includes three families of aquatic plants with floating, submerged, or, more rarely, emergent leaves that extend out of the water. The family *Nymphaeaceae* includes water lilies, which are grown in ornamental ponds around the world for their showy flowers.

Native range Africa, Asia, Australasia, North America, South America

The huge lily pads of *Victoria boliviana* can be up to 10 ft (3 m) wide.

Fragrant water lily | *Nymphaea odorata*
This species, often seen in the lakes and streams of North and Central America, has showy, white flowers, and large, waxy leaves.

▽ PROTEALES

Families 4 **Genera** 85
Species 1,750

Of the four *Proteales* families, the largest is the *Proteaceae*—evergreen trees and shrubs from the southern hemisphere. The *Platanaceae* are northern deciduous trees; the *Sabiaceae* are tropical trees or lianas; while the *Nelumbonaceae* has just two species—aquatic plants from Asia, Australia, and North/Central America.

Native range Every continent except Antarctica

Tight heads of flowers have long, yellow styles

Leaves are narrow and grayish green, with fine hairs

Honeysuckle grevillea |
Grevillea juncifolia
This erect Australian shrub is found in drier, mainly inland, regions of the continent.

▷ RANUNCULALES

Families 7 **Genera** 199
Species 4,510

The order Ranunculales consists of seven families. Four are relatively obscure, with few species, but the buttercup family, *Ranunculaceae*—after which the order is named—contains around 3,200 species. Together with members of the poppy and barberry families, these include some of the most common agricultural weeds worldwide and many familiar garden plants.

Native range Every continent except Antarctica

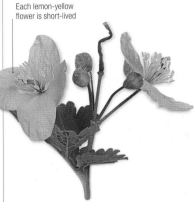

Each lemon-yellow flower is short-lived

Matilija poppy | *Romneya coulteri*
A species of scrub and grassland in California and Mexico, this poppy has fragrant flowers and is often grown in gardens.

Japanese staunton vine |
Stauntonia hexaphylla
This vigorous evergreen climber is native to woodland in Japan and South Korea.

Leaves are the sole food of the barberry carpet moth

Oblong-shaped fruits are edible and rich in vitamin C

Barberry | *Berberis vulgaris*
A European species of hedges and scrub, barberry has distinctive triple spines, hanging flower clusters, and red berries.

Greater celandine | *Chelidonium majus*
Formerly cultivated by herbalists, greater celandine is native to Europe and northern Asia, growing in woodland, scrub, and rocky places.

A characteristic spur extends from the flower

Scarlet larkspur |
Delphinium cardinale
This short-lived perennial grows on dry hillsides in California and Mexico.

Moonseed | *Menispermum canadense*
The fruits of this climber resemble black grapes, but are extremely poisonous. It inhabits woodland and stream banks in Canada and the US.

Leontice | *Leontice leontopetalum*
Native to cultivated ground and dry hillsides in north Africa and eastern Mediterranean countries, leontice grows from a tuber.

Berberis are particularly important in traditional medicine and the diet of Iranians.

▽ BRASSICALES

Families 19   **Genera** 405
Species 5,035

The order Brassicales has 19 families. Many members have bitter or fragrant oils in their leaves, stems, or swollen roots. Although these oils evolved to deter grazers, they make many species pleasantly edible for humans, and have culinary, perfumery, or herbal uses. The cabbage family (*Brassicaceae*) is the largest group, with 3,300 species.

Native range Every continent except Antarctica

Annual honesty | *Lunaria annua*
Native to southwestern Europe, honesty is often grown in gardens. Its seed pods are used in dried flower arrangements.

— Nectar-rich flowers attract a wealth of pollinating insects

▽ CELASTRALES

Families 2   **Genera** 94
Species 1,355

The two families in this diverse order, which mostly occur in tropical and subtropical regions, are characterized by a nectar-secreting disk in the flower. The *Lepidobotryaceae* comprises just two tropical tree species, but the *Celastraceae*, or spindle-tree family, has 1,200 species, mainly vines, shrubs, and trees.

Native range Every continent except Antarctica

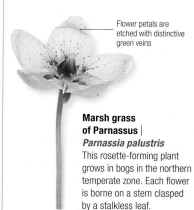

Flower petals are etched with distinctive green veins

Marsh grass of Parnassus | *Parnassia palustris*
This rosette-forming plant grows in bogs in the northern temperate zone. Each flower is borne on a stem clasped by a stalkless leaf.

▽ CROSSOSOMATALES

Families 7   **Genera** 12
Species 66

This small order of Eudicots is found in tropical and subtropical regions except Africa. Its members are mostly deciduous trees and shrubs, with flower parts in fives. Those of the *Staphylea* genus have seeds enclosed in a papery, bladderlike capsule.

Native range Every continent except Antarctica

Caucasian bladdernut | *Staphylea colchica*
This shrub from the Caucasus region, east of the Black Sea, has scented, pendant flowers.

▽ CUCURBITALES

Families 7   **Genera** 107
Species 2,985

Seven families of trees, shrubs, herbs, and climbers, mainly tropical, make up this order. Six have few members, but the begonia family (*Begoniaceae*) has 1,400 species, 130 of which are horticultural plants. The 850 species in the gourd family (*Cucurbitaceae*) include food plants, such as squash and pumpkins. Both of these families have male and female flowers on the same plant.

Native range Every continent except Antarctica

Sutherland begonia | *Begonia sutherlandii* This is a tuberous, trailing perennial from subtropical southern Africa, where it grows in damp forests or by streams or waterfalls.

▽ FABALES

Families 4   **Genera** 773
Species 22,190

Growing on every continent except for Antarctica, plants in the order Fabales have compound leaves with tiny outgrowths (stipules) at the base and seed pods that open when mature. Called legumes, these plants have swellings on their roots that contain *Rhizobium* bacteria, which help them fix nitrogen from the air into a form that is available for plant growth. The family *Fabaceae* includes the peas (*Pisum*), whose flowers have a large upper petal and several smaller adjacent petals.

Native range Every continent except Antarctica

Phyllodes are not true leaves but modified leaf stems

Globular yellow flowers bloom in spring and early summer

Flat wattle | *Acacia glaucoptera*
The globular flowers of this spreading shrub from southwest Australia grow from a modified stem that looks like a twisted leaf.

Stems reach a height of 12 in (30 cm)

Nicean milkwort | *Polygala nicaeensis*
This perennial from France and Italy has flowers with two sepals and three joined petals, one of which is fringed, and a small capsule as a fruit.

Sensitive plant | *Mimosa pudica*
The leaves of this South American plant close when touched. Its flower heads usually have pink flowers and long, pink-purple stamens.

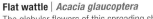

Crown vetch | *Securigera varia*
This rapidly spreading perennial of Southern Europe and Western Asia has deep roots, good for binding soil and controlling erosion.

Flowers are followed by horseshoe-shaped seed pods

Horseshoe vetch | *Hippocrepis comosa*
The leaves of this perennial are a major food plant for blue butterfly caterpillars (*Polyommatus* species).

Slightly zigzag stem grows 23–39 in (0.6–1.0 m) long

Licorice milk vetch | *Astragalus glycyphyllos*
With similar leaves to true licorice (*Glycyrrhiza glabra*), this European grassland herb has curved pods.

Elliptical leaflets grow to ¹⁄₂–1¹⁄₂ in (1.5–4 cm) long

Perennial sweet pea | *Lathyrus latifolius*
Distributed throughout southern Europe and North Africa, this vigorous, climbing perennial has winged stems and clusters of 5–15 pinkish flowers.

Stem is winged and hairless

Fabaceae is the most important plant family in the production of human food.

▽ FAGALES

Families 7 **Genera** 33
Species 1,599

The seven families in this order include some of the world's best-known trees: beech trees (family *Fagaceae*), birches (*Betulaceae*), southern beeches (*Nothofagaceae*), walnuts (*Juglandaceae*), and Australian she-oaks (*Casuarinaceae*).

Native range Every continent except Antarctica

Kermes oak | *Quercus coccifera*
An evergreen, shrubby tree from the Mediterranean region, it has holly-like leaves and yellow-brown male catkins.

▽ GERANIALES

Families 2 **Genera** 14
Species 815

Two families make up the Geraniales order. The geranium family (*Geraniaceae*) contains around 800 species, including 400 cranesbills in the genus *Geranium*. Many of the 200 species in the African genus *Pelargonium* are of horticultural importance, including the garden plants called geraniums. The new family *Francoaceae* includes the herbaceous perennials known as bridal wreaths.

Native range Every continent except Antarctica

Giant honeybush | *Melianthus major*
Nectar drips from the bronze flower spikes of this South African native. Touching the leaves makes them give off a strong odor.

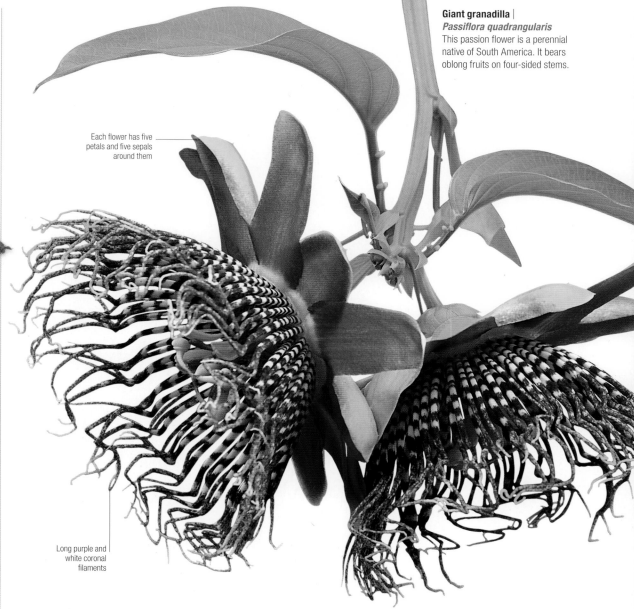

Giant granadilla |
Passiflora quadrangularis
This passion flower is a perennial native of South America. It bears oblong fruits on four-sided stems.

Each flower has five petals and five sepals around them

Long purple and white coronal filaments

▷ HUERTEALES

Families 4 **Genera** 6
Species 27

The mostly evergreen shrubs and trees in this small order of eudicots have a very scattered distribution in East Asia, Australasia, Central and South America, and southeast Africa. All are woody plants that produce berries and bear alternate leaves with toothed edges. The flowers usually have five petals and five sepals, and the bases of their calyx, corolla, and stamens form a cup-shaped tube, called a hypanthium.

Native range Africa, Asia, Australasia, North America, South America

Perrottetia sandwicensis
Native to wet forests in the Hawaiian Islands, this evergreen shrub or small tree has smooth, gray bark and grows to 23 ft (7 m) tall.

△ MALPIGHIALES

Families 36 **Genera** 759
Species 19,019

This large and diverse order of plants consists of 36 mainly tropical families, grouped together by their DNA but widely different in form, from small herbaceous plants to large trees. It contains plants as varied as violets (*Violaceae*) and passion flowers (*Passifloraceae*) to mangroves (*Rhizophoraceae*), coca trees (*Erythroxylaceae*), and willows (*Salicaceae*). The spurge family (*Euphorbiaceae*) has 6,300 species.

Native range Every continent except Antarctica

▽ MALVALES

Families 10   **Genera** 338
Species 6,005

The ten families in the Malvales include many shrubs and trees, found mainly in tropical and warm temperate regions, but extending into cooler parts. The main members are the rockrose family (*Cistaceae*), mostly shrubs from the northern hemisphere; the more widespread mallow family (*Malvaceae*) of herbs, shrubs, and massive trees; and the dipterocarp family (*Dipterocarpaceae*).

Native range Every continent except Antarctica

Mezereon | *Daphne mezereum*
Damp woods and shady gorges are the typical habitat of this deciduous shrub, which is found across most of Europe.

All parts of mezereon are toxic to humans, particularly the fruits, sap, and bark.

▷ MYRTALES

Families 9   **Genera** Around 380
Species 13,005

The nine families in the Myrtales are most common in warmer regions. The 5,800 species in the myrtle family (*Myrtaceae*) provide essential oils, spices, and fruits such as guava. They include more than 700 species of eucalypts from Australia and New Guinea. The loosestrife family (*Lythraceae*) consists mainly of tropical trees and shrubs, producing fruits such as pomegranate and various dyes.

Native range Every continent except Antarctica

Thin leaves are 1–1½ in (2.5–4.0 cm) long and arranged alternately

Green bottle bush | *Melaleuca virens*
Resisting snow, frost, and drought, this sprawling subalpine shrub from Tasmania, Australia, attracts birds and butterflies.

Cigar flower | *Cuphea ignea*
A densely branched, perennial shrub, this garden ornamental is native to Mexico. Its fruits are paperlike capsules.

Leaves grow on branched stems

Godetia | *Clarkia amoena*
This annual is native to coastal hills of western North America. Cultivated in gardens, its flower has four broad petals and forms a dry capsule.

Buds held in groups of three

Urn-fruited gum | *Eucalyptus urnigera*
This tree from Tasmania, Australia, has urn-shaped fruits, blue-gray juvenile leaves, and white flowers in clusters of three.

Water chestnut | *Trapa natans*
This floating plant is from Europe and Asia. It has an edible, starchy seed in a nut with four hornlike, barbed spines.

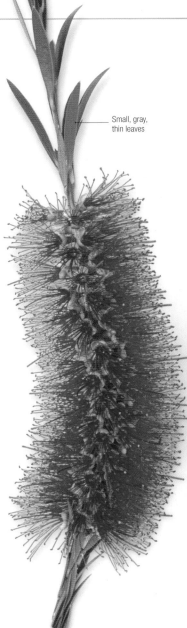

Small, gray, thin leaves

Tonghi bottlebrush | *Melaleuca subulata*
A spreading shrub with small, woody fruits containing hundreds of seeds, it is found mainly in New South Wales and Victoria, Australia.

Swamp loosetrife | *Decodon verticillatus*
Native to eastern North America, this shrub grows in swamps. It has arching stems and red or purple flowers up to 1 in (2.5 cm) across.

Velvety leaves have red edges

Princess flower | *Tibouchina urvilleana*
This Brazilian ornamental blooms for most of the year in warm regions.

Seedbox | *Ludwigia alternifolia*
Native to eastern North America, this is a plant of damp places. It has box-shaped seed pods borne on angled stems.

Small panicles of white flowers with yellow stamens

Red gum | *Eucalyptus camaldulensis*
Widespread in Australia, this riverside tree with smooth, pale bark has durable timber and its nectar makes good honey.

Flowers borne in tall spike

Long, thin leaves

Rosebay willowherb | *Epilobium angustifolium*
This herbaceous perennial is widespread in the northern hemisphere.

Scarlet kunzea | *Kunzea baxteri*
Kunzea species are unusual in having colorful stamens much longer than their petals, which add to their showy appearance.

▽ OXALIDALES

Families 7   **Genera** 58
Species 1,845

Of the families that comprise this order, *Cephalotaceae* contains only one species—the carnivorous Albany pitcher plant (*Cephalotus follicularis*). The *Cunoniaceae* are woody plants that produce tough fruit capsules containing small seeds. The wood sorrel family (*Oxalidaceae*) is the largest in the order, with about 800 species of herbaceous plants, plus shrubs and small trees.

Native range Every continent except Antarctica

PICRAMNIALES

Family 1   **Genera** 4
Species 50

A single family (*Picramniaceae*) and a small number of genera make up this order of eudicots, the bitterbushes. Most constituent species are shrubs and trees growing in wet tropical areas of southern North America and South America. All have bitter bark and alternate, compound leaves. Some—including *Picramnia pentandra*—provide valuable chemicals for the manufacture of pharmaceuticals.

Native range North America, South America

Albany pitcher plant | *Cephalotus follicularis* This carnivorous plant is native to the coast of southwest Australia. It has a liquid-filled pitcher that traps insect prey.

▷ ROSALES

Families 9   **Genera** 288
Species 10,583

This order of plants contains nine families, among them the *Rosaceae* (rose family), *Cannabaceae* (hemp family), *Moraceae* (mulberry family), *Rhamnaceae* (buckthorn family), *Ulmaceae* (elm family), and *Urticaceae* (nettle family). Members of the Rosales are often grown for their fruits or other products. Plants in this order are often thorny or hairy, and tend to have flowers with five sepals and numerous stamens. Most are insect-pollinated.

Native range Every continent except Antarctica

Prairie crab apple | *Malus ioensis*
One of several crab apples native to North America, this species is one of many cultivated for its rather tart fruits.

Orange fruits form on spherical, female flower heads

Paper mulberry | *Broussonetia papyrifera*
Fine paper is made from the inner bark of this tree from Japan and southeast China. Male catkins produce large quantities of pollen.

Stems grow to 4½ in (12 cm) tall

Silverweed | *Potentilla anserina*
This silky-haired, creeping perennial is native to wasteland, pastures, and dunes in Europe, Asia, and North America.

Willowlike leaves have a silvery, downy underside

Pendent branches give this tree a weeping habit

Willow-leaved pear | *Pyrus salicifolia*
Cultivated for its pendulous, silvery foliage, not for its inedible fruits, this Middle Eastern tree is endangered in the wild in Türkiye.

Leaf surfaces have fine hairs

New Jersey tea | *Ceanothus americanus*
This bush, native to North America, has purple, three-lobed capsules, containing seeds. Its red roots and its leaves have been used to make tea.

Flowers are highly scented

Firehorn | *Pyracantha rogersiana*
This thorny, evergreen shrub from eastern China belongs to a genus often planted for its attractive but inedible, orange, berrylike fruits.

Jujube | *Ziziphus jujuba*
This thorny, shrubby tree is widely cultivated for its fruits in China and Korea. The immature, smooth, oval, green-stoned fruit tastes like apple.

Creamy-white flowers are borne in spring

Toothed leaves have hairy surfaces

Glossy, deciduous leaves

Wrinkled fruits grow to 5in (13cm) across

Plants in the Rosales order grow in varied habitats, from lush forests to arid deserts and from sea level to high mountains.

Glands on the leaves produce an apple scent when crushed

Flowers have eight petals, giving the species its Latin name

Crimson blooms emerge from knobbly green flower heads in summer

Water avens | *Geum rivale*
This downy perennial grows in damp places in Europe, Anatolia, and North America. Hooked hairs on its fruits latch onto animals for dispersal.

Strawberry | *Fragaria vesca*
The wild strawberry is a perennial in European and North American woodlands. Tiny edible fruits form from the swollen flower receptacle.

Osage orange | *Maclura pomifera*
Native to southeastern regions of the US, this tree is used for hedging; its roots and wood were valued by Indigenous peoples.

Sweet briar rose | *Rosa rubiginosa*
One of the most deeply colored wild roses, sweet briar rose enlivens hedgerows and scrub around Europe, Asia, and Africa.

Mountain avens | *Dryas octopetala*
The flowers of this Arctic and mountain undershrub turn to follow the sun to warm their centers and attract pollinating insects.

Salad burnet | *Sanguisorba minor*
Native from Europe to Iran, and introduced in North America, this perennial of lime-rich grassland has edible leaves, hence its name.

Thought to resemble a cloak, the leaves give this plant its common name

Wild cherry | *Prunus avium*
The wild ancestor of orchard cherries grows in woods and hedges in Europe, Asia, and North Africa and is naturalized in North America.

Stinging nettle | *Urtica dioica*
Nettles grow on disturbed ground in Europe, Asia, North Africa, and North America. Stinging hairs discourage animals from eating the leaves.

Lady's mantle | *Alchemilla vulgaris*
The common name of this plant encompasses several closely related grassland species from Europe, Asia, and eastern North America.

▽ SAPINDALES

Families 9   **Genera** 473
Species 6,567

The Sapindales is an important order of mostly trees, shrubs, and woody vines. It includes many dominant woodland plants and commercially important species, such as citrus fruits. More than half its members belong to two families: the maple family (*Sapindaceae*), which has around 1,900 species; and the rue family (*Rutaceae*), with 1,700 species that mostly originate in Australia and South Africa.

Native range Every continent except Antarctica

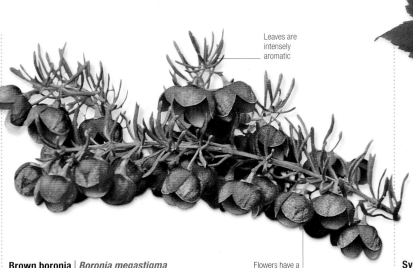

Leaves are intensely aromatic

Flowers have a strong fragrance and are used in essential oils

Brown boronia | *Boronia megastigma*
This erect shrub from wet, sandy sites in Western Australia has bell-like flowers, brownish on the outside and gold-green inside.

Leaves have five lobes

Flowers develop in panicles up to 6 in (15 cm) long

Sycamore | *Acer pseudoplatanus*
Native to mountain woods in Europe and Asia, sycamore is widely planted elsewhere. Its winged seeds are dispersed by the wind.

Frankincense | *Boswellia sacra*
Cuts made in the trunks of these Arabian trees exude a milky juice. This is frankincense, a gum resin used in incense and to fix perfumes.

Fruit ripens from green to red or pink-red

Lychee | *Litchi chinensis*
Probably originating in southern China, this tree is cultivated for its fruits. Their sweet flesh is encased within a tough shell.

Smoke bush | *Cotinus coggygria*
Finely branched clusters of yellowish-pink flowers give this bush a smoky appearance. It is found in southern Europe and Asia.

Leaves are aromatic

Some fruits have green peel

Seville orange | *Citrus × aurantium*
Unlike the sweet oranges we eat raw (*Citrus × sinensis*), this species' bitter fruits are only good for cooking. Both originated as Asian hybrids.

Leaves comprise 3–5 leaflets

Petals remain closed

Leaf stems are winged

Bitterwood | *Quassia amara*
Boiled extracts from the bark and leaves of this tree are used to make tonics against malaria in tropical regions of northern South America.

Fruits turn from green to yellow as they ripen

Hardy orange | *Citrus trifoliata*
The small, inedible yellow fruits of this spiny shrub resemble oranges with a downy skin. They have several medicinal uses.

Fringed rue | *Ruta chalepensis*
A native of rocky habitats in southern Europe and southwest Asia, this plant is thought to be the rue mentioned in the Bible.

Mature flowers have maroon throats

Yellowhorn | *Xanthoceras sorbifolium*
This small tree grows wild in China. Its species name references its leaves, which resemble those of rowan (*Sorbus*).

▽ VITALES

Family 1   **Genera** 15
Species 1,018

This order consists of a single family, the *Vitaceae* or grape family, which includes the grapevine and the ornamental Virginia creeper. Members of the *Vitaceae* are mainly native to the tropics or warm temperate regions. Mostly vines or lianas, they usually have swollen nodes (where leaves fork from the stem) and tendrils for climbing. Their flowers are usually held in flat-topped clusters.

Native range Asia, Australasia, North America, South America

Leaves turn bright orange and red in the fall

Virginia creeper |
Parthenocissus quinquefolia
This prolific climber from North and Central America clings on to smooth surfaces using the adhesive pads on its small, forked tendrils.

▽ ZYGOPHYLLALES

Families 2   **Genera** 27
Species 304

This eudicot order has a wide distribution through the subtropical and tropical regions of the world. Most are annuals or short-lived perennial plants, often from arid or desert regions. Flower parts are in fives. Several genera have fruits with multiple strong spines, hence their common name of caltrop.

Native range Every continent except Antarctica

Sea grape | ***Zygophyllum fontanesii***
The fleshy, succulent leaves of this cushion-forming plant resemble small grapes.

▽ SANTALALES

Families 8   **Genera** 184
Species 2,488

Found mainly in tropical and subtropical regions, families in the order Santalales include several species that are important timber trees. They also feature many parasitic and semiparasitic plants, notably the 900 species in the showy mistletoe family (*Loranthaceae*), which are native to the southern hemisphere. These live attached to other plants, from which they obtain all or most of the water and nutrients they need for growth.

Native range Africa, Asia, South America

Golden flowers are sweetly honey-scented

Fire tree | ***Nuytsia floribunda***
This species is semiparasitic, deriving moisture and nutrients from the roots of surrounding plants in woodland in southwestern Australia.

▷ SAXIFRAGALES

Families 15   **Genera** 115
Species 3,082

Of the 15 diverse families in the Saxifragales, five have just two members each and only three have more than 500 species. Best known is the saxifrage family, after which the order is named. The Latin *saxifraga* literally means "rock breaker," as these plants often grow in cracks in rocks and walls. The largest family is the stonecrops, *Crassulaceae*, which includes many succulent or water-retaining plants that are adapted to dry conditions.

Native range Every continent

▷ TROCHODENDRALES

Family 1   **Genera** 2
Species 2

This order comprises a single family (*Trochodendronaceae*) and only two genera, *Trochodendron* and *Tetracentron*, each of which has a single species. Both are temperate east Asian trees with unusual, petalless green flowers that have flower parts in fours. *Trochodendron aralioides* is an evergreen, whereas *Tetracentron sinense* is deciduous.

Native range Asia

Wheel tree | ***Trochodendron aralioides***
Spirals of glossy, leathery leaves surround the unusual flower clusters of this compact tree.

The saxifrage family includes currants and gooseberries.

Flaming Katy | ***Kalanchoe blossfeldiana***
Arid areas of Madagascar are home to this bushy species with glossy, succulent leaves and brightly colored flowers.

Fungi

Once classified as plants, fungi are now recognized as a distinct kingdom of living organisms. Growing in or through their food, they digest organic matter, and often become visible only when they reproduce. Fungi are both allies and enemies to other forms of life: vital recyclers and mutually benefiting partners, they also include parasites and pathogens.

Orange peel cup | *Aleuria aurantia* The orange peel fungus is a good example of the simple cup-shaped fruit body adopted by many fungi species. It is a member of the order Pezizales.

Sac fungi

The Ascomycota, or sac fungi, produce their spores in rounded to elongate sacs called asci, which are located on the fertile surface of the fruit body. They are the largest group of fungi and include many cup- or saucer-shaped species.

CAPNODIALES

Families 12 **Genera** 106
Species 749

Commonly called sooty molds, these sac fungi are frequently found on leaves, where they feed on the honeydew excreted by insects or on liquid exuded from the leaves. Some species cause skin problems in humans, and others are responsible for economically important diseases in trees and crops.

Native range Every continent

PLEOSPORALES

Families 56 **Genera** 500
Species 9,411

Typical members of this order develop their asci within a flask-like fruit body. The asci have two wall layers: at maturity, the inner wall protrudes beyond the outer wall, ejecting the spores. Most species decay plant material in aquatic or terrestrial environments. Others grow on living plants; some form lichens.

Native range Every continent

▽ EUROTIALES

Families 4 **Genera** 45
Species 1,364

Widespread, abundant, and better known as the blue and green molds, this order includes the Penicillium species—some of which produce penicillin, the first discovered antibiotic—and the toxin-producing Aspergillus species, some of which are carcinogenic in humans.

Native range Every continent

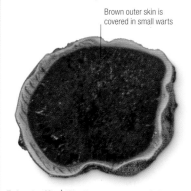

Brown outer skin is covered in small warts

False truffle | *Elaphomyces granulatus* Common in sandy soils below conifers in Eurasia and North America, this reddish-brown truffle has a purple-black inner spore-mass.

ERYSIPHALES

Family 1 **Genera** 30
Species 991

Parasitic on the leaves and fruit of flowering plants, the Erysiphales are powdery mildews—producing powdery white spots on infected leaves and stems. The hyphae (filaments) of their mycelium (the vegetative part of the fungus) penetrate the cells of the host plant and take up nutrients from it. They have developed fungicide resistance.

Native range Every continent except Antarctica

▽ HELOTIALES

Families 18 **Genera** 667
Species 7,323

The fungi of this order are distinguished by their disk- or cup-shaped fruit bodies, unlike similar cup fungi. Their saclike spore-producing cells, or asci, do not have an apical lid (a flap through which they open). Most of these fungi live on humus-rich soil, dead logs, and other organic matter. Some of the most damaging plant parasites are members of this order.

Native range Every continent

Black bulgar | *Bulgaria inquinans* Found in Eurasia and North America, it has a brown outer surface. Its spore-producing inner surface is smooth, black, and rubbery.

▽ RHYTISMATALES

Family 4 **Genera** 92
Species 769

Commonly called tar spot fungi, the species in this order infect plant matter, such as leaves, twigs, bark, female conifer cones, and occasionally berries. Many species attack the needles of conifers, causing needle drop. The tar spot of maple leaves is perhaps the most frequently seen.

Native range Every continent except Antarctica

Tar spot | *Rhytisma acerinum* Abundant on maple trees in North America and Eurasia, this fungus causes irregular spots with paler yellow margins, which disfigure the leaves.

▷ PEZIZALES

Families 16 **Genera** 266
Species 2,660

Members of this order produce spores inside saclike structures, or asci, which typically open by rupturing to form an operculum (terminal lid) and eject the spores. The order includes a number of species of economic importance, such as morels, truffles, and desert truffles.

Native range Every continent

Margin of cup is toothed when fully mature

Elongated cup is split down short side

Toothed cup | *Tarzetta cupularis*
A common species in alkaline soils in woodlands in Eurasia and North America, its goblet-like cup has a short stem.

White saddle | *Helvella crispa*
Possibly poisonous, this fungus is common in mixed woods in Eurasia and North America. Its saddlelike cap sits on a fragile, ribbed stem.

Hollow stem grows to 4 in (10 cm) tall

Hare's ear | *Otidea onotica*
Clusters of this species are often found in broadleaf forests in Eurasia and North America. Its tall cups are split down on one side.

Black morel | *Morchella elata*
Common in woods during spring in Eurasia and North America, this species has a pinkish-buff to black cap, with cross-connected black ridges.

Half-free morel | *Morchella semilibera*
This hollow morel looks like a dark, ridged thimble on a scurfy, pale stem. It is common in mixed woods in Eurasia and North America.

Bleach cup | *Disciotis venosa*
Growing in spring in damp woodland in Eurasia and North America, this short-stemmed species has a chlorine-like odor.

Yeast is a sac fungus that has been used in bread making since 1500 BCE.

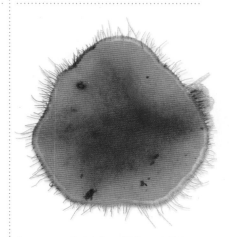

Cellar cup | *Peziza cerea*
Found across Eurasia and North America, this fungus often occurs on damp brickwork. It is dark ocher on the inside and paler outside.

Elfin saddle | *Helvella lacunosa*
A species of mixed woods in Eurasia and North America, this common fungus has a lobed, dark cap on a gray, fluted and columned stem.

Common eyelash | *Scutellinia scutellata*
This is one of many similar species; its fruit body is a scarlet cup. This fungus is common on wet, rotten wood in Eurasia and North America.

Candlesnuff fungus | *Xylaria hypoxylon* Common on dead wood in Eurasia and North America, this species resembles a snuffed-out candle with a velvety-gray stem.

▽ HYPOCREALES

Families 11 **Genera** 419
Species 4,779

The fungi in this order are commonly distinguished by their brightly colored, spore-producing structures. These are usually yellow, orange, or red. The Hypocreales are often parasitic on other fungi and also on insects. The best known among them is the genus Cordyceps, which has club- or branchlike fruit bodies.

Native range Every continent

Cap of bolete discolored and dimpled by mold

Bolete eater | *Hypomyces chrysospermus*
This common mold, which grows on boletes (family *Boletaceae*) in North America and Eurasia, turns bright golden yellow as it ages.

◁ XYLARIALES

Families 13 **Genera** 187
Species 2,640

Members of this order often have their spore-producing cells in chambers, which are embedded in a woody growth called stroma. Although many species live on wood, some also occur on animal dung, fruit, leaves, and soil, or are associated with insects. The order includes many damaging plant parasites.

Native range Every continent

TAPHRINALES

Families 2 **Genera** 8
Species 150

This order contains many plant parasites, with most species in the genus *Taphrina*. All species have two growth states: in the saprophytic state, they are yeast-like and propagate by budding; in the parasitic state, they emerge through plant tissues, causing distorted leaves and galls.

Native range Every continent

Mushrooms

The phylum Basidiomycota includes the majority of what are commonly called mushrooms and toadstools. Found in almost every major habitat type, nearly all share the ability to form sexual spores externally on special cells called basidia.

▽ AURICULARIALES

Families 2   **Genera** 41
Species 288

Although often grouped with other jelly fungi, the Auriculariales are separated by their unusual basidia (spore-producing cells). These vary in shape but all are partitioned by dividing membranes into four divisions, with each division producing a spore. Auriculariales fungi are mostly saprotrophic, growing on dead wood, where their fruit bodies can form into large masses. Several species are edible.

Native range Every continent

▷ CANTHARELLALES

Families 7   **Genera** 55
Species 750

The species of the Cantharellales order may look like agarics (members of the Agaricales order) but differ in several important respects. They may have fleshy fruit bodies with a cap and stem, but they lack true gills, having instead a smooth, wrinkled, or folded gill-like spore-producing surface on the underside. The spores are smooth and usually white to cream. Several species are edible.

Native range Every continent

The tips of the branches have tiny crests

Crested coral | *Clavulina coralloides*
Very common in woods in Eurasia and North America, this fungus forms a coral-like mass of white branches, each dividing into fine points.

▽ GLOEOPHYLLALES

Family 1   **Genera** 11
Species 42

This is an order of wood-decay fungi that is characterized by the ability to produce a brown rot of wood. The order Gloeophyllales has a single family, the *Gloeophyllaceae*, which includes the genus Gloeophyllum. Some well-known bracket fungi on conifer trees are members of this genus.

Native range Every continent

Anise mazegill | *Gloeophyllum odoratum*
This fungus, which grows on decayed conifer wood, is found in Eurasia and North America. It has irregular brackets with yellow pores.

▽ HYMENOCHAETALES

Families 4   **Genera** 78
Species 1,119

This group contains a number of diverse types of fungi including some crust fungi, polypores, such as those in the genera *Mensularia* and *Phellinus*, as well as several agaric species, such as those in *Rickenella*. The *Hymenochaetales* are defined through molecular studies and have few uniting physical characteristics. Many feed on wood and may cause a white rot of timber.

Native range Every continent

Witches' butter | *Exidia nigricans*
Present in the temperate northern hemisphere, frequently on hardwood trees, it resembles a wrinkled mass of gelatinous tar. It shrivels when dry to a hard, black mass.

Fruit body has brain-like folds

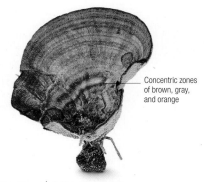
Concentric zones of brown, gray, and orange

Tiger's eye | *Coltricia perennis*
Frequently found on acidic heathlands, this fungus's goblet-shaped, thin fruit bodies are concentrically zoned.

The fruit bodies of many mushroom species grow rapidly at night, giving rise to the phrase, "to mushroom."

▷ POLYPORALES

Families 13   **Genera** 311
Species 3,553

The Polyporales form a large group of diverse fungi. All are saprotrophs, and most are polypores, wood decomposers whose spores are formed in tubes (rather like the tubes of the boletes) or sometimes on spines. Most lack fully developed stems and grow shelf-, bracket-, or crust-like fruit bodies on wood, but some have a short, more or less central stem, for example *Lentinus tigrinus*.

Native range Every continent

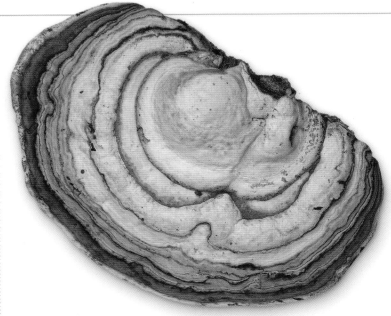

Tinder bracket | *Fomes fomentarius* This gray-brown, hoof-shaped, perennial bracket grows on birches and other deciduous trees. It is found in Eurasia and North America.

The cap's upper surface is smooth and often darkens with age

Winter polypore | *Lentinus brumalis*
This small species grows on fallen branches. It has relatively large, decurrent (running down the stem) pores.

Blushing bracket |
Daedaleopsis confragosa
A common bracket fungus, this species has cream pores that bruise pinkish-red.

Smoky bracket | *Bjerkandera adusta*
This common bracket, found in Eurasia and North America, can be identified by the ash-gray pore surface on its underside.

Black footed polypore | *Polyporus durus*
The funnel-shaped, leathery cap of this fungus is distinctive, and its stem is black at the base. It grows on fallen beech (*Fagus*) logs.

Jelly rot | *Phlebia tremellosa*
Found on logs in Eurasia, this species has a pale, velvety upper side and a yellow-to-orange underside with dense ridges.

Fruit body grows to 16 in (40 cm) across

Wood cauliflower | *Sparassis crispa* Growing at the base of conifers in Eurasia and North America, this species has cream lobes that are flattened and fleshy like a cauliflower.

Hairy bracket | *Trametes hirsuta*
This semicircular bracket is covered in minute hairs. It grows on dead deciduous wood or old gorse stems in Eurasia and North America.

Tuberous polypore | *Polyporus tuberaster*
Growing on fallen branches in Eurasia and North America, this species may root into the ground and form a large, tuberous mass.

Bracket fungi grow annually from their base and can live for 30 years.

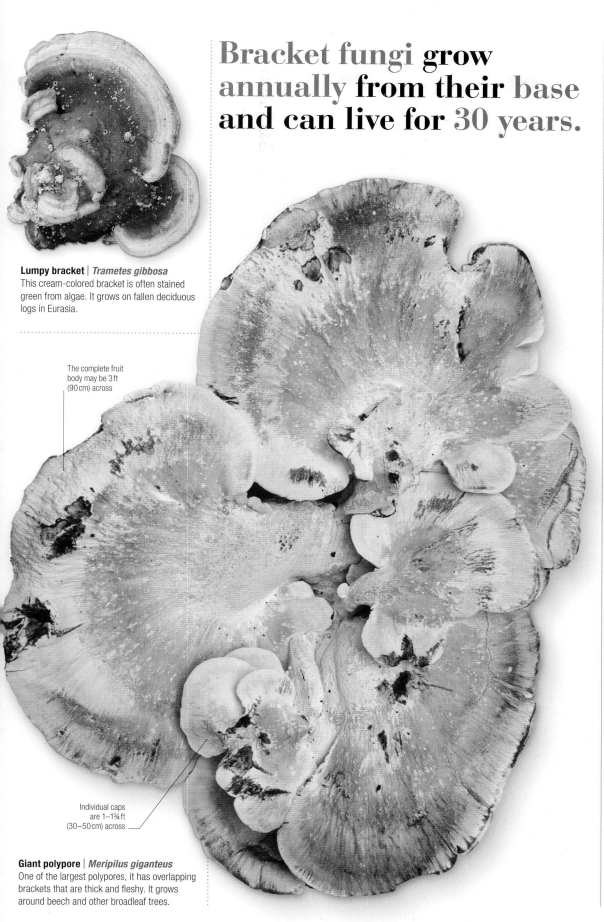

Lumpy bracket | *Trametes gibbosa*
This cream-colored bracket is often stained green from algae. It grows on fallen deciduous logs in Eurasia.

The complete fruit body may be 3ft (90cm) across

Individual caps are 1–1¾ft (30–50cm) across

Giant polypore | *Meripilus giganteus*
One of the largest polypores, it has overlapping brackets that are thick and fleshy. It grows around beech and other broadleaf trees.

▽ RUSSULALES

Families 13   **Genera** 115
Species 3,137

The best-known genera within this large order are *Russula* and *Lactarius*, which, although resembling typical mushrooms, with convex to funnel-shaped caps, are not related to the true Agaricales. Apart from the cap-and-stem shapes, Russulales produce fruit bodies in a wide range of forms. Most also have spores with warts that stain blue-black in iodine.

Native range Every continent

Root rot | *Heterobasidion annosum*
Usually parasitic on conifers in Eurasia and North America, this species has a pale brown crust that darkens with age.

▽ THELEPHORALES

Families 2   **Genera** 20
Species 356

This diverse and varied order includes bracket fungi, crust fungi, toothed fungi, and earthfans. Many of these have tough, leathery flesh, and commonly feature knobbed or spiny spores. The group was only identified as a result of molecular studies, because the Thelephorales have few physical features in common.

Native range Every continent

Earthfan | *Thelephora terrestris*
Common on sandy soils in parts of Eurasia and North America, this fungus grows on soil or woody debris. It has fan-shaped fruit bodies.

▷ AGARICALES

Families 33   **Genera** 586
Species 23,224

Many of the most familiar mushrooms and toadstools belong to this order. They include fungi with fleshy—not woody—fruit bodies. They are grouped together based on their genetic relatedness rather than structural similarities. Many have caps and stems with gills; some also have pores. Other forms include bird's-nest fungi, brackets, crusts, and puffballs. Most live on leaf litter, soil, or wood; others are parasitic or live in association with plant roots. The oldest Agaricales fossil dates from more than 113 million years ago.

Native range Every continent

Flowerpot parasol |
Leucocoprinus birnbaumii
Common worldwide, this species grows on the soils of potted plants.

The slender stem is more "hairy" toward the base

Amethyst deceiver | *Laccaria amethystina*
This slender fungus from Eurasia and North America has an intense violet coloration when fresh, and powdery spores dusting the gills.

The ivory fruit body turns gray-brown with age

White dapperling |
Leucoagaricus leucothites
Common in meadows and grassy roadsides, this fungus has gills that are white to pale pink.

Branching oyster | *Pleurotus cornucopiae*
Growing in clusters on fallen logs, usually of elm (*Ulmus*), this fungus has trumpet-shaped caps with gills running down the short, frequently branching stems.

Pleurotus species are carnivorous—they kill and feed on nematodes.

Convex when young, the cap later becomes funnel-shaped

The greasy cap is bright orange when wet, drying to pale orange-brown

Several stems fuse together at the base

The stem has a rusty-brown base

Conifer tuft | *Hypholoma capnoides*
Found in Eurasia and North America, this uncommon species occurs on conifer wood. Its whitish gills mature to grayish lilac.

The thin cap bears honey-colored gills on its underside

The stem grows to 3 in (8 cm) long

Deadly galerina | *Galerina marginata*
This species has an orange-brown cap and a small stem ring. It grows on fallen timber in Eurasia and North America.

The cap is very slimy in wet weather

Golden waxcap | *Hygrocybe chlorophana*
Found in Eurasia, this is the most common waxcap found in meadows. It has a bright yellow-orange, slightly sticky cap.

Jack o'lantern | *Omphalotus illudens*
Found across Eurasia and North America, this bright orange, poisonous fungus is famous for gills that glow greenish in the dark.

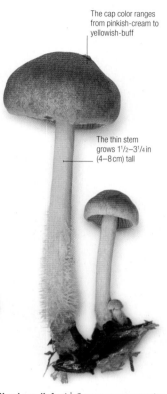

The cap color ranges from pinkish-cream to yellowish-buff

The thin stem grows 1$\frac{1}{2}$–3$\frac{1}{4}$ in (4–8 cm) tall

Wood woollyfoot | *Gymnopus peronatus*
The common name of this species from Eurasia refers to the stiff, fuzzy hairs at the base of the stem.

White scales contrast with a gray-brown background

The stem grows up to 8 in (20 cm) tall

Magpie ink cap | *Coprinopsis picacea*
Usually found on chalky soils in Eurasian woodlands, this uncommon species has a distinctively colored cap.

As it ages, the cap changes from golden to an orange-brown tone

Big laughing gym | *Gymnopilus junonius*
Occurring in Eurasia, this fungus is found in clumps, usually at the base of a tree. It has a dry cap with crowded, shallow, yellowish gills.

White fragments of the universal veil contrast with the red cap

The stem base is swollen

Fly agaric | *Amanita muscaria*
Common in Eurasia and North America, this mushroom is common under birches. Its white warts may wash off after rain.

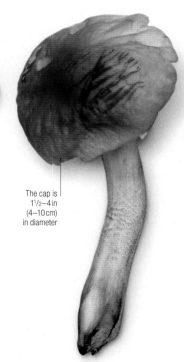

The cap is 1$\frac{1}{2}$–4 in (4–10 cm) in diameter

Popular fieldcap | *Cyclocybe cylindracea*
Found in Eurasia, this rare species grows on poplar and willow wood. The cap cracks when dry, and the stem has a ring.

▽ BOLETALES

Families 18 **Genera** 151
Species 2,173

This order contains fleshy fungi and includes those with both pored and gilled fruit bodies. Most species have a cap and stem, but some are crusts, puffballs, or have a star-shaped or truffle-like structure. The majority live in association with trees (they are mycorrhizal), but some feed on dead wood and cause a brown rot, while others are parasitic. The spore-producing layer (hymenium) is easily loosened from the flesh.

Native range Every continent

As it ages, the cap frequently splits and develops a wavy edge

Bitter bolete | *Tylopilus felleus*
This species, found in Eurasia and North America, is characterized by pores that turn pink with age and a strongly netted stem.

Barometer earthstar | *Astraeus hygrometricus* Common in Eurasia and North America, this species has starlike arms that peel back to reveal the inner spore-filled ball, but close again in dry weather.

Rosy spike | *Gomphidius roseus*
Growing in association with the bolete *Suillus bovinus* under pines in Eurasia, this fungus has a slimy, rose-pink cap with grayish gills.

Gills are deeply decurrent (extend down the stem)

Copper spike | *Chroogomphus rutilus*
Common under pines in Eurasia and western North America, this species has a conical-shaped fruit body with a coppery-brown cap.

Summer bolete | *Boletus reticulatus*
A matte, brown cap with a cracked surface and a stem with a fine white net extending to its base distinguish this species.

Bay bolete | *Imleria badia*
Common among conifers or beech (*Fagus*) trees in Eurasia and North America, its color varies from orange-brown to chestnut.

Bitter beech bolete | *Caloboletus calopus*
From Eurasia and western North America, its cap varies from white to buff. Its yellow pores and cream flesh bruise blue.

Orange birch bolete | *Leccinum versipelle*
Found in Eurasia, this species has a yellow-orange fleshy cap. The stem has black, woolly flecks, and the flesh stains lilac-black.

Brown birch bolete | *Leccinum scabrum*
This fungus is from Eurasia and North America. Its flesh may flush pink when cut, and the cap is sticky when wet.

▽ GEASTRALES

Family 1 **Genera** 10
Species 115

The Geastrales, or earthstars, share the common character of a thick outer layer—the peridium—which splits apart and peels back to form starlike arms. These reveal a central spore-sac, like a puffball, from which the dark brown, warted spores exit via a pore at the apex. Earthstars are found in varied habitats, including leaf litter in conifer or broadleaf woodland, and bare, sandy soils—for example, in sand dunes.

Native range Every continent

Spores are released through ostiole pores

Pepper pot | *Myriostoma coliforme*
Found on dry, sandy soils in Eurasia and North America, this rare species has a distinctive, large spore-sac with several pore openings.

Drops of rain trigger the release of spores from the pores of earthstars.

▽ GOMPHALES

Families 3 **Genera** 19
Species 486

Although some species were included with the chanterelles in the order Cantharellales, DNA analysis of the Gomphales fungi suggests that they are more closely related to the stinkhorns in the Phallales. They often form large fruit bodies, varying in shape from simple clubs (*Clavariadelphus* spp.) to trumpet-, chanterelle-, or coral-like structures (*Phaeoclavulina* spp.)

Native range Every continent except Antarctica

Greening coral | *Phaeoclavulina abietina*
Found in conifer woods in Eurasia and North America, this yellow-olive fungus has densely packed branches that bruise green.

Branches have deep red tips

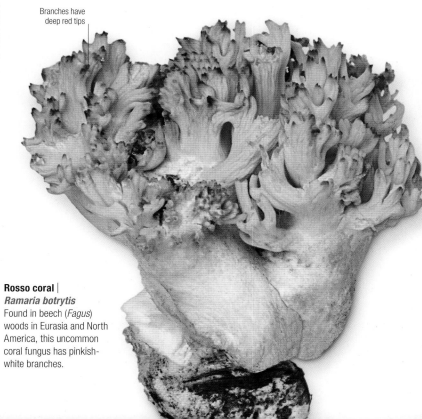

Rosso coral |
Ramaria botrytis
Found in beech (*Fagus*) woods in Eurasia and North America, this uncommon coral fungus has pinkish-white branches.

Scaly vase chanterelle |
Gomphus floccosus
Common in North America, this fungus resembles a fleshy, trumpet-shaped vase.

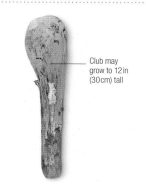

Club may grow to 12 in (30cm) tall

Giant club | *Clavariadelphus pistillaris*
This fungus forms a large, swollen club, with a smooth to slightly wrinkled surface, which bruises purple-brown.

▷ PHALLALES

Families 2 **Genera** 39
Species 172

Named for the phallic shape of many of the species in this group, the Phallales contains the stinkhorns and some false truffles. The former "hatch" from an egg-like structure, often in just a few hours. They are named for their foul-smelling, sticky spore mass, or gleba, which attracts flies, beetles, and other insects.

Native range Every continent except Antarctica

Netlike "skirt," or indusium, surrounds the hollow stem

Basket stinkhorn |
Phallus merulinus
This tropical species is mainly found in Australasia. It hatches from a white "egg." Some similar species have brightly colored "skirts."

Conical cap has a small hole in the top and is covered with pungent slime

▽ DACRYMYCETALES

Family 1 **Genera** 13
Species 171

This order forms very simple, rounded or branched gelatinous fruit bodies, usually with bright orange coloration. Smooth or wrinkled, the Dacrymycetales have unusual spore-producing cells (basidia), which typically have two stout stalks (sterigmata), each bearing a spore. They feed mostly on dead wood.

Native range Every continent except Antarctica

The branched, orange-yellow branches are greasy

Yellow stagshorn | *Calocera viscosa*
Attached to conifer wood, this fungus is found in Eurasia and North America. Its clubs usually divide into gelatinous, rubbery branches.

The upper surface of each arm is covered with spores

Devil's fingers | *Clathrus archeri*
The red arms of this fungus emerge from a white "egg" and have blackish spores that smell fetid.

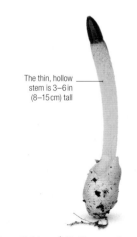

The thin, hollow stem is 3–6 in (8–15 cm) tall

Dog stinkhorn | *Mutinus caninus*
This common stinkhorn is found in mixed woodlands. The tip of the spongy stem is covered in greenish-black spores.

Red cage fungus | *Clathrus ruber*
Found in parks and gardens in Eurasia, this rare species has a red cage with black, foul-smelling spores. The cage hatches from a small "egg."

Some fungi have a foul scent that attracts insects, which help to spread their spores.

▽ PUCCINIALES

Families Around 15 **Genera** 205
Species 8,014

One of the largest orders of fungi with more than 7,000 species, the rust fungi include numerous serious parasites of crop plants. Some have very complex life cycles with multiple hosts, and they can produce spores from different structures at different stages in their life, each spore type typically infecting just one plant species.

Native range Every continent except Antarctica

Raspberry yellow rust |
Phragmidium rubi-idaei
This rust causes pustules to form on the upper surface of leaves. It survives winter with the help of black spores on the underside of leaves.

Fungus causes yellowish galls

Alexanders rust | *Puccinia smyrnii*
Found across Eurasia, this common rust fungus forms raised plaques or warts on the leaves of alexanders (*Smyrnium olusatrum*).

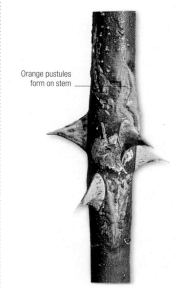

Orange pustules form on stem

Rose rust | *Phragmidium tuberculatum*
This common rust causes orange pustules on the undersides of leaves and on distorted stems. The pustules turn black in late summer.

Reddish-brown galls form on the undersides of leaves

Hollyhock rust | *Puccinia malvacearum*
This serious pest of hollyhocks (*Alcea*) covers the plants' leaves with small pustules. Older leaves die and fall off.

Hypericum rust | *Melampsora hypericorum*
This common Eurasian species is visible as scattered, raised pustules on the undersides of *Hypericum* leaves.

EXOBASIDIALES

Families 4 **Genera** 19
Species 166

This small group consists mainly of gall-forming plant parasites whose spore-producing cells form a layer on the leaf surface. Some cause disease in cultivated plants of the *Vaccinium* genus, which includes the common blueberry, *V. corymbosum*.

Native range Every continent except Antarctica

UROCYSTIDALES

Families 6 **Generaa** 17
Species 313

This order contains some well-known smut fungi, in particular species of the genus *Urocystis*. These are parasites of cultivated plants such as onions and garlic (*Allium*), wheat (*Triticum*), and rye (*Secale*), as well as wood anemones (*Anemone nemorosa*), often causing serious injury to the host.

Native range Every continent

Additional fungi

The fungi kingdom is vast, and includes many orders that consist of microscopic and single-celled species that are yet to be described.

Archaeorhizomycetales	Microascales	Pachnocybales
Lahmiales	Boliniales	Platygloeales
Triblidiales	Calosphaeriales	Septobasidiales
Arthoniales	Chaetosphaeriales	Malasseziales
Acrospermales	Coniochaetales	Ceraceosorales
Botryosphaeriales	Diaporthales	Doassansiales
Hysteriales	Ophiostomatales	Entylomatales
Jahnulales	Sordariales	Georgefischeriales
Koralionastetales	Lulworthiales	Microstromatales
Patellariales	Saccharomycetales	Tilletiales
Trypetheliales	Neolectales	Ustilaginales
Dothideales	Pneumocystidales	Blastocladiales
Microthyriales	Schizosaccharomycetales	Chytridiales
Myriangiales	Entorrhizales	Lobulomycetales
Meliolales	Wallemiales	Neocallimastigales
Mytilinidales	Corticiales	Olpidiales
Chaetothyriales	Sebacinales	Rhizophlyctidales
Pyrenulales	Trechisporales	Rhizophydiales
Coryneliales	Atheliales	Spizellomycetales
Onygenales	Hysterangiales	Monoblepharidales
Mycocaliciales	Cystofilobasidiales	Archaeosporales
Laboulbeniales	Filobasidiales	Diversisporales
Pyxidiophorales	Tremellales	Glomerales
Candelariales	Agaricostilbales	Paraglomerales
Acarosporales	Spiculogloeales	Basidiobolales
Cyttariales	Atractiellales	Entomophthorales
Geoglossales	Classiculales	Asellariales
Leotiales	Cryptomycocolacales	Dimargaritales
Mediolariales	Cystobasidiales	Harpellales
Thelebolales	Erythrobasidiales	Kickxellales
Eremithallales	Naohideales	Mortierellales
Lichinales	Hetrogastridiales	Endogonales
Orbiliales	Leucosporidiales	Mucorales
Phyllachorales	Microbotryales	Zoopagales
Trichosphaeriales	Sporidiobolales	
Coronophorales	Mixiales	
Melanosporales	Helicobasidiales	

Lichens

From exposed, coastal outcrops to desert areas, where they have to grow inside rocks, lichens survive in the harshest habitats in the world. There, they are some of nature's pioneers, creating the foundations on which other organisms can establish.

Hoary rosette lichen | *Physcia aipolia* This gray to brownish-gray species forms rough patches with lobed margins on tree bark in Eurasia and the Americas. It has black, cupped, reproductive structures.

▷ VERRUCARIALES

Family 1   **Genera** 56
Species 1,000

Most lichens in the order Verrucariales have a prostrate, crust-like body that clings tightly to their substrate—usually rock. However, some species have a bushy or shrubby form, and others are scaly. They are found widely in temperate regions of the northern hemisphere, and include some marine lichens that grow in intertidal zones.

Native range Every continent

Black tar lichen | *Verrucaria maura*
Found on rocks along seashores in Eurasia and North America, this species has a dark gray crust that contains spore-producing structures.

▽ UMBILICARIALES

Families 5   **Genera** 18
Species 117

The Umbilicariales includes many crust-like lichens, and some that are scaly. Many genera in this order contain only one species, but a few, such as *Fuscidea* and *Umbilicaria*, are larger. These lichens grow on rocks and on the bark of trees in forests in the northern hemisphere.

Native range Every continent

△ CALICIALES

Families 2   **Genera** 56
Species 910

Some members of this order live as fungi, but most partner with green algae and take the form of a lichen. These lichens vary greatly in appearance, with some crust-like, some leaflike, some scaly, and others taking a shrubby or tufted form. Most species are from tropical or subtropical mountainous areas, but some are able to withstand Antarctic conditions.

Native range Every continent

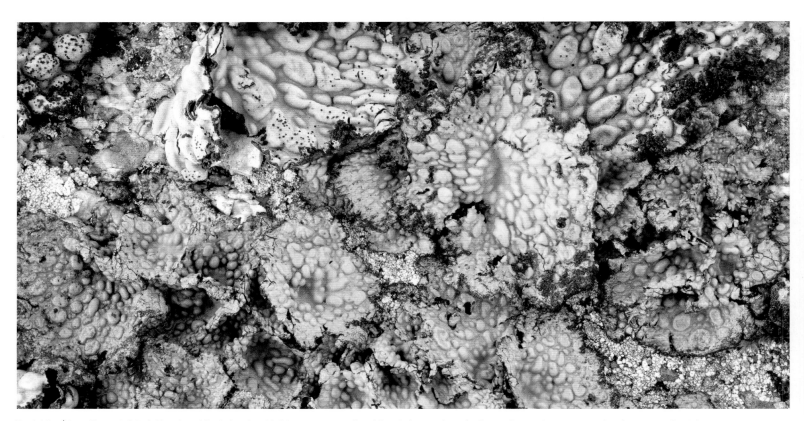

Rock tripe | *Lasallia pustulata* In Eurasia and North America, this lichen grows on nutrient-rich rocks in coastal or upland areas. Its gray-brown upper surface has many oval pustules.

About seven percent of Earth's land surface is covered by lichens.

▷ LECANORALES

Families 20 **Genera** 207
Species 3,991

The order of Lecanorales includes some species that take the form of fungi, but most live as lichens. These are found all over the world and are variable in form. Some live on rock or bark and are crust-like, scaly, leaflike, or shrubby. Other species—the beard lichens—form hanging tassels or bushy growths on tree branches.

Native range Every continent

▽ LECIDEALES

Families 2 **Genera** 30
Species 270

Most lichens in this order form a thin crust on bare rocks and some are adapted to survive extreme cold in the Antarctic. They vary in color from almost black to white, and have sunken, dark, spore-producing structures across their surface.

Native range Every continent

Lecidea lichen | _Lecidea fuscoatra_
Found on siliceous rocks and old brick walls in North America and Eurasia, this species forms a gray crust with black spore-producing structures.

Beard lichen | _Usnea filipendula_ Found mainly in northern regions, this species forms green-gray, pendent clumps on trees. Spiny spore-producing structures develop at the tips of the branches.

Dog lichen | *Peltigera praetextata* Found on rocks in Eurasia and North America, this lichen has large gray-black lobes with paler margins, and reddish-brown spore-producing structures.

◁ PELTIGERALES

Families 9   **Genera** 54
Species 668

Most fungi in this order form symbiotic associations with green algae in the genus *Coccomyxa* or with cyanobacteria (usually *Nostoc* species) and live as lichens. They are found all over the world and grow on soil, tree bark, and rocks. The lichens may be scaly, leaflike, or shrubby in form. They include the dog lichens, named for the rootlike structures (rhizines) on their lower surfaces that resemble dog teeth. Species within the *Peltigeraceae* family have medicinal properties.

Native range Every continent

▽ RHIZOCARPALES

Families 2   **Genera** 6
Species 85

These lichens are crust-like (crustose) in form; a few species are parasitic on other lichens. They are found mainly in arctic and alpine habitats, although some species also occur in temperate and subtropical regions, most commonly growing on rocks. They are collectively known as "map lichens," because of the pattern created when they grow next to each other.

Native range Every continent

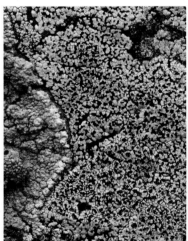

Map lichen | *Rhizocarpon geographicum* Common on rocks in mountains in northern regions and Antarctica, this lichen forms a flat patch bordered by a black line of spores. When growing in groups, these lichens have a patchwork appearance.

Lichens should be regarded as a community of organisms, not just as an algae-fungi association.

The disks are reproductive fruit bodies that form spores

Golden-eye lichen |
Teloschistes chrysophthalmus
A critically endangered species in Eurasia, America, and tropical regions, this lichen grows on shrubs and small trees in old orchards and hedgerows. Its branched lobes produce large, orange disks.

◁ TELOSCHISTALES

Families 4   **Genera** 54
Species 1,007

Most members of the order Teloschistales form lichens in association with green algae; a few live as fungi. The lichens may be crust-like, leaflike, or branched and shrubby in habit. They are usually yellow, red, or orange in color, with some species known as sunburst lichens. They grow on rocks, often near the sea, and on tree bark, mainly in warm regions in conditions where high levels of nitrogen are present.

Native range Every continent

Brown beret lichen | *Baeomyces rufus* Forming gray-green crusts on sandy soil and rocks, this lichen has brown, ball-like, reproductive fruit bodies on stalks a few millimeters high. It is found in Eurasia and North America.

△ BAEOMYCETALES

Families 3   **Genera** 16
Species 97

Most of the lichens in this order are crust-like in form, although some can be scaly. Several species in the *Arthrorhaphis* genus are parasitic on other lichens and have no body of their own. Members of the order have a wide global distribution, but mainly inhabit temperate, mountainous regions. They grow on rocks, soil, and the bark of trees. Some species live on decaying organic matter.

Native range Every continent

▷ OSTROPALES

Families 9   **Genera** 103
Species 1,358

The order Ostropales includes fungi that decompose organic matter or live as parasites on plants, and others that take the growth form of a lichen. The lichens are found on rocks or tree bark in the northern hemisphere, where they may live alongside non–lichenized examples of the same species that take a fungal body form.

Native range Every continent

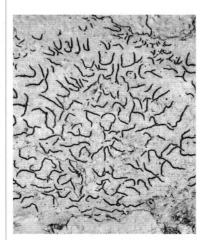

Common script lichen | *Graphis scripta*
Often seen on tree bark in North America and Eurasia, this lichen forms a thin, gray-green crust with slit-like openings.

▽ PERTUSARIALES

Families 5   **Genera** 16
Species 376

Most members of this order of fungi form lichens in association with green algae. They are mainly crust-like in habit and are frequently found in maritime habitats, close to the shoreline. Species include the peppermint drop lichen, named for its green, crust-like body form covered with drop-shaped, pink fruit bodies. Other species have a leaflike or scaly form.

Native range Every continent

Crab-eye lichen | *Ochrolechia parella*
This lichen forms patches on walls and rocks in North America and Eurasia. Its surface usually has many pink-brown reproductive structures.

Glossary

ACCESSORY FRUIT
A fruit that is formed from the flower's ovary and another structure, such as the swollen base of the flower—for example, apples and figs.

ALKALOID
Bitter, sometimes toxic, chemicals produced by certain plants and fungi to deter predators.

ALTERNATE
Describes leaves that form an ascending spiral, with one leaf per plant node and on alternate sides of the stem.

ANGIOSPERM
A seed-producing plant that encloses its seeds in a fruit and produces flowers. *See also* Gymnosperm.

ANNUAL
A plant that completes its life cycle, from germination to death, in a single season of growth.

ANTHER
In flowering plants, the podlike structure on the stamen that produces pollen.

ARIL
An extra coat that covers certain seeds. This layer is often hairy or fleshy and brightly colored.

ASCOMYCETES
The largest class in the fungal kingdom, which includes cup fungi. Their fruit bodies produce sexual spores in sacs called asci.

ASCUS (PL. ASCI)
Microscopic saclike structure of sac fungi (Ascomycota) that produces spores.

ASEXUAL REPRODUCTION
A form of reproduction that involves just one parent, producing offspring that are genetically identical to each other (clones).

BARK
The protective outer layer or "skin" of the trunk, branches, and roots of woody plants. It overlays the inner tissues, and protects the plant from water loss, cold, and other types of damage. The bark stretches as the plant grows.

BASAL ANGIOSPERMS
Five orders of flowering plants with certain primitive features that diverged from the main evolutionary line of flowering plants before others. The group includes water lilies.

BASIDIOMYCETES
The division of fungi that includes mushrooms. Their fruit bodies vary greatly in order to spread their spores, which are released from cells called basidia.

BASIDIUM (PL. BASIDIA)
A microscopic, club-shaped, spore-producing structure in the fruit bodies of fungi within the Basidiomycetes division.

BERRY
A fleshy many-seeded fruit of a plant that develops from a single ovary. Many fruits popularly called berries are not true berries but compound fruits—an example of which is the raspberry.

BIENNIAL
A plant that completes its life cycle, from germination to death, in two years. It typically stores up food in the first season that can be used for reproduction in the second season.

BRACKET
A shelflike fruit body of a fungus.

BRACT
Modified, usually small, leaflike structure typically found at the base of a flower or inflorescence, or in the cone of a conifer. It can resemble normal foliage.

BROMELIAD
Flowering plant of the family *Bromeliaceae*. Almost exclusively from tropical America, most live as rainforest epiphytes, perched in the branches without getting nourishment from the trees.

BRYOPHYTE
An early form of photosynthetic plant that lacks a developed vascular system. Bryophytes have no roots and reproduce using spores. The group includes mosses, hornwort, and liverworts.

BUD
A small swelling on a plant's stem that can develop into a flower, leaf, or shoot. This protuberance consists of immature leaves or petals protected by a tight layer of modified leaves called scales.

BULB
The underground shoot of a plant, consisting of modified leaves used for food storage during periods of dormancy, and asexual reproduction.

BURR
A fruit, seed head, or flower that has hooks or teeth. A burr is also a term for a woody outgrowth found on the trunk of some trees.

BUTTRESS
Large and wide roots surrounding a shallowly rooted tree. They help the tree maintain stability, especially in shallow and nutrient-poor soil conditions.

CALYX
The outer, cuplike whorl of a flower, made up of sepals.

CANOPY
The layer of high-level foliage, continuous or discontinuous, found in a forest, and made up of the crowns of individual trees.

CARPEL
The female reproductive part of a flower, divided into ovary, style, and stigma. Also known as the pistil.

CATKIN
A type of inflorescence, usually pendulous, in which scalelike bracts and tiny, stalkless, often petalless flowers are arranged on an unbranched axis.

CELLULOSE
A complex carbohydrate found in plants. It is used by plants as a building material, and has a resilient chemical structure that animals find hard to digest. Plant-eating animals break it down in their stomach with the aid of microorganisms.

CHLOROPHYLL
The green pigment found within the chloroplasts of plant cells. It is used to capture energy from sunlight during photosynthesis.

CHLOROPLAST
Structures found within the tissues of plants and algae that contain the green, photosynthetic pigment chlorophyll.

CLIMBER
A plant that grows up a vertical surface, such as a rock or a tree, using it for support. Climbers do not gain nourishment from other plants, but may weaken them by blocking out light and competing for moisture.

CLONE
A plant or fungus that is genetically identical to another. This results from asexual reproduction, where the parent organism splits or fragments into an identical offspring.

COMPOUND LEAF
A leaf with a blade divided into smaller leaflets. *See also* Simple leaf.

CONE
The reproductive structure of a plant, consisting of a cluster of scales or bracts used for producing spores, ovules, or pollen. Cones are found on various trees, particularly pine trees.

CONIFER
A cone-bearing seed plant. They are usually evergreen, with small, needle- or scalelike leaves.

CORM
The underground storage organ of certain seed plants, formed from a swollen stem base.

COROLLA
Inner whorl of a flower made up of petals.

CORTINA
Fine, cobweb-like threads, usually joining the cap margin to the stem on certain types of mushroom.

COTYLEDON
The food-containing seed leaves situated within the embryo of a seed. Cotyledons aid the supply of nutrition that a plant embryo requires in order to germinate.

CROWN
The topmost part of a tree made up of branches growing out from the main trunk.

CULTIVAR
Contraction of "cultivated variety." A plant originally bred for a desired trait and subsequently maintained in cultivation.

CUTICLE
A general term referring to the outermost layer or skin of plant leaves and fungal fruit bodies.

DECIDUOUS
A woody plant that is leafless for several months of the year during dormancy. This is usually in winter (in temperate zones) or the dry season (in tropical zones).

DIOECIOUS
A plant that has either male or female flowers, not both.

DISPERSAL
The way in which seeds and spores are transported away from the parent plant or fungus that produces them. The main methods of dispersal are wind, water, animals, and mechanical (such as exploding seed capsules).

DORMANCY
A period when the growth and development of a plant (or animal) is suspended. It may occur temporarily during adverse conditions, such as during drought, or seasonally, such as in winter.

DROUGHT
A period when rainfall is lower than normal, which may last for weeks or even years.

DRUPE
A fleshy fruit that usually contains a large single seed that has a hard outer shell, such as a peach or olive.

ECOSYSTEM
A collection of plant, fungal, and animal species living in the same habitat that form a complex interdependent relationship.

EMBRYO
A young plant that is at a rudimentary stage of development. In seed plants, including seed trees, the embryo is encased in a seed until it grows into a seedling during germination.

ENDEMIC
A species that is native to a particular geographic area, such as an island, forest, mountain, or country, and does not naturally occur elsewhere.

ENZYME
A group of substances produced by all living things that promote a specific chemical process, such as photosynthesis or digestion.

EPIPHYTE
A plant or plantlike organism (such as an alga or lichen) that lives on the body of another plant without getting any nourishment from it.

EUDICOT
A large group of flowering plants. Together, the higher eudicot orders contain the majority of flowering plants.

EVERGREEN
A plant that bears leaves all year round.

FAMILY
A unit of classification, grouping together related units called genera. For example, the species *Amanita muscaria* belongs to the genus *Amanita*, which is placed in the family *Amanitaceae*.

FERTILIZATION
The union of a male and female cell, which creates a cell capable of developing into a new organism.

FLOWER
The reproductive structure of the largest group of seed plants, typically consisting of sepals, petals, stamens, and carpels.

FRAGMENTATION
A common form of asexual reproduction, where parts of a parent plant or fungus detach to produce new, separate individuals.

FRUIT
A fleshy structure of a plant that develops from the ovary of the flower and contains one or more seeds. Fruits can be simple, like berries, or compound, where the fruits of separate flowers are merged. *See also* Accessory fruit.

FRUIT BODY
The fleshy spore-producing structure of a fungus, typically a mushroom or bracket above ground, or a truffle below it.

GALL
A tumorlike growth in a plant that is induced by another organism (such as a fungus or an insect). By triggering the formation of galls, insects provide themselves with a safe hiding place and a convenient source of food.

GENUS
A term applied to a group of closely related species and denoted by the first part of the botanical name. For example, in *Pinus pinea* (stone pine), the genus is *Pinus*.

GERMINATION
The developmental stage where a seed or a spore begins to grow.

GILLS
The bladelike, spore-bearing structures found under the caps of fungi fruit bodies.

GYMNOSPERM
A seed plant that does not enclose its seeds in a fruit. Many gymnosperms carry their seeds in cones, such as conifers. *See also* Angiosperm.

HABIT
The characteristic form of a plant, including its size, shape, and orientation.

HEARTWOOD
The dead, inner, central wood of a tree, strong and resistant to decay. Over time, layers of living sapwood cells are converted to heartwood.

HERBACEOUS PLANT
A plant whose stem does not become woody (as in a tree or shrub) but remains soft, and dies completely or down to the root after flowering. Herbaceous plants include annuals, biennials, and most perennials.

HERMAPHRODITE
An organism that has both male and female reproductive organs, such as a plant where the male and female reproductive organs are borne within the same flower.

HUMUS
The decayed, soil-like remains of leaves and other organic debris.

HYBRID
The result of cross-pollinating two distinct plants to form a new plant. A hybrid's name comprises the genus name, followed by ×, and the hybrid's specific name. For example, *Ilex × koehneana*.

HYPHA (PL. HYPHAE)
A microscopic, threadlike structure making up the body of a fungus. Many such hyphae make up a mass that is known as a mycelium.

HYPHAL CORDS
Tightly spun hyphae in a ropelike fashion that a fungus can use to exploit its surroundings.

INFLORESCENCE
A flower cluster or a single flower.

LANCEOLATE
Describes a leaf shaped like a lance head—broadest below the center, narrow, and tapering to a point at each end.

LEAFLET
A small leaf that makes up one part of a compound leaf. Also known as a pinna (pl. pinnae).

LEGUME
Plants of the pea family of flowering plants, the *Fabaceae*. They are important for having root nodules that contain nitrogen-fixing bacteria.

LENTICEL
One of many raised pores found on the surface of bark or some fruits that allow air to access the inner tissues of a plant.

LICHEN
The mutualistic association between a fungus and a photosynthetic algae. From this relationship, the fungus obtains sugars, and the algae receives minerals.

LIFE CYCLE
The developmental sequence of an organism from gametes (sex cells) to death.

LIGNIN
An organic polymer central to the support tissues of most plants. Lignins are found in the cell walls of woody tissue and make timber hard and rigid.

LOBE
A protruding part of a leaf or a flower, which is typically rounded or pointed.

LYCOPHYTE
An early form of photosynthetic plant, and the first to evolve with a complex vascular system to transport nutrients and water between the roots and leaves.

MAGNOLIIDAE
A group of flowering plants consisting of four orders with certain primitive characteristics, such as undifferentiated tepals instead of sepals and petals.

MARGIN
The edge of a leaf blade. There are many kinds of leaf margins, including smooth (entire), lobed, or serrated.

MERISTEM
Tissue consisting of unspecialized cells within a plant that divide to form new tissues and organs, such as leaves, stems, and roots.

MIDRIB
The main vein of a leaf or leaflet. Usually central, it runs from the stalk to the tip of a leaf or leaflet. It is also known as mid-vein.

MONOCOT
A group of flowering plants with a single seed leaf (cotyledon).

MONOECIOUS
A plant that has separate male and female parts on the same individual.

MUTATION
A permanent alteration in the genetic makeup of an organism. Mutations can be passed on through generations.

MUTUALISM
A relationship between organisms of two different species in which each benefits, such as mycorrhiza and lichens.

MYCELIUM
The vegetative body of a fungus (usually below the surface) formed by a mass of fine, threadlike cells called hyphae.

MYCORRHIZA (PL. MYCORRHIZAE)
The mutualistic association between a fungus and the roots of a plant. The fungus obtains sugars, while the plant increases its mineral uptake by absorbing them via the mycelium produced by the fungus.

NATURALIZED
A nonnative plant or species introduced to a foreign region by human activity that has adapted successfully, and now forms self-sustaining populations in that region.

NODE
The point where two sections of a plant's stem join, from which one or more leaves, shoots, branches, or flowers arise.

NUT
The dry, hard-shelled fruit of some plants, usually a single seed.

ORDER
One of the eight taxonomic ranks, it is a unit of classification that groups together related units called families. Orders are grouped within classes.

OVARY
The lower, wide, vessel-like section of the female part of a flower that contains one or more ovules. After fertilization, the ovules become seeds and the ovary develops into a fruit.

OVULE
The section of the flower that contains the egg cell. In flowering plants, ovules are encased in an ovary, but in gymnosperms, they are naked. After fertilization, the ovule develops into the seed.

PALMATE
Describes the shape of a type of compound leaf that is lobed or divided into five parts, like an open palm or a hand with the fingers extended. The leaflets arise from a single basal point.

PANICLE
An elongated flower cluster in which each flower has its own stalk (or pedicel) attached to the branch.

PARASITE
An organism that lives on or in another host organism, gaining advantage (such as nourishment) while causing the host harm. Parasites often weaken their host but generally do not kill them.

PERENNIAL
A plant that normally lives for more than two growing seasons. Some perennials can be very long-lived.

PERIANTH
The outer two whorls of a flower (the calyx, made up of sepals, and the corolla, made up of petals); especially where the two are undifferentiated.

PETAL
One of the parts of the corolla of a flower. Petals are often brightly colored to attract pollinating animals.

PETIOLE
The stalk of a leaf that attaches it to the stem of the plant.

PHLOEM
These are vessels within the vascular system of plants that conduct water and sugars between tissues during photosynthesis.

PHOTOSYNTHESIS
A process whereby organisms use light energy to make food and oxygen; photosynthesis occurs in plants, algae, and many microorganisms.

PINNATE
A compound leaf arrangement in which the leaflets (pinnae) are arranged so as to resemble a feather. The leaflets are arranged either alternately or in opposite pairs on a central axis. Pinnately lobed leaves have lobes arranged in this fashion.

PISTIL
The female reproductive organ of a flower.

POLLEN
Tiny grains produced by seed plants that contain male gametes for fertilizing the female egg of either a flowering plant or a coniferous plant.

POLLINATE
To fertilize a plant with pollen. This is commonly done by wind dispersal, or by insects and animals as they transfer pollen from the male anther of a flower to the female stigma.

POLYPORE
Common name for fungi with woody or tough fruit bodies, and with a pored, tubular spore-producing layer.

PORES
The openings of the tubular spore-producing layer on fungi, such as boletes and polypores.

RECEPTACLE
The section of a plant stem that bears the organs of an individual flower or the florets of a flower head. After pollination, the receptacle can swell to form a fruit.

RHIZOME
A creeping or underground plant stem that can send out new shoots.

RHIZOMORPHS
Thick, cord-like strands of fungal mycelium in a rootlike structure.

ROOT
The part of the plant that is usually underground, anchoring it in the soil. Roots also absorb water and minerals, and store reserve foods.

ROOT NODULE
Spherical swelling on the root of a legume that contains nitrogen-fixing bacteria.

SAP
A watery or milky fluid found in plants. It contains dissolved minerals that are carried from the roots to the leaves via the vascular system. Sap may also contain chemicals that deter predators.

SAPLING
A young tree—specifically, one that is no greater than about 4 in (10 cm) in diameter when measured at an average adult's chest-height.

SEED
The mature, fertilized ovule of a plant. Inside the seed case is the embryo and some stored food. Fruits, berries, nuts, pods, and cones all have different types of seeds. When given the appropriate conditions, a seed will grow (germinate).

SEEDLING
The young plant that develops out of a plant embryo from a seed.

SEMIEVERGREEN
A plant that loses its leaves for only a short period during the year. This term can also refer to a tree that sheds a proportion of its leaves periodically—usually over fall and winter—but is never entirely leafless.

SEPAL
One of the parts of the calyx of a flower, usually small and leaflike and enveloping the unopened flower bud.

SEXUAL REPRODUCTION
A form of reproduction that involves two parents, producing offspring that contain genetic material from both.

SHOOT
The aerial part of a plant. It is a new growth, usually developing upward.

SHRUB
A woody perennial plant that has multiple stems. Most shrubs live for several growing seasons.

SIMPLE LEAF
A leaf with an undivided blade.

SPECIES
A classification category used to group similar plants together that can interbreed with one another and reproduce.

SPORANGIUM
The structure in which reproductive spores are produced and released in plants such as mosses, liverworts, hornworts, and ferns, and some fungi.

SPORE
A single cell containing half the quantity of genetic material of typical body cells. Unlike gametes, spores can divide and grow without being fertilized. Spores are produced by fungi, algae, and plants.

SPOROPHYTE
The spore-producing stage of a plant. It is the dominant stage of ferns and seed plants.

STAMEN
The male reproductive part of a flower. It has an anther borne on a long filament.

STIGMA
The female part of the flower positioned at the tip of the pistil that receives the pollen. The stigma is usually elevated above the ovary on the style.

STIPE
The stem or stalk that supports the cap of a mushroom, composed of sterile hyphal tissue.

STIPULE
A small leaflike or bract-like structure occurring on one or both sides of the base of a leafstalk (petiole), where it arises from a stem.

STOMA (PL. STOMATA)
A tiny adjustable pore on the surface of a plant that allows the exchange of gases during photosynthesis and respiration.

STYLE
The slender, sterile part of the plant ovary that bears the stigma so it is positioned in an effective location for pollination.

SUBSPECIES
A category of classification, below species, defining a distinct variant within a species, usually isolated based on geographical location. Subspecies can interbreed successfully with others of the same species.

SUBSTRATE
The medium, such as soil or stone, in/on which plants and fungi grow.

SUCKERS
A growth that usually develops from the roots of a plant, or sometimes the lower part of the stem. Suckers arise from below the soil, some distance away from the main stem or trunk, and divert nourishment away from the plant.

TEPAL
The outer part of a flower, undifferentiated into sepals and petals. Tepals collectively make up the perianth.

TERMINAL
Usually used to describe a bud or inflorescence growing at the end of a shoot, stem, branch, or other organ.

THALLUS
The vegetative body of fungi, lichens, and liverworts that is undifferentiated into roots, stems, or leaves, and lacks a vascular system.

TRANSLOCATION
The movement of nutrients, mainly sugars, in plants from the leaves to other parts of the plant during photosynthesis.

TRANSPIRATION
The movement of water through the plant, via the vascular system, from the roots to the leaves during photosynthesis.

TREE
A woody perennial plant usually with a well-defined stem, or trunk, and a crown of branches above.

TRUNK
The main stem of a tree and the tree's main organ. It is made up of the bark, inner bark, cambium, sapwood, and hardwood. On most conifers, the trunk grows straight to the top of the tree. On most broadleaf trees, the trunk does not reach the top, but divides into branches.

UNIVERSAL VEIL
The thin skin or weblike tissue that covers the immature fruit body of a mushroom, which splits as it grows. It may leave a volva at the stem base or loose scales on the cap.

VARIEGATED
Usually used to describe leaves that are more than one color, owing to a lack of chlorophyll in some of the leaf's cells. Variegated sections can appear as stripes, circles, borders, and other shapes. Variegation is a rare natural phenomenon.

VASCULAR SYSTEM
In plants, the vascular system transports water, nutrients, and sugars between the roots, stems, and leaves. The system consists of xylem and phloem vessels.

VEIN
A vascular bundle of transportation vessels at or near the surface of a leaf and running through it. Veins provide support for a leaf and are used to transport both water and food.

VOLVA
A saclike remnant of a veil at the base of a fungus's fruit body stem.

WHORL
A radial, vertical arrangement of three or more identical structural parts—such as petals, stamens, or leaves—around a stem. For example, petals make up the whorl of the corolla.

WOODY PLANT
A plant that has wood—a type of strengthening tissue found in plants consisting of thick-walled water-transporting vessels.

XYLEM
These are vessels within the vascular system of plants that conduct water and dissolved nutrients between tissues during photosynthesis.

Index

Page number in **bold** refer to main entries; page numbers in *italics* refer to illustrations

A

abacá 339, *339*
abal 143, *143*
Abelmoschus manihot 300, *300*
Abies 22
    A. alba 385, *385*
    A. balsamea 59, *59*
    A. grandis 67, *67*
    A. holophylla 60, *60*
    A. magnifica 385, *385*
    A. nordmanniana 384, *384*
    A. sibirica 61, *61*
    A. spectabilis 108, *108*
acacia 140–41, **143**
    bullhorn acacia *141*
    umbrella thorn acacia 142, *142*
Acacia 140–41, **143**
    A. dealbata 116, *116*
    A. glaucoptera 404, *404*
    A. longifolia 117, *117*
açaí palm 123, *123*, 291, *291*
Acer 29, *29*, 36
    A. griseum 354, *354*
    A. palmatum 100, 355, *355*
    A. platanoides 87, *87*
    A. p. 'Drummondii' *35*
    A. pseudoplatanus 410, *410*
    A. saccharum **76–77**
Achillea millefolium 167, *167*
Achimenes longiflora 195, *195*
achiote 125, *125*
acid frillwort 379, *379*
aconite, winter 161, *161*
Acorales 393
acorn banksia 265, *265*
Acorus calamus 252, *252*
Actinidia deliciosa 278, *278*
Adams, Ansel 355
Adansonia 150
    A. rubrostipa 149, *149*
    A. za 149, *149*
adaptations **69**
adder's-tongue ferns 380
Adenium multiflorum 144, *144*
    A. socotranum 250–51, *251*
Adiantum capillus-veneris 12, 163, *163*
Adonis annua 180, *180*
Adoxaceae 388
adzuki beans 311, *311*
Aechmea nudicaulis 244, *244*
Aegilops neglecta 398, *398*
aerial roots *263*
Aerides odorata 207
Aeschynanthus pulcher 194, *194*
    A. speciosus 193, *193*
Aesculus californica 83, *83*
    A. hippocastanum 86, *86*
Aextoxicaceae 391
Africa
    deserts **226–27**
    living stones **226–27**
    rainforests 346
    savanna **142–43**
    tropical Africa **136–39**, 194
    Welwitschia mirabilis **230–31**
African breadfruit 136, *136*
African cabbage 301, *301*
African eggplant 284, *284*
African fan palm 142, *142*
African lily 24, 213, *213*
African mahogany 346, *346*
African tulip tree 269, *269*
aganisia 207, *207*

Aganisia cyanea 207, *207*
Agaonidae 283
Agapanthus praecox 24, 213, *213*
Agaricales **418–19**
Agaricus bisporus 42, 316, 317, *317*
    A. campestris 168, *168*
Agastache rugosa 13
agave 394
    Queen Victoria agave 225, *225*
Agave amica 362, 363, *363*
    A. fourcroydes 339, *339*
    A. sisalana 339, *339*
    A. victoriae-reginae 225, *225*
Ahmed III 363
aibika 300, *300*
Ailanthus altissima 101, *101*
air 15
air plant 245, *245*
airy shaw 237, *237*
Alabaster towers 224, *224*
Alaska 155
    boreal forests 59
Albany pitcher plant 232, *232*, 407, *407*
Alcea rosea 183
Alchemilla vulgaris 409, *409*
alcohol 42
    alcoholic beverages **329**
alder
    red alder 67, *67*
    Siberian alder 61, *61*
Aldrovanda vesiculosa 237, *237*
Aleuria aurantia 45, *45*, 412, *412*
Aleurina argentina 129, *129*
Aleurites moluccanus 295, *295*
Alexanders rust 423, *423*
alfalfa 310, *310*
algae 13, 39
    aquatic algae **12**
    green algae 12, 50, *50*, 426, 427
Alismatales **393**
alizarin 350
alkaloids 337
Alkekengi officinarum 391, *391*
Allen, Richard 117
Alliaria petiolata 161, *161*
Allioni's primrose 215, *215*
Allium 423
    A. ampeloprasum 302, *302*
    A. cepa 302, *302*
    A. sativum 302, *302*
    A. schoenoprasum 303, *303*
    A. sphaerocephalon 160, *160*
    A. triquetrum 184, *184*
    A. ursinum 161, *161*
allspice, California 82, *82*
almond 294, *294*, 295, *295*
Alnus hirsuta 61, *61*
    A. rubra 67, *67*
aloe
    aloe vera 335, *335*
    Namibian aloe 224, *224*
Aloe helenae 149, *149*
    A. namibensis 224, *224*
    A. vera 335, *335*
Aloidendron dichotomum 142, *142*
Alpine forget-me-not 155, *155*
alpine plants
    alpine flowers **214–17**
    leaves 36, *36*
Alpine rock jasmine 214, *214*
Alpine toadflax 215, *215*
alstonia 136, *136*
Alstonia congensis 136, *136*
alstroemeria family 396
Alternanthera reineckii 253, *253*
Alyogyne huegelii 264, *264*
Amanita 48, 49, *49*
    A. muscaria 48, *48*, 419, *419*
    A. pantherina 49
    A. phalloides 272, *272*, 317, *317*
amaranth, green 301, *301*
Amaranthus viridis 301, *301*
amaryllis 394, *394*
Amazon basin, seed plant species 195

Amazon frogbit 252, *252*
Amazon rainforest 123, 346, 347
    plant species found 128
    rubber trees 239
Amazon water lily **258–59**
Amborella trichopoda 386
Amborellales 386
Ambrosia psilostachya 178, *178*
Ambuchanania leucobryoides 373
Ambuchananiales 373
Amelanchier alnifolia 59, *59*
    A. lamarckii 354, *354*
America *see* North America; South America
American cranberry 278, *278*
American sweetgum 74, 75, *75*
amethyst deceiver 418, *418*
amia 277, *277*
Ammi majus 181, *181*
Amorpha canescens 178, *178*
Amorphophallus konjac 315, *315*
    A. paeoniifolius 202, *202*
    A. titanum 202, **204–205**
Anacardium occidentale **296–97**
Anagyris foetida 99, *99*
ancient grains 305
Andean violet 216, *216*
Andes mountains 216
Andreaeales 367
Andreaeobryales 367
Andreaeobryum macrosporum 367
Androcymbium melanthioides 212, *212*
Andropogon gerardii 179, *179*
androsace, hairy 388, *388*
Androsace alpina 214, *214*
    A. villosa 388, *388*
anemone
    crown anemone 187, *187*
    wood anemone 161, *161*
Anemone blanda 187, *187*
    A. coronaria 187, *187*
    A. nemorosa 161, *161*, 423
Anemopsis californica 264, *264*
Anethum graveolens 319, *319*
angel's fishing rod 213, *213*
Angiopteris evecta 162, *162*, 380
angiosperms 13, 24–25, **386–411**
    Acorales **393**
    Alismatales **393**
    Amborellales 386
    Apiales 386
    Aquifoliales 386
    Arecales 393
    Asterales 387
    Austrobaileyales 391
    Berberidopsidales 391
    Boraginales 387
    Brassicales 403
    Bruniales 387
    Buxales 391
    Canellales 400
    Caryophyllales 392
    Celastrales 403
    Ceratophyllales 393
    Chloranthales 400
    Commelinales 396
    Cornales 388
    Crossosomatales 403
    Cucurbitales 403
    Dasypogonales 396
    Dilleniales 393
    Dioscoreales 396
    Dipsacales 388
    directory **386–411**
    Ericales 388
    Escalloniales 389
    Fabales 404
    Fagales 405
    flowers 26–27
    Garryales 389
    Gentianales 389
    Geraniales 405
    Gunnerales 401
    Huerteales 405
    Icacinales 386
    Lamiales 390
    Laurales 400
    Liliales 396

Magnoliales **401**
Malpighiales **405**
Malvales **406**
Myrtales **406–407**
Nymphaeales **401**
Oxalidales **407**
Pandanales **397**
Paracryphiales **391**
Petrosaviales **397**
Picramniales **407**
Piperales **401**
Proteales **402**
Ranunculales **402**
reproduction **24–29**
Rosales **408–409**
Santalales **411**
Sapindales **410**
Saxifragales **411**
Solanales **391**
Trochodendrales **411**
Vitales **411**
Zingiberales **400**
Zygophyllales **411**
see also individual species
Angraecum sesquipedale 207, *207*
animals
    seed dispersal 276
    spore dispersal 47
    see also individual species
anise mazegill 415, *415*
aniseed 320, *320*
Anisodontea scabrosa 145, *145*
Anisotome latifolia 248, *248*
Annona mucosa 123, *123*
    A. squamosa 401, *401*
annuals and perennials 16
    alpine flowers **214–17**
    Amorphophallus titanum **204–205**
    aroids **202–203**
    Asian bamboos **198–99**
    bee orchids **174–75**
    bucket orchids **208–209**
    cycads **210–11**
    death 17
    desert annuals **188–89**
    desert blooms **190–91**
    Ensete ventricosum **200–201**
    forest ferns **162–63**
    fungal agriculture **170–71**
    grassland fungi **168–69**
    grasslands and scrub **166–67**
    jade vine **196–97**
    Mediterranean **180–81**, **184–87**
    Mediterranean basin **182–83**
    mosses **220–21**
    North American prairies **176–79**
    northern latitudes **154–55**
    pioneer plants **218–19**
    temperate orchids **172–73**
    tree ferns **164–65**
    tropical orchids **206–207**
    tropical plants **192–95**
    tundra plants **156–57**
ant plant 141, *141*
antheridia 379
Anthoceros agrestis 246, *246*, 374, *374*
Anthocerotales 374
anthocyanins 37
Anthriscus sylvestris 351, *351*
Anthurium andraeanum 202, *202*
Anthyllis vulneraria 218, *218*
antibiotics 337
Antrodia crassa 64
ant tree 123, *123*
ants 141, *141*
Aphelandra squarrosa 390, *390*
aphyllanthes 394, *394*
Aphyllanthes monspeliensis 394, *394*
Apiaceae 386
Apiales 386
apical lid 412
Apium graveolens 302, *302*
    A. g. var. rapaceum 313, *313*
Apocynaceae 389
apple 280, *280*
    ancestry of **281**
    wild apple 280, *280*

apple-moss, common 367, *367*
apricot *277*
aquatics
    aquatic algae **12**
    temperate zone **252–53**
    tropical aquatics **252–53**
    types of aquatic plants 253
Aquifoliaceae 386
Aquifoliales 386
Aquilegia bertolonii 214, *214*
    A. canadensis 218, *218*
Arabian jasmine 112, *112*
Araceae **202–203**, 205, 393
Arachis hypogaea 294, *294*, 324, *324*
Araucaria 134
    A. angustifolia 122, *123*
    A. araucana **134–35**
Araucariaceae family 134
arbuscular mycorrhiza 53
arbuscules 53
Arbutus andrachne 96, *96*
    A. menziesii 83, *83*
Arceuthobium americanum 238, *238*
Archaeopteris hibernica 53
archegonia 379
Archidiaceae 369
Archidiales 369
Archidium 369
Arctic mosses 19
Arctic region, boreal forests 59
Arctium lappa 29, *29*
Areca catechu 291, *291*
Arecaceae 291
Arecales 393
argan tree 264, *264*
Argentine senna 132, *132*
arid pincushion 145, *145*
Arisarum proboscideum 186, *186*
    A. vulgare 186, *186*
Arizona hedgehog cactus 228, *228*
Arizona lupine 189, *189*
armadillo's tail 216, *216*
Armeria maritima subsp. *californica* 261, *261*
Armillaria **72–73**
    A. gallica 73
    A. ostoyae 72, 73
aroids **202–203**, 393
    titan arum **204–205**
arracacha 313, *313*
Arracacia xanthorrhiza 313, *313*
arrowhead 252, *252*
arrowroot 314, *314*
art
    plants and **97**
    trees in 355
Arthrobotrys oligospora 235
Arthrorhaphis 427
artichoke, globe 303, *303*
artichoke cactus 229, *229*
Artomyces pyxidatus 106, *106*
Arum italicum 186, *186*
arum lily **34–35**, 35
Arum maculatum 393, *393*
asarabacca 401, *401*
Asarum europaeum 401, *401*
asci 44, *44*, 412
    in fruit bodies 44, *44*, 45
Asclepias curassavica 195, *195*
    A. syriaca 339, *339*
ascomycetes **44–45**, 50, 92, **93**
    special spore sacs 44
    types of fruit bodies 45, *45*
Ascomycota 39, **412–13**
ascospores 44
ascus 39
asexual reproduction **16**
    bryophytes 18
    fungi 40, **41**
ash
    common ash 87, *87*
    white ash 342, *342*
ash dieback 87
Asia
    bamboos **198–99**
    boreal forests **60–61**
    fungi **106–107**
    rainforests 347

Acknowledgments

Dorling Kindersley would like to extend thanks to the following people for their help with making the book: Alison Gardner for designing The Science of Plants and Fungi section; Daksheeta Pattni for additional illustrations and design assistance; Christine Stroyan and Kingshuk Ghoshal for editorial support; Diana Vowles for proofreading; Priyanka Lamichhane for fact-checking; and Vanessa Bird for compiling the index.

DK India would like to thank Ira Sharma, Anukriti Arora, Aanchal Singal, Priyal Mote, Sulagna Das, and Ananya Gyandhar for design assistance; Mrunali Sanjay Likhar for additional illustrations; Nandini D. Tripathy for editorial assistance; Nunhoih Guite, Ridhima Sikka, Manpreet Kaur, and Sumedha Chopra for picture research assistance.

Smithsonian Enterprises:
Avery Naughton, Licensing Coordinator
Paige Towler, Editorial Lead
Jill Corcoran, Senior Director, Licensed Publishing
Brigid Ferraro, Vice President of New Business and Licensing
Carol LeBlanc, President

Smithsonian Gardens:
Matthew Fleming, Horticulturist

The publisher would like to thank the following for their kind permission to reproduce their photographs:

(Key: a–above; b–below/bottom; c–center; f–far; l–left; r–right; t–top)

2 naturepl.com: MYN / Marc Pihet. **6 Dreamstime.com:** Evgenii Kazantsev. **8–9 naturepl.com:** Klein & Hubert. **10–11 Getty Images:** Science Photo Library—STEVE GSCHMEISSNER. **12–13 Dreamstime.com:** Yap Kee Chan. **12 Alamy Stock Photo:** Panther Media GmbH (bc). **Dreamstime.com:** Chuyu (fbr); Czuber (fbl); Muslih Muslih (bl). **13 Alamy Stock Photo:** filmfoto–02 (fbl). **Dreamstime.com:** Efesan (ca); Serhiy Shullye (clb). **Getty Images / iStock:** Ninell_Art (br). **Prague National Museum:** Lenka Vchov (cra). **14 Shutterstock.com:** Elena Zajchikova. **15 Alamy Stock Photo:** Vladwitty (cra). **16 Alamy Stock Photo:** Nigel Cattlin (bl). **naturepl.com:** Heather Angel (ca). **Shutterstock.com:** Firn (cra). **17 Dreamstime.com:** Irochka (l). **18 Alamy Stock Photo:** Scott Sim (b). **Dreamstime.com:** Febrika Nurmalasari. **Wikipedia:** BerndH (cr). **19 Alamy Stock Photo:** Robert Hoetink (br). **Dorling Kindersley:** Malcolm Storey (tr). **Dreamstime.com:** Andreistanescu (bc). **Science Photo Library:** Eye of Science (cl). **20 Alamy Stock Photo:** Bailey–Cooper Photography (tr). **Dreamstime.com:** Jamraslamyai. **Getty Images:** Corey Ford / Stocktrek Images (br). **21 Dreamstime.com:** Jochenschneider (tr). **23 Dreamstime.com:** Alisali (tr); Melissa Sherron (cr); Alena Vihkareva (br). **naturepl.com:** Chris Mattison (bc). **24 Alamy Stock Photo:** Richard Griffin (bc). **25 Dreamstime.com:** Robyn Mackenzie (tr). **27 Alamy Stock Photo:** Rolf Nussbaumer Photography (br). **Shutterstock.com:** Dave Massey (clb). **28–29 Shutterstock.com:** Anton–Burakov. **29 Alamy Stock Photo:** Alan Keith Beastall (ca); Wagner Campelo (tc); blickwinkel (cra); TT50 / Stockimo (c). **Dreamstime.com:** Verdateo (cla). **Getty Images / iStock:** Cohncentric (tr). **30–31 Getty Images / iStock:** pjohnson1. **31 Science Photo Library:** Dr Jeremy Burgess (cl); Dr Keith Wheeler (c). **32 Dreamstime.com:** Ievgenii Tryfonov (cra). **32–33 Getty Images / iStock:** ranasu. **33 Dorling Kindersley:** © Sally Caulwell, 2023 (clb). **Dreamstime.com:** Wasana Jaigunta (bc); Vaeenma (crb). **34 Getty Images / iStock:** ByMPhotos (bc). **36–37 Alamy Stock Photo:** David Cook / blueshiftstudios. **36 Alamy Stock Photo:** Paula Dillinger (c); DianaThomas / Stockimo (cl). **Dreamstime.com:** Chuyu (fbr). **Getty Images / iStock:** DmitriyKazitsyn (bc). **Shutterstock.com:** Yingna Cai (br). **37 Alamy Stock Photo:** Tim Gainey (bl); Frank Hecker (fbl). **38 Alamy Stock Photo:** Dr_Microbe (br); Sanamyan (ca). **naturepl.com:** Nick Upton (bc). **Science Image, CSIRO:** (bl). **39 Alamy Stock Photo:** Xinhua (cra). **Alexander Hyde** (tl). **naturepl.com:** Duncan Mcewan (bl); Robert Thompson (br). **40 Shutterstock.com:** Liubomyr Tryhubyshyn (cl). **41 Alamy Stock Photo:** Arthit Buarapa (bl); Science Photo Library (crb). **Science Photo Library:** Eye of Science (br). **42 Getty Images:** Science Photo Library—STEVE GSCHMEISSNER (cra). **42–43 Shutterstock.com:** MakroBetz. **43 Alamy Stock Photo:** HHelene (ca); J Marshall—Tribaleye Images (cla); Panther Media GmbH (cra). **Dreamstime.com:** Empire331 (cl). **44 Dreamstime.com:** Taiftin. **45 Dorling Kindersley:** Neil Fletcher (tr). **Dreamstime.com:** Tetiana Rizanenko (bl). **naturepl.com:** Guy Edwardes (bc). **Shutterstock.com:** Svitlyk (c). **46 Alamy Stock Photo:** Martin Bergsma (b). **Science Photo Library:** BIOPHOTO ASSOCIATES (cra). **47 Alamy Stock Photo:** Andrew Chisholm (tr); Perry van Munster (bc). **Dreamstime.com:** Christian Weinktz (cr). **Shutterstock.com:** godi photo (c). **48 Dreamstime.com:** Empire331 (ca). **49 Alamy Stock Photo:** Anatoliy Berislavskiy (bc); M & J Bloomfield (t); Universal Images Group North America LLC / DeAgostini (br). **50 Shutterstock.com:** Rattiya Thongdumhyu (cla). **51 Alamy Stock Photo:** Sabena Jane Blackbird (tc); Gillian Pullinger (tr); Papilio (cl); Chris Howes / Wild Places Photography (cr). **52 Alamy Stock Photo:** Jolanta Dbrowska (bl). **53 Alamy Stock Photo:** The Natural History Museum (tc). **Dorling Kindersley:** © Sally Caulwell, 2023 (br). **Dreamstime.com:** Oleksandr Kostiuchenko (bc). **54 Alamy Stock Photo:** robertharding (c). **Dreamstime.com:** Unicusx (br). **54–55 Getty Images:** imageBROKER / AVTG. **55 Alamy Stock Photo:** imageBROKER.com GmbH & Co. KG (ca); Emmanuel LATTES (bc). **58 Getty Images:** AS Photovisions / 500px. **59 123RF.com:** valengilda (clb). **Alamy Stock Photo:** Florilegius (cb); Evgenii Zadiraka (cra). **Dreamstime.com:** Sally Scott (tl). **60 Alamy Stock Photo:** Lubo Ivanko (tr); Zoonar GmbH (cl). **Dreamstime.com:** Digitalimagined (cla); Drnn79 (bc). **61 Alamy Stock Photo:** Botany vision (cl); WILDLIFE GmbH (tc). **Dreamstime.com:** Valentyn75 (c). **Getty Images / iStock:** bksrus (tr); Luda311 (cr). **naturepl.com:** Philippe Clement (bc). **62–63 Getty Images / iStock:** yanikap. **63 Alamy Stock Photo:** Bill Waterson (br). **64 Alamy Stock Photo:** AGAMI Photo Agency (bl); Roland Knauer (crb); imageBROKER.com GmbH & Co. KG (br). **Jorma Pennanen:** (tr). **64–65 naturepl.com:** Niall Benvie. **66 Alamy Stock Photo:** Matthew Taylor (cl). **Getty Images / iStock:** kazakovmaksim (cr); Photoshopped (cra). **66–67 naturepl.com:** David Noton (b). **67 Alamy Stock Photo:** John Eveson (tr); John Richmond (c); Roger Phillips (cr). **Dreamstime.com:** Jolanta Dabrowska (tl). **68–69 naturepl.com:** Doug Gimesy. **69 Alamy Stock Photo:** jordi clave garsot (br). **Getty Images / iStock:** Stefan Sutka (cra). **70 Alamy Stock Photo:** BIOSPHOTO (bl). **Science Photo Library:** Dr Jeremy Burgess (tr); Eye of Science (br). **Andy Taylor:** (cr). **70–71 Alamy Stock Photo:** Emmanuel LATTES. **72 Alamy Stock Photo:** Andrew Kearton (bl). **Getty Images:** James Brey (tl); imageBROKER / Frank Sommariva (cl). **72–73 Alexander Hyde. 73 naturepl.com:** Nick Upton (cr). **74 123RF.com:** scis65 (tl). **Alamy Stock Photo:** Bruce Montagne / Dembinsky Photo Associates (cl). **Dreamstime.com:** Manfred Ruckszio (cr). **Getty Images / iStock:** lightphoto (bl). **75 Alamy Stock Photo:** Derek Harris (bc); Anna Maloverjan (ftl). **Depositphotos Inc:** prill (tl). **Dreamstime.com:** Tetiana Kovalenko (tr). **Getty Images:** Adrian Burke (br). **76–77 naturepl.com:** Chris O'Reilly. **77 Alamy Stock Photo:** Marc Bruxelle RF (bl); Vince F (cla). **Getty Images:** Bettmann (br). **naturepl.com:** Philippe Clement (cra); Thomas Lazar (tl); Jerry Monkman (clb). **78–79 Alamy Stock Photo:** inga spence. **79 Alamy Stock Photo:** inga spence (br). **Dreamstime.com:** Alfio Scisetti (cra). **80–81 Alamy Stock Photo:** Rosey.. **81 Alamy Stock Photo:** Avalon.red (cla); david speight (clb); Steve Holroyd (bl). **Getty Images:** Tim Graham (br). **Science Photo Library:** Dr. John Brackenbury (tl). **82 123RF.com:** Natalie Ruffing (br). **Alamy Stock Photo:** Ed Callaert (bl). **Dreamstime.com:** Alfio Scisetti (cl); Iva Vagnerova (cra). **83 Alamy Stock Photo:** Botany vision (cr); Roger Phillips (bc); Brian Overcast (br). **Dreamstime.com:** Melinda Fawver (cl). **Getty Images:** Jeff Rose Photography (t). **84 Alamy Stock Photo:** Associated Press (bc). **naturepl.com:** David Welling (cl). **84–85 Alamy Stock Photo:** Danita Delimont Creative. **86 Alamy Stock Photo:** John Richmond (cra). **Dreamstime.com:** Labemax (cr); Osoznaniejizni (tl); Manfred Ruckszio (bl). **87 123RF.com:** ajhill262 (br). **Alamy Stock Photo:** geogphotos (br); npict (bl). **Dreamstime.com:** Jolanta Dabrowska (t). **Shutterstock.com:** spline_x (bc). **88 Alamy Stock Photo:** John Richmond (clb). **Getty Images:** Arterra (crb); Travelpix Ltd (tr); Mike Powles (cra); R A Kearton (br). **88–89 Getty Images:** Cavan Images. **90–91 Alexander Hyde. 91 Sarah Christofides:** (cr). **Richard Wright:** (br). **92 123RF.com:** weinkoetz (fbl). **Dreamstime.com:** Empire331 (cr); Empire331 (bl); Jukka Palm (bc). **Getty Images / iStock:** Junjarus Srichaiyachana (c). **93 123RF.com:** olko1975 (cra). **Alamy Stock Photo:** Richard Becker (tr); Premaphotos (cla); blickwinkel (br). **Dreamstime.com:** Empire331 (cr). **naturepl.com:** Guy Edwardes (ca). **Shutterstock.com:** Feng Yu (bl). **94–95 naturepl.com:** Staffan Widstrand / Wild Wonders of China. **95 Dave Genney:** (cla)(clb)(bl)(br)(tl). **96 Alamy Stock Photo:** Bob Gibbons (bl); user685475 (cra); Penta Springs Limited (bc). **97 123RF.com:** waldemarus (cla). **Alamy Stock Photo:** Emilio Ereza (tc); Lamax (r). **Dreamstime.com:** Taiga (bc). **98 123RF.com:** photohampster (c). **Alamy Stock Photo:** Album (br). **Dreamstime.com:** Rob Lumen Captum (bc); Denira777 (tr); Geert Huysman (tc); Jean Paul Chassenet (cr). **Getty Images:** Jasenka Arbanas (l). **99 123RF.com:** scis65 (tc). **Alamy Stock Photo:** Florilegius (cla); History and Art Collection (ca); Nature Picture Library (bl). **Dorling Kindersley:** Mark Winwood / RHS Wisley (tr). **Dreamstime.com:** Wirestock (crb). **100 naturepl.com:** Hiroya Minakuchi / Minden. **101 123RF.com:** sterna (cr). **Alamy Stock Photo:** P Tomlins (cra). **Dorling Kindersley:** Gary Ombler / Batsford Garden Centre and Arboretum (cl). **Dreamstime.com:** Nikolai Kurzenko (c). **102 Alamy Stock Photo:** Mohammed Anwarul Kabir Choudhury (bl); Tetiana Kovalenko (cla); Margaret Welby (tr); MELVIN GREEN (c); Imagebroker (br). **Dreamstime.com:** Cogent (ca); Alfio Scisetti (bc). **Getty Images:** Mandy Disher Photography (cr). **103 Alamy Stock Photo:** Corbin17 (tr); Nature Photographers Ltd (ca); Formatoriginal (cr). **Dreamstime.com:** Alfio Scisetti (cl). **Getty Images:** I love Photo and Apple. (b); Science Photo Library (tc). **104–105 Alamy Stock Photo:** Chronicle. **105 Alamy Stock Photo:** fabio formaggio (br). **Getty Images:** YuenWu (cr). **106 123RF.com:** anolis01 (cr). **Alamy Stock Photo:** All Canada Photos (bl); John Quixley—Australia (c). **Dreamstime.com:** Jianghongyan (tl); Pavel Parmenov (cra); Rajesh (br). **Stephen Axford @Planet Fungi:** (bc). **107 Alamy Stock Photo:** John Quixley—Australia (cl). **Dreamstime.com:** Vectortone (c). **Stephen Axford @Planet Fungi** (br)(tc)(tl). **naturepl.com:** Alex Hyde (cra). **Shutterstock.com:** puttography (bc). **108 Alamy Stock Photo:** REDA &CO srl (crb); John Richmond (bl); Universal Images Group North America LLC / DeAgostini (cb). **Dorling Kindersley:** Mark Winwood / RHS Wisley (cr). **Dreamstime.com:** Simona Pavan (cl); Alfio Scisetti (tl); Björn Wylezich (tr). **naturepl.com:** Felis Images (c). **109 Dorling Kindersley:** Colin Keates / Natural History Museum, London (cr); Mark Winwood, Courtesy of RHS Wisley (br). **Dreamstime.com:** Digitalfestival (l). **110–111 naturepl.com:** Yashpal Rathore. **111 Alamy Stock Photo:** imageBROKER.com GmbH & Co. KG (cra); Xinhua (br). **112 Alamy Stock Photo:** India Stock (bl). **Dreamstime.com:** Pittawut Junmee (br); Likit Supasai (tl); Tetiana Kovalenko (cra); Nuttapol Noprujikul (cr). **113 123RF.com:** anatskwong (tr). **Dreamstime.com:** Airubon (c); Mollynz (bl); Jon Benito Iza (bc). **Shutterstock.com:** duchy (br); wasanajai (cl). **114–115 Alamy Stock Photo:** Jamie Pham. **115 Alamy Stock Photo:** Heritage Image Partnership Ltd (br); Zoonar GmbH (bl). **Shutterstock.com:** Mazur Travel (tl). **Wikipedia:** N. Aditya Madhav (cl). **116 Alamy Stock Photo:** Alfio Scisetti (cra); Dave Watts (cr). **Shutterstock.com:** Wattlebird (bc). **117 Alamy Stock Photo:** Album (bc); Balfore Archive Images (tl); phototrip (tr); The Natural History Museum (bl). **Getty Images / iStock:** Alika Obrazovskaya (br). **118 Alamy Stock Photo:** Genevieve Vallee (bc). **Getty Images / iStock:** janaph (cl). **118–119 naturepl.com:** Steven David Miller. **120–121 Getty Images:** Robin Bush (b). **120 Alamy Stock Photo:** Album (c); blickwinkel (tl); imageBROKER.com GmbH & Co. KG (cra); Krystyna Szulecka (cl). **Dreamstime.com:** Alfio Scisetti (cr). **Te Motu kairangi–Miramar Ecological Restoration:** (clb). **121 Dorling Kindersley:** Mark Winwood / RHS Wisley (tc). **122 Shutterstock.com:** Lisandro Luis Trarbach. **123 Alamy Stock Photo:** Charles Stirling (cra). **Dreamstime.com:** Gabriela Bertolini (c); Adilson Sochodolak (tl); Wasana Jaigunta (fcl); Horst Lieber (cl); Àlvaro Bueno Lumbreras (fbl); Angela Macario (bl); Dlida (br). **Getty Images / iStock:** edsongrandisoli (bc). **124 123RF.com:** dewins (tr). **Alamy Stock Photo:** Uwe Bergwitz (bl); blickwinkel (br). **Dreamstime.com:** Noppharat (cr); Simona Pavan (ca). **Shutterstock.com:** litchima (cla). **125 Alamy Stock Photo:** Florilegius (cl); adrian hepworth (cra). **Dreamstime.com:** Mamik Slamet Asrori (bl); Alf Ribeiro (c); David Gonzalez Rebollo (bc). **naturepl.com:** Klein & Hubert (br). **Shutterstock.com:** Ailisa (tl). **126–127 naturepl.com:** Johannes Melchers / BIA / Minden. **127 Alamy Stock Photo:** Jon G. Fuller, Jr. (cla); Raquel Mogado (tl). **Getty Images:** sergey hmelevsky / 500px (clb); Stefan Huwiler (bl). **128 Alamy Stock Photo:** Henri Koskinen (cra); Nature Picture Library (br). **Dorling Kindersley:** Neil Fletcher (tl). **Giuliana Furci** (cr). **Matthew E. Smith** (bc)(c)(clb). **129 Dr Camille Truong:** (tl). **Dreamstime.com:** Miriam Rizzuti (cra); Miriam Rizzuti (c). **Giuliana Furci:** (br). **Matthew E. Smith** (bc)(bl)(cl)(tc). **130 Alamy Stock Photo:** Album. **131 Alamy Stock Photo:** John Richmond (bc); RM Floral (cra). **132 Alamy Stock Photo:** Nigel Cattlin (l); WILDLIFE GmbH (tc); Colin Varndell (br). **Getty Images / iStock:** PFMphotostock (cra). **Shutterstock.com:** Ailisa (ca). **133 123RF.com:** bzh22 (cl); tunedin123 (c). **Alamy Stock Photo:** John Richmond (bl); John Richmond (bc). **Dreamstime.com:** SI Photography (tl). **Getty Images:** Priscilla Burcher (cr). **134–135 Getty Images:** Fotografas Jorge León Cabello. **134 Alamy Stock Photo:** Roger Phillips (cl); Rob Walls (bc). **136 africanplants.senckenberg.de:** Meike Piepenbring (cr). **Deni Brown:** (clb). **Jean–Louis Doucet:** (c). **Dreamstime.com:** Elena268 (cra); Md Sojibul Islam (tl). **Paul Latham** (br). **Wikipedia:** Len Worthington (bc). **137 naturepl.com:** Florian Mollers. **138 Alamy Stock Photo:** Regis Martin (b). **Dreamstime.com:** Wagner Campelo (cla). **Bernard Dupont:** (cra). **Paul Latham:** (ca). **139 Stefan Porembski / africanplants.senckenberg.de:** (bc). **Alamy Stock Photo:** AfriPics.com (tr); Wirestock, Inc. (fcl); Premaphotos (cl); Florilegius (bl); Tamara Kulikova (br). **Dreamstime.com:** Wagner Campelo (tl). **Shutterstock.com:** Cheng Wei (cr). **Nicholas Case Wightman:** (c). **140–141 naturepl.com:** Gerry Ellis / Minden. **141 Alamy Stock Photo:** Roberto Nistri (clb). **Dreamstime.com:** Sergey Kolesnikov (cr). **naturepl.com:** Piotr Naskrecki / Minden (cla); Cyril Ruoso (tl); Mark Moffett / Minden (bl); Mark Moffett /

Minden (br). **142 Alamy Stock Photo:** AfriPics.com (cra); Westend61 GmbH (cl); Sonia Bonet (bl). **Dreamstime.com:** Uskarp (tl); Znm (c); Christian Weiß (br). **Getty Images / iStock:** znm (bc). **143 Alamy Stock Photo:** karenfoleyphotography (cl); Morgan Trimble (tr); RM Floral (bl). **Dreamstime.com:** Gerald D. Tang (br). **naturepl.com:** Mark Payne–Gill (bc). **144 123RF.com:** annytop (cra). **Alamy Stock Photo:** allotment boy 1 (bc); Lukas Anthonie (c); imageBROKER.com GmbH & Co. KG (br). **Dreamstime.com:** Alfio Scisetti (bl); Jj Van Ginkel (tl). **Shutterstock.com:** Dominique de La Croix (cr). **145 Alamy Stock Photo:** Sabena Jane Blackbird (tl); Steffen Hauser / botanikfoto (cl); Kevin Schafer (tr); Geraldine Buckley (bl); José María Barres Manuel (bc). **Dreamstime.com:** Iakov Filimonov (br); Wirestock (c). **146–147 Getty Images:** Paul Bruins Photography. **147 Alamy Stock Photo:** Grobler du Preez (clb); Pete Titmuss (cla); Ann and Steve Toon (bl); Mike Wesson (br). **naturepl.com:** Tony Phelps (tl). **148 Dreamstime.com:** Le Thuy Do (tl); Kamonrutm (cra). **Getty Images / iStock:** mirecca (br). **naturepl.com:** Pete Oxford / Minden (bl). **149 Alamy Stock Photo:** BIOSPHOTO (tc); Florapix (cl); Ariadne Van Zandbergen (c); Chris Mattison (bl). **Dreamstime.com:** Prapat Aowsakorn (tl). **Getty Images / iStock:** Gam1983 (crb). **naturepl.com:** Chien Lee / Minden (tr). **G.E. Schatz:** (bc). **150 Alamy Stock Photo:** Emilio Ereza (cl). **Getty Images:** Marcus Valance / SOPA Images / LightRocket (bc). **150–151 Alamy Stock Photo:** Panoramic Images. **154 Alamy Stock Photo:** All Canada Photos (cra); Suzanne Goodwin (c). **Dreamstime.com:** Klemen Cerkovnik (bc); Dave Willman (tl); Agata Pietrzak (cl); Nataliia Vyshneva (crb); Ihor Hvozdetskij (br). **155 Alamy Stock Photo:** Galaxiid (bl); H. Mark Weidman Photography (t). **Dreamstime.com:** 404045 (br); Remus Cucu (cl); Andrei Stepanov (c). **156–157 naturepl.com:** Espen Bergersen. **157 naturepl.com:** John Abbott (br). **158 Getty Images:** R A Kearton. **159 Alamy Stock Photo:** Premaphotos (cr); WILDLIFE GmbH (cra); Matthijs Wetterauw (cl). **Dreamstime.com:** Emberiza (c); Richard Griffin (bl). **160 Alamy Stock Photo:** Panther Media GmbH (br). **Dreamstime.com:** Richard Griffin (bc). **Getty Images:** Guenter Fischer (cla). **161 Alamy Stock Photo:** Richard Griffin (ca); Anthony Hatley (bl). **Dreamstime.com:** Harald Biebel (cr). **Getty Images / iStock:** AntiMartina (cl); MariaBrzostowska (tr). **Shutterstock.com:** Manfred Ruckszio (br). **162 Alamy Stock Photo:** Nigel Cattlin (bl); John Richmond (br). **Dreamstime.com:** Jon Benito Iza (tl); Vaclav Volrab (cra); Taweesak Sriwannawit (cr). **163 Alamy Stock Photo:** aroundtheworld.photography (tr); Elizabeth Whiting & Associates (bl). **Dreamstime.com:** Sanskar Hardaha (cla); Jon Benito Iza (tc); Jobrestful (c); Luis Echeverri Urrea (br). **164–165 Alamy Stock Photo:** Dennis Frates. **165 Alamy Stock Photo:** Sergey Kuznetsov (br). **166 Alamy Stock Photo:** Ernie Janes (b). **Dreamstime.com:** Angelacottingham (c); Rbiedermann (tl). **167 Alamy Stock Photo:** Historic Images (tr); imageBROKER.com GmbH & Co. KG (crb). **Dreamstime.com:** Jolanta Dabrowska (bc); Elena Odareeva (cb); Rbiedermann (bl). **Getty Images:** Chushkin (tc). **168 Alamy Stock Photo:** blickwinkel (cr); Bob Gibbons (tl). **Dreamstime.com:** hsvrs (cra). **Getty Images / iStock:** Michel VIARD (br). **naturepl.com:** Jean E. Roche (bl). **Shutterstock.com:** AleksandarMilutinovic (c). **169 Alamy Stock Photo:** Bob Gibbons (c); Nature Photographers Ltd (tc); Roel Meijer (bc); Jonathan Need (br). **Dreamstime.com:** Christian Weinktz (tr). **Getty Images / iStock:** Matthew Pennini (cl). **170–171 Getty Images / iStock:** jeridu. **171 Alamy Stock Photo:** imageBROKER.com GmbH & Co. KG (br); Rolf Nussbaumer Photography (bl). **Getty Images / iStock:** KenCanning (tl). **Science Photo Library:** Thierry Berrod, Mona Lisa Production (cla). **Wikipedia:** Mushroom Observer (clb). **172 Alamy Stock Photo:** Jon Dunn (bc); Hideo Kurihara (cl); imageBROKER.com GmbH & Co. KG (r); Florilegius (bl). **Dreamstime.com:** Krishnakumar Nagaraj (tl); Alfio Scisetti (cr). **173 Alamy Stock Photo:** Bill Gozansky (t); Nature Photographers Ltd (bc); Krystyna Szulecka (br). **Dreamstime.com:** Armando Frazo (bl). **174–175 Getty Images:** Valter Jacinto. **175 Alamy Stock Photo:** MIKEL BILBAO GOROSTIAGA–NATURE & LANDSCAPES (br); Simon Stirrup (tl). **Getty Images:** Friedhelm Adam (clb); Christian Handl (cla); imageBROKER / Erhard Nerger (bl). **176 Dorling Kindersley:** Mark Winwood / RHS Wisley. **177 Alamy Stock Photo:** agefotostock (br); Steffen Hauser / botanikfoto (c); Andrey Nekrasov (cr). **Dreamstime.com:** Tracy Immordino (tl); Rbiedermann (cra); Pavel Parmenov (cl); Kazakovmaksim (clb); Gerald D. Tang (bl); Vasiliybokov (bc). **178 Alamy Stock Photo:** BIOSPHOTO (ca); WILDLIFE GmbH (cla); PureStock (cra); Clint Farlinger (bl); Universal Images Group North America LLC / DeAgostini (br). **179 Alamy Stock Photo:** Florapix (tc); Gina Kelly (bl); Gina Kelly (bc); Steffen Hauser / botanikfoto (br). **naturepl.com:** Ingo Arndt (tr). **Shutterstock.com:** Doikanoy (tl). **180 Alamy Stock Photo:** blickwinkel (bl). **Dreamstime.com:** Homydesign (tl); Nadin333 (br). **Getty Images / iStock:** Tirex (bc). **181 123RF.com:** domnicky (bc); rachel_a_bennett (c). **Dreamstime.com:** Tamara Kulikova (cr); Saba11 (tl). **Getty Images / iStock:** firina (bl). **Getty Images:** Paroli Galperti / REDA&CO / Universal Images Group (br). **182–183 Getty Images:** YONCA60. **183 Alamy Stock Photo:** imageBROKER.com GmbH & Co. KG (tl); Alfio Scisetti (cra). **Dreamstime.com:** Anmbph (clb); Barmalini (bl). **Getty Images:** DeAgostini (br); Jacky Parker Photography (cla). **184 Alamy Stock Photo:** Chris Burrows (cra); Marcos Veiga (bc). **Dreamstime.com:** Vetre Antanaviciute–meskauskiene (cr); Jtbob168 (tl); Ncristian (bl); Nadin333 (cl); Nadin333 (c); Ksushsh (br). **185 Alamy Stock Photo:** Florilegius. **186 Alamy Stock Photo:** ART Collection (cla); Nature Picture Library (tc); Nature Photographers Ltd (bc). **Dreamstime.com:** Tamara Kulikova (tr); Manfred Ruckszio (ca). **186–187 Alamy Stock Photo:** Tetiana Vitsenko. **187 123RF.com:** kongxinzhu (tc). **Alamy Stock Photo:** FLPA (bl). **Dorling Kindersley:** Mark Winwood / RHS Wisley (tl); Mark Winwood / Alpine Garden Society (tr). **Dreamstime.com:** Tetiana Kovalenko (bc); Sergei Razvodovskij (cr); Multik (br). **188 Alamy Stock Photo:** Cephas Picture Library (bl); Nature Picture Library (cra). **Dreamstime.com:** Daniel Larson (br); Gene Zhang (tl). **189 Alamy Stock Photo:** Richard Broadwell (bc); Fabiano Sodi (tc); donna Ikenberry / Art Directors (cra); Craig Lovell / Eagle Visions Photography (cr). **Dreamstime.com:** Eutoch (br); VinceZen (c). **Getty Images / iStock:** TheYDP (cl). **naturepl.com:** Jeff Foott (bl). **190–191 naturepl.com:** Jack Dykinga. **191 Alamy Stock Photo:** Cesar Santana (br). **192 Alamy Stock Photo:** Minden Pictures. **193 Alamy Stock Photo:** imageBROKER.com GmbH & Co. KG (c); P Tomlins (tl); Aleksandr Puludi (cra); m.schuppich (cl). **Getty Images / iStock:** Dewin ' Indew (crb). **Shutterstock.com:** Nick Pecker (bl); wasanajai (bc). **194 123RF.com:** paulettestuff (c). **Alamy Stock Photo:** Florilegius (tc); Nick Kurzenko (tl); Steffen Hauser / botanikfoto (tr); SJ Images (cr); Karol Kozlowski Premium RM Collection (bl). **naturepl.com:** Cyril Ruoso (br). **195 Alamy Stock Photo:** Florilegius (r); imageBROKER.com GmbH & Co. KG (tl); Panther Media GmbH (bl); positivesoundvision (bc). **Dreamstime.com:** Alfio Scisetti (tc). **Shutterstock.com:** Detiga (c). **Wikipedia:** Natalia Reyes Escobar (cl). **196–197 Getty Images:** Pete Orelup. **197 Alamy Stock Photo:** Wirestock, Inc. (cra). **Shutterstock.com:** sez (br). **198 Dreamstime.com:** Tania Bertoni (c); Subas Chandra Mahato (tl). **Getty Images / iStock:** pixhook (r). **Isidro Martínez:** (cl). **Shutterstock.com:** GYAN PRATIM RAICHOUDHURY (bc); Wut_Moppie (bl). **199 Alamy Stock Photo:** Arterra Picture Library (cl); ERIC LAFFORGUE (tr). **Dreamstime.com:** Simona Pavan (tl); Sanjiv Shukla (bl). **Shutterstock.com:** DEVIKA PRODUCTION (br); Babo Sembodo (tc). **200 Department of Agriculture and Fisheries, the State of Queensland 2024:** Jeff Daniells (bc). **Getty Images:** wilatlak villette (cl). **200–201 Alamy Stock Photo:** Zoonar GmbH. **201 Alamy Stock Photo:** Florapix (cra); GRANT ROONEY PREMIUM (crb); Glen Pearson (br). **Shutterstock.com:** Davis Dorss (tr). **202 123RF.com:** taxiboat (ca). **Alamy Stock Photo:** Elena Odareeva (cb); Kobus Peche (bl). **Getty Images / iStock:** Nurma Agung Firmansyah (br). **Shutterstock.com:** Izzah Khaliifah (cr); Natalia van D (bc). **203 Alamy Stock Photo:** overwateringkills (br). **Dorling Kindersley:** Gary Ombler: Centre for Wildlife Gardening / London Wildlife Trust (bl). **Dreamstime.com:** Aquamarine4 (t); Safrida Vida (bc). **204 Getty Images:** Fadil Aziz (tl); Fadil Aziz (bl). **204–205 Alamy Stock Photo:** Aleksandra Kossowska. **205 Getty Images:** Adi Prima / Anadolu Agency (br). **206 Alamy Stock Photo:** Avalon.red (crb); Stephanie Jackson—Gardens and flowers collection (cb). **Dreamstime.com:** Amphawan Chanunpha (tl); Umaporn Thongta (cra); Le Thuy Do (bl). **207 Alamy Stock Photo:** blickwinkel (tr); The Picture Art Collection (tl); Maria Mosolova (cl); The History Collection (bl); Ken Griffiths (br). **Dreamstime.com:** Martin Battiti (cr); Jimbophotoart (tc); Roberto Dziura Jr. (c); Chirasak Tolertmongkol (bc); Otsphoto (crb). **208–209 naturepl.com:** Christian Ziegler / Minden. **209 Alamy Stock Photo:** MInden Pictures (br). **210 Alamy Stock Photo:** Karind (bc); VIRENDER SINGH (tr); shapencolour (cra); Ariadne Van Zandbergen (br). **Getty Images:** Gail Shotlander (crb). **210–211 Dreamstime.com:** Andrei Stancu. **212 123RF.com:** wernerl (tl). **Alamy Stock Photo:** agefotostock (c); Florapix (bc); Friedrich von Hörsten (br). **Dreamstime.com:** Andre201313 (cra); Alfio Scisetti (cr); Aris Astriana (clb). **213 123RF.com:** avapeattie (bc). **Alamy Stock Photo:** imageBROKER.com GmbH & Co. KG (t); RM Floral (br). **Dreamstime.com:** Markspirit (bl); Gene Zhang (fbl). **214 Alamy Stock Photo:** ams images (cra); Nature Picture Library (bl); blickwinkel (c); blickwinkel (br). **Dreamstime.com:** Alviseziche (cr); Onlyfabrizio (tl). **naturepl.com:** Adrian Davies (bc). **215 Alamy Stock Photo:** shapencolour (bl); C J Wheeler (c); shapencolour (br). **Dreamstime.com:** Rob Lumen Captum (cl); Christian Weiß (tl); Wiertn (tc); Alfio Scisetti (cra); Jacques Vanni (bc). **216 Alamy Stock Photo:** Album (cb); Florapix (tl); christopher miles (tr). **Dreamstime.com:** Cathywithers (br); Julian Popov (c). **Maria Teresa Eyzaguirre:** (cl). **Claudina Jirón:** (tc). **217 Alamy Stock Photo:** The Africa Image Library. **218 123RF.com:** simicv (br). **Alamy Stock Photo:** Gerry Bishop (bc); Nature Photographers Ltd (tr). **Dreamstime.com:** Nedim Bajramovic (cr); Sgoodwin4813 (cl); Belaruslady (c). **Getty Images / iStock:** scisettialfio (bl). **219 Alamy Stock Photo:** Peter de Clercq (cr); Katya Tsvetkova (br). **Dreamstime.com:** Pjhpix (tl); Alfio Scisetti (bl). **220–221 naturepl.com:** Orsolya Haarberg. **221 Alamy Stock Photo:** Frank Blackburn (cra); Nature Picture Library (br). **224 Alamy Stock Photo:** imageBROKER.com GmbH & Co. KG (c); Chris Mattison (cra); imageBROKER.com GmbH & Co. KG (bl). **Dreamstime.com:** Alessandrozocc (cr); Andreistanescu (tl); Fritz Hiersche (cb); Sarah Jane Duran (crb). **225 Alamy Stock Photo:** GFC Collection (tl); Anton Sorokin (tr); Zoonar GmbH (c); Jamie Pham Photography (br). **Dreamstime.com:** Barmalini (bc); Soniabonet (cla); Supitcha Mcadam (bl). **226–227 Alexander Hyde. 227 Alamy Stock Photo:** REDA &CO srl (br). **naturepl.com:** Chris Mattison (cr). **228 Alamy Stock Photo:** David Chapman (bc). **Dreamstime.com:** Rinus Baak (cl); William Perry (tl); Katharina Notarianni (cra); Katharina Notarianni (c). **naturepl.com:** Jeff Foott (crb). **229 Alamy Stock Photo:** blickwinkel (bc); Sam Oaksey (cb); Chocoholic (bl). **Dreamstime.com:** Jonmanjeot (t). **Shutterstock.com:** Darrel Guilbeau (clb). **230–231 naturepl.com:** Jen Guyton. **231 naturepl.com:** Ann & Steve Toon (br). **232 Alamy Stock Photo:** Carol Dembinsky / Dembinsky Photo Associates (bc); Minden Pictures (cr); SBS Eclectic Images (bl); NatureOnline (br). **Dreamstime.com:** Julie Feinstein (cra). **naturepl.com:** Chien Lee / Minden (c); MYN / Krista Schlyer (tl). **233 Alamy Stock Photo:** anjahennern (tc); Avalon.red (tl); Shawn Hempel (c); Minden Pictures (cr); Sklifas Steven (bl). **Dreamstime.com:** Anastasiia Skorobogatova (cra). **naturepl.com:** Chris Mattison (br); Chien Lee / Minden (bc). **234–235 Paul Williams / Iron Ammonite. 235 Science Photo Library:** BIOPHOTO ASSOCIATES (br). **Paul Williams / Iron Ammonite** (bl)(cl)(tl). **236 Alamy Stock Photo:** BIOSPHOTO (bl); Steffen Hauser / botanikfoto (c). **Dreamstime.com:** Rob Lumen Captum (br); Digitalimagined (tl). **naturepl.com:** Dave Watts (cr). **237 Alamy Stock Photo:** blickwinkel (bl); Carol Dembinsky / Dembinsky Photo Associates (cl); Makoto Honda (c); Florapix (bc/flycatcher bush). **W. Barthlott, lotus-salvinia.de:** (br). **Dreamstime.com:** Verastuchelova (tl). **Getty Images:** Paul Starosta (tr). **naturepl.com:** MYN / Niall Benvie (crb). **Shutterstock.com:** anjahennern (cr). **238 123RF.com:** mguntow (cl). **Alamy Stock Photo:** Nature Picture Library (clb). **Dreamstime.com:** Andreistanescu (c); Mirror Images (cra); Ncristian (tl); Dana Kenneth Johnson (bl); Jeyaprakash Mariaselvam (bc); David Steele (br). **Shutterstock.com:** alybaba (cr). **239 Alamy Stock Photo:** Tim Gainey. **240 123RF.com:** adwo123 (fcra). **Alamy Stock Photo:** agefotostock (cl); blickwinkel (b). **Dreamstime.com:** Rbiedermann (ca); Christian Weiß (cra). **241 Alamy Stock Photo:** Wallace Garrison (l); Nature Picture Library (bl). **Dreamstime.com:** Julia Pivovarova (cl); Gene Zhang (tc); Pkzphotos (tr); Whiskybottle (c); Pnwnature (cr); Wirestock (br). **Getty Images:** Paroli Galperti / REDA&CO / Universal Images Group (bc). **242–243 Alamy Stock Photo:** Aliaksandr Mazurkevich. **243 Alamy Stock Photo:** southeast asia (cr); A & J Visage (br). **244 123RF.com:** dextorth (br). **Alamy Stock Photo:** Colouria Media (cra). **Dreamstime.com:** Wagner Campelo (tl); Nancy Ayumi Kunihiro (cr). **naturepl.com:** Luiz Claudio Marigo (bl). **245 Alamy Stock Photo:** 916 collection (tc); Chris Mattison (tl); Pat Canova (c); D3WI / Stockimo (br). **Dreamstime.com:** Pras Boonwong (bl); Ricardo De Paula Ferreira (cl); Mansum008 (bc). **Shutterstock.com:** isarescheewin (cra); Salparadis (ftl); NANCY AYUMI KUNIHIRO (fcl). **246 Alamy Stock Photo:** Archive PL (c); Jonathan ORourke (cl); David Whitaker (br). **Dreamstime.com:** Digitalimagined (tl); Ian Redding (cra); Oliver Risteski (bc). **Getty Images / iStock:** Robert Winkler (cr). **Robert Harding Picture Library:** Daniel Vega (bl). **247 Alamy Stock Photo:** imageBROKER.com GmbH & Co. KG (bl); Henri Koskinen (cla). **Dreamstime.com:** Evgenii Mitroshin (cra); Olga Popova (tc); Febrika Nurmalasari (br). **Shutterstock.com:** HHelene (ca). **248 Alamy Stock Photo:** agefotostock (cr); GM Photo Images (cra); Gillian Moore (c); GM Photo Images (br). **Dreamstime.com:** Vladvitek (tl). **Getty Images / iStock:** Gerald Corsi (bc). **naturepl.com:** Tui De Roy (bl). **249 Alamy Stock Photo:** Avalon.red (br); thrillerfillerspiller (tl); Cool–pix (cl); imageBROKER.com GmbH & Co. KG (tr). **Dreamstime.com:** Agami Photo Agency (tc); Sergey Mayorov (c). **naturepl.com:** Tui De Roy / Minden (bl). **250–251 Getty Images / iStock:** Lukas Bischoff. **251 Alamy Stock Photo:** blickwinkel (br); FLPA (bl). **Getty Images / iStock:** zanskar (tl). **Getty Images:** Csilla Zelko (cla). **naturepl.com:** Sylvain Cordier (clb). **252 Alamy Stock Photo:** Julie Pigula (bl); Oleksiy Yakovlyev (c). **Dreamstime.com:** Antonel (tr); Rita Puteikyte (tl); Slowmotiongli (cr); Harald Biebel (bc). **Getty Images:** Cuveland / ullstein bild (br). **253 Alamy Stock Photo:** Nigel Cattlin (tr); Mick Durham FRPS (cl); pytyczech (bl). **Dreamstime.com:** Dm Stock Production (fcl); Alfio Scisetti (tc); Kazakovmaksim (c); Sgoodwin4813 (crb). **254–255 Alamy Stock Photo:** John Cancalosi. **255 Dreamstime.com:** Jolanta Dabrowska (cra). **Shutterstock.com:** Tikta Alik (br). **256 Alamy Stock Photo:** Juniors Bildarchiv GmbH (crb); Alessandro Mancini (cl); Frank Teigler / Hippocampus Bildarchiv (c); Alessandro Mancini (bl); Armands Pharyos (br). **Dreamstime.com:** David Carillet (tl); Debbie Ann Powell (bc). **257 123RF.com:** maulejobs (tr); sakarai (cr). **Alamy Stock Photo:** Marcus Harrison—plants (bl); imageBROKER.com GmbH & Co. KG (cla); Y Kumar (tc); Alessandro Mancini (bc); mauritius images GmbH (br). **258–259 Alamy Stock Photo:** myLAM. **259 Alamy Stock Photo:** Joe Blossom (tl); YAY Media AS (cla); SAWASSAKORN MUTTAPRAPRUT (br). **Getty Images / iStock:** Gerald Corsi (clb). **Getty Images:** Norberto Duarte / AFP (bl). **Science Photo Library:** Ted Kinsman (cra). **260 Alamy Stock Photo:** Nature Photographers Ltd (cra). **Dreamstime.com:** Kazakovmaksim (tl); Wirestock (bl); Carlos Neto (br). **Shutterstock.com:** Hugh Lansdown (cr). **261 Alamy Stock Photo:** AGAMI Photo Agency (cra); Charles O. Cecil (tl); Anton Sorokin (bl). **Dreamstime.com:** Geraldo F Filho (cl); Magryt (tc); Seadam (bc). **naturepl.com:** Sue Daly (c); Jiri Lochman (br). **262–263 Getty Images / iStock:** Damocean. **263 Getty Images / iStock:** Hamid Photography (br). **264 Alamy Stock Photo:** Nature Photographers Ltd (cr); P Tomlins (c). **Dorling Kindersley:** Alan Keohane (br). **Dreamstime.com:** Anitasstudio (tl); Czuber (cra); Iva Villi (bc). **naturepl.com:** Erlend Haarberg (bl). **265 Alamy Stock Photo:** Bramwell Flora (tr); Zoonar GmbH (ftl); Panther Media GmbH (bc). **Dreamstime.com:** Alcaproac (tl); Ken Griffiths (tc); Jay Pierstorff (cl); Iva Villi (c). **Getty Images / iStock:** Gerald Corsi (br). **266 Alamy Stock Photo:** robertharding (bl). **266–267 Alamy Stock Photo:** J K Lovelace. **268 123RF.com:** griffin024 (clb). **Alamy Stock Photo:** Stephanie Jackson—Agriculture (c); William Mullins (bc); Craig Joiner Photography (br). **Dreamstime.com:** Boonchuay Iamsumang (cra); Tanja Mikkelsen (tl); Watcharee Suphakitudomkarn (cr). **269 Alamy Stock Photo:** Pat Bennett (tl); Holmes Garden Photos (bl); Vintage Archive (br). **Dreamstime.com:** Chernetskaya (cr); Tetiana Kovalenko (cra); Takepicsforfun (cl); Le Thuy Do (c). **270–271 Getty Images /**

iStock: Robert John Photography. **270 Alamy Stock Photo:** Valsa / Stockimo (cr). Bugwood.org: Ronald F.Billings, Texas A&M Forest Service (tr); Rebekah D. Wallace (br). **Getty Images / iStock:** chengyuzheng (cl). **272 Alamy Stock Photo:** Hemis (crb); Christine Whitehead (tr); ian west (cra); Juniors Bildarchiv GmbH (br). **272–273 Getty Images / iStock:** EstuaryPig. **274–275 Getty Images:** Image Professionals GmbH. **276 Alamy Stock Photo:** Nick Greaves (bl); Nature Photographers Ltd (tr); Przemysaw Nieprzecki (bc). **Dreamstime.com:** Emilio100 (cr); Anna Kucherova (tl); Vladimir Tomovic (cl); Yvdavyd (c); Olgachwa (br). **277 Alamy Stock Photo:** blickwinkel (t); Shotshop GmbH (crb); Jacquelin Grant (br). **Dreamstime.com:** Tukaram Karve (fbl); Toon Sang (bl); Picture Partners (bc). **278 Alamy Stock Photo:** Alfio Scisetti (tl); WILDLIFE GmbH (c); The Picture Pantry (bl). **Dreamstime.com:** Nedim Bajramovic (cra); Draghicich (cl). **279 Alamy Stock Photo:** Valentyn Volkov (tl). **Dreamstime.com:** Chernetskaya (ca); Roman Samokhin (cb); Kittiphong Lakajit (cra); Maxim Tatarinov (c); Evgenii Kazantsev (cr); Jirattawut Domrong (br). **Getty Images:** Fine Art Images / Heritage Images (bc). **280 Dreamstime.com:** Emilio100 (tr); Liligraphie (tl); Dmitry Strizhakov (cl); Oskanov (c). **Getty Images:** Josef Mohyla (br). **281 Dreamstime.com:** Czuber (br); Richard Griffin (tr); Montypeter (cr). **Getty Images:** Universal Images Group / Hulton Fine Art (bl). **282–283 Science Photo Library:** Steve Lowry. **283 Alamy Stock Photo:** Ernesto Rosé (tl); Zoonar GmbH (cla); C J Wheeler (crb). **Getty Images / iStock:** Anzhela Shvab (bl). **naturepl.com:** Christian Ziegler / Minden (clb). **284 Alamy Stock Photo:** Ammit (c); Anamaria Mejia (cl); Fabrizio Troiani (cr). **Dreamstime.com:** Ava Peattie (tr). **Getty Images:** MIXA (bl). **285 Alamy Stock Photo:** Panther Media GmbH (cr); Pulsar Imagens (cla); Valentyn Volkov (c). **Dreamstime.com:** Anmbph (tr); Sommai Sommai (cl); Elizaveta Smirnova (bl); Passakorn Umpornmaha (tc). **Mauricio Mercadante:** (ca). **286 Alamy Stock Photo:** agefotostock. **287 Alamy Stock Photo:** Oleksandr Perepelytsia (br); Björn Wylezich (cl). **Dreamstime.com:** Alexan24 (tl); Cristina Dini (cra); Katerina Kovaleva (bl). **Shutterstock.com:** Valentyn Volkov (cr). **288 Alamy Stock Photo:** Yllar Hendla (tr); WILDLIFE GmbH (tc); imageBROKER.com GmbH & Co. KG (cla); Picture Partners (cra). **Getty Images / iStock:** pjohnson1 (cl). **288–289 Alamy Stock Photo:** Alice Musbach. **289 Alamy Stock Photo:** Md.Sohorab Ali (cr); Diane Randell (cl). **Dreamstime.com:** Pongsak Keawmanaprasert (tc); Sarah Marchant (tr); Phana Sitti (br). **Getty Images / iStock:** baona (c); xijian (bc). **Shutterstock.com:** aimpol buranet (tl). **290 Alamy Stock Photo:** imageBROKER.com GmbH & Co. KG. **291 123RF.com:** diogoppr (cl). **Dreamstime.com:** Sarot Chamnankit (fcl); Anamaria Mejia (cra); Jcsmilly (cr); Luboslav Ivanko (fcr); Shuttersyndicate (bc). **Getty Images:** Werner Forman / Universal Images Group (br). **naturepl.com:** Oriol Alamany (bl). **Shutterstock.com:** COULANGES (tl). **292–293 Alamy Stock Photo:** WaterFrame. **293 Alamy Stock Photo:** Classic Image (br); Zoonar GmbH (clb). **Dreamstime.com:** Draftmode (cr). **Getty Images:** Pavel Gospodinov (tl); Mark Newman (cla); Kunal Patil / Hindustan Times (bl). **294 Dreamstime.com:** 470117407 (cr); Anitasstudio (c); Dinosmichail (bc); Nevinates (br). **295 Alamy Stock Photo:** agefotostock (cr). **Dreamstime.com:** Raphael Chay (c/ candlenut); Ntdanai (tc); Dmuratsahin (cl); Phong Giap Van (c/pecan); Tetyana Lyapi (bc); Anton Ignatenco (br). **296–297 Science Photo Library:** Natural History Museum, London. **297 Getty Images / iStock:** Alexander Rubanov (cra). **Shutterstock.com:** tawanroong (br). **298 Alamy Stock Photo:** inga spence. **299 Dreamstime.com:** Belman (bl); Photooasis (tl); Feldarbeit (c). **300 123RF.com:** savett03 (br). **Alamy Stock Photo:** Tetiana Kovalenko (clb); Bowonpat Sakaew (tc); Leavector (c). **Getty Images / iStock:** ian al amin (bc). **301 123RF.com:** ninetechno (cr). **Alamy Stock Photo:** Panther Media GmbH (br); Zoonar GmbH (c). **Dreamstime.com:** Mohammed Anwarul Kabir Choudhury (cra); Poonsak Pornnatwuttikul (cl); Lertwit Sasipreyajun (bl); Pannarai Nak–im (bc). **Shutterstock.com:** COULANGES (tl). **302 123RF.com:** dianazh (cl); valery121283 (cr). **Alamy Stock Photo:** P Tomlins (c). **Dreamstime.com:** Aquariagirl1970 (bc); Milosluz (clb). **Shutterstock.com:** MaraZe (br); zcw (cra). **303 Dreamstime.com:** Le Thuy Do (cla); Mohamed Osama (cl); Iakov Filimonov (bl). **Getty Images / iStock:** Christian–Fischer (bc). **Shutterstock.com:** Diana Taliun (r). **304 123RF.com:** ruckszio (tl); ruckszio (fcl). **Dreamstime.com:** Artem Honchariuk (cr); Fabrizio Troiani (cl); Rangizzz (bl). **Getty Images / iStock:** ansonsaw (c/oat). **Shutterstock.com:** Lotus Images (r). **305 Alamy Stock Photo:** Joerg Boethling (cr). **Dreamstime.com:** Cerealphotos (bc); Ksena2009 (cla); Supamas Lhakjit (c); Cerealphotos (br). **Getty Images / iStock:** Azure–Dragon (ca). **Shutterstock.com:** Claudio Rampinini (bl); spline_x (tc). **306–307 Alamy Stock Photo:** RooM the Agency. **307 Alamy Stock Photo:** Antony Ratcliffe (br). **308 Alamy Stock Photo:** David Bleeker Photography (clb); Nigel Cattlin (tl); David Cole (cra); Tomasz Klejdysz (c); Nigel Cattlin (bc); Morley Read (br). **Dorling Kindersley:** Alan Buckingham (cr). **309 Alamy Stock Photo:** Album (br); Nigel Cattlin (t); Tetiana Kovalenko (cr); Design Pics Inc (bl). **Dreamstime.com:** Floriankittemann (c). **naturepl.com:** Simon Colmer (cl). **Science Photo Library:** NIGEL CATTLIN / SCIENCE SOURCE (bc). **310 123RF.com:** aalaimages (cra); kolesnikovserg (c). **Alamy Stock Photo:** Sunny Celeste (crb); The History Collection (cl). **311 Dreamstime.com:** Barmalini (c); Nipaporn Panyacharoen (ca); Jevtic (tr); Tom Meaker (cr); Jianghongyan (b). **Getty Images / iStock:** chengyuzheng (tc). **Shutterstock.com:** Lotus Images (cl); phive (tl). **312 Alamy Stock Photo:** Tony Baggett (br); WILDLIFE GmbH (c). **Dreamstime.com:** Lepas (cr); Nevinates (cra); Snowwhiteimages (bc). **Getty Images / iStock:** pjohnson1 (bl). **313 Alamy Stock Photo:** Design Pics Inc (tr); PA Images (tl); Juniors Bildarchiv GmbH (fcl). **Dreamstime.com:** Sergii Figurnyi (b); Slowmotiongli (cl); Anamaria Mejia (c). **Getty Images / iStock:** Floortje (cr). **314 Alamy Stock Photo:** Florilegius. **315 123RF.com:** airdone (cl); tsunamicloud (br). **Alamy Stock Photo:** Historic Illustrations (bl). **Dreamstime.com:** Picture Partners (bc); Ppy2010ha (tl); Toon Sang (c); Slallison (cb). **316 123RF.com:** cynoclub (br). **Alamy Stock Photo:** FotoHelin (bl). **Dreamstime.com:** Sommai Sommai (cr); Weerapat Wattanapichayakul (tl). **317 123RF.com:** kolesnikovserg (bc/morel). **Alamy Stock Photo:** positivesoundvision (tl); pawita warasiri (tr). **Dreamstime.com:** Wasana Jaigunta (cl); Akepong Srichaichana (c); Picture Partners (cr); Picture Partners (bc). **Getty Images / iStock:** adrianam13 (br). **318 Alamy Stock Photo:** Paul Bradforth (br). **Dreamstime.com:** Supamas Lhakjit (c); Alfio Scisetti (tl). **Getty Images / iStock:** Yana Boiko (bl); fermate (cra). **319 123RF.com:** peterhermesfurian (tl); nanthawan suwanthong (cl). **Alamy Stock Photo:** blickwinkel (tc). **Dreamstime.com:** Chaiyon021 (bl); Maxim Tatarinov (ca); Fotyma (bc/dried leaves). **320 Dreamstime.com:** Charles Brutlag (tr); Colourdream (cl); Tetiana Kovalenko (c); Eyewave (cr). **Shutterstock.com:** Roman Mikhailiuk (b). **321 Dreamstime.com:** Vivek Devasya (tc); Klickmr (fcl); Jolanta Dabrowska (fbl); Alfio Scisetti (cr). **Getty Images:** Universal Images Group / Hulton Fine Art (tr). **Shutterstock.com:** Valentyn Volkov (c). **322–323 Bridgeman Images:** Royal Asiatic Society. **324 123RF.com:** Koosen (bl). **Dreamstime.com:** Mohammed Anwarul Kabir Choudhury (cl); Troichenko (tl); Dipak Shelare (cra); Jackimage520429 (br). **Fotolia:** Zee (clb). **325 123RF.com:** Carolyn Franks (bc/soybean). **Alamy Stock Photo:** JORGE JEREZ MOLIMA (tr). **Dreamstime.com:** Digitalpress (cl); Jose Marques Lopes (tl); Ovydyborets (c); Alexey Kamenskiy (br); Anastasiia Malinich (crb). **326 Alamy Stock Photo:** John Bennet (clb); Aliaksandr Mazurkevich (tl). **naturepl.com:** Juergen Freund (cla); Chien Lee / Minden (bl). **326–327 Shutterstock.com:** muhd fuad abd rahim. **327 Alamy Stock Photo:** imageBROKER.com GmbH & Co. KG (br); Scenics & Science (cra). **328 Dreamstime.com:** Zeynel Cebeci (br); Eric Gevaert / Enjoylife25 (cb). **329 Dreamstime.com:** Nancy Ayumi Kunihiro (c); Kaiskynet (tl); Marazem (tr); Picture Partners (fcl); Sergey Kolesnikov (cr); Supamas Lhakjit (br). **Getty Images / iStock:** seamartini (cl/ rooibos). **330–331 naturepl.com:** Thomas Marent / Minden. **331 Bridgeman Images:** Pictures from History (br). **332 123RF.com:** aneva (c); domnicky (bl). **Alamy Stock Photo:** LianeM (bc). **Dreamstime.com:** Alexan24 (br); Jared Quentin (cl); Anastasiia Malinich (r). **Getty Images:** Avalon_Studio (cr). **333 Alamy Stock Photo:** Botanic World (tr); Heinz Tschanz–Hofmann (cl); GRANGER—Historical Picture Archive (bc). **Dreamstime.com:** Banprik (tc); Tetiana Kovalenko (c). **334 123RF.com:** katerinamore (tr). **Alamy Stock Photo:** blickwinkel (br); Yakov Oskanov (cr); WILDLIFE GmbH (bl); Hervé Lenain (bc). **335 Dorling Kindersley:** Colin Keates / Natural History Museum, London (cr). **Dreamstime.com:** Aakriti Stock (ca); Lev Kropotov (cl); Marilyn Barbone (cla); Zz3701 (c). **Getty Images:** Science & Society Picture Library (bc). **336–337 Science Photo Library:** Eye of Science. **337 Science Photo Library:** Science Source (crb). **338 Alamy Stock Photo:** Bengal Picture Library (bl); Sunny Celeste (tr). **Dreamstime.com:** Rob Lumen Captum (cr); Le Thuy Do (tl); Aleksander Kovaltchuk (c); Dadalia (br). **Shutterstock.com:** Photoongraphy (bc). **339 123RF.com:** adsniks (cr). **Alamy Stock Photo:** Dennis K. Johnson (cl); Alexey Lesik (fcl); Shamil (cr/fibers); Yulia.Panova (br). **Dreamstime.com:** Fotomak (tr); Irina Khudoliy (c); Slowmotiongli (bl); Georgesixth (bc). **340 Shutterstock.com:** Asimm Graphics (bl). **340–341 Getty Images:** dszc. **342 123RF.com:** amorozov (bl). **Alamy Stock Photo:** Frank Hecker (br); imageBROKER.com GmbH & Co. KG (cra); TMI (c). **Dorling Kindersley:** Gary Ombler / Westonbirt, The National Arboretum (cr). **343 123RF.com:** scis65 (b). **Alamy Stock Photo:** All Canada Photos (cl); Wolstenholme Images (tr); Panther Media GmbH (cr). **Dreamstime.com:** Oleg Prigoryanu (c). **344 Alamy Stock Photo:** Ben Schonewille (bl). **Dreamstime.com:** Mihalec (cl). **344–345 naturepl.com:** Juan Carlos Munoz. **346 Alamy Stock Photo:** Wolfgang Kaehler (cra); Nature Picture Library (bl); Michael Wald (cr). **naturepl.com:** Simon Colmer (br). **Shutterstock.com:** Muslianshah Masrie (tl). **347 Alamy Stock Photo:** blickwinkel (bl). **Dreamstime.com:** Oskanov (cl); Narah Sookaew (bc); Nontakorn Phakphoom (crb). **naturepl.com:** Jabruson (tr). **Shutterstock.com:** Jakkrit Orrasri (br). **Wikipedia:** Sybil Kaesedick (cla). **348–349 Dreamstime.com:** Passakorn Umpornmaha. **349 Alamy Stock Photo:** Dinodia Photos (clb); Travel Wild (tl); thitimon toyai (crb). **Dreamstime.com:** Chonticha Wat (cla). **Getty Images:** Anuwar Hazarika / NurPhoto (bl). **350 123RF.com:** marilyn barbone (br). **Alamy Stock Photo:** Tetiana Kovalenko (fbl). **Dorling Kindersley:** Clive Streeter / The Science Museum, London (tl). **Dreamstime.com:** Olga Bungova (c); Iquacu (bl); Macro Studio (bc). **351 Alamy Stock Photo:** Danita Delimont (tr); Manfred Ruckszio (cla); Steffen Hauser / botanikfoto (tl); Panther Media GmbH (cr). **Dreamstime.com:** Key1234 (bl); Manfred Ruckszio (c). **Getty Images / iStock:** DeeNida (cb). **352–353 Getty Images:** Heritage Art / Heritage Images. **353 Alamy Stock Photo:** ERIC LAFFORGUE (br). **Dreamstime.com:** Tetiana Kovalenko (cra). **354 Alamy Stock Photo:** Bailey–Cooper Photography (bc); Peter Jordan_NE (br). **Dorling Kindersley:** Mark Winwood / RHS Wisley (cra). **355 Alamy Stock Photo:** John Anderson (t); mahir ates (bl); Peter Horree (br). **Dorling Kindersley:** Debbie Patterson / Ian Cuppleditch (cl). **356 Alamy Stock Photo:** Album (bl). **356–357 Dreamstime.com:** Ippeito. **358 Alamy Stock Photo:** John Richmond. **359 123RF.com:** elen1 (fbr). **Alamy Stock Photo:** Photimageon (tl); Olaf Simon (cra). **Dreamstime.com:** Vilor (br). **360 Alamy Stock Photo:** flowerphotos (tc); RM Floral (br). **Dreamstime.com:** Valerii Maksimov (tl); Voltan1 (tr); Tetiana Zbrodko / Taratata (bl). **361 Alamy Stock Photo:** Panther Media GmbH (cl). **Dorling Kindersley:** Tatton Park (c); Mark Winwood / RHS Wisley (tl). **Dreamstime.com:** Michael Gray (br); Likefermat (cr). **Getty Images:** View Pictures / Universal Images Group (bc). **Shutterstock.com:** Lopatin Anton (c/lily). **362 Alamy Stock Photo:** Buddy Mays (bl); Nadezhda Nesterova (cl). **Dreamstime.com:** Wieslaw Jarek (br); Tetiana Kovalenko (tl); Valery Prokhozhy (cr). **363 Alamy Stock Photo:** gokhan dogan (bl); Kyoko Uchida (tl); thrillerfillerspiller (tc). **Dorling Kindersley:** Mark Winwood / RHS Wisley (r). **Dreamstime.com:** Roksana Bashyrova (ftl); Simona Pavan (cb). **366 Alamy Stock Photo:** Design Pics. **367 Alamy Stock Photo:** BIOSPHOTO (br); Tommi Syvänperä (c). **Shutterstock.com:** Nancy J. Ondra (tc). **368 Alamy Stock Photo:** fishHook Photography (cra); Bob Gibbons (tl). **Sharon Pilkington:** (br). **369 Alamy Stock Photo:** Henri Koskinen (bl). **Dreamstime.com:** Danolsen (tr). **370 Alamy Stock Photo:** Chris Mattison (tr). **Dorling Kindersley:** David Fenwick (tc). **371 Alamy Stock Photo:** Henri Koskinen (tc). **Shutterstock.com:** Jeff Holcombe (bl). **372 Alamy Stock Photo:** Nature Picture Library. **373 Alamy Stock Photo:** Henri Koskinen (b). **Dorling Kindersley:** Malcolm Storey (tl). **374 Australian Plant Image Index, https://www.anbg.gov.au/photo:** B.Fuhrer (bl). **Stepan Koval:** (br). **Sharon Pilkington. 375 Alamy Stock Photo:** José Mara Barres Manuel (cra); Mikko Suonio (cla). **376 John Braggins:** (tr). **377 Alamy Stock Photo:** BIOSPHOTO (cl). **Dreamstime.com:** Jeffrey Holcombe (br). **378 Alamy Stock Photo:** Penta Springs Limited. **379 Alamy Stock Photo:** Archive PL (bc); Bob Gibbons (tc). **Dorling Kindersley:** David Fenwick (bl); Malcolm Storey (cra). **380 Alamy Stock Photo:** Martin Shields (cla). **Dorling Kindersley:** Jens Christian Schou (tr). **381 Alamy Stock Photo:** Nature Picture Library (r). **Dorling Kindersley:** Jens Kristian Overgaard (cl). **382 Alamy Stock Photo:** blickwinkel (tr); Premaphotos (cla); Chris Mattison (bl). **383 naturepl.com:** Ann & Steve Toon (br). **386 Dreamstime.com:** Toni Genes (clb). **387 Alamy Stock Photo:** Nature Picture Library (bl). **388 Alamy Stock Photo:** Botanic World (bc). **389 Alamy Stock Photo:** Yon Marsh Natural History (tr). **Shutterstock.com:** Madlen (br). **390 Alamy Stock Photo:** Jon Wilson (tc). **391 Alamy Stock Photo:** The History Collection (cra). **naturepl.com:** MYN / Marko Masterl (bl). **Danny Schissler:** (ca). **393 Alamy Stock Photo:** Les Archives Digitales (clb). **Dreamstime.com:** Roman Ivaschenko (tl). **Science Photo Library:** HISTORICA GRAPHICA COLLECTION / HERITAGE IMAGES (bc). **394 Alamy Stock Photo:** Richard Becker (cl); Matthew Taylor (bc); Historic Collection (tr). **Dreamstime.com:** Coplandj (tc). **395 Alamy Stock Photo:** Zoonar GmbH (tr). **396 Alamy Stock Photo:** Bob Gibbons (cr); Robert Wyatt (bl). **397 Dreamstime.com:** Pawel Papis (tr). **398 Alamy Stock Photo:** Steffen Hauser / botanikfoto (br). **Dorling Kindersley:** Neil Fletcher (tr). **399 Alamy Stock Photo:** blickwinkel (cl); Living Levels Photography (r); Wagner Campelo (c); Nature Photographers Ltd (bc); Florida Images (tc/Xyris). **Dreamstime.com:** LariBat (tl). **Getty Images / iStock:** Karin de Mamiel (tc). **400 Alamy Stock Photo:** amana images inc. (br). **401 Dreamstime.com:** Ileana Marcela Bosogea Tudor (br). **402 Alamy Stock Photo:** Jimlop collection (cr); Alessandro Zocchi (c). **403 Alamy Stock Photo:** History and Art Collection (crb). **Dreamstime.com:** Christian Weiß (bc). **404 naturepl.com:** Adrian Davies (c). **405 Alamy Stock Photo:** imageBROKER.com GmbH & Co. KG (bc). **Getty Images:** R A Kearton (bl). **406 Alamy Stock Photo:** Steffen Hauser / botanikfoto (br); Liudmila Prymak (tc); Nick Kurzenko (bl). **407 Alamy Stock Photo:** BIOSPHOTO (br). **Dreamstime.com:** Tamara Lee Harding (cl). **408 Alamy Stock Photo:** Ognyan Yosifov (br). **Colin Walton:** (bc). **409 Alamy Stock Photo:** WILDLIFE GmbH (tc). **Dorling Kindersley:** Gary Ombler: Centre for Wildlife Gardening / London Wildlife Trust (cl). **410 Alamy Stock Photo:** Oleg Znamenskiy (cl). **Dreamstime.com:** Wasana Jaigunta (c). **411 Alamy Stock Photo:** Steffen Hauser / botanikfoto (tr). **Dreamstime.com:** Tamara Kulikova (bl). **412 Alamy Stock Photo:** Mike P Shepherd (cla). **Dorling Kindersley:** Neil Fletcher (c); Neil Fletcher (br). **413 Alamy Stock Photo:** GFC Collection (cl). **naturepl.com:** Duncan Mcewan (bl). **414 Alamy Stock Photo:** imageBROKER.com GmbH & Co. KG (l). **Dorling Kindersley:** David Fenwick (cra). **418 Shutterstock.com:** Anne Powell (tl). **420 Alamy Stock Photo:** flafabri (tr). **421 Alamy Stock Photo:** All Canada Photos (tr); Minden Pictures (cl). **422 Taylor Lockwood:** (tl). **423 Dorling Kindersley:** David Fenwick (tc); David Fenwick (cl, c, bc); Neil Fletcher (bl). **424 Alamy Stock Photo:** Bob Gibbons (b). **Dorling Kindersley:** Paul Diederich (ca). **naturepl.com:** Chris Mattison (tr). **425 Alamy Stock Photo:** Klaus Reitmeier (r). **naturepl.com:** Robert Thompson (bl). **426 Alamy Stock Photo:** Bob Gibbons (b). **Dorling Kindersley:** Paul Diederich (tl); Paul Diederich (cra). **427 Alamy Stock Photo:** Clarence Holmes Wildlife (bl). **Dorling Kindersley:** Paul Diederich (br). **naturepl.com:** Alex Hyde (t).

All other images © Dorling Kindersley Limited

DEFINITIVE VISUAL GUIDES

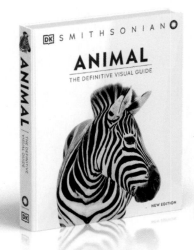

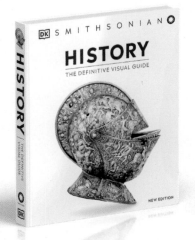